Assessing Young Children *Thurs.*

THIRD EDITION

GAYLE MINDES
DePaul University

PEARSON

Merrill
Prentice Hall

Upper Saddle River, New Jersey
Columbus, Ohio

Library of Congress Cataloging-in-Publication Data

Mindes, Gayle.
    Assessing young children / Gayle Mindes.— 3rd ed.
      p. cm.
    Includes bibliographical references and index.
    ISBN 0-13-171821-5
1. Child development—United States—Testing. 2. Early childhood education—United States—Evaluation.
3. Educational tests and measurements—United States. I. Title.
    LB1131.M6146 2007
    371.26—dc22

                                      2006001467

Vice President and Executive Publisher: Jeffery W. Johnston
Publisher: Kevin M. Davis
Acquisitions Editor: Julie Peters
Editorial Assistant: Michelle Girgis
Production Editor: Linda Hillis Bayma
Production Coordination: Barb Tucker, Carlisle Editorial Services
Design Coordinator: Diane C. Lorenzo
Photo Coordinator: Monica Merkel
Cover Designer: Terry Rohrbach
Cover Image: Index Stock
Production Manager: Laura Messerly
Director of Marketing: David Gescll
Marketing Manager: Amy Judd
Marketing Coordinator: Brian Mounts

This book was set in Palatino by Carlisle Publishing Services. It was printed and bound by R.R. Donnelley & Sons Company.
The cover was printed by R.R. Donnelley & Sons Company.

First edition © 1996 by Delmar Publishers.

Photo Credits: Laura Bolesta/Merrill, p. 47; Scott Cunningham/Merrill, pp. 98, 145, 258, 266; George Dodson/PH College,
p. 135; Laima Druskis/PH College, pp. 171, 312; Dan Floss/Merrill, p. 235; Ken Karp/PH College, p. 63; KS Studios/Merrill,
p. 87; David Mager/Pearson Learning Photo Studio, pp. 2, 35, 128, 160; Anthony Magnacca/Merrill, pp. 138, 214, 286, 322;
Liz Moore/Merrill, p. 130; Val Schultz/Merrill, p. 30; Barbara Schwartz/Merrill, pp. 18, 89; Teri Leigh Stratford/PH College,
pp. 58, 226; Anne Vega/Merrill, pp. 4, 33, 60, 78, 109, 114, 136, 170, 228, 229, 260, 284, 327, 330; Tom Watson/Merrill,
p. 201; Todd Yarrington/Merrill, p. 190.

Pearson Education Ltd.   Pearson Education Australia Pty. Limited
Pearson Education Singapore Pte. Ltd.   Pearson Education North Asia Ltd.
Pearson Education Canada, Ltd.   Pearson Educación de Mexico, S.A. de C.V.
Pearson Education—Japan   Pearson Education Malaysia Pte. Ltd.

10 9 8 7 6 5 4 3 2 1
ISBN: 0-13-171821-5

To friendship and walking . . . 4 years and counting . . . thanks,
Baila, Gail, and Rae

Preface

We live in a challenging time for American education. Some of the important issues facing educators today include accountability (No Child Left Behind, Head Start Outcomes), high-stakes tests, management of scarce resources and shortage of highly qualified early childhood teachers, multicultural curriculum, and inclusion. For early childhood educators, the first formal teachers in the lives of young children, the challenges are enormous. Parent partnership, respect for cultural diversity, appropriate early intervention assessment, and linking curriculum and assessment practices appropriately are just a few of the demands.

ASSESSMENT IS A REQUIRED COMPETENCY FOR EARLY CHILDHOOD TEACHERS

Crafting an assessment system is one of the most important tasks and challenges for early childhood educators. Early childhood teachers must therefore be mindful of the responsibilities they assume as they assess and participate in teaching, evaluation, and placement of the young children and families they serve. Thorough knowledge of child development, formal and informal assessment measures, statistics and characteristics of standardized measures, variables in consultation with parents, and portfolio and performance assessment are required competencies for the professional early childhood educator. Early childhood assessment decisions affect infants, young children, and their families for life.

ABOUT THIS TEXT

This book addresses theory, provides illustrations of appropriate practice for prospective teachers, and discusses current trends for experienced teachers. It approaches assessment as an integral part of the teaching and learning process. Key components of the assessment system advocated include cultural sensitivity, parent collaboration, and a vision of inclusionary practice in all early childhood environments—child care and school. Relevant professional standards are addressed throughout. The text is written in nontechnical language with support from the most current research. All "hot topics" are included—standards-based and outcomes-based teaching, high-stakes testing, coping with legislative demands, as well as relevant incorporation of technology in the assessment process. This book reflects the knowledge base of early childhood and early childhood special education. It is meant for the teacher who wants to understand and deliver an effective educational program for all young children from birth through age 8.

The book is organized holistically. Chapter 1 begins with an orientation to assessment through the age span of early childhood: birth through age 8. Parent collaboration and involvement is introduced in Chapter 2 as an important element in assessment. Chapter 3 discusses observation as the beginning of all assessment. Chapters 4 and 5 describe the basic concepts of measurement and where and how an educator can put them into practice. Chapter 6 addresses the use of alternative assessment strategies to facilitate individualization of instruction and behavioral management. Chapter 7 shows how an educator records and reports assessment to others, with an emphasis again on parent involvement. Chapter 8 consists of real-life examples and ten case studies to guide the student on how to build a child study. Chapters 9 through 11 focus on the special assessment issues for infants and toddlers, preschoolers, and children in the primary grades.

KEY FEATURES OF THE TEXT

- Throughout the text there is a focus on inclusion of children with disabilities.
- Issues related to English language learners are woven into the discussion.
- Collaboration with parents is emphasized.
- The No Child Left Behind legislation is discussed thoroughly throughout the text.
- Each chapter includes terms to know, focus questions, reflection questions, technology links, out-of-class activities, and suggested further readings. New to this edition for each chapter are case vignettes and activities for classroom discussion and exploration.
- The book includes a test review guideline, reviews of commonly used tests, a glossary, a pretest of assessment terminology for readers, guidelines for choosing technology and software, and practical examples throughout. Features new to this edition include a portfolio template, additional example checklists and rating sheets, and blank templates that can be reproduced for teacher use.

ACKNOWLEDGMENTS

Thanks to the thousands of children, parents, undergraduate and graduate students, and colleagues who have influenced my thinking and practices over the years. In particular, I appreciate the contributions of Carol Mardell-Czudnowski and Harold Ireton, who collaborated with me on the first edition of this book. I value the care and hard work of Josh Sheppard, DePaul University, who compiled and updated the reviews of early childhood tests. Thanks to my colleagues at DePaul University and early childhood educators elsewhere for their assistance and support in discussing the revisions for this edition. In particular, I appreciate the suggestions of Marie Donovan and Alice Moss, who critiqued the second edition as they used it in teaching. Bridget Amory, DePaul alumna and Assistant Principal of Morris Early Childhood Center, Milford School District, Delaware, always keeps me grounded in the real world with her enthusiasm and stories from the field. Finally, I am especially indebted to my son, Jonathan, for his never-ending support and contribution of his professional, editorial opinions throughout the writing process.

I appreciate the support, encouragement, and vision from Julie Peters, Michelle Girgis, and others behind the scenes at Merrill/Prentice Hall.

My appreciation is extended to the reviewers for their constructive criticism and helpful suggestions: Alice Atkinson, The University of Iowa; Judy Hudson, San Juan College; Rebecca Huss-Keeler, University of Houston, Clear Lake; Lynda Nelson, Central Missouri State University; and Paulette Shreck, University of Central Oklahoma.

Finally, I appreciate the wonderful copyediting by Kirsten Balayti and the overall production facilitation by Barb Tucker at Carlisle Editorial Services.

Discover the Companion Website Accompanying This Book

THE PRENTICE HALL COMPANION WEBSITE: A VIRTUAL LEARNING ENVIRONMENT

Technology is a constantly growing and changing aspect of our field that is creating a need for content and resources. To address this emerging need Prentice Hall has developed an online learning environment for students and professors alike—Companion Websites—to support our textbooks.

In creating a Companion Website, our goal is to build on and enhance what the textbook already offers. For this reason, the content for each user-friendly website is organized by topic and provides the professor and student with a variety of meaningful resources. Common features of a Companion Website include:

- **Introduction** - General information about the topic and how it will be covered in the website.
- **Web Links** - A variety of websites related to topic areas.
- **Timely Articles** - Links to online articles that enable you to become more aware of important issues in early childhood.
- **Learn by Doing** - Put concepts into action, participate in activities, examine strategies, and more.
- **Visit a School** - Visit a school's website to see concepts, theories, and strategies in action.
- **For Teachers/Practitioners** - Access information you will need to know as an educator, including information on materials, activities, and lessons.
- **Observation Tools** - A collection of checklists and forms to print and use when observing and assessing children's development.
- **Current Policies and Standards** - Find out the latest early-childhood policies from the government and various organizations, and view state, federal, and curriculum standards.

- **Resources and Organizations** - Discover tools to help you plan your classroom or center and organizations to provide current information and standards for each topic.
- **Electronic Bluebook** - Paperless method of completing homework or essays assigned by a professor. Finished work can be sent to the professor via email.

To take advantage of these and other resources, please visit Merrill Education's **Early Childhood Education Resource Website.** Go to **www.prenhall.com/mindes**, click on the book cover, and then click on "Enter"at the bottom of the next screen.

TEACHER PREP

MERRILL
PRENTICE HALL

Teacher Preparation Classroom

See a demo at
www.prenhall.com/teacherprep/demo

Your Class. Their Careers. Our Future. Will your students be prepared?

We invite you to explore our new, innovative and engaging website and all that it has to offer you, your course, and tomorrow's educators! Organized around the major courses pre-service teachers take, the Teacher Preparation site provides media, student/teacher artifacts, strategies, research articles, and other resources to equip your students with the quality tools needed to excel in their courses and prepare them for their first classroom.

This ultimate on-line education resource is available at no cost, when packaged with a Merrill text, and will provide you and your students access to:

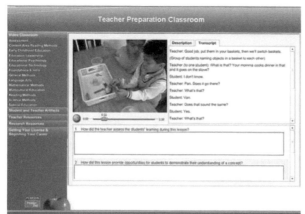

Online Video Library. More than 150 video clips—each tied to a course topic and framed by learning goals and Praxis-type questions—capture real teachers and students working in real classrooms, as well as in-depth interviews with both students and educators.

Student and Teacher Artifacts. More than 200 student and teacher classroom artifacts—each tied to a course topic and framed by learning goals and application questions—provide a wealth of materials and experiences to help make your study to become a professional teacher more concrete and hands-on.

Research Articles. Over 500 articles from ASCD's renowned journal *Educational Leadership.* The site also includes Research Navigator, a searchable database of additional educational journals.

Teaching Strategies. Over 500 strategies and lesson plans for you to use when you become a practicing professional.

Licensure and Career Tools. Resources devoted to helping you pass your licensure exam; learn standards, law, and public policies; plan a teaching portfolio; and succeed in your first year of teaching.

How to ORDER *Teacher Prep* for you and your students:
For students to receive a *Teacher Prep* Access Code with this text instructors **must** provide a special value pack ISBN number on their textbook order form. To receive this special ISBN please email **Merrill.marketing@pearsoned.com** and provide the following information:
  • Name and Affiliation
  • Author/Title/Edition of Merrill text
Upon ordering *Teacher Prep* for their students instructors will be given a lifetime *Teacher Prep* Access Code.

Brief Contents

Contents

Note: Every effort has been made to provide accurate and current Internet information in this book. However, the Internet and information posted on it are constantly changing, so it is inevitable that some of the Internet addresses listed in this textbook will change.

Case study details are based on experiences of the writer and early childhood students' work in assessment courses. Details are altered and situations combined so no real persons are featured.

Assessing Young Children

1

A Comprehensive Assessment System for Birth Through Age 8

Chapter Overview

Assessment is an integral part of the total picture of child care and education. Information gathered through informed observation and other methods guides the countless decisions at the heart of solid and appropriate instruction and intervention. Some of these decisions can be made easily and as a matter of course: Should the program move on to the next theme in the curriculum? Are children growing in their abilities to follow directions and to share cooperatively? Other decisions, by their nature, require more systematic and intensive assessment information collection due to the life consequences that may result. Does this child need to be enrolled in a special program? What opportunities will result? What, if any, stigma may be attached to such placement?

By definition, best practice dictates that all decisions be based upon assessment information gleaned from multiple sources. In addition, all everyone involved in the care and education of the child—parents, teachers, and other related service personnel—must be included in the process. Because the techniques for gathering information and the steps involved in intervention and educational decision making are varied, the task of assessing young children is a tremendous responsibility. The aim of this book is to help you begin to learn the rudiments of assessment: the why, the how, and what to do with assessment information gathered. Toward this end, this initial chapter focuses on exploring the early childhood assessment system.

Assess as You Read

- What is assessment? How is assessment the same or different than a test?
- What assessment methods are most suitable for infants and toddlers? Preschoolers? School-age children?
- How do you use your knowledge of child development in assessment?
- What do parents, principals, and others want to know about assessment results?

THE AGE SPAN OF EARLY CHILDHOOD

Birth through age 8 . . . wow . . . think of the differences: Cute and help-less babies depending on the adults in their lives for care, nurturance, and development; energetic and determined toddlers moving away from the adults to stake out and explore their world through play while helping themselves to feed and dress; fanciful and creative preschool-ers launching into friendships and dramatic play; earnest and curious young school-agers attacking the challenges of reading, writing, math-ematics, and technology. In these 8 intervening years, children change more than during any other life period.

Beginning with the reflexes of the newborn, through the first smile, words, and step, the infancy years fly by quickly. Toddlers establish au-tonomy, self-help skills, and sophistication in their language and move-ment. Preschoolers cooperate with each other, develop themes in their play, and learn elaborate cognitive and gross- and fine-motor skills. At school age, young children engage their curiosity for the purpose of learning, become even more self-sufficient in their own care, and play games with rules in their leisure. These developmental changes and milestones, and others, occur in a social/cultural context that influences the acquisition and elaboration of this growth (cf. Berk, 2005).

Parents, caregivers, teachers, and others who impact the lives of young children must not only be familiar with the broad aspects of de-velopment in this period—the usual and typical growth patterns—but must also be sensitive to variations within typical development that af-fect temperament, learning style, fine- and gross-motor skills, and lan-guage acquisition. These significant adults must remember that developmental processes in young children occur in a social context shaped by diverse familial, cultural, geographic, social, and economic factors influencing developmental progress. In a major way, the age span of early childhood contributes to the complexity of developing a

comprehensive assessment system. Intricately intertwined with the issue of the age span is the difference in types of settings where infants, toddlers, and young children are served. Along with diverse purposes for the implementation of care, education, and intervention, the complexity of the assessment task is staggering. Before looking at types of assessment, you must consider the places where the care and education of young children occurs.

MATCHING ASSESSMENT METHODS TO EARLY CHILDHOOD SETTINGS

The care and education of infants and toddlers occurs at home, in home child care, and in group child-care settings. Often, those with special needs are found in early intervention settings. Among other things, caregivers in these settings need to know

- what the crying baby wants.
- when to feed, diaper, and soothe babies.
- when to talk with and stimulate with toys.
- when to allow "me do it."
- when something is "off" with the baby and whether the problem is serious.

In each of these situations, caregivers assess the needs of the baby by observation. They compare their knowledge of the individual baby to past experience with the baby, to their experiences with babies in general, and to their knowledge of infant/toddler development. After reflecting on their observations, caregivers change the intervention, routine, or educational plan. When caregivers believe that their capacity to care appropriately and responsively for a particular infant/toddler is limited, the next assessment step is parent involvement. This conversation evolves from the regular and routine conversations that have set the tone for parent partnerships and collaboration. Thus, the discussion of concern can proceed more naturally when a basic rapport is already established between the caregiver and parent. So, by comparing caregiver knowledge with parent knowledge regarding a troubling problem, the difficulty can be resolved or referred for specialist evaluation.

Preschoolers can be found in all of the locations previously described (home, home-based child care, and child-care centers). In addition, young children are located in compensatory educational programs for the "at risk"; special programs for those with disabilities; and increasingly, in inclusive environments. Among other things, caregivers and teachers in these settings need to know

- when to move the story time to closure.
- when to change the curricular theme.

- when to intervene in conflicts between children.
- when to provide enrichment activities for a precocious reader.
- when to ask the speech therapist or other related service person to observe and/or assess a particular child.

Many of the decisions of preschool caregivers and teachers in these and other situations involve a consideration of the group of children and the group's best interests. These are teaching decisions that teachers and caregivers make based on the overall plan for the center or program and the pacing decisions that teachers make based on the needs of the group for the particular day. Assessment methods for these situations can be accomplished through the use of observation. Informed observation consists of knowledge of child development, curricular goals, and expected learning outcomes. An integral part of the use of informed observation is the choice of a record-keeping system.

For those decisions that involve a question or concern about developmental progress or process, the first step is conversation and collaboration with the child's parents. If parents and caregivers or teachers have serious concerns, a referral for specialists' assessment may be in order. The use of tests for these occasions is discussed. Special issues of preschool-age children and the current events influencing philosophy and program practice are considered.

Young school-age children receive care in locations similar to those of infants and toddlers (at home, in home child care, and in center-based child care), and in public and private settings where they begin "school" and are introduced to the privileges and responsibilities associated with formal education. Teachers of primary-age children and their caregivers need to know

- when to use cooperative group activities for the curricular goal.
- how to incorporate phonics or character education in the teaching theme.
- how to prepare children for the accountability tests in their school.
- what kind of "homework" will meet the needs of the children, the after-school setting, and the parents.
- how to mainstream, or include, the young child with special needs in the group.

Assessment decisions in these situations appropriately rely primarily on teacher observation. Tests appear as a feature of the primary years. Special assessment techniques for including and referring children with special needs are important features of the teacher's knowledge base. The special issues of the primary years, including accountability in its current form, are a feature. Each of these assessment situations rely on the components illustrated in Figure 1.1.

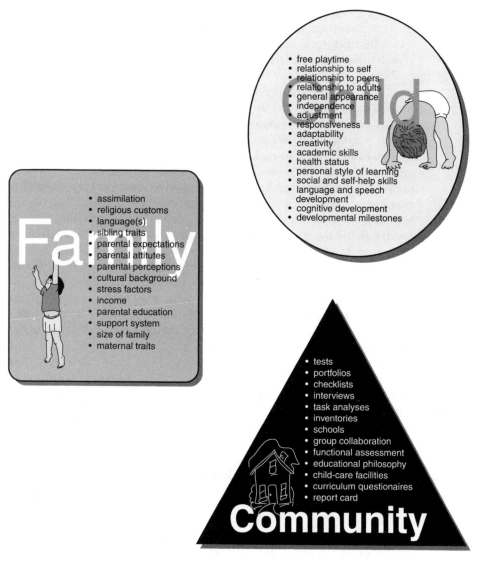

Figure 1.1
Essential components for total assessment.

STAKEHOLDERS IN THE PROCESS

In each early childhood setting, the need for information about infant/toddler/child progress varies. Collecting information, choosing appropriate methods, thinking about the information gathered, and planning the next step based on the assessment are all approached and handled in different ways by each of the young child's "important people." The primary "important people," or **stakeholders,** in the "need to know" loop or assessment system are each child's parents and

stakeholder
people important in the lives of children, especially regarding the assessment of children.

caregivers/teachers. These, however, are not the only stakeholders in the process; others include related service personnel, program funders and administrators, legislators, and the public at large. Each of these stakeholders seeks different pieces of information.

Parents want to know how their children are developing and learning. They are interested not only in their own opinions, but also informed opinions shared by caregivers and teachers in informal and formal conversations, conferences, and reports. Because paraprofessionals want to meet the needs of the child in the particular setting, they will want to be able to make decisions about particular children and groups based on the guidelines developed by the teachers they collaborate with. Teachers and specialists need information to keep programs running well for the groups of children and for particular children with special needs. Administrators, policy boards, and legislators are accountable for the progress of groups of children. They need to know that programs are working.

Each stakeholder comes with varying degrees of knowledge about the unfolding of development during the early childhood age span. Parents, paraprofessionals, policy boards, and legislators have practical knowledge, diverse experiential knowledge, and various pieces of contextual information. Most do not have professional information. The professionals—caregivers/teachers, administrators, and related service personnel—have diverse training experiences that shape their notions of the best ways to gather assessment information. All stakeholders have the best interests of young children in mind. The definition and criteria for the demonstration of the progress of development and education vary with the stakeholders (see Table 1.1). Thus, defining a comprehensive assessment system for young children is extremely complicated. It requires teachers and others to keep assessment firmly in mind when thinking about what to teach? How? To whom? And when?

DEFINING AND CREATING A COMPREHENSIVE ASSESSMENT SYSTEM

In view of the myriad and differing needs of stakeholders previously outlined, creating and implementing a truly comprehensive assessment system is an enormous task. It is not an insurmountable one, however, as you will learn by reading this book. Keep in mind that as a teacher, you will be one of the important stakeholders in the lives of young children. You will plan to gather information to assist you in guiding learning for the children you serve. In addition, you will need to document child progress and communicate regularly with the other stakeholders—the child, his or her parents, administrators, boards, and ultimately, legislative bodies. The procedures for

TABLE 1.1   Method of assessment of frequency of use

Stakeholder	Observation	Special alternative method	Test and performance assessment
Parent	daily and routinely	rarely	never
Paraprofessional caregiver	daily and routinely	rarely	under supervision
Infant teacher	daily and routinely	rarely	screening, regularly
Infant specialist	daily and routinely	often	diagnostic
Paraprofessional preschool caregiver	daily and routinely	rarely	under supervision
Preschool teacher	daily and routinely	sometimes	screening and performance tasks
Preschool specialist	daily and routinely	often	diagnostic
Primary paraprofessional caregiver	daily and routinely	never	under supervision
Primary teacher	daily and routinely	sometimes	screening, diagnostic, performance tasks, accountability
Primary specialist	daily and routinely	often	diagnostic
Administrators	rarely	never	review results for accountability
Policy boards	rarely	never	review results for accountability
Legislators	rarely	never	review results for accountability

gathering information discussed in this book are drawn from the following beliefs:

- Children learn best when their physical needs are met and they feel psychologically safe and secure.
- Children construct knowledge.
- Children learn through social interaction with adults and other children.
- Children's learning reflects a recurring cycle that begins in awareness and moves to exploration, to inquiry, and finally to utilization.
- Children learn through play.
- Children's interests and "need to know" motivate learning.
- Human development and learning are characterized by individual variation. (Bredekamp & Rosegrant, 1992, pp. 14–17; see also *Young Children*, 2005)

With these beliefs in mind, you will choose assessment techniques suited to the needs of your program from those discussed in the text. Your decisions will be based on knowledge of the needs of the particular age span you serve and the setting for your program. An illustration of the components in the assessment process follows. Each is multidimensional and interactive with the other components.

Definition of Assessment

Before considering the design of an assessment system, it is important to define what is meant by *assessment*. The definitions are many. Common elements of the definitions include the ideas that assessment

- is a process.
- is a decision-making tool.
- can apply to an individual or a group.
- generates products.

assessment process for gathering information to make decisions.

In this book, **assessment** *is a process for gathering information to make decisions about young children. The process is appropriate when it is systematic, multidisciplinary, and based on the everyday tasks of childhood. The best assessment system is comprehensive in nature. That is, the assessment yields information about all the developmental areas: motoric, temperament, linguistic, cognitive, and social/emotional.*

A comprehensive assessment system must consider the following factors:

- the child as an individual and as a group member
- the other stakeholders—parents, teachers, administrators, policy-board members, and legislators—as participants in the process as well as consumers of the products
- the program philosophy and the curriculum or intervention strategy of the program
- the purpose for evaluating, measuring, or documenting progress
- available methods and the accuracy, usability, and meaning of the results

The settings for the age span contribute to the immense task of developing a comprehensive assessment system, because the meaning of assessment varies with each of the factors just listed.

techniques methods, whether formal or informal, for gathering assessment information.

Assessment information may be gathered in a variety of formal and informal ways. **Techniques** employed for gathering information must be nondiscriminatory, continuous, and must result in meaningful documentation of child progress. The technique also must yield information that can be used easily and accurately by stakeholders.

Techniques for assessment decisions must be matched to purpose: Why is the information needed? What will happen when the information is gathered? Will changes in care or education follow? Will stakeholders document existing knowledge? The answers to each of these questions will influence the choice of technique for information gathering. An analogy to consider is as follows. Suppose you are cooking a dinner. If the dinner is a picnic, you may choose to fry a chicken at home or buy a bucket on the way to the park. You make this choice based on the weather (hot), food safety (no refrigeration), ease of serving, your skill as a cook, and so on. If the dinner is a celebration for a friend who is retiring after 40 years of teaching, you will use your best recipe for chicken that may take several hours to prepare (or cater from the best). You make this choice based on the occasion (celebration), your skill as a cook, and the time you have available for preparation. If the dinner is for 200 at the local community center, you grab a friend or two and choose a baked chicken recipe that can be made easily by several cooks. You make the decision based on the equipment available, the food interests of the group, and the ease of preparation and serving.

In each of these situations, you considered the purpose of the dinner, the social context, the expectations of the participants, the techniques available in your repertoire, and the skill that you have in using them. No matter how casually you gathered information for this dinner decision, you matched the purpose of the dinner to the techniques employed. It is the same with assessment; you must choose the techniques to suit the purpose. If you choose a test to gather information, you must know the important technical qualities of the test. You must consider factors of efficiency, accuracy, usability, appropriateness for the children you wish to examine, limits of the test, and others. All of these factors are discussed.

All assessment activities must be conducted for a particular purpose at a particular point in the lives of young children.

Decisions

Why are you gathering information on the children in your program? Reasons may include: it is time to decide what to teach or how to modify your instruction or intervention; it is time to report progress to parents; there is a concern about developmental progress of an individual or group on the part of parents or others; it is required to determine eligibility for service for special needs; or it is time to be accountable to the program or legislative body. *All of these occasions should be ongoing and routine in the lives of teachers and children.* These are important assessment situations in the lives of young children. It is important that their caregivers and teachers understand the stakes as they choose the technique to answer the questions. At best, an assessment not matched to purpose may just yield no important information related to purpose. At worst, assessment decisions based on incomplete, inaccurate, or otherwise technically flawed information may damage the life of a child.

Methods

The most basic technique that sustains most early childhood assessment is informed observation of the infant/toddler or child in action. To be an effective and accurate observer, the watcher must have the capacity to separate judgment from watching. For example: You look out your window and see several buildings of various ages. You describe the three brick buildings: one with concrete pillars and balconies, one with neo-classic Greek ornamentation, and one with a chain-link fence on top of it. You judge the one with the fence on top as "ugly," according to your (previously defined) criteria for "ugly" city skyscrapers. Contrast this with saying simply: "There are three brick buildings outside my window. One of them is ugly!"

Notice the missing information in the two descriptions. If the observation report were on a child, much information would be lost and decisions would be made based on fragmentary information. Another important consideration for the teacher or professional observer is knowledge of child development and all the other variables that affect development.

In addition to observation, techniques of assessment include interview and presentation of task to an individual or group. These may be structured or open-ended. There may be criteria for judging the information gathered or the assessor may be expected to bring clinical and contextual knowledge to bear when interpreting the way in which the child completes the interview or task. Some assessment procedures are specialized teaching techniques that give you an opportunity to gather information to solve an individualization of instruction problem. These techniques are called *task analysis*, a procedure for gathering detailed information about the learning activity of a particular child, and *functional analysis*, a procedure for reviewing behavior that may be inhibiting learning for a particular child in a particular program.

Finally, some techniques require that the child read, interpret, and solve paper-and-pencil activities that relate to definitions of development or curriculum. These measures are usually group achievement tests that are used primarily as accountability information (information gathered to see if the program is working). These paper-and-pencil measures are least appropriate for the youngest pupils in our age span. When choosing paper and pencil, you will need to be aware of the issues surrounding the limitations, use, and misuse of these measures.

Each of these techniques may be employed in a standardized or performance-based setting. The rules for interpretation and the limits for use of the results will vary accordingly. Each of these methods has strengths and limitations. Issues of accuracy, usability, defined limitations, and bias must be considered when applying any assessment technique. In all cases, the interpretation of an assessment measure must be related to the program and purpose for its use. For example, to be eligible for public services for children with special needs, standardized instruments must be used and applied with the appropriate limitations. This is the case because eligibility for service definitions includes test scores as one of the criteria. Of course, the score must be considered as only one of the pieces of information needed to make a final determination for program placement and participation.

Whenever information is gathered by assessment techniques, the information must then be applied to practice. That is, the information gathered for the purpose of program eligibility in the previous example becomes the baseline information that is used to plan intervention strategies. Interpreting assessment information and decision-making is an ongoing process. Information is continuously compared to standards, theory, and curricula so it can be evaluated. Evaluation occurs through matching information to standards for developmental and educational practice. The stakeholders in the assessment system then draw plans to advance and facilitate development. The assessors must remember that assessment results indicate the child's situation at only that moment in time. Further assessment may yield similar results, but only then is a pattern suggested. Even a pattern of assessment results, however, must be subjected to verification. For if the assessment measure is biased or if only some players in the system are in action, then the results may present only part of the story. "Any assessment results are like a photograph of a child: they only give one picture of the many-sided child" (Deno, 1990).

Table 1.2 lists some assessment decisions accompanied by examples of methods to address the questions. Column 1 lists some common assessment decisions. Column 2 lists methods for gathering information to make decisions for the questions. Column 3 raises contextual ambiguities that influence the choice of assessment method.

Assessment decisions are never as easy as they first appear. By keeping an open mind, having an awareness of the complexity of the task, and using your knowledge of child development, appropriate curricular implementation based on these principles will assist you in the development of a repertoire of assessment techniques to apply in the situations where you must determine child progress and report your decisions to parents and others. Throughout this book, you will be shown a range of assessment techniques appropriate for the children who you serve. After choosing appropriately from among these techniques, you will consider the issues of reporting to parents and others. Assessing children for teaching, for monitoring individual progress, and for the reports that you make are among your most important duties and responsibilities.

Ethics and Responsibilities

The foundation of ethical behavior is personal recognition of the rights of children and families, the limits of personal knowledge, and the choice of appropriate assessment methods for programmatic decisions. Another key factor is keeping personal biases out of the process. This is particularly important when serving children whose social and cultural experiences may be different from your own. You must keep in mind that your sociocultural lens may affect your objectivity when you interact with children and families from diverse cultures. You must also remember that families do not exist in a static definition of a particular

TABLE 1.2   Assessment decision

Decision	Methods to consider	Contextual ambiguities
1. Shall I introduce a new food to baby Shiloh?	observation of adjustment to previous foods; expert consultation	For Shiloh, critical variables include which stakeholder is making the decision and Shiloh's age. The decision is appropriately made by parents. If she is 1 month old, hopefully, the parents will consult an expert. If she is 18 months old, previous experience and knowledge of the expert's previous advice may guide the decision.
2. Is baby Nicholas getting a long enough nap?	observation of waking state and comparison to knowledge of his previous patterns	Nicholas and the nap is an assessment decision that may be made by parents or caregiver, based on knowledge of Nicholas. Even then, issues of teething, overstimulation, and other variables may come into play here. Care interventions will vary depending on the available information. An ongoing adjustment to Nicholas' sleeping routine will be made.
3. Is toddler Debbie's speech developing typically?	observation of Debbie in various situations requiring conversation; interview of Debbie's parents; developmental screening	If Debbie is saying only a few words, the assessment decision may seem to point to developmental screening. The decision changes, however, if the context includes a bilingual situation. Intervention and teaching activities will then support both languages and a hasty judgment of deficient will be curtailed.
4. Are the children in my preschool group playing cooperatively?	observation and comparison to definition of cooperative play; performance task	Group process evaluation seems to contain no ambiguity for the assessment decision-maker. However, definition of cooperation and previous experiences of children influence the context of this decision. Teachers must provide descriptors for those tasks that they wish to use as evaluation markers. If the purpose of the assessment is to judge whether more experience is needed, then teachers observe and intervene accordingly.
5. Are the children tired of easel painting?	collection of paintings; frequency checklists	No one is easel painting. What is the reason? Maybe you need to change the paint colors. Maybe you need to see what else is available. Maybe it is not important that no one is painting. You make a teaching decision for yourself based on reflection about these and other hypotheses.
6. Shall the preschool class study "our families"?	review of curricular goals; evaluation of child interest through discussion	Several children in your class report that they will soon have new brothers and sisters. Your program guide calls for the inclusion of a theme on families. You make teaching plans based on this and other information.
7. Is Oswald's conflict with peers as expected developmentally?	observation of Oswald in diverse settings; interview of Oswald's parents; developmental screening; diagnostic assessment by specialist	Oswald is indeed combative. He kicks, screams, bites, spits, and throws toys. This pattern of behavior has been consistent since September. In conversations with his mother you note that she is similarly bothered at home with these outbursts. It is indeed time to seek an expert. If, however, Oswald started this stream of acting out following a major life crisis (new sibling, loss of family member, move, and so on), you may first plan intervention in the program geared toward reassuring Oswald.

Decision	Methods of consider	Contextual ambiguities
8. Do the first graders in my program understand the concept of a story?	review of checklist record according to criteria for the definition; performance task	Concept of a story, as empirically defined by your program, seems to be critical piece of information most first graders will need to know. Your choose an appropriate technique (e.g., story map) to gather the information and plan further teaching for those who have not developed an awareness or mastery of this concept. The contextual variables include definitions of the task, child experience with stories, and language development.
9. Are the third graders mastering the mathematical knowledge required by the state goals?	checklist comparison to the state goals: performance tasks; required achievement tests.	Third-grade teachers are indeed responsible for state learning goals. So you plan to meet the goals through the implementation of a curriculum that is derived from these as well as other goals. You teach, you assess, you reteach. But, what if the goals, are unrealistic? You do not have an assessment question; you have a policy problem that you and other stakeholders, parents, principals, and others must solve in the best interest of the children.
10. Is Louis demonstrating a talent for visual arts?	collection of art products; expert consultation	Louis seems to produce paintings and drawings unlike and that you have seen in second grade. You can enjoy these paintings, assist Louis in developing his talent, or refer to an expert. You must consider the wishes and interests of Louis and his parents before following up, since there may be important sociocultural variables that influence whether Louis should be encouraged in artistic activities.

culture. Our society is composed of socioeconomic variables that impact family identification as well as the "traditional" cultural norms. In addition, families choose, on the basis of their experiences, whether or not to identify with "mainstream American values" some or all of the time. Thus, it is crucial to take your cues from the family when considering issues of culture, social class, and ethnicity that may affect an assessment plan. You want the family to know that you accept and value the learner, that you have knowledge of the family's cultural and linguistic background, that you recognize and appreciate the differences in school and home culture, and finally that you grasp the cultural transitions and other support needed by the family (Lynch & Hanson, 2004; National Association for the Education of Young Children, 2005; Stefanakis, 1998). Failure to consider the complexity of the social and cultural context can result in serious damage.

The dreadful history of improper decisions for children includes the mismatch of method to purpose, interpretation of results beyond the limits of the technique employed, and failure to consider the role of contextual factors. Currently, early-childhood educators must wrestle with the demands for accountability and whether or not the measures employed are appropriate for the children and families that they serve. The risk in ignoring this responsibility is lifetime stigmatization of young children and the foreshortening of educational opportunity. As well, teachers should recognize the messages that they send to children about learning achievement through the decisions that they make about the placement of children in work-groups, the materials that they use with individuals and groups, the ways they motivate (or don't) to try various learning experiences, the choices and responsibilities available for young children to engage, and the overall learning climate as well as relationships with the other stakeholders—parents, community, and so on (Weinstein, 2004).

An important responsibility of child-care and teaching personnel is providing information to parents and others about the developmental process and progress of individual children. This information must be held and shared in confidence.

In addition, teachers have a central role in "Child Find." This means that teachers must screen and refer children in their care who may need special intervention. Neisworth and Bagnato (2000) outline best practice for this screening that links to program planning. Best practice includes the need to be sure that the assessment methods are acceptable, authentic, collaborative, convergent, equitable, sensitive, and congruent. In short, this means assessment for identification for special programs is a process with many technical components that require careful planning, implementation, and interpretation. Equal protection under the law requires that teachers must use techniques appropriate for the situation and the child, as well as participate in the multidisciplinary team that develops the Individualized Education Plan (or the Individualized Family Service Plan for children birth to age 3). Federal legislation (i.e., the Individuals with Disabilities Education improvement Act [IDEA] of 2004) delineates the rights of children for entitlement to special intervention and education to meet special needs so that they may have an equal educational opportunity. Special educational decisions will involve you, the classroom teacher, as a member of a team. You will have help in assuming these responsibilities.

In your own program, however, you must assume the responsibility for the *match of* child, curriculum, and assessment technique. You must apply the current knowledge of early childhood education theory and principles in making this match. "Above all, we shall not harm the child. We shall not participate in practices that are disrespectful, degrading, dangerous, exploitative, intimidating, psychologically damaging, or physically harmful to children" (Feeney & Kipnis, 1989; see also NAEYC, 2005).

In the past, good intentions regarding the gathering of assessment information about children have resulted in inappropriate evaluation decisions. This has happened in large part because one or more elements of the comprehensive assessment system have been ignored or unknown to the individual making the judgments. For example, IQ tests, a form of structured interview and tasks presented individually to children, have often been applied as single-technique options for assessment and placement decisions. The factor of English-language facility has sometimes been ignored. Life chances for children have been affected. When these instruments are used as part of an assessment system, usually when attempting to diagnose disabilities so that a child may be entitled to special educational or intervention services, it is imperative that the instruments themselves be reviewed for cultural bias and that the results found be applied fairly to the child assessed with this standardized format (Baca & Cervantes, 2004; Rhodes, Ochoa & Ortiz, 2005; Valenicin & Suzuki, 2001). In the present, early childhood educators struggle with some of the same issues, particularly those surrounding the use of achievement tests in the primary years.

CURRENT ISSUES IN THE ASSESSMENT OF YOUNG CHILDREN

An early childhood assessment system has many players. The central figure is the infant/toddler/child who can participate in more informed and self-conscious ways as maturity and experience are acquired. The second crucial players are the child's parents. Parents have expectations and personal social/cultural knowledge and information to add to the assessment mix. Teachers, child-care providers, and related service personnel enter as important figures in children's lives and contribute to the information pool. Administrators and boards, as those responsible for program excellence and evaluation, participate in the system. Often administrative and board participation is at the policy level—setting standards, prescribing methods, and designating curricula that match the outcomes for learning. Administrators, of course, are responsible for monitoring the policy requirements of boards, local, state, and federal governmental requirements. Finally, a society that cares for the youngest of our citizens—babies, toddlers, and young children—participates as standard setter and judge. Who are our children? What are their skills, knowledge, and attitudes? The players in the assessment system grapple with many current assessment issues, including accountability, high-stakes decisions, authentic and portfolio assessment, and outcomes-based reporting. None of these issues is simple; many overlap in their origins and complexity. In the next section, each is briefly outlined. These issues are further addressed throughout the book in the context of their impact on the assessment system being described.

Accountability

Stakeholders most concerned with broad social interests, in the provision of equal opportunities for all and the problems inherent in such efforts, have concerned themselves with **accountability.** As well, other

accountability being responsible for the proper education of all children.

17

national interests result in calls for accountability—improvement and educational reform to improve "results." "[P]ersistent criticism of schools began with the onset of the Cold War soon after World War II ended in 1945. The steady stream of negativity probably accounts for much of our openness to negativity. At that time, politicians, generals, defense specialists, and university professors came to see schools for the first time as integral to national defense and, at the same time, as lacking" (Bracey, 2004, p.1). Educational accountability is not a new idea (Flesch, 1955), and professionals have usually made their best effort to teach "all" the children. Efforts have sometimes fallen short, as highlighted in the 1983 report *A Nation at Risk* (National Commission on Excellence in Education, 1983). This report suggested that large numbers of American youngsters were being miseducated. In response, across the country, states enacted legislation to "check up" on school districts. These checks were shown in the form of state-mandated testing, state-mandated learning goals, and learner outcomes.

Then came No Child Left Behind (NCLB; P.L. 107–110, 2002), a reauthorization of the Elementary and Secondary Act of 1965, requiring increased emphasis on adequate yearly progress of all learners in public school and third-grade achievement testing in reading and math, state plans for assessment, as well as the mandate for highly qualified teachers across the nation. Failure to comply with these federal demands places school districts at risk for loss of federal funds. With the passage of this law, the debate about what to test—mostly reading and math—how to use the results, and whether the imperatives of the law are realistic and obtainable heightened awareness about schools and schooling. The law is advertised on the U.S. Department of Education's website as one that provides "stronger accountability results, more freedom for states and communities, encouraging proven methods, more choice for parents" (http://www.nclb.gov).

In the parent information publication that accompanies NCLB, the "The Facts About No Child Left Behind" states that school districts must provide:

- *School District Report Cards:* NCLB legislation gives parents report district-wide cards so they can see which schools in their district are succeeding and why. With this information, parents, community leaders, teachers, principals, and elected leaders have access to the information they need to improve schools.

- *Public School Choice:* NCLB legislation may let parents transfer their child to another public school if the state says that the child's school is "in need of improvement." The school district may pay for transportation for the child. Contact your school district to find out if your school district offers this opportunity.

- *Extra Help with Learning:* NCLB may also provide a child with free tutoring and extra help with schoolwork if the state says that child's school has been "in need of improvement" for at least 2 years. This extra help is often referred to as "supplemental educational services." Contact the child's school district to find out if a child qualifies.

- *Parental Involvement:* NCLB requires schools to develop ways to get parents more involved in their child's education and in improving the school. Parents should contact their child's school to find out how they can get involved.

- *Scientifically Based Research:* NCLB focuses on teaching methods that have been proven by research to work. "Experimenting" on children by using educational fads is not advocated.

- *Reading First:* NCLB provides more than one billion dollars a year to help children learn to read. Reading First is the NCLB segment dedicated to ensuring that all children learn to read on grade level by the third grade. Reading First provides money to states and many school districts to support high-quality reading programs based on the best scientific research. Contact your school district to find out if its reading program is based on research. (http://www.nclb.gov)

Each of these federally required components of NCLB legislation that states must observe are geared toward educational reform, appealing to parents and other stakeholders who remain concerned about the achievement gaps across our country between middle-class children, affluent children, and young children living in poverty. Not many disagree with the above components that seek parent involvement in their children's education and the assurance that schools will provide appropriate and adequate learning experiences—instead, the crux of the debate about NCLB centers around testing, particularly, the role that

high-stakes decision is
any test applied to make
life-affecting decisions for
the educational futures of
young childlren.

testing plays in making important, life-altering decisions about child
education—**high-stakes decisions.** Examples of high-stakes decisions
include decisions for placing children in special programs away from
peers made on the basis of one test experience and decisions to retain
young children in third grade based on performance on a single standardized test. *While state departments of education make and implement
plans and school districts implement various ways to demonstrate compliance
with the law, as a teacher you will need to keep up to date on this legislation
because the curricular interpretations by states will have a profound impact on
your practice as an educator.* Various organizations and journal publications regularly post and publish updates about this law; check the
Internet sites provided in this chapter's Technology Links section. In the
meantime, remember as you read that *this reform legislation influences
your teaching—everyday.* For, "(m)easuring student learning is a central
focus of the NCLB. In fact, U.S. Secretary of Education Margaret
Spelling has referred to testing as "the linchpin of the whole doggone
thing." Spelling has insisted states strictly follow the law's requirement
of testing students each year in grades 3–8, but new opportunities may
open up for states that want to change the way they assess student
learning (ASCD, 2005, p. 1).

There are, however, some difficulties with this approach. For example, "California projects that by the witching year of 2014, when
100 percent of the nation's students are supposed to be 'proficient,'
99 percent of the state's schools will be labeled as 'failing' under NCLB"
(Bracey, 2004, p. 67). "If we assume that we will continue to make the
same progress on National Assessment of Educational Progress
(NAEP, the federal report card, http://www.ed.gov) in the future as in
the previous decade, we can get 100 percent of our students to reach
proficiency in mathematics in 61 years at the 4th grade, 66 years at the
6th grade, and 166 years at the 12th grade" (Linn, 2003). Also, "to a very
great extent, NCLB equates teaching quality and students' learning
with high-stakes test scores . . . this equation precludes the use of multiple measures of progress toward goals and multiple assessments of
learning . . . which provide a more complex picture of both students'
learning and effective teaching" (Cochran-Smith, 2005, p. 101).

Other problems based on an "intuitive" understanding of test theory
on the part of legislators and other important stakeholders are the following beliefs: "a test measures what it says at the top of the page; a
score is a score is a score; any two tests that measure the same thing can
be made interchangeable with a little 'equating' magic; . . . score a test
by adding up scores for items; an A is 93%, a B is 85%, a C is 78%, 70%
is passing; multiple choice questions measure only recall; . . . can tell an
item is good by looking at it" (Braun & Mislevy, 2005, pp. 489–497).
None of these assertions are particularly true, even though they may
make intuitive sense. Thus, ". . . we need to do a much better job of
communicating to a variety of audiences the basics of testing and the
dangers we court when we ignore the principles and methods of
educational measurement" (Braun & Mislevy, 2005, p. 497). Beyond the

statistical improbability of meeting the law's requirements, there are many practical issues that affect the everyday lives of teachers, children, and families. For example, for English-language learners (ELLs) who must reach high standards in English-language arts and mathematics by 2014, there are special challenges, including:

1. Historically low ELL performance and slow improvement.
   a. State tests show ELL performance oftentimes 20–30 percentage points below other students and little improvement across many years.
2. Measurement accuracy.
   a. . . . Language demands of tests negatively influence accurate measurement of ELL performance. For the ELL, tests measure both *achievement* and language *ability*.
3. Instability of the ELL subgroup, i.e., the population of children in the group varies across time, adding newly arrived ELLs whose language ability and achievement is typically lower.
4. Factors beyond school control.
   a. Such as the variability of parental educational achievement within the population that seems to influence student performance on standardized tests" (Abedi & Dietel, 2004, p. 1).

It is also important to recognize that the ELL population is diverse. In Colorado, for example, Escamilla, Chavez, and Vigil (2005) show that the Spanish speakers in English-language acquisition/bilingual classrooms are among the highest achieving students in their schools. The bilingual program no doubt supports the achievement gains, so it is not the students who are a problem, but the program that may be needed to promote achievement. The educational issues are indeed complex. "One-size thinking" can't possibly fit everyone.

"In summary, the NCLB mandated a method for designing achievement standards that . . . depended on each state's political and educational authorities to apply the (standards setting) method as they saw fit. This process has resulted in marked differences across states in the content and difficulty level of tests and in the rigor of achievement standards" (Thomas, 2005, p. 65). Thus, there is some "collateral damage"—high incidence of failing schools, excellent schools dubbed failures, one-size-fits-all error, increased retention in grade rates, high school graduation rates reduced, rule changes continue, and inconsistency across states (Thomas, 2005, pp. 66–75). Finally, does research-based mean "value" neutral? Often research begins from a philosophical stance—a case to be made for an approach. As a result, though most of the national curricular organizations promote practices that center on learner development as well as student achievement, the wary teacher will want to be aware of the philosophical underpinnings that shape district assessment requirements, even if they are research-based.

High-Stakes Decisions

Accountability decisions become high stakes when funding is appropriated based on the results of tests and when the names of schools "not achieving" are published in the newspaper (i.e., school report cards). Such efforts are thought to call attention to educational malpractice. This may well be so in some cases. Often it is a case of not considering the context of the learning environment, not matching the assessment instrument to the curriculum, interpreting tests beyond their limits, or other errors of measurement application. In early childhood, the error most commonly made is the use of screening and readiness tests to deny kindergarten entrance; retention in kindergarten on the basis of test scores; choice of primary curriculum based on test scores; and third-grade retention on the basis of test scores. Historically, tests have placed children in special education programs on the basis of IQ alone. These decisions are not only wrong, they have lifelong consequences for the individuals involved—affecting the opportunity for education, self-esteem, and chances to change life goals. When it comes to serving the most vulnerable of our young—those with disabilities—appropriate ethical principles include:

- *Autonomy:* supporting the family in ethical decision-making.

  This is the opposite of the past paternalistic practice of the family as client with the expert telling what should be done. Often the plans were made without regard to the family context, resulting in plans that were not suitable for particular families—they were too "cookie cutter" and not responsive.

- *Beneficence and nonmalfeasance:* a balance of benefits and harms.

  This is the "first, do-no-harm" orientation of traditional medical ethics balanced with the accountability orientation—will there be a benefit?

- *Justice:* weighing of risks, costs, and benefits.

These principles apply to making services accessible to all young children (Epps & Jackson, 2000; see also The Children's Defense Fund Mission Statement and Leave No Child Behind® movement).

Such principles should guide actions and decisions with regard to the moral issues involved in assessment. Because assessment goals will continue to evolve from NCLB and other federal initiatives, you will want to be familiar with the tenets of professional use of achievement testing programs as declared in the American Educational Research Association (2000) position statement that outlines good practice for high-stakes tests:

- Validity statements regarding a test must match the purpose for the high-stakes use.

- Avoid one test for decisions that affect an individual student's life chances or education opportunities.

- When achievement testing is part of reform efforts, students should have adequate resources and an opportunity to learn.
- Policy-makers should be informed of any negative consequences of a testing program.
- The test and the curriculum must be aligned.
- Validity of passing scores and achievement level must be obtained before using them as a high-stakes indication.
- Those who fail must have opportunities for meaningful remediation.
- Attention must be given to those with language differences, as well as disabilities.
- Careful attention must be given to the rules for who should be tested and how.
- Sufficient reliability must be established for each intended use.
- Ongoing evaluation of the testing program is necessary.
- Of fundamental importance to all teachers is the knowledge of the statistical aspects of testing.

You will want to be sure that you understand the technical qualities and limitations of all kinds of tests so that you can advocate for children, especially those who are most vulnerable due to economic, personal, or social conditions that affect learning opportunities. "Bell curve thinking is the enemy of millions of children who have unrecognized genius . . . savage inequalities in schools' services are eliminated by giving students equal access to good teachers. The power of good teaching has overwhelming support in the literature. The high-stakes standardized testing movement advocates cannot ignore the connection of such uses to the pessimists who are, in fact, enemies of the poor . . . in the final analysis, what do we really want? Will we keep weighing the elephant to make it grow? . . . We need high-stakes services for our children. Then, any testing will be a matter of small concern" (Hilliard, 2000, pp. 293–304). As an early childhood teacher you can make a difference in the lives of children by knowing about the limits of high-stakes assessment and by becoming familiar with the authentic assessment techniques that are part of the curricular planning process. **Authentic assessments** are those that are most similar to the tasks of the classroom. Thus, they are the ways that teachers judge everyday whether children are learning and lessons are working. These are the assessment methods that are described by early childhood educators in position statements.

authentic assessment
determining developmental progress of children through a variety of means, including observations and special problems or situations.

Authentic Assessment and Portfolios

As advocates for the best interests of young children, scores of early childhood educators are concerned with appropriate practice that includes authentic assessment (Bredekamp & Rosegrant, 1992; Kamii, 1990; Meisels, 2000; Shepard, Hammerness, Darling-Hammond, & Rust, 2005). Many leaders have articulated the link from theory about child learning to the application for appropriate curriculum. In turn, assessment practices must be consistent with this theoretical knowledge. From the field of early childhood and elsewhere have come assessment activities that more closely resemble the activities of the preschool and primary classroom. This is part of the current trend toward authentic assessment, performance-based assessment, and portfolio assessment. Authentic, performance-based assessment is the evaluation that engages children and teachers daily, in many ways in answer to the basic questions: What learning is occurring? How do we know? What shifts in practice should we make? Portfolios are the vehicles used to gather the documents of learning. An integral part of the gathering of this documentation is reflection on the documents themselves as well as the process of learning. Although these performance-based portfolio assessment trends are promising, the measures are not without limits. In sum, though, authentic assessment and the collection of child work samples in portfolios is at the heart of the everyday work of the early childhood educator. It is through this work that children learn to judge their own progress and begin their journeys as learners in an educational system that demands accountability.

SUMMARY

Each of the players (child, parent, caregivers, teachers, administrators, boards, legislators) in the rearing (care and education) of a child comes to the stage with a distinct knowledge base, potentially dissimilar goals, and often diverse notions of how to gather information for the purpose of judging developmental process and progress. Each of the players applies information to the standards/outcomes that relate to their ideas of important questions and issues to be documented, measured, or otherwise assessed and evaluated. Because of the complexity surrounding the interface of these various players, each must be considered separately, and each must be careful to practice responsible/responsive assessment so that the assessment system and the stakeholders treat children fairly and equitably, both individually and collectively.

FIELD ACTIVITIES

1. On your campus, ask students not enrolled in education to define assessment. With your classmates, review the definitions collected. How do these definitions compare to those discussed in this chapter? What kind of public awareness plan should be made to address students on your campus?

2. Review the week's newspapers or television coverage on education. Note any stories that involve assessment. How are these stories treated? What would you do differently if you were the reporter or newscaster?

3. At the college level, portfolio assessment currently is a part of the way that students document progress. Find out who among your friends—those in education and those who major in the arts or business—is required to participate in the process. Look at the syllabi; talk with your friends about the experiences with the directions and the judgments made. What works?

4. Gather two or three news reports about stakeholders' views of testing in your community. Identify community concerns. Share your information with colleagues.

5. Visit one of the websites listed in the Technology Links section of this chapter. Present information to your colleagues about the site and what you learned about assessment and the policy issues you reviewed.

IN-CLASS ACTIVITIES

1. Reflect on your own experiences with assessment. Which have you enjoyed the most? Which do you hope no one will ever have to repeat? How do your experiences influence what you believe should be done for young children?

2. With a partner, list all of the details that you have heard or read about NCLB. Compare your list to NCLB the http://www.nclb.gov site. Did you get all of the details? Then shift to your state department of education website. What else did you learn about the law and its provisions?

STUDY QUESTIONS

1. Identify the issues related to the development of a comprehensive assessment system for the early childhood years.

2. Who are the important stakeholders? How are they involved?

3. For which assessment decisions must early childhood teachers assume primary responsibility? How is this assessment process developed?

4. Which techniques do early childhood teachers use in their assessment activities? What techniques do other stakeholders use?

5. Where do teachers fit in the accountability process? What high-stakes decisions must early childhood teachers prepare for?

REFLECT AND RE-READ

- I can define assessment and describe its components.
- I am becoming aware of the diverse views of stakeholders in the assessment process.

- I can explain *high-stakes decisions*. And give examples.
- I have preliminary familiarity with the complexity of assessment issues in early childhood education.

CASE VIGNETTE

Leisel is a 5-year, 11-month-old girl who attends full-day kindergarten in Cincinnati. Leisel has hazel eyes, brown hair, and a fair complexion. She is of average weight and height. Born in Germany, Leisel lived there with her parents until she came to the United States at age 3 1/2. She has no brothers or sisters. Mr. Braun, her father, was transferred to the United States by his employer for a 5-year contract; Mr. Braun is fluent in English. Mrs. Braun is enrolled in English as Second Language courses at Cincinnati State Technical and Community College and works as a nanny in the mornings. Everyone speaks German at home. At the beginning of Leisel's kindergarten year, she spoke no English. Now in the spring, she speaks English and enjoys friendships with peers in school and outside of school. To date, Leisel's school performance is average according to her teacher, Mrs. Barnes. Is she ready for first grade? How would you find out? What should Mrs. Barnes do to prepare Leisel for first grade?

Source: From L. Spalding, 2003, submitted in partial fulfillment of T&L 411, Assessment in Early Childhood Education: DePaul University. Used by permission.

TECHNOLOGY LINKS

http://apa.org

American Psychological Association. Position papers and books about assessment.

http://www.aera.org

American Educational Research Association. Position papers and books about assessment.

http://www.annenberginstitute.org

Annenberg Institute for School Reform. Position papers on standardized testing.

http://catalyst-chicago.org

School reform journal in Chicago. Articles applicable to urban settings across the country.

http://www.childrensdefense.org/

Children's Defense Fund. Statistics and position papers on the lives of children.

http://www.ccsso.org

Council of Chief State School Officers. Position papers and policy statements on best practices in education.

http://www.csteep.bc.edu

Center for the Study of Testing, Evaluation, and Educational Policy (CSTEEP). Position papers and policy statements on assessment and evaluation.

http://www.ecs.org/

Education Commission of the States. Resources for state leaders and others on educational policy issues.

http://www.learningfirst.org

Learning First Alliance. Coalition of associations with projects, resources, and position papers available online.

http://www.cse.ucla.edu

National Center for Research on Evaluation, Standards, and Student Testing (CRESST). Research center that publishes updates and a newsletter, and holds conferences on assessment and standards.

http://www.fairtest.org

National Center for Fair and Open Testing. An advocacy organization with position papers on tests and assessment, a newsletter, and other activities.

http://www.aecf.org/kidscount/

Kids Count is a project of the Annie E. Casey Foundation that tracks the status of children.

http://www.naeyc.org

National Association for the Education of Young Children. With particular interest in children birth to age 8, this site contains links to position papers, best teaching practices, and other items of educational importance to young children and their families.

http://nga.org

National Governors Association. Best practices and position papers of the states, including many resources on NCLB.

http://www.ed.gov

U.S. Department of Education. A source for legislation, government reports, and links to educational issues.

SUGGESTED READINGS

Bredekamp, S., & Copple, C. (Eds.). (1997). *Developmentally appropriate practice in early childhood programs serving children from birth through age eight.* Washington, DC: National Association for the Education of Young Children.

Gullo, D. F. (2005). *Understanding assessment evaluation in early childhood education* (2nd ed.). New York: Teachers College Press.

Kleinert, H. L., & Kearns, J. F. (2001). *Alternate assessment: Measuring outcomes and supports for students with disabilities.* Baltimore: Paul H. Brookes.

Kohn, A. (2004). *What does it mean to be well educated? And other essays on standards, grading and other follies.* Boston: Beacon Press.

Popham, W. J. (2004). *America's "failing" schools.* New York: Routledge/Falmer.

Sacks, P. (1999). *Standardized minds: The high price of America's testing culture and what you can do about it.* Cambridge, MA: Perseus.

Salvia, J., & Ysseldyke, J. E. (2004). *Assessment* (9th ed.). Boston: Houghton Mifflin.

School readiness: Closing racial and ethnic gaps. (2005) *The Futures of Children, 15.*(1).

2

Developing Family Partnerships in Assessment

Terms to Know

- parent perspective
- parental reports
- parent questionnaires
- behavior questionnaires
- parent interview
- parents' rights

Chapter Overview

The early childhood assessment process needs parents and family members as key partners. This partnership shapes the nature of future school and child-care communication in the lives of young children. Questionnaires and interviews with parents are part of an early childhood assessment system. The assessment process links families to parent education programs and parent–teacher collaboration efforts. The partnership assessment process lends itself to problem-solving, prereferral activities, and, finally, the formal process for identifying young children who may have disabilities. This chapter rolls out the underpinnings for partnership relations with parents, setting the stage for collaboration in all assessment practices described throughout the book.

Assess as You Read

- What do parents know about their children that they can share with teachers?
- What are the best methods for getting information from parents or other significant family members?
- What are the key elements in educating parents about school and schooling?
- Who makes decisions about intervention plans for young children?

FAMILY PARTNERSHIPS IN THE ASSESSMENT SYSTEM

When families enroll their child in a program, the parents— either casually, formally, or informally—will be interviewed by a teacher, director, social worker, or other early childhood education professional. (See Box 2.1 for a sample enrollment interview form). This interview forms the foundation for the group care and education process for the life of the child; That is, the first experience that families have with intervention programs, child-care centers, or schools forms a lasting impression. It is your responsibility as an early childhood professional to appreciate the family perspective. In this way, you can care responsively for the young children and families served in your programs. When teachers begin the enrollment process, they need to keep in mind the **parent perspective**, as well as the infant program, child-care center, or school's "need to know."

parent perspective a parent's perception of a child's development, learning, and education.

Teachers Want to Know

Typically, teachers want to know what families think about their child's development, learning, and education. It is also important to know about the cultural and family traditions that shape the family's view on these important parts of child life. Depending on the enrollment situation, teachers and caregivers will need more information and will require special interview skills to acquire this information. Often the teacher is a member of a team in the more specialized situations. The information you need depends on your teaching role.

Ms. Vogel, a home-caregiver, requires basic health, safety, and emergency contact information when enrolling baby Leslie. In addition, she needs to know Mr. and Mrs. Jefferson's preferences for naps, feeding, and any special toys that will comfort Leslie. If Ms. Vogel and the Jeffersons are neighbors, the need for additional formal interview may even be less.

As situations become more formal in child-care settings for groups of children, the teacher's "need to know" and the structure for obtaining information becomes more formal. In addition, the issues of cultural group values, language, and social class affect the initial trust for the budding partnership. In situations where young children have special needs and diagnosed disabilities, the teacher needs to know more. In any of these more specialized situations, the teacher relies on consultation or social work intervention that facilitates understanding of the family perspective. The family perspective is the foundation for the development of the Individualized Family Service Plan and an important component of the Individual Educational Plan required by the Individuals with Disabilities Education Act (P.L. 101–476). Sensitive teachers in any child-care or early education setting are familiar, however, with the many facets that influence the giving and receiving of information to and from families (cf. Berger, 2004; Berns, 2004; Gestwicki, 2004; Gonzalez-Mena, 2006).

Family Contribution

Families can contribute critical information regarding their children's abilities, strengths, possible problems, and educational needs. Family members have observed their children's behavior in a wide range of situations over a long period. They know whether their child is coordinated enough to play baseball, soccer, or basketball. They know how much sleep their second grader requires to avoid "cranky" behavior. Their descriptions of what their baby or child is doing can provide valuable information about that child's development and personal adjustment. Their questions, concerns, and interpretations regarding their children add an important perspective.

Parents of young children wonder about their child's development: "How is my child doing?" "Is my child doing well enough?" "Will my child learn to read?" "Will my child have friends?" At any given time, the child's parents may be more, or less, satisfied with what the child is doing, perhaps concerned about the child's development, or may at least have questions regarding the child. Teachers need to know how satisfied the parents are and how and whether they are concerned about something. Often family members are the first people to recognize that their children are not developing well. They may know that their child is "fidgety" or "flighty." Although parents recognize problems and potential problems, they may not be willing to share everything they know or all of their worries. Skillful and sensitive interviews will permit parents a greater opportunity for sharing their knowledge and concerns.

There is little question that "parents have the most information about the present functioning and past history of the child . . . the parent is the first and often best assessor of his/her child's functioning and problems" (Walker & Wiske, 1981). This important principle is one of those highlighted by the National Education Goals established in 1990. "Parents should be a valued source of assessment information, as well as an audience for assessment results" (U.S. Department of Education, 1991, p. 6). More than 40 years ago, Gesell and Amatruda (1954) emphasized the importance of involving parents in the identification of developmental problems of their young children. Even then, the point must have seemed self-evident. The Interdisciplinary Council on Developmental and Learning Disorders(ICDL) Clinical Practice Guidelines for Infants, Children, and Families with Special Needs (2000) stress the need for family co-leadership in planning and delivering intervention with their babies and children. This perspective is a shift from mere "family involvement" in which the "expert" determines the intervention or teaching prescription for a child or family. Thus, the foundation for co-leadership is the sharing of information.

Crucial Importance of Family Information

Information from families may cover a wide range of material: medical history and any current symptoms or concerns; the child's current developmental functioning and developmental history; personality and social-emotional adjustment, including behavioral/emotional problems; family information, including relevant stress factors such as loss of a parent through death or divorce; and other situational factors that might bear on the child's functioning.

Although parents possess a wealth of information about their children, one critical question is whether their reports are reliable or accurate. **Parental reports**—information collected by interview or questionnaire about a child, a situation, or problem—are not uniformly dependable; some parents are better observers of children than others. Also, some parents may give biased responses due to their own personal needs. A number of factors influence the accuracy of parental information including: (a) the parent's willingness to participate, (b) the parent's ability to comprehend the request for information and to provide accurate data about the child, and (c) the professional's ability to create useful parent-involving ways of obtaining information from parents.

However, research demonstrates that parental reports of children's current behavior are usually reliable, especially when teachers obtain these developmental reports through structured interviews or inventories (Liechtenstein & Ireton, 1984). In these situations, parents provide information about their young child's developmental abilities (e.g., Can your child draw pictures that can be recognized?) in screening and follow-along programs. In some of the first research of this type, Knobloch, Steren, Mulone, Ellison, and Risernberg (1979) used a parent-completed questionnaire including items taken from the Gesell Developmental and Neurological Evaluation to follow high-risk newborns for the first 2 years of life. In this study, parents' reports were quite similar to the results of professional evaluations. However, parental reports of history or early developmental milestones are not as reliable (Glascoe, MacLean, & Stone, 1991). Parents' concerns about their children's present development and behavioral problems are reliable indicators of problems (American Academy of Pediatrics, 2001; Glascoe, 1998). So, how can families become involved? The best methods flow from the daily or other conversations that teachers have with parents.

parental reports
information from a parent concerning a child.

METHODS FOR OBTAINING INFORMATION FROM FAMILIES

Information from families comes to teachers in a variety of ways: informally, in parents' comments about Suzy or Alex; in casual conversations; and in the questions parents ask and the concerns they express. More in-depth information may come in response to your questions at parent–teacher conferences. Sometimes teachers ask families to provide information more systematically through interviews and by completing **parent questionnaires.** Parent questionnaires are sets of questions that collect information from families about the facts and perceptions that families have regarding their child's development and behavior.

parent questionnaires
questionnaires given by child-care professionals to parents for obtaining information about a child.

When a child-care center is the first point of entry for a child into the care and education systems, teachers may find an enrollment questionnaire appropriate. Boxes 2.2 and 2.3 show other examples of questionnaires. These questions could form the basis for a systematic interview or the parent could complete the questionnaire alone. An interview conference follows the questionnaire completion.

Parent Questionnaires

Parent questionnaires obtain information similar to that obtained through interviews. Questionnaires completed by families prior to children's enrollment in a program are typically extensive and include questions about the child's health, development, personal habits and preferences, family information, and so on. Usually, such questionnaires include present status and history, such as medical history. These questionnaires serve as an adjunct to the Child Find screening process used by Head Start and other programs that seek to identify young children with disabilities. Typically, the parent questionnaires do not provide any guidelines for interpretation. Sometimes, briefer questionnaires determine more narrowly the child's present development, learning, or adjustment.

Using parent questionnaires routinely prior to parent-teacher conferences often sets an agenda or focus for the meeting. Sometimes parent questionnaires assist teachers in understanding parental perceptions of developmental or educational issues when children present learning or behavioral concerns. Using parent questionnaires can benefit parents and teachers in the following ways:

- Parents have an opportunity to thoughtfully describe their child, answer questions, and express questions and concerns.
- Teachers have advance information, so surprises may be limited.
- Teachers can assess whether the parents and teacher are in accord.
- Questionnaires may inform a later discussion.
- Teachers have an opportunity to educate or communicate program goals to families.

Box 2.2 *Example of a Program Enrollment Questionnaire*

Program Enrollment Questionnaire

Date _____ Time _____

Child name _____

Nickname (preferred name) _____

Parent(s) name(s)_____

Address _____

Phone number _____

Parent(s) present _____

With whom does the child live? _____

What do you expect your child to learn and do in preschool? _____

Have you or has your child lived in or visited other places? _____

What types of things do you do together as a family? (vacations, celebrating birthdays and holidays) _____

Of these, what does your child enjoy most? _____

What does your child do with free time? (favorite activities and interests, likes and dislikes)
_____

Has your child had experience with scissors _____ paint _____
play dough_____?

Does your child listen to stories? _____

Do you spend time reading with your child _____ coloring _____ drawing
_____ making things _____ cutting things out _____ cooking
_____?

Does your child know colors _____ numbers _____ write _____
emergency procedure _____ phone number and address _____?

Does your child have brothers or sisters? _____

Name(s)
Age/Grade

_____   _____
_____   _____
_____   _____
_____   _____

How does your child get along with siblings? _____

How does your child get along with other children? _____

continued

Box 2.2 *continued*

Has the child been to a babysitter, preschool; or religious school? _____

What is the child's reaction when you leave? _____

How does your child respond to new situations and people? Shy _____ bold _____ curious _____ slow to warm up _____ initiates conversation _____

Are there other significant adults in the child's life? (grandparents, aunts, uncles) _____

Does your child pretend in play? Does your child make up friends or places? _____

Is your child attached to a favorite toy, blanket, or stuffed animal? _____

Name of toy? _____

Is your child easily upset? By what kinds of things? Emotional? Fearful? Temper tantrums? _____

What do you do for discipline for misbehavior? _____

How does your child respond? _____

Does your child have chores or other responsibilities? _____

Are there any changes in the family—expecting, separation or divorce—that could affect your child? _____

Are there any physical limitations? (sight, hearing, walking, speech) _____

Is your child frequently ill? (colds, flu, earache, allergies) _____

Does your child take a nap? _____ Sleep patterns: early or late riser? _____

What are your child's eating habits? (meals, snacks, small or large appetite, uses fork and spoon or hands) _____

Does your child have toilet training problems? (accidents, bed wetter) _____

In what ways can we help your child this year? _____

Is there anything else you would like us to know about your child? _____

• Families may feel included, respected, and empowered through the responsibility acknowledged for completing the questionnaire.

Questionnaires are of limited value when parent literacy in English is an issue. As well, oftentimes questionnaires do not reflect the nuances of cultural values that may influence the parent's view of development, learning, and behavior. Nevertheless, they may be useful in some situations. One such situation may be when the parent or teacher is concerned about behavioral problems.

Box 2.3 *Child Information Collected at Enrollment by Interview or as Questionnaire*

Date _____

Child's name is _____ but likes to be called _____

Parent/guardian name _____

Medical conditions that affect child' activities _____

Emergency contact relative? _____

Don't ever contact _____

Allergies _____

Fears _____

Favorite toy _____

Favorite game _____

What does your child do well? _____

After-school activities (e.g., What does the child do? Go home? Go to a babysitter? Go to an after-school program?) _____

_____

Getting ready for school on a typical day: _____

_____

Weekend routines: _____

_____

How do you handle problem behaviors? What are some that you deal with regularly? Occasionally? _____

_____

How would you like to be involved with the school? Is there anything that would make it difficult for you to come to school?

_____

_____

Behavior Problem Questionnaires

The design of behavior problem questionnaires gives parents an opportunity to report any behavior problems, usually not to describe the child's overall adjustment. Typically, these questionnaires couch behavior in terms of problems or symptoms and may include a few related questions (Perrin, 1995). Usually these brief **behavior questionnaires** do not have norms but may be useful in early childhood settings as part of a screening process for the identification of children who are at risk of disability.

One limitation with most of these questionnaires is that they address one primary area (e.g., behavior) to the exclusion of other areas. Comprehensive questionnaires that address children's development, learning, adjustment, and health, including both strengths and problems, are more useful for teachers. An example of one such overall instrument is the Child Development Review–Parent Questionnaire (CDR–PQ) described in the next section.

Child Development Review–Parent Questionnaire

The Child Development Review–Parent Questionnaire (CDR–PQ) (Ireton, 1997) is a comprehensive survey of the child's present functioning that covers development, learning, adjustment (including behavior problems), health, vision, and hearing. The CDR–PQ includes six open-ended questions and a 26-item problems list. The CDR–PQ is standardized and there are norms for parents' responses to the six questions and the frequencies of the problem items by age and sex. Validity studies have shown that certain problem items are associated with placement in early childhood special education: These items include difficult-to-understand speech, clumsiness (poor walking and running), poor comprehension, and immaturity (Ireton, 1994). The instrument functions as an adjunct to an enrollment parent conference that follows a month or so after children begin in a program. An example of its use is as follows.

One early childhood teacher used this systematic approach with more than 100 parents of 3- to 6-year-olds in her preschool program (Ofstedal, 1993, personal communication). She found that parents welcomed the opportunity to complete the questionnaire, that completing it contributed to rapport, and that parents and teachers discussed and dealt with many more issues than in past conferences. Parents' reports helped the teacher prepare for the conference, including bringing along relevant materials for parents. Ms. Ofstedal reports that Bill was 4 when he started at the center. She immediately noticed how bright and curious he was, and was interested to see how his parents filled out the review, wondering what they thought about their son's progress. As she read the report, she saw that Bill's mom addressed so many concerns. Ms. Ofstedal soon met with her to sort out her thoughts. She gathered information for the parents concerning disobedience, poor listening skills, and hyperactivity. Bill's mom was excited to have concrete methods for handling situations. Ms. Ofstedal assured her that Bill was busy, but delightful, in school. He just needed structure and guidelines. The parents and Ms. Ofstedal met several times and the parents soon began to see positive changes in their son at home. They spent some "quality time" each day with him and established "rules" for him to follow.

Ms. Ofstedal noted: "Bill is the type of child a teacher loves to have in school. He is excited about everything and anything and flourishes in a structured environment. Our conference could have been 20 minutes of me praising their son without hitting on any of the serious problems they were having at home."

This example illustrates the importance of knowing something about how parents are doing with their children. The teacher and the parents formed a partnership that affirmed mutual interest and respect to start this child's educational career. (See Figure 2.1 for an example of a questionnaire used with a 2-year-old child named Matthew.)

Glascoe (1999) describes how parent questionnaires facilitate the communication process when children may be at risk of developmental delays or disabilities. She suggests that the questionnaire helps parents share a concern by serving to identify an important development issue for the parent. Questionnaires may also help parents know whether they should be worried because they compare the questions to typical developmental norms. The questionnaire may help teachers and others in planning screening or diagnostic assessment.

Another popular questionnaire process that is widely used in early childhood programs is the *Ages and Stages Questionnaires* (Bricker & Squires, 1999). Parents complete this 30-item, illustrated questionnaire at designated intervals. The questionnaire functions as a way to help parents and teachers know about any potential developmental issues in five key developmental areas: communication, gross motor, fine motor, problem solving, and personal-social. The questionnaires begin at age 4 months and continue through 5 years of age. Once completed, teachers convert the parent response to determine a child's progress in each developmental area. In addition to the questionnaires, learning activities are available for both family and teacher use. The activities support early childhood teachers and programs by identifying ways to enhance development related to the five key areas (Twombley & Fink, 2004).

Limitations of the Questionnaire Process

Use of parent questionnaires depends on how comfortable and able parents are to respond to paper-and-pencil forms. One advantage of questionnaires is that they provide advance information that can help focus an interview with the parents. Another advantage is that they may save some professional time because teachers can read the questionnaires more quickly than they can ask questions and listen for responses. However, questionnaires are a one-way communication device. That is, the teacher cannot observe the parent response. Thus, valuable clues about comfort with the questions and knowledge of their purpose may be lost.

In addition, questionnaires have serious limitations when parents and teachers are communicating in different languages. Paper forms may inhibit the candor with which parents approach the center when

child development review

Parent Questionnaire

Child's Name ___ Matthew _____ Sex ☑ Male ☐ Female
                   Last   First   Initial

Birthdate [   ][   ][   ] Today's Date [   ][   ][   ] Age [2] [0]
         Month Day Year   Month Day Year   Years Months

Your Name _____ Relationship to Child _____

Your Address _____ Telephone ___ Mother _____

A WORD TO PARENTS: Your answers to these questions can help us to understand your child. They also let us know what questions and concerns you may have about your child. The possible problems list at the bottom of the page provides another way of knowing your concerns about your child.

1. Please describe your child briefly? Very happy kid. Loves to play. Some "terrible twos" stuff.	4. Does your child have any special problems or disabilities? What are they? Health—urinary reflux. Healthy otherwise.
2. What has your child been doing lately? Loves to climb on things. Puts train track pieces together.	5. What questions or concerns do you have about your child? Not talking very much. Eating—skips meals—used to eat everything.
3. What are your child's strengths? A real sweet kid.	6. How are you doing, as a parent and otherwise, at this time? Three children—very busy. Hard to find time for self. Doing pretty well.

The following statements describe possible problems that your child may have. Read each statement carefully and check (✓) those statements that describe your child.

1. (✓) Health problems.
2. ( ) Growth, height, or weight problems.
3. (✓) Eating problems — eats poorly or too much, etc.
4. ( ) Bowel and bladder problems, toilet training.
5. (✓) Sleep problems. –up at night
6. ( ) Aches and pains; earaches, stomachaches, headaches, etc.
7. ( ) Energy problems; appears tired and sluggish.
8. ( ) Seems to have trouble seeing.
9. ( ) Seems to have trouble hearing.
10. ( ) Does not pay attention; poor listener.
11. (?) Does not talk well for age.
12. ( ) Speech is difficult to understand (Age 3 and older).
13. ( ) Does not seem to understand well; is slow to "catch on."

14. ( ) Clumsy; walks or runs poorly, stumbles or falls (Age 2 and older.)
15. ( ) Clumsy in doing things with his/her hands.
16. ( ) Immature; acts much younger than age.
17. ( ) Dependent and clingy.
18. ( ) Passive; seldom shows initiative.
19. ( ) Disobedient; does not mind well.
20. (✓) Temper Tantrums.
21. ( ) Overly Aggressive.
22. ( ) Can't sit still; may be hyperactive.
23. ( ) Timid, fearful, or worries a lot.
24. ( ) Often seems unhappy.
25. ( ) Seldom plays with other children.
26. ( ) Other?

STOP

Figure 2.1
Child development review
Source: Ireton, Harold R. (1990). *Child development review—Parent questionnaire.* Minneapolis: Behavior Science Systems, Inc. Used by permission.

42

Child Development Chart – First Five Years

Harold Ireton, Ph.D.

	SOCIAL	SELF-HELP	GROSS MOTOR	FINE MOTOR	LANGUAGE	
5-0 yrs.	Shows leadership among children	Goes to the toilet without help	Swings on swing, pumping by self	Prints first name (four letters)	Tells meaning of familiar words	**5-0** yrs.
4-6	Follows simple game rules in board games or card games	Usually looks both ways before crossing street	Skips or makes running "broad jumps"	Draws a person that has at least three parts - head, eyes, nose, mouth, etc.	Reads a few letters (five+)	**4-6**
4-0 yrs.		Buttons one or more buttons	Hops around on one foot, without support	Draws recognizable pictures	Follows a series of three simple instructions	**4-0** yrs.
	Protective toward younger children	Dresses and undresses without help, except for tying shoelaces			Understands concepts - size, number, shape	
3-6	Plays cooperatively, with minimum conflict and supervision	Washes face without help	Hops on one foot, without support	Cuts across paper with small scissors	Counts five or more objects when asked "How many?"	**3-6**
				Draws or copies a complete circle	Identifies four colors correctly	
	Gives directions to other children	Toilet trained	Rides around on a tricycle, using pedals		Combines sentences with the words "and," "or," or "but"	
3-0 yrs.		Dresses self with help	Walks up and down stairs - one foot per step	Cuts with small scissors	Understands four prepositions - in, on, under, beside	**3-0** yrs.
2-6	Plays a role in "pretend" games - mom-dad, teacher, space pilot	Washes and dries hands	Stands on one foot without support	Draws or copies vertical (|) lines	Talks clearly - is understandable most of the time	**2-6** Matthew's Age Line
	Plays with other children - cars, dolls, building				Talks in two-three word phrases or sentences	
	"Helps" with simple household tasks	Opens door by turning knob	Climbs on play equipment - ladders, slides	Scribbles with circular motion		
2-0 yrs.	Usually responds to correction - stops	Takes off open coat or shirt without help	Walks up and down stairs alone	Turns pages of picture books, one at a time	Follows two-part instructions	**2-0** yrs.
	Shows sympathy to other children, tries to comfort them	Eats with spoon, spilling little	Runs well, seldom falls		Uses at least ten words	
		Eats with fork		Builds towers of four or more blocks		
	Sometimes says "No" when interfered with		Kicks a ball forward		Follows simple instructions	
18 mos.	Greets people with "Hi" or similar	Insists on doing things by self such as feeding	Runs	Scribbles with crayon	Asks for food or drink with words	**18** mos.
	Gives kisses or hugs	Feeds self with spoon	Walks without help	Picks up two small toys in one hand	Talks in single words	
	Wants stuffed animal, doll or blanket in bed	Lifts cup to mouth and drinks	Stands without support	Stacks two or more blocks	Uses one or two words as names of things or actions	
12 mos.	Plays patty-cake	Picks up a spoon by the handle	Walks around furniture or crib while holding on	Picks up small objects - precise thumb and finger grasp	Understands words like "No," "Stop," or "All gone"	**12** mos.
	Plays social games, peek-a-boo, bye-bye		Crawls around on hands and knees		Word sounds - says "Ma-ma" or "Da-da".	
9 mos.	Pushes things away he/she doesn't want		Sits alone . . . steady, without support	Picks up object with thumb and finger grasp	Wide range of vocalizations (vowel sounds, consonant-vowel combinations)	**9** mos.
	Reaches for familiar persons	Feeds self cracker	Rolls over from back to stomach	Transfers toy from one hand to the other	Responds to name - turns and looks	
6 mos.	Distinguishes mother from others	Comforts self with thumb or pacifier	Turns around when lying on stomach	Picks up toy with one hand	Vocalizes spontaneously, social	**6** mos.
	Social smile	Reacts to sight of bottle or breast	Lifts head and chest when lying on stomach	Looks at and reaches for faces and toys	Reacts to voices Vocalizes, coos, chuckles	
Birth						**Birth**

Figure 2.1
(Continued)

43

parent literacy is a factor, when cultural norms find paper-and-pencil formats "less than friendly," or when parents are enrolling children for less than "choice" reasons.

For example, the public aid caseworker tells Susan Teenager that she must enroll her 3-year-old in the local "at risk" program and attend classes to secure her GED. Susan may have many mixed reactions about "the fact" of her child being "at risk", sending her baby to school, attending school herself, and—not the least—"growing up" as another single parent in her peer group. A questionnaire may heighten her feelings of vulnerability or attack her autonomy. After all, she may feel uncertain of her mothering capacities, as well. Susan may choose to answer the questions haphazardly or she may not answer them at all, thus starting the baby's career with "a bad taste" toward teachers in the early childhood setting. A paper cannot answer her questions, comment on what a happy baby she seems to have, and so on.

In addition, many questionnaires lack any kind of standardization. Standardization of formal assessment instruments is an important issue that you must consider when choosing questionnaires. Both the *Child Development Review* and the *Ages and Stages Questionnaires* are notable exceptions; both are standardized. In the technical reports available for these questionnaires, you will find ample documentation of research conducted to support both the development and use of these instruments. When choosing or developing your own questionnaire, you must ask yourself "Why am I asking the questions?" "Will the information help me teach Johan better?" "Am I just being nosy?" If Johan is allergic to chocolate, this is an important piece of information; therefore, asking about allergies is important. Discovering who lives in the home may be an interesting fact to know about, but Johan's parents may find it intrusive. Maybe you will learn this information later in the collaborative partnership. If Arlene's mother is worried about whether her daughter is too "shy" as a 3-year-old, this is valuable information that establishes a conversational base for a discussion. You will be able to share your observations from the class and be able to clarify her mother's concern.

Teachers need not know everything immediately. Teachers and parents can communicate regularly and elaborate their partnership. One of the ways that this may happen is through the interview process.

Parent Interviews

Conversations with family members are the most natural situations for teachers to talk with them about their children. There is no substitute for talking with family members about their children. Parents usually enjoy this if they feel comfortable and respected. Sometimes a more systematic **parent interview** that uses set questions or prompts can provide a survey of what the child is doing and tentatively determine how well the child is doing. Particular attention and sensitivity is

parent interview an interview of a child-care professional with a parent for determining how well a child is doing.

important when interviewing parents from a culture other than your own. In addition to being respectful, you will want to ask about such things as how long the family has lived in Los Angles? Denver? Or Des Moines? Do they have any relatives in the area? What languages are spoken at home, whether the family uses TV to help them learn English, what languages the child speaks at home and elsewhere, what a typical day at home is like for the family, and so on. Interviews work best when the process keys to parental perceptions, concerns, if any, and questions about the child.

For example, Ms. Hawk, a teacher at Corporate Center Child Care, is curious about Tina. Tina entered Corporate Center Child Care about a month ago. She is making some friends and has explored the room and the activities with enthusiasm. Ms. Hawk wants to meet with Tina's mother, Ms. Banker, to check out Ms. Banker's perceptions and to sustain the budding teacher/parent partnership. Ms. Hawk asks the following questions:

- What interests Tina lately?
- How do you see Tina as a person?
- What do you see her strengths to be? How is she special?
- Do you have questions or concerns about her development? Learning? Behavior? Health? Other?
- How are you doing as a parent?
- Is there anything else you can tell me that would help me to understand Tina?

It is usually best to begin by asking parents for their current observations of their child. Asking about their questions and concerns helps to determine how satisfied or concerned they are about their child. When there are concerns or problems, asking them for their ideas about what is wrong involves them in all aspects of the assessment and educational process. Parents' spontaneous observations of their children may include three kinds of "observations":

1. Descriptions of what the child is doing, including comments about what the child is not doing yet.
2. Questions and concerns regarding whether this is "normal" or not.
3. Attempts to explain "why" this is the case.

For example, a 2-year-old child's mother may say, "He is not talking a lot yet, not as much as he should be, but his big sister is always there, handing him things when he makes noises." Please notice that parents engage in the same processes of observation and interpretation that professionals do. An example of another instrument that facilitates the gathering of information to create parent-teacher partnerships is the *Infant-Toddler and Family Instrument* (Provence & Apfel, 2001). The *Infant-Toddler and Family Instrument* (ITFI) "help(s) home visitors and other frontline staff members organize their impressions of family and child well-being. The ITFI includes three components—a parent/care-giver interview, a developmental map, and a checklist of concerns about the child and family" (Apfel, 2001, p. 29). In addition to the ITFI and other questionnaires found in many early childhood screening kits, some teachers choose to use interviews. As you will see, a variety of formats and issues relate to interviewing.

Interview Formats

Formats differ in the amount of structure prescribed and the amount of latitude allowed the interviewer and the parent. Even a so-called "open-ended" interview has a limited purpose and encompasses a finite amount of territory. Within these boundaries, the interviewer begins with broad questions and continues with focus questions to elicit information from the outlined scope. Teachers tailor the selection, phrasing, and sequence of questions in an open-ended interview by parents' preceding replies. Thus, no two interviews proceed exactly the same way.

Hirshberg (1996) describes the critical importance of listening and withholding judgment as the interview goes along. He also identifies the importance of being clear about the purpose of the interview and ending it with a summary of learned information so that the parent and teacher leave the experience on the same footing. This clinical approach to interview is widely used by social workers, psychologists, and psychiatrists. Teachers and others can employ the principles while sticking to the dimensions of their knowledge (i.e., education and development). Some guidelines to help move the interview along include using transitional phrases such as, *I see, umm;* paraphrasing and restating to be sure that you understood what Mr. Halsted really said; summarizing your understanding based on what you heard to allow Mr. Halsted or Ms. Delta to say "Oh, no, I meant . . ."; and expressing empathy with what Ms. Delta or Ms. Gazelle said, such as "Oh, how wonderful that your daughter qualifies for gymnastics," or "My, that will be a challenge to have your husband's family move into your three-room house for a month," and so on. Another interview format used widely in early childhood settings is the structured interview—a format that may be more comfortable for the novice teacher to employ.

In a structured interview, the interviewer asks a predetermined set of questions, usually with the same wording. A branching structure for these interviews introduces some flexibility. For example, if the parent answers "yes" to a question about noticing unusual speech behavior, the interviewer would then ask "What seems to be unusual?" or a related series of questions (e.g., "Is your child's speech intelligible? Does your child speak in sentences?"). The branching questions use some preestablished rule. A structured interview requires less interviewing skill than an open-ended interview, where the professional is simultaneously interpreting data and deciding what to ask next.

Such approaches to interviewing ascertain developmental and curricular concerns of families, as well as serving as information-seeking tools for teachers. This involves answering questions about curriculum and instruction as well as behavioral expectations and home support of the child-care and education program. These conversations help the family–teacher partnership identify goals and topics for educational programs. For example, many parents of preschoolers want to know about "nightmares." What causes them? How do other parents handle them? Do they ever go away? Parents of third graders may wonder whether their children will pass the state-mandated tests. Teachers can delineate both the curricular support for required outcomes and identify ways that parents may support the learning of their children. These concerns and others may come from the conversations, questionnaires, and interviews and can form the basis of the parent-education agenda.

PARENTS' EDUCATIONAL PROGRAMS

When talking with parents about their children, teachers also learn a lot about how they are doing as parents. Conversations with parents often show how much parents enjoy their child, or identify how frustrated or discouraged they are, and give some idea if there are particular or unusual stressors in their lives. When trying to appreciate how well a parent is doing, it is wise to avoid "diagnosing" them. Instead, try to appreciate their efforts and strengths, as well as recognize their difficulties. This knowledge can form the backdrop to develop parent-education programs. Develop such programs in collaboration with families. This avoids the past tradition of parent education that treats the parent as someone who needs to know rather than someone who brings a set of understandings and curiosities to the process. More appropriately, families assess their own needs, seeking assistance from teachers and others when needed.

The following example shows parents' responses to different parent programs. Inner City Preschool Program A offered "parent education programs" on topics selected by the staff. Topics included "Discipline for 3-Year-Olds," "Nutritious Snacks," and so on. Two parents out of 40 came to each of the sessions. Inner City Preschool Program B scheduled a craft-making meeting. Informally, while making "bleach bottle" baskets for their children, the 20 (out of 40) parents shared experiences and discussed alternatives. Topics ranged from child discipline to managing coupon shopping to new ways to make macaroni. The parents planned to meet again and asked the teacher to schedule a child literacy expert as speaker. The difference between the two scenarios was that parents were in power in Program B. They were assessing their own needs and seeking resources as necessary.

This same parent empowerment can happen at the primary level when teachers find out what parents want rather than try to give parents what they think they need. For example, the teacher may want parents to learn how to teach their children multiplication or may want them to get their kids to bed before 10 P.M. Parents may be more inclined to come to a meeting about science fair projects using household objects or coming to support a special event at the school. Through the informal conversation, teachers have a chance to introduce some of the "parents need to know" items on their agenda. In addition, teachers and parents may increasingly avail themselves of electronic options for informal contact: e-mail, web page chat rooms, or blogs. The point is that whatever the age and stage, parents and teachers can collaborate in the best interests of children. Some out-of-the-box thinking on both sides facilitates a parent education program that accomplishes teacher and parent goals.

There are exceptions to cooperative parent interactions. That is, sometimes teachers must face challenging parents. These include hostile parents, uncooperative parents, perfectionist parents, arrogant parents, dependent parents, overly helpful parents, overprotective parents, and neglectful parents (Seligman, 2000). Using a family systems view, teachers can try to understand the context that leads parents to adopt these roles. Teachers can then appreciate the strengths that parents bring to the care and education session and call on support staff (i.e., social worker or counselor) to assist those who need the extra intervention to support themselves and their children. Before assigning the "difficult" descriptor to parents, teachers need to be sure that they do not stigmatize parents or children, particularly those with disabilities. Parents who have watched adults withdraw from their children may fear this attitude when they have children who drool, speak unclearly, or in other ways seem "different." Teachers need to avoid "blaming the victim," because parents are sensitive about their children who may display symptoms of disability. They may be doing all they can with Sally, who is constantly in motion. Try to remember that teachers and parents are usually on the same side—wanting the best interests of young children to be at the forefront.

Sensitivity to family interests and understandings is particularly important in settings with a diverse population. A special challenge is often the monolingual English-speaking teacher and parents who speak different languages. Conversations through a translator are often stilted and strained. As well, the choice of translator and understanding of parental perceptions of trust related to the translator influence the validity of the conversation. Keep in mind, as well, that families may choose to listen rather than offer their own perceptions due to their view of status differences between teachers and parents (Ramsey, 2004). Additional important considerations that affect teacher–parent communication and collaboration are teacher assumptions that parents share the same belief structure and values. Both may assume that the "home" culture is superior. Prejudice and stereotypes may influence trust in relationship building. Finally, each may be more, or less, comfortable with the communication styles and procedures of the "other" (Taylor, 1998). As teachers are in the "power" or "expert" position, respect for each child's home culture must be clear and valued (NAEYC, 1996). As part of the assessment process, culture influences all aspects of parent collaboration and communication. A particularly delicate time for honor and respect of diversity is when the family is the client.

Even in these situations, the family must be empowered to prioritize the family intervention plan in collaboration with the relevant professionals. In these cases, a family specialist is the point person in developing rapport and helping parents to establish priorities. Teachers in these situations participate as team members who will follow the directions developed by the family specialist and parent.

In all situations, teachers must establish relationships with parents. These serve to facilitate the young child's adjustment and success in child-care and education settings.

FAMILY–TEACHER COLLABORATION

Knowing the families and their priorities, as well as their child, contributes to effective collaboration. Working with families is a basic tenet of "best practice" in early childhood instruction and assessment. The challenge of finding ways of involving families in the assessment of their children's developmental and educational strengths and problems continues. While useful methods for obtaining developmental information from parents do exist, professionals' skepticism regarding parental ability to be objective about their children limits the use of this information source. It does appear that teachers and others often give less credit to parents than they deserve for providing valuable information regarding their children's development. In fact, parents may be quite useful in rating the everyday cognitive abilities of their children. Using the *Parent Ratings of Everyday Cognitive and Academic Abilities* (Dewey, Crawford, Creignton, & Sauve, 2000), a recent study showed that parent ratings may be a useful aid to the clinical determination of reading disabilities and attention-deficit/hyperactive disorder (Dewey, Crawford & Kaplan, 2003). Doctoroff and Arnold (2004) report similar findings using parent structured interviews, teacher observation, and parent rating scales.

Collaboration at the assessment level sets the stage for collaboration at other levels. Family involvement begins by providing the parent with an opportunity to report on the child's development and to raise concerns or questions, if any. Assessment data collected and based upon both parent information and on teacher observation, as well as any testing of the child, provides a sound basis for appreciating the child's abilities and educational needs. A positive, informative relationship with parents will be helpful to the parents as well as the child. A school program with these elements optimizes the prospects for making appropriate decisions and lays the groundwork for effective parent-school relationships.

When teachers know the family priorities, as well as observe and record carefully, they can share meaningful examples of child learning with families. Hannon (2000) shares first-hand experience of her growth as a teacher when applying this technique. Besides observing and recording specific behavioral examples for kindergartners, Hannon interviewed the children about their progress, choosing what to say to parents in collaboration with the kindergartners. Thus, Hannon modeled the partnership of teacher, learner, and parent from the earliest days of education. This partnership forms the foundation for pre-referral collaboration of parents and the school or child-care setting. "Best practice" includes parents in the assessment process from program beginning through the year and into the transition for the next program. Particularly, when parents and teachers use a problem-solving approach (Kroth & Edge, 1997), they display a spirit of cooperation that focuses on "the issue" rather than assigning responsibility. For example:

Parents' Thoughts

- If you were a better teacher, this wouldn't be happening.
- Don't bother me with this school stuff.

Teacher's Thoughts

- You're not a good parent; you don't care.
- Didn't you teach your child manners?

Before these tentative perceptions are hardened into beliefs and distrust, teachers and parents need to meet to discuss problems, perceptions, and differences. Then, child, parent, and teacher can feel comfortable about the resolution.

You also need to be familiar with the cultural values for each of the children and their individual families. This includes knowing how the family defines deviancy or difference, as well as their behavioral norms or expectations . . . which can influence the family's opinions and actions, in addition to acceptable places for the family to seek guidance (Takushi & Uomoto, 2001). This knowledge is particularly important when considering whether to suggest a formal referral for specialized assessment when you suspect that a young child may have disabilities. In addition, you must be thoroughly familiar with the legal and ethical rights of the parents whose child you may refer for evaluation.

PARENTS' RIGHTS

Referral of a child for evaluation by a specialist—psychologist, speech therapist, social worker—is a formal step in the life of the child and family. Federal, state, and local legislation govern the process. At the federal level and since the first legislation requiring that all children with disabilities would have a free appropriate public education (P.L. 94–142, 1975), the law assures parents of the following best practices and **parents' rights:**

- Notice that you intend to refer their child will be given.
- Written permission will be obtained from parents for any formal evaluation.
- All evaluation information will be kept in strict confidence.
- Assessment must be conducted with instruments that are nonbiased.
- Assessment must be multidimensional.
- Assessment must be conducted in the child's native language.
- No single test score may be used to place a child in a program.
- Assessment results will be shared with parents.
- When parents disagree with the school's assessment, they have the right to an independent assessment at public expense.
- Permission will be obtained for any specialized educational services.
- Parent involvement in the development and annual review of Individualized Family Service Plans (IFSP) or Individualized Educational Plans (IEP) is manded.
- Parent have the right to appeal plans and decisions made by the educational agency or school.

In addition, the 1997 amendments to the Individuals with Disabilities Education Act (IDEA) assure parents that schools and teachers

- Will secure *informed* parental consent prior to evaluation or reevaluation. This means that teachers and schools must explain the rationale and process for assessment to parents in ways that

parents' rights as specified in state and federal law, parents are assured that schools and agencies will fully involve and inform parents in the care and education of their children.

they understand. Thus, signing on the dotted line of a generic form—"test my kid"—is no longer possible.

- Will provide notice to parents that they may seek an external evaluation.
- Must collaborate with parents in the development of the IEP. This provision is strengthened with the latest reauthorization of the legislation (IDEA 2004). Now collaboration is similar to the process that already exists in the birth-to-3-years range, where the plans take the lead from parents.

Ethical practice grounds all of these legal requirements regarding co-operating and planning with families. Parents have a vested interest in their child's learning, know aspects about their child's strengths and interests that may be helpful in planning educational interventions, and can rehearse or in other ways assist their child with becoming an effective student. However, parents of children with disabilities have special challenges as parents. Often, extra care and teaching at home is required so that their child can keep up. They must help the other children in the family understand the limitations as well as the strengths of their sibling. Sometimes they must cope with the special challenges of child behavior in public that may seem unusual to passersby.

All of these stresses and particular issues may be present even before you consider referring a child for assessment. So, sometimes parents are not ready to hear what you have to say even though they may share some of your impressions about the developmental progress of their child. When such is the case, you must support the parent's decision to wait and see before embarking on a formal assessment. You can encourage parents to think about assessment and from time to time bring data forward about their child. With permission from other parents, you can link them to others who may have faced similar challenges. In many cases, parents will be ready for the assessment step. Therefore, ethical practice principles will be a natural outgrowth of your work with families when you are discussing any special need regarding their child. Some behaviors on your part that will contribute to a breakdown in the process include treating parents as vulnerable clients, being aloof in your conversations about their child, treating all parents as if they need counseling, blaming parents for the behaviors of their child, treating parents as if they were not intelligent, and treating parents as adversaries and labeling them as "difficult," "resist-ant," or "denying" (Heward, 2006, pp. 112–113). Thus, you must be prepared to meet the parents where they want to start and responsively engage in problem-solving in the best interest of their children.

SUMMARY

When embarking on the road to family partnerships, teachers must remember that partnership implies *partner.* Respect and appreciation for the complex roles of families will ensure the beginning of a smooth and productive relationship in the best interests of children. Parents must be involved in providing information about their children so that teachers may effectively care for and educate them. Child-care and school personnel must understand the values and conventions that shape parent practices and perceptions. Together, families and teachers nurture children so that they may grow to be self-confident, happy, and capable young students. Teachers of young children bear the responsibility for setting the stage for all future school relationships. Many parents of young children have learned to be advocates for their children through the partnership relationships established and utilized in the best interests of young children.

FIELD ACTIVITIES

1. Visit a child-care facility in your community. Ask for a description of enrollment policies and procedures. How are families involved in the process? Do you think the procedures match the potential population?

2. Choose a questionnaire or structured interview. Try it out on a volunteer parent. Summarize the results of your experience. What conclusions can you draw about the parent and about the process? Compare your experiences to those of your classmates.

3. With permission, review the entrance forms or other parent-interview material in the files of two children. Observe the children. Make a tentative judgment about the progress of the children from the time of entrance into the program. Discuss your assessment with the classroom teacher.

4. With permission of the teachers and parents involved, observe several interviews. Write up your understandings, protecting the confidentiality of the parents. Share your experience with your colleagues.

IN-CLASS ACTIVITIES

1. Identify family child-rearing customs—feeding, sleeping, toileting, chores, and so on —and child management techniques—time out, withholding privileges, reasoned discussion, and so on—that members of the class use with their children or that they remember from their experiences as children. Develop an interview protocol to capture this knowledge and experience. Describe how the results fit into an assessment partnership.

2. Think about a child in your program (or a program that you observe) that presents problems. Describe the problem behaviorally. For example: Florence often interrupts children in the story circle when they are responding to questions or making comments. Decide whether she interrupts in other parts of the day. Identify any other behavioral issues that Florence presents. Plan a parent conference to

discuss the matter with Florence's parent(s). Pair up with another student in your class to critique and revise your plans.

STUDY QUESTIONS

1. What biases might a teacher carry that may influence family participation? How can teachers overcome biases they may have?
2. How important are parent reports? What information gleaned from parent reports will be most useful to teachers?
3. How are parent questionnaires most effective? What are their limits?
4. What may influence a teacher's decision in using a behavioral or developmental questionnaire? What are some strategies to implement in requesting parental input on such questionnaires?
5. How can the teacher use parent-teacher interviews most effectively? What approaches are most effective in encouraging participation in family education programs?

REFLECT AND RE-READ

- I know some ways to gather information from families.
- I have some ideas about establishing rapport with families.
- I could develop an outline for a parent education program.
- I can identify preliminary questions to problem-solve with parents about educational or developmental issues.

CASE VIGNETTE

Jasmine, your new third grader, lives with her parents—Mr. and Mrs. Burling—and an older brother, Jarrett, who is 12. Anecdotal notes in Jasmine's file depict Jarrett as very protective of Jasmine on the playground and around school; they seem to enjoy a very close relationship. Until this September, Mrs. Burling stayed home with the children and volunteered at an Arts Club after school where Jasmine spent many happy hours. According to records, Jasmine is a bright, motivated, and capable learner. Mr. Burling learned in late August that his job as a computer programmer is in danger; he may be laid off. Mrs. Burling is thinking of looking for work, as the family worries about medical insurance coverage that may be jeopardized with Mr. Burling's unemployment. What classroom plans will you make to support Jasmine through the family crisis? How might you see the effect of the crisis in the classroom? What referral support may you need to be prepared to offer Mr. and Mrs. Burling?

Source: From Y. Jeong, 2002, submitted in partial fulfillment of T& L 411, Assessment in Early Childhood Education: DePaul University. Used by permission.

TECHNOLOGY LINKS

http://clas.uiuc.edu/

Culturally and Linguistically Appropriate Services Research Institute. This site "identifies, evaluates, and promotes effective and appropriate early intervention practices and preschool practices that are sensitive and respectful to children and families from culturally and linguistically diverse backgrounds."

http://www.eparent.com/

Exceptional Parent. Covers all aspects of parenting children with disabilities.

http://www.famlit.org

National Center for Family Literacy. Contains program suggestions, statistics, and links to research about the relationships of family literacy, parent involvement, and child success.

http://www.familiesandwork.org/index.html

Families and Work Institute. Information about for working families.

http://www.pta.org

National Parent Teacher Association. Hints for parents to promote school success, resource guide on diversity, and other current issues. Some resources available in Spanish.

http://www.thefamilyworks.org

The Family Works, Maryland's Goals 2000 Parent Information and Resource Center. Parenting tips and suggestions about parent/school partnerships.

http://www.nhsa.org

The National Head Start Association. This is the advocacy organization for families and children in Head Start. There are links to family-friendly information.

SUGGESTED READINGS

Brooks, J. B. (2004). *Process of parenting* (6th ed.). New York: McGraw-Hill.

Gaitan, C. D. (2004). *Involving Latino families in schools: Raising student achievement through home-school partnerships.* Thousand Oaks, CA: Corwin.

Gonzalez-Mena, J. (2006). *The child in the family and the community* (4th ed.). Upper Saddle River, NJ: Merrill/Prentice Hall.

Hale, J. E. (2001). *Learning while Black: creating educational excellence for African American children.* Baltimore: Johns Hopkins University Press.

Lynch, E. W. (2004). *Developing cross-cultural competence: A guide for working with children and their families* (3rd ed.). Baltimore: Paul H. Brookes.

Polakow, V. (2004). *Shut out: Low income mothers and higher education in post-welfare America.* Albany: State University of New York.

Seligman, M., & Darling, R. B. (1999). *Ordinary families, special children: A systems approach to childhood disability* (2nd ed.). New York: Guilford.

Turnbull, A., & Turnbull, R. (2006). *Families, professionals, and exceptionality: Collaborating for empowerment* (5th ed.). Upper Saddle River, NJ: Merrill/Prentice Hall.

3

Observation as the Key Method in the System

Terms to Know

- observations
- observation records
- anecdotal notes
- running records
- class journals
- checklists
- frequency records

- event sampling
- time sampling
- rating scales
- portfolios
- documentation panel
- formative evaluation
- summative evaluation

Chapter Overview

The cornerstone of an assessment system is child observation. This chapter describes the observation process, methods for recording information, and procedures for interpreting and using the results of observation. Emphasized in the discussion are the important procedural and ethical responsibilities and variables that lie beneath this seemingly straightforward activity that is anything but casual. Incorporated in the discussion is the role of observation in the development of portfolios and documentation panels.

Assess as You Read

- What is the difference between watching children play or work and observing them?
- How do you choose a recording method?
- What goes in the portfolio? How is it different from a "laundry basket of stuff"?
- Why do we need tests if we observe the children regularly?
- Why must time be budgeted for observation?
- What are the limitations of observation? How do you avoid bias in the process?

OBSERVATION IN THE ASSESSMENT SYSTEM—PLANNING, DECIDING, AND RECORDING

Teachers make many important decisions that affect the lives of children. Observation is the basis for many child-care and educational decisions, both informal and formal. Teachers decide what to teach on a

day-to-day basis for a group of children and how to individualize activities for particular children. Teachers decide what kinds of materials and equipment to use to carry out the curriculum. Teachers decide whether to use themselves in the teaching process as models, as guides, or as directors of the learning task. Finally, teachers set up rules and expectations about how the children will interact with each other.

Teachers Are Decision-Makers

observations systematic means of gathering information about children by watching them.

Observations of the children in the program inform the decisions of teachers. Observations are the most important assessment tool, more so than any book or set of packaged tests. Teachers spend several hours a day with the children they teach. Teachers who regularly and systematically observe young children use the soundest informational basis for curricular and instructional planning. By knowing what to look for and how to observe children, teachers make accurate inferences regarding the needs of children.

Both preschool and primary teachers learn more about young children by using the observation process. Also, family intervention specialists observe babies as part of their work. By keeping their eyes open, teachers and interventionists gather the information needed to assess developmental progress. They find out how well the children in the program are learning and how they get along with other children, teachers, and other adults. Teachers decide whether to begin, continue, or change an activity. They decide which children to group in various activities based on what they see.

observation records written records of the observations of a child including anecdotes, daily logs, and in-depth running records.

The records of these observations allow teachers to reflect and to inform decision making. Thus, early childhood education programs must include all of the following forms of **observation records:**

- brief, casual anecdotal observations of various children throughout the day, perhaps recorded on Post-it notes

60

- daily logs written at the end of each day
- in-depth running record observations, about 10 minutes long, of particular children or situations
- samples of children's artwork or other graphic depictions
- documentation of the curriculum with display panels, large charts, or other visuals
- teacher- or program-developed prepared forms that include focus points for notes
- reflective journals focusing on group issues regarding curriculum or behavior
- concept map that shows how children are processing information (e.g., what do they know about fractions?)
- graphic organizers that show the curricular topics explored by individuals or the class

Regular, data-based decision-making is important to the early childhood program. Teachers want to avoid "hit or miss" decisions so that they do not misjudge children and their progress. All teachers want to help children learn and adjust. No one wants to be judged on the performance of an "off day." Nor do teachers want to base all curricular decisions simply on a child's "peak performance." Spotty observation notes may not catch the whole picture of the child. Think of observation notes and records as snapshots in the classroom lives of children. Teachers want notes to show all the angles: front, side, back, and three-dimensional. Choosing one or several of the ways to record observations suggested here and using them regularly for all the children in the program ensures "full color portraits."

In summary, the questions teachers ask and answer while teaching include the following:

What does Jon know about the alphabet?

What can Helen do in math?

How does Marvin get along with other children?

How does Paul get along with teachers?

How does Brad get along with his parents?

How can I help Juanita learn to tie her shoes?

Does Carol understand how to sum two-digit problems?

Can Alan illustrate his understanding of the story?

Shall I put all the 3-year-olds together for finger painting?

Should I put the story time before lunch?

What memories does the class have about our trip to the apple orchard?

My class seems to be humming along; shall I make any changes?

The answers to these questions come from observing the children. In fact, teachers make assessment decisions several times a day.

Insights from observation are the basic tools of assessment for early childhood education. Further testing of a formal nature may be necessary in some cases. Insights gained through observation will help decide when, whether, and how to use formal tests as part of the program. Observation records serve as a "check" on formal tests or as a valuable baseline for deciding whether to refer a child for formal study. Teachers gather important insights from observations to share with parents in conferences and in reports. With parents, teachers use observational insights to decide whether to refer an individual child for further assessment that may lead to the provision of special services for a particular child.

Summarized observational information on all the children in the program provides important evidence for administrators and other decision-makers. Such material can help in program evaluation that shapes and directs plans for the future. These summaries can serve as documentation of effective practice and prove the need for continued or enhanced funding of programs.

Because teachers want to make these decisions and reports effectively, they must develop assessment plans that are comprehensive, yet realistic. Not every procedure suggested in this chapter is necessary for every child. However, the plan for each child must represent techniques that will provide insights on all aspects of each child's development and learning in the program. To ensure that a plan is comprehensive, use many methods (multiple measures) to observe each child in multiple settings. This practice also enables the teacher to gather insights about how the group is behaving and learning. For each child, report on the basic areas of development: motor skills, language, intellect, social skills, and self-esteem. More detail will be required if there is a specific concern about David, Walter, Jose, Esther, or Chelsea.

Practicing Being a Better Observer

Observation is a skill sharpened with practice. Teachers have already had considerable practice in it. Teachers observe children in a variety of situations throughout the day. To practice observing more keenly, begin in a small way by watching the children's interaction—for instance, in the block corner—for 5 or 10 minutes a day or at the science learning center. Also, be aware of what you bring to the situation—your culture with beliefs about child rearing, appropriate ways to communicate, child independence, and so on; your personality, your temperament, interests, and feelings; and your professional experience (Jablon, Dombro, & Dichtelmiller, 1999).

Thus, as Ms. Wolf watches and records what she observes in good detail, she considers whether she is objective as she writes notes about Albert, Pablo, and Keisha, who are building in the block corner. She asks Ms. Brown—as a second teacher, a supervisor, or a teacher aide—to observe the scene with her and to listen to the report. Through the discussions, Ms. Wolf sees whether she observed similar behavior as the second adult and whether their conclusions match. This is a good check on the accuracy of the data. Almost certainly one of them will pick up a detail or two that the other missed.

To sharpen your observation skills, imagine that you are looking at a video recorded on your first birthday. At first, the camera shows the whole party scene: the balloons, grandparents laughing and watching, and the older children at play. Then it moves closer to capture you diving into the cake with two hands. With this favorite scene on film, you can review it and enjoy the experience all over again, seeing things that you may have forgotten—the color of the napkins and balloons, the exact expression of Aunt Mimi, and so on.

Think of yourself as that camera. First, note the complete "party" of your classroom. Then observe smaller groups of children involved in various activities. Then move in on the group in the doll corner, with close-ups of the individual children. At even closer range, you record one child's facial expression and wonder about the emotions reflected by it. At this natural level of observation, you are primarily noticing and describing. Your observations will be of great use when it comes to discussing a child with parents. However, your observations will be of use long before that. Observations will reinforce (or perhaps lead you to question) your general impression of the child— individual style, peer relationships, problem-solving skills, and so on. Observations will contribute to your appreciation of each child in your care as a unique individual, and to your empathy for each child—even for a misbehaving child. Too, the observations will teach you much about your class as a group, material that can be applied to future planned activities. Your observations help you to read situations and children.

Planning for Observations

To plan for observations, first list your questions. Decide what insights you want to be able to write down about all the children in your program. Decide which children you may want to learn more about. Here you are defining what to observe and the focus of your observation. Is Jeanie really in constant motion? Can Elton work by himself on a writing project? Is Anita pinching other children? How long does Charles work in the block corner? Is Erica directing the play in the doll corner? How is Christopher doing as chair of the social studies project? Decide what you want to be able to tell parents at report time. Decide what information your principal or director will require about the children in your class. After you have the questions, choose the ways to record that will give you the insights you want.

The outlines in Box 3.1 and Box 3.2 highlight the kinds of questions you may want to keep in mind so that you can report completely on each child. You do not have to answer all questions for every child, but use the questions to help you pinpoint descriptions for each child.

Box 3.1 *Suggested Observation Outline*

General Overview

- Expressions: cheerful, bland, angry, and so on?
- General tempo: active, plodding, and so on?
- Alert, energetic, or listless and apathetic? Variable? If so, why?
- Dressed well or disheveled?
- Runny nose, eyes, and so on?
- Specific personal habits you notice (e.g., chewing hair, sucking thumb, and so on)?

Gross-Motor Skills

- Seems agile?
- Uses climbing apparatus well?
- Runs smoothly?
- Jumps on two feet?
- Hops on one foot?
- Gets up and down stairs?
- Throws and catches a ball?

Fine-Motor Skills

- Strings beads?
- Grasps a crayon, marker, or pencil well?
- Stacks a tower of blocks?

Box 3.1 *continued*

- Manipulates a puzzle?
- Chooses small manipulatives to work with (small blocks, and so on)?

Speech and Language

- Uses language to express needs?
- Speaks clearly or mumbles?
- Speaks both to children and adults?
- Understands what you say?
- Follows directions?
- Answers questions?
- Speaks only one language or parts of two languages in a bilingual home and/or school environment?

Cognitive Skills

- Can identify objects?
- Can identify objects in pictures or books?
- Can name some colors?
- Can count to 2? 10? 20? 100?
- Can learn new words quickly?
- Can recognize letters or numbers?
- Can solve problems: reflective, impulsive?

Relationship to Adults

- Discriminates between teachers and visitors?
- Calls teachers by their names or calls them "teacher"?
- When asked, knows teacher's name?
- Seems overdependent on adults?
- Appears defiant toward adults?
- Is cooperative, resistant, too compliant?

Relationship to Other Children

- Plays cooperatively?
- Shares materials?
- Becomes anxious when other children want to share?
- Teases or provokes other children?
- Hits or behaves in an aggressive manner?
- Is withdrawn or uninvolved?

continued

Box 3.1 *continued*

Relationship to Self

- Appears self-confident?
- Appears to know who he/she is?
- Can tell own full name?
- Can tell about own likes and dislikes?
- Can tell about own family? house?
- Possesses self-help skills?

Free Play or Self-Selected Activities and Interests

- Finds occupations during free time or self-selected time?
- Plays with other children (solitary, parallel, cooperative, games with rules, rough and tumble)?
- Stays with activity or flits frequently?
- Uses materials appropriately, creatively?
- Requires an adult to initiate activity?

Group Activity

- Makes required oral or movement tasks?
- Sits with group during activities?
- Is attentive and cooperative?
- Needs the help of an adult to attend?

Transitions

- Moves easily from one activity to another?
- Requires frequent reminders from adults?
- Responds to prewarnings or announcements that a change of activity is coming?

Routines

- Follows schedule?
- Is self-reliant?
- Remembers structure?
- Challenges rules and expectations?

General Impressions

- General areas of strength?
- Any weakness?
- General areas of skill?
- Any particular impressions?

(Modification of Baumann, McDonough, & Mindes, 1974.)

Object Manipulation

- Play with toys? Which toys? How?
- Uses specific features of the toy (pulls string, pushes buttons)? Which? Ignores other features (e.g., lifting lid)?
- Combines toys or real objects (spoons, cups) in pretend play? How?
- Imitates actions observed in the environment (pushes stroller with dolls)? How? What kind?
- Users any strategies to solve problems? How? Amount of persistence?

(Derived from Higginbotham & Pretzello, nd.)

Recording Observations

There are many ways to record observations, varying from brief notes to extensive running records. Some ways require lots of time, so teachers need to plan what the children will be doing while they are observing. For example, it is very hard to record detailed observations while you (as a teacher) are telling a story, leading a song, or taking children on a walk. The detailed observations are best conducted during free play or while primary children are engaged in project work. If there is extra help in the classroom, a teacher can sit and record details during large-group time. Also, teachers can train assistants and others to help in this kind of observation or invite a supervisor or colleague to help with the task.

Some observational records can be done more casually and even by reflection. In planning for observational assessments, you need to be sure that you include different kinds of observations for each child. The *first rule* of any assessment plan is to make multiple measures, so be sure to collect several samples of observations on all the children. Three of the most common methods for recording observations—anecdotal notes, running records, and logs or notebooks—are described in the next section.

These are naturalistic observations: "live" recordings that allow you opportunities to look at the same notes at different times and to gain new information or insights about what you saw each time. The following guide in Box 3.3 was created from ideas presented in various forms by early childhood professionals who have worked hard to make observation a skill that is available to our field. Included are ideas from Almy and Genishi (1979); Cohen, Stern, and Balaban (1997); Cook, Tessier, and Klein (2004); and Greenspan (2003).

Anecdotal Notes

Anecdotal notes are brief, accurate notes made of significant events or critical incidents in a particular child's day. For example, if a child who

anecdotal notes brief notes of significant events or critical incidents in a particular child's day.

Box 3.3 *What Should I Do to Record Anecdotes and/or Running Record Observations?*

1. Look at one child or situation. Be sure to observe all children at different times in the day over the course of the year. By the end of the year, you can probably answer questions about each child and how the child fits into the routine of your classroom. Questions that you may wish to answer to give a complete description of Gene, Lorraine, Bernadine, or Stephen include the following:

    a. description: physical appearance, expressions, agility, general tempo, moods, problem-solving style, and communication style

    b. attendance and arrival: start of the day, response to overtures from friends and teachers

    c. relationship to teachers and children

    d. relationship to materials

    e. relationship to routines

    f. approach to tasks

2. Write down exactly what a child is doing. You should be like a camera; recording what you can see. All the details should be recorded so you can remember later what happened and can interpret the behavior. For example, "Joshua played in the block corner for 20 minutes" is a sparse note. All that you can interpret from this note is that Joshua can concentrate. Details describing what he built, whether he constructed things by himself, and whether he was using a theme or merely stacking blocks and knocking them down gives you much more information to work with in figuring out later what Joshua's development is like.

3. Focus on one child at a time, recording peer interactions as they affect the focus on that child. It may be hard to write down the language of several children. They are all talking at once and may not be talking to each other. It is also easier to file materials about one child and to be sure that you have a range of material on one child if you focus on one child at a time. Occasionally, however, when two children interact, the observation can serve a dual purpose.

4. Be sure to record the observation in the same order that events occurred. For example, "Sara cried, threw a doll at Marcia, and grabbed her arm in pain." What really happened is that Marcia socked Sara. Sara grabbed her arm in pain, cried, and then threw a doll at Marcia. The interpretation of Sara's behavior will be different depending on the order in which the events are recorded.

5. If group dynamics are the focus of the observation, do not try to record every word said. Record key phrases and use arrows to show action between children. You probably will use this approach when you are trying to solve a classroom grouping problem or a social-behavior problem. That is, can Kevin and Arthur ever be placed in the same small group? How can I get Sylvia and Rose to broaden their jump rope group to include Suzanne?

6. Record in a style that is convenient for you. You may wish to develop your own abbreviations and symbols to help you in writing quickly. For example, T for teacher, first initials for children's names, and shorthand for objects (e.g. hse for house, blk for block, bk for book, and so on).

Box 3.3 *continued*

The purpose of the observation will shape the way you record. For example, if you wish to keep a record of all your 35 third graders using art media, you will need to know which students you have observed. One way to remember is to write each child's name on a flag that you put around a pencil—one pencil for each child. Place all the pencils in a cup on your desk; have an empty cup beside the full one. As you record a note on each child, move the pencil to the empty cup. Watch your progress as one cup fills and the other empties (Greenberg, 1991, personal communication).

The major advice in keeping observational records is to make the system easy for you. Keep pens and pencils handy—in your pocket, around your neck, in magnetic boxes attached to furniture, and so on. Notebooks and papers of various kinds should be readily available. Some teachers like to use Post-it notes on the spot and place them on paper for filing. Various-sized cards can be arranged and rearranged with notes for the summarization process.

Letter-size paper can be divided into sections for four to six children. After observations are entered, the paper can be cut into pieces for filing.

Dot	Harold
Ryan	Elsie
Jon	Gavriela

7. Collect regular information on a child; observe the child at different times in different settings. Avoid recording only negative incidents or only positive behaviors.

8. Be sure to schedule observations. Plan to observe only a few children each day. It is too hard to teach and record lots of observation notes each day. You want to participate in the play or discussion, so you have to think about what you are teaching, as well as the effect of the teaching on each child. Four children are a suggested number to observe in a whole day. Four observations on each child each month will give you 36 to 48 notes for the year. You then have many rich details to share in reports to parents and information on

continued

Box 3.3 *continued*

which to base trend statements about each child in your program. For example: Veronica enjoys putting puzzles together. She has put puzzles together every day for the last 6 weeks. Donna organizes the play in the housekeeping corner. She decides whether the girls will be ballet dancers or whether they will be psychologists and then gives everybody a part to play. The girls cooperate with her.

Avoid recording running records on stressful days (e.g., parent night, first day after vacation, field trip days, and so on). Of course, if a critical incident occurs, by all means jot down the anecdote.

9. Another way to organize the scheduling aspect of observations is to pick a subject. Observe art one week, science the next, math the next, and so on. Collect information on Keisha, Andy, Arnold, Alex, and Otto for each subject.

10. Be discreet when observing. That is, record your notes so that the child's work or play is not disturbed. If children ask what you are doing, you can say that you are writing, because you like to write about children's play or work, and you are making notes to help you remember.

11. Be aware of your reactions as you are observing. What are you feeling about the action that is occurring? In a separate section of the notes, jot down these notions. Refer to them later as you try to understand what your opinion is about an individual child. For example, as I watched Luz-marie struggle to communicate with Tom, I felt pleased that she was making an effort to make her self understood. Or, as I watched Leo flit round and round the room, bumping into things, I felt exhausted and frustrated. These notes to yourself will help in the interpretation of the observations.

12. When you finish an observation session, jot down any question, ideas, and conclusions that pop into your mind about the observation. These notes will be useful for the summarization.

13. Maintain confidentiality of notes. Don't leave them out where the casual visitor can find them. Stress the need for confidentiality to all staff and volunteers who may be involved in recording observations.

has never talked in class begins speaking, the teacher writes down what she said and under what circumstances she spoke.

- Valerie, age 3, arrives breathless, having run from the corner of the street. Valerie's mother trails a few steps behind, smiling broadly. Valerie jumps up and down in front of you, yelling "puppy, puppy." Her mom confirms that indeed the family now has a new puppy at home. Valerie's teacher, Ms. Sizemore, records this dated and timed note on the notebook in her pocket and makes a note to add books about puppies to the book corner. She does all of this while listening to Valerie, her mother, and the other children who are arriving. Alternately, Ms. Sizemore records the incident as soon as she can, keeping track of all the relevant details for Valerie's file.

- In another case, Ms. Weffer is working with Maureen, who often hits other children. One day Maureen and Peg are playing in the block corner. Maureen has used almost all of the blocks of the foot-length size for her house. Peg has been asking her for some of them to complete her own house structure. She gives up on asking and begins to pull her foot back, as if to kick at Maureen's house. Maureen screams at Peg, "STOP, don't you dare knock my house down! I told you to get out of my way." Maureen starts to march toward Peg with her hand outstretched. Peg, anticipating the slap, retreats hastily away. Ms. Weffer moves quickly to the block corner before Maureen has a chance to swing. She commends Maureen for talking about the problem (though it was at scream pitch) and tries to help the girls figure out an agreeable way of sharing the blocks. Ms. Weffer records this anecdote as soon as possible for Maureen's record, so that she can begin to mark her progress toward verbal problem-solving strategies.

- For science time in first grade, the class divides into groups to make charts about caring for the classroom plants, fish, and gerbil. You notice that Rhoda is sitting silently in her group. Roger, a member of the group, asks Rhoda a direct question. She doesn't answer. Rose asks her a question and she answers. You make a note of this *anecdote*. You will want to follow up on whether Rhoda only responds to the girls in the room, had some special stress that day, whether she habitually daydreams, or whether the observation is a isolated experience not seen in other small- or large-group experiences.

The anecdotes serve as notes for further substantiation, documentation, and ways to explore behavior for patterns. (See Boxes 3.4 and 3.5 for sample blank forms to use in your program.) A more detailed form of this kind of observation is the running record.

BOX 3.4 *Example of an Anecdotal Note Form*

Anecdotal Note Form

Name of child observed: _____

Date: _____   Time Period: _____

Context (who is involved, where, what preceded the event)

_____

_____

continued

Box 3.4 *continued*

What exactly is happening? Be sure to record in the order of the events. Write down exactly what is said. Use abbreviations to be sure to get the detail.

_____

_____

_____

_____

Questions that you have. Ideas to explore. Tentative conclusions—to be verified with other observations or sources.

_____

_____

_____

_____

_____

Teacher signature _____

*When observing interactions among children, list all children. Use arrows and other abbreviations to show interactions and conversation.

Box 3.5 *Example of an Anecdotal Note Observation Form*

Anecdotal Note Observation Form

Name of child: _____

Time: _____   Date: _____

Objective for this observation:

_____

_____

List of others in the context (by initials to protect confidentiality; only for reference in determining any patterns of interaction, friendships): _____

_____

Context (when, where, etc.): _____

_____

_____

Running Records

Running records are narrative notes made of routine functioning of an individual child or a small group of children. For example, Ms. Ryan plans to observe Rachel for 10 minutes during the free-play period. She then writes down everything that Rachel does or says; she does not participate or interact with Rachel while writing. Ms. Ryan collects the record at different times throughout the year. Ms. Ryan saves each record for later analysis.

running records notes made of routing functioning of an individual child or a small group of children.

In another instance, a group of second graders is planning a way to use attribute blocks for a new game. As they establish rules, Mr. Sanchez observes and records the process in detail, using good descriptive words. When he analyzes this record, he makes decisions about child progress and grouping plans and gains information about what further details he should provide to the group about attribute blocks, game development, and so on. (See Box 3.6 for a template to use to record running records.)

This running record approach to note taking is a widely used method for documenting reading progress (Clay, 1993). Ms. Anderson watches Bonnie read a passage, and uses a blank paper and a code to note any problems that Bonnie has with the passage. Ms. Anderson will want to note substitutions, attempts, omissions, insertions, self-corrections, and repetitions; instances when she must tell Bonnie the word; times when she asks Bonnie to try again; and times when Bonnie asks for help (Gunning, 2005). Box 3.7 shows some of the symbols for this approach and Box 3.8 provides a blank template for your use. You can adapt one-to-one work with children on other subject areas in a similar manner.

Running Record Template

Name: _____   Date: _____

Objective for this observation: _____

_____

_____

Context (who is involved, where, what preceded the event): _____

_____

Reflections/Questions	Notes

Continue on text sheet as needed.

Teacher signature at the bottom of last page. Initials and page numbers on all other.

Box 3.7 *Running Reading Record*

Text	Bonnie's Record
Humpty Dumpty sat on the wall Humpty Dumpty had a great fall All the kings horses and all the kings men Couldn't put Humpty Dumpty together again ✓ Read correctly SC Self-corrected T Told a word TTA Try that again / Mispronounced ○ Asked for word	

Box 3.8 *Example of a Reading Running Record Form*

Reading Running Record Form

Name: _____

Date: _____

Copy of text read attached or duplicated here.	Child's Record

✓   Read correctly
SC Self-correct
T   Told a word
TTA Try that again
/   Mispronounced
○   Asked for a word

Recording narrative notes. Before beginning to record an observation on a child or a situation, you should make a few notes that will help in remembering important issues and details. This includes a sketch or mention of the part of the room where the action takes place and a note about the context (i.e., who is playing, acting, where, and so on). Record the date, time, and any relevant preceding events. For example, if you are recording that Theda is crying, note what happened before—that Ronald hit her, she smashed her finger, or you saw nothing that tells you why she is crying. Box 3.9 illustrates a naturalistic observation.

Box 3.9   *Sample Observation (In a Child-Care Center) of Two Boys at Play*

This center is in a large house. It is a cozy, warm old house with many nooks and crannies for children to explore. During the free-play period, children can be inside or outside as their play takes them.

On this day, Ronald is inside in the living room of the house. This is the area where the housekeeping equipment is set up. Besides the standard equipment of wooden stove, refrigerator, and sink, there are large cardboard boxes set up in the area. The boxes are there to invite creative play. The boxes vary in size, but most will easily hold one or two children.

Ronald is a tall, slender, well coordinated 4-year-old. He is dressed in a tee-shirt and comfortable cotton pants. Ronald is always clean and neat. He is regarded as a leader in this program. Most of the time he leads children in a play activity of his choice. Today, he is playing alone in the housekeeping corner. His expression is bland today, although he is usually peppy and expressive. He appears to be a little bit tired, not his usual energetic self.

9:09 Ronald is sitting on the table pulling knobs off the stove. He is waving the knobs in the air, as if they were airplanes. He announces, "Take off, take off."

He pauses in his play to command Jon, who has strolled near Ronald at the stove, "You ain't playing here." He states this not in an angry way, but to clearly show that he wants to be alone and that he has the authority to direct the play of his peers.

Brad tries to join the play by handing Ronald a large cardboard box the size of an orange crate. Ronald tosses the box back to Brad.

Brad kicks the box around the housekeeping area. He really seems to want Ronald's attention. They usually play together. Ronald continues to ignore Brad and Jon. Jon wanders away.

Ronald continues his airplane play alone, with much buzzing sound.

He then declares, "Take off, man." He continues, "flying" the stove knobs. He is becoming more excited and enthusiastic about the flying. His voice is louder, clearly imitating his notion of airplane sounds.

9:13 "BBBBBBBBBBBBBBBBB"

"uum oo oo"

"Buzz—"

"5 4 3 2 1 blast off." (Have the knobs become a rocket?)

Brad, who is sitting near Ronald in one of the boxes, turns to Ronald and entreats, "Pow, your turn to drive. Ronald, your turn to drive the car."

Brad, with resignation, says, "OK, I'll drive one more time."

Brad continues to badger Ronald, "Your turn to drive the car."

Box 3.9 *continued*

Pleadingly, Brad turns to Ronald, "Would you drive the car for me?"

Ronald finally climbs into the box with Brad. (Brad smiles broadly. He seems pleased to have finally recruited his friend Ronald into play.)

Ronald asks, "Where we going to—your house?" (He seems to be enjoying himself and seems good-naturedly going along with Brad in the shift to the car play.)

Brad exclaims, "Go real fast." They scoot around the floor in the box. Ronald hops out.

9:15 Ronald grabs some dishes from the stove.

Brad asks with puzzlement, "Ronald, what are you doing?"

Ronald responds matter-of-factly, "Putting gas in it."

Brad pronounces, "Just drive the car." Ronald hops back into the box.

Ronald sits in the box with Brad, but does not begin to drive. He turns his hands over and over (like wings).

Brad, frustrated, says, "Will you drive the car?" Ronald ignores Brad, and continues making wing-like movements.

Brad agrees reluctantly: "OK, I'll drive the car."

Ronald jumps out of the box.

9:16 Ronald throws more dishes into the box.

He turns to Brad and announces, "OK, we'll throw these out as we go."

Brad says excitedly, "I got my foot on brake. We gotta get more food."

Ronald adds more dishes to the box.

Brad drops in a telephone.

Ronald throws in another phone.

Ronald shouts, "Get cover, get cover."

Both boys throw blankets in the box. (They seem to be getting a little silly. They are giggling and laughing. The play has shifted from driving a car to throwing things into the box.)

9:17 Ronald turns to Brad and shouts as he gives him toy fruit, "Here, Mr. Smith. Here Mr. Smith."

Brad rejoins, "My name is Cool Joe."

Ronald says commandingly to Kevin, "Don't play with us." (Kevin has come in and sat on the table.)

Brad falls on Kevin and laughs. Kevin joins the laughter. Brad and Kevin are rolling playfully on the floor.

9:20 Ronald threatens Kevin, "You better not laugh, kid."

Tony calls Kevin from across the room. He runs to join Tony.

Ronald and Brad settle back to the initial car game. They seem to have calmed down. Together, they plan a trip in the car to Brad's house.

Impressions from this observation. Record your impressions from the observation. For example, Ronald seems to have had an "off day"; that is, he was quiet and subdued and tried to resist the offers of others to play. He is usually so peppy. (Is he feeling well? Did something happen at home?) Brad finally succeeded in dragging him into play. He seems to have a way of pulling Ronald out of his withdrawn mood. The other children really seem to depend on Ronald's leadership skills. Both boys could pull themselves together when the play was beginning to get out of hand. They are developing good self-control. Ronald's play shows a good imagination (use of dishes as gas); Brad is more concrete in his play (dishes as symbols of food).

The teacher, Ms. Perez, saves this running record for Ronald's file. Ms. Perez may also summarize her impressions of Brad and place them in his file. When doing this, Ms. Perez will want to protect Ronald's and Brad's privacy as she uses the files. She collects notes on each child in the program once or twice a month. At the end of the year, or when she wishes to report to parents, she reviews the notes to help clarify her thoughts about the developmental progress of each child in the program. Running record observation is the most time-consuming kind of observation. As you can see from the previous example, Ms. Perez's primary occupation during the 10 minutes is recording notes about Ronald and Brad. She sits close to the boys and watches and records their play. The rest of the group is playing in their respective areas of the classroom. Ms. Cobbler, the assistant teacher, is keeping an eye on the total group. This kind of observation may not always be possible in a program. The children in the class may need all the adults in the room to help them maintain smooth play. Sometimes, teachers may also need to collect observations while they are one of the participants in the action. Running records will not work then. Alternatives include making notes in logs or notebooks or on Post-its or cards as soon as possible after the action, discretely during the action, or asking an assistant, volunteer, or child to help remember an incident. For example, you turn to the 4-year-old at your elbow during story time and say, "Keisha, let's write down your comment. It added so much to our discussion." Then jot a note on the Post-it in your pocket. This serves to remind you of the high-level cognitive functioning of Keisha that you want to note with examples.

Logs or notebooks are records accumulated throughout the year on each child. For example, Ms. Myers gets spiral notebooks for each child. She keeps the notebooks in a basket on the side of the room with a pen handy. Nearby, she hangs a calendar with the names of four children written on the days of the week when the program is running regularly. The calendar is her appointment schedule for recording observations for the children in the program. Therefore, she does not schedule observations on days when the class will be on a field trip, the day before or after vacation, or at other high-stress times in the life of the program. Throughout the year, Ms. Myers collects observations on each child in the various areas of the room. The log is a developmental progress record. Ms. Myers records in her lesson plan book when she will collect these developmental progress records (Figure 3.1).

Some teachers like to make notes about each child on each day of the year. Teachers complete these daily logs at the end of each day, and then summarize at the end of each week. These are collected anecdotes like the previous examples. They are brief, filled with one's own notes and abbreviations, sketches, and so on. You write enough information so that you can remember the event, but the notes do not have to be so complete that their completion wears you out. These are impressions or memories of what children have been doing for the day rather than live observation notes. The impression or memory material can be useful, but "live" observations must be included as well. Keep in mind that impressions and memory material are interpreted or filtered, and conclusions drawn.

Written notes are not the only observational method for the busy teacher. The following sections describe some additional methods for

Time	Week of Jan 3 2006					
	Mon	Tues	Wed	Thurs	Fri	Notes
9:00–10:15	Indiv. Activities				→	Observe Anthony
10:15	Snack				→	
10:30	Story Time				→	Observe Lakesha
10:45–11:30	Outdoor Play				→	
11:30	Dismissal	Call Ms. Johnson	Bring Fish Food		Look for Pix for Train Theme	

Figure 3.1
Observation in the teacher's schedule.

recording information. These methods do not provide the rich insight data, but they do help teachers collect information. For example, Mr. Psujek, the third-grade teacher, plans a science project. He wants to be sure that everyone in the class uses the telescope at some point in the 8 weeks. It is not necessary for him to record anecdotes or running records to assess the accomplishment of this goal—he can keep a checklist. As teachers, we do not always need to use the most complex method to assess children. We must match the knife to the purpose (e.g., a butter knife for bread, a steak knife for steak). For example, if you are interested in formative evaluation of your curriculum or of the day, you may wish to keep a class journal.

Journals for the Class

class journals diaries that teachers keep about a group's progress toward meeting educational goals.

Class journals are records that teachers make at the end of the day. In a few minutes at the end of the day, teachers jot notes of the events of the day with attention to salient details. These notes offer time for teachers to reflect on the curricular, instructional, and behavioral events that took place. The notes are subject to bias, since a few hours have passed, specific details are lost, and you solidify impressions before writing. For example, think about a traffic accident at an intersection. When it happens, you see which car turned left and hit the mailbox and newspaper stands and how the light pole went through the back of a second car. If you were there, in a few hours you may forget whether a taxi was involved, how far the mailbox leapt in the air, and whether the pavement was wet or dry. This is because you have other things on your mind. The formative evaluation form in Box 3.10 illustrates a series of focus questions for directing your class journal reflections. No matter which method you choose to use for observing and recording child behavior, you will need to make a plan to incorporate the time in your day.

Checklists as Records

checklists forms for recording the skills or attributes of the children in a class.

Checklists are useful for recording the skills or attributes of the children in your class. Choose checklists that are commercially available, if these are compatible with your instructional goals. These are increasingly available as test companies try to capture the performance assessment market. Make checklists that match your teaching plans for the class. Make checklists to record progress that Zachary is making toward the goal you have set for him.

frequency records checklists for recording the presence or absence of, frequency of, or quality of selected behaviors.

Frequency records are teacher-developed or commercially designed checklists that teachers use to record the presence or absence of selected behaviors, how often a certain behavior occurs, or the quality of the behaviors. For example, you may want to know how often Mary Irene drinks milk at lunch. You make a list for this and check off the days Mary Irene drinks milk. Your colleague wants to know which students can add single-digit numbers. As she observes their play at the

Box 3.10 *End of the Day Formative Evaluation*

As you think about the day, what worked well?

____

____

____

____

List three or four ideas or concerns that you will ponder:

____

____

____

____

What additional information do you need to solve any concerns or teaching issues?

____

____

____

____

		Yes	No
Adds single digits:	Ellen	X	
	Toni	X	
	George		X
	Albert	X	
	Bernard	X	

Figure 3.2
Addition skill checklist.

math center, she can check off which children can accomplish this task (Figure 3.2).

As teachers develop checklists, they must be aware that they are developing "assessment" instruments. Thus, the instruments must be derived from the philosophy and curriculum. The lists must describe

Teacher's Name _____					Week of _____				
	Puts jacket in cubby					**Washes hands before lunch**			
Name	**M**	**T**	**W**	**T**	**F**	**M**	**T**	**W**	**T**	**F**
Shirley	X	X	X	X	X	X	X	X	X	X
Elly	X	absent	absent			X	absent	absent		
Laurita	X	X	X	X	X	X	X	X	X	X
Charles	X					X				

Figure 3.3
Self-help checklist for the Main Street School.

skills (Figure 3.3) or target behaviors in a way that reflects the appropriate developmental sequence and subject matter progression. Otherwise, these seemingly benign lists become a biased instrument. Sources for the development of checklists include program goals, child development milestones, and district-wide scope and sequence charts.

Because we value the program goal of independence, we operationalize the goal for the age of the child we teach. For example, Ms. Potenza, a second-grade teacher, operationalizes the independence goal for her students as follows: Second graders arrive, hang up their coats, and choose an activity from their file of "things to do." Children may work together on their projects and share experiences. During this time, Ms. Potenza collects lunch money, conducts writing conferences, and provides individual guidance for those requesting assistance. At 9:45, the class meets to review the status of projects, to plan the day's agenda, and to listen to a story.

If Modesto, California, teachers want to assess the development of the children referred to their early intervention program, they check a child development milestone list to remind themselves of the typical sequence for the development of communication skills. They use the list as one indicator of progress, with interpretation dependent on the nature of each child's particular special need and with understanding of the issues involved in bilingual language development.

Math teachers at Middle Sized City have studied the National Council of Teachers of Mathematics (NCTM) Guidelines (2000) and invited experts to visit. They created a chart with skills identified for each age level, K–12. Ms. Park uses the kindergarten list to record which skills Kelly has developed. She finds that Kelly has mastered all of the skills. It is October. What next? Ms. Park can consult the first-grade scope and sequence material, and use the first-grade list to record Kelly's accomplishments.

Activity checklists are lists of activities that teachers prepare to record which child engages in an activity during a given period. For example, you may wish to know who is using puzzles, clay, blocks, the easel, books, geoboards, and so on. List the activity across the top of the page.

Figure 3.4
Activity checklist.

Name	Puzzles	Small Blocks	Books	Clay	Geoboards
Laurita	1/2	1/3			2/15
Regina			3/1	1/3	
Cheryl			3/2		
Mary			2/4		
Lisa			1/2		
Larissa					2/10
Nancy				3/15	
Jack	2/1				
Dennis		1/4	3/5		
Duncan		2/6			
Rosalind			3/6	3/7	
Sam	2/1				
Susan				2/10	

Then, down the side of the page, list the children in your class. You check or date when each child is doing one of the activities (Figure 3.4). Widerstrom (2005) includes checklists and matrices as part of the tools for developing a play-based curriculum. These prepared checklists may be useful as you learn to develop those keyed to your curriculum.

Event Sampling

Event sampling is a record of skills or behaviors that you want the children in your class to know or to do in a specified amount of time. For example, you may want to know how often William asks to share a toy during the 40-minute play period; how often Lonnie is writing at the writing table during the 30-minute choice time; and how often Perry is at the computer center during the hour allowed for self-selected activities. Additional skills and attributes that can be observed and recorded in this way include:

- *Social skills:* cooperation, group cohesion, sense of fair play, competitiveness, and loyalty
- *Affective expressions:* joy, pleasure, satisfaction, self-confidence, shyness, and fear

event sampling record of skills or behaviors a teacher wants the children to know or to do.

- *Cognitive attributes:* decision-making, problem-solving, expressive language, and exploration
- *Creativity:* divergent response, fluency of ideas, spontaneity, flexibility, and originality
- *Enhancement to self:* sense of humor, leadership, and curiosity

Note that these skills and attributes are important life skills—ones not assessed with tests. Observation, therefore, is a critical method for assessing developmental progress. For example, Mr. Friedman, a second-grade teacher, values creativity and wants to assess whether children in his room are showing creative behavior (see Box 3.11).

Box 3.11   *Cognitive Event Sample Record*

Name	Divergent	Fluency	Spontaneity	Original
Arthur	3/5	3/6	3/8	3/12
Herb	3/5			
James	3/5	3/9		
Tom				
Betty				
Susan		3/6		
Dick			3/12	
Jane				3/12
Sally	3/7			
Frances		3/8		
Joey		3/8		
Marilyn			3/13	
Debbie				3/15
Billy				
Shawn	2/28			
Sharon				
Tony				
Melissa			3/25	

Box 3.11 *continued*

Deanne			3/24	
Alan				3/30
Tiffany				
Angela				
Jeff	2/27			
Linda		2/24		
Rick				
Joyce				
Bob			3/9	
Christie	2/24			3/16
Michael				
Brian	2/22	2/23	2/23	3/16

Time Sampling

Time sampling is a way to check to see what is happening at a particular time with one or more children. For example, you may wish to know what is happening between 1:00 and 1:15 on Mondays. You collect this information by using a running record on Martin or by using a checklist to record the activities of several children. This technique may be helpful when you feel that the program is not working smoothly. There may be a lot of running about, bickering, or waiting in line. By sampling the period, you get an idea of who is where and begin to make some different plans. This technique also works to assess concentration and persistence for Mari. Ms. Carr is curious whether Mari can stick to one activity on the playground, so she makes the time sample chart shown in Box 3.12 to check whether Mari can concentrate in outdoor play.

time sampling checklist for determining what is happening at a particular time with one or more children.

Rating Scales

Rating scales require teachers to judge child performance on some predetermined behavioral description. For example, "Hermes matches English color words to color swatches: never, some of the time, all of the time." Frequently, rating scales are part of a report card. As teachers, we are asked to decide whether an individual child possesses a particular

rating scales methods of recording whether or not children possess certain skills or attributes and to what extent.

Example of a Time Sample Record

Time Sample Record				Week of April 15, 2006	

Playground Activities for the Hummingbird School

Fifteen-minute record. Observer samples once each minute.
Observer watches one child at a time.

Child's Name	Big Wheel	Climber	Ball	Jump Rope	Not Playing
Judy	x----15				
Vincent	xxxx		x-10		
John		xxxxx	x-10		
Mari	xx	xx	xx	xx	x-6

skill or attribute and to what extent. For example, Clarence turns in homework on time (always, often, seldom, never); Arnetta writes clearly (excellent, satisfactory, needs improvement). Such procedures are subject to error and bias. For example, as teachers, you may hesitate to use the extreme positions of *never* and *always*. Unless, of course, Clarence, a third grader, needs to get a "wake up call." Never turning in homework may be a serious problem. It may also mean that the homework is irrelevant, and Clarence knows it. These rating scales may lack a common definition in the minds of teachers. What does it mean that Gloria, a 4-year-old, has emerging or accomplished conversation skills? What are the expectations in conversation for a 4-year-old? Do all the teachers in the center have a shared definition? Do Gloria's parents know that "emerging" may be a problem at age 4? Is it a problem at age 4?

When developing or using rating scales, look for well-defined categories and those that are observable behaviors; for example, "recognizes five words (yes, maybe, not reading)," or "asks questions about the story (often, sometimes, never)." You can quickly observe each of the children in your class and "rate" each child's performance on these criteria. Keep in mind, then, that the more complicated the behavior is to rate, the greater the chance of error unless you and your colleagues have participated in extensive training to learn the definitions for the complicated behaviors to be rated.

Using Photographs, Videotapes, and Audiotapes

Photographs enhance observational notes. These are particularly useful in recording sculpture, block designs, and group dynamics. Videotape

and audiotape are very helpful in recording storytelling and dramatic play. Use tapes sparingly, however, especially if you will transcribe the material to paper when the material is used for accountability. Transcription frequently takes two to three times as long as the original observation. For instance, a 10-minute observation may take 20 to 30 minutes to transcribe. As a permanent record of a child's work, tapes can be a rich source of information because they show not only the words, but also the effect and group dynamics as well. The environment is as important as the players in video recordings. Revisiting videotapes may be an important adjunct to therapeutic interventions by therapists, diagnosticians, teachers, and parents when solving knotty problems (Guidry, van den Pol, Keely, & Nielson, 1996). As well, videotapes or other electronic recordings can be used to revisit an activity with children to review and reinforce learning or solve a class problem (Beaty, 2006).

Portfolios

Technically speaking, **portfolios** are one type of performance-based assessment, a strategy for deciding the competency of children in a particular area or areas. The portfolio is the place to keep all the information known about each child. Observational notes form the foundation of the portfolio. To enrich the observational record, add to the collection of each child's work. A collection of children's paintings, drawings, and stories shows what children know. Besides these artifacts, include lists of books read, transcripts of discussions with children about their work, and other products collected throughout the year to provide a good progress report. Save these materials in places

portfolios places, such as folders, boxes, or baskets, for keeping all the information known about the children in a class.

87

such as individual file folders, portfolio envelopes, file boxes, scrapbooks, or other convenient containers. Collect the materials to answer questions about progress in developmental areas: social/ emotional skills and attitudes, language/cognitive knowledge, and gross- and fine-motor coordination. Pictures and sketches of projects that you make aid in illustrating child progress. Be sure to include reflection as part of the process for selecting child work. Why is this work/artifact in the portfolio? What does it show about Monte's work? How would Monte improve or change the document if it were to be done again? These and other questions prompt children to consider learning as a process with stopping points—judgment spots along the way. Interviews of children about their interests, such as their favorite books, games, and activities, add details of each child's year in the program. Notes of parent conferences and questions add to a well-rounded picture of each child.

Why Use Portfolios?

The first and most important reason to use portfolios as part of an assessment plan is that these documents involve the teacher, parent, and child in the system. Some reasons to use portfolio assessment to support children as readers and writers are that the process itself

- Increases language learning.
- Emphasizes both content and performance, or holistic learning.
- Links between learning across the curriculum.
- Facilitates children's learning about audience awareness as they write.
- Is individualized. (Farr & Tone, 1998)

Deciding What to Include in the Portfolio

When first choosing what to include, you may collect a "laundry basket full of stuff." To be useful, however, the portfolio should contain selections carefully matched to answer the assessment question. You need to think about a number of things before filling a milk crate for each child, which is a common tendency for early portfolio builders. Will the portfolio represent a child's best work, selected drafts, a random sample of work, or only child-chosen or only teacher-chosen items? Will you develop several portfolios for each child, such as an ongoing portfolio and one for the end-of-the-year? The answers to these questions vary depending on whether the portfolio is

- *a working one*—to be used by you and the children during the course of a unit
- *a formative one*—to show parents at the end of 6 weeks
- *a summative one*—to pass to the kindergarten teacher

Some questions to guide you and your students in the selection of work include (Shanklin & Conrad, cited in Gullo, 2005):

- Will the work samples tell the consumer—child, parent, teacher— about the level of development or academic progress?
- Will the sample show what to modify in the curriculum or what to individualize?
- How do the selected products help the consumer—child, parent, teacher—understand the developmental or academic progress?

There are no right answers to these questions, only answers that match the purpose for collecting the information. (A sample portfolio template is shown in Appendix F.)

Involving Children in the Portfolio Process

As children grow older, they will want to be involved in the process of portfolio development; even preschoolers can begin judging their work (Shores & Grace, 2005). When you hold writing conferences with primary-aged children, you can ask them to select writing samples for their permanent record. Marcia can choose which math paper shows that she has learned to add single digits. Eloise can select the painting that shows a complete story. At conference time with children, you can involve them in writing notes about their progress in social studies. Jacob may tell you that he is more comfortable in his assigned social studies project than he was at the beginning of the assignment. Then you translate the conversation into a note that says, "Jacob is feeling more comfortable in small-group assignments." Harvey may tell you that he enjoys reading "bigger" or "longer" books. A conference note is included that says, "Harvey is reading books of 15 pages now."

By involving the children in the selection of work to be included in a portfolio and by showing them some notes that you make at individual conferences, you are showing how to conduct assessment. You collect samples of work that show skills, collecting *multiple* pieces of information, and demystify the assessment process for children. As well, you show them how to assess their own progress. Regularly examining the portfolio and setting new goals shows children that learning evolves. Children can be proud of their accomplishments and will help decide where they want to go next.

To help children select work products that document their learning, some questions include (Hebert, 2001):

- How has your writing changed since last year? Since January?
- What do you know about numbers that you didn't know in October?
- Let's compare a page in the book that you read in first grade with one that you are reading now.
- What is special or unique about your portfolio?
- What do you want to show your parents about your learning? How can you organize your portfolio to show this?

You are helping children understand assessment and evaluation at their developmental level by choosing questions that focus on the process appropriate to their age and stage of development.

This kind of review sets the stage for programs that want to move toward involving children in decision-making and responsibility for their own learning, including student-led conferences specifically in the primary years (Bailey & Guskey, 2001). Another approach to documenting child progress, called **documentation panel,** has gained favor in preschools across the country. This is part of the philosophy and practice of education known as *Reggio Emilia* (Edwards, Gandini, & Foreman, 1998).

documentation panel is the part of the Reggio Emilia process that shows, publicly, the learning accomplishements of young children.

formative evaluation assessment an approach to examining young children that holds assessment is an ongoing process. It is similar to the scientific approach where a query is generated, validated or not, and then another query is formed.

summative evaluation reports the final results of a given assessment. For teachers, this often means the end-of-the-year summary of child progress.

Documentation Panels

The application of the Reggio Emilia documentation panel (Helm, Beneke, & Steinheimer, 1997; Krechevsky et al., 2003) to the classroom provides a focus for the accounts of individual child growth and for whole class summaries of knowledge, skills, and dispositions. This is a technique much like that used in program evaluation and is commonly called formative and summative evaluation. **Formative evaluation** is a review of the program or work as it is in process. **Summative evaluation** is the decision, judgment, or opinion regarding the work at the end. Thus, the visual display of work in progress serves to show all constituencies—children, teachers, parents, administrators, and community—what children know and are able to do. The panels include pictures, narratives, charts, and illustrations that show children's experience, memories, thoughts, and ideas. Assess these artifacts during the implementation of the curriculum—formative evaluation—and as a reflection later—summative evaluation. Whenever using observation and the related tools, you must remember that there are some limitations to the application of the method. As an early childhood teacher who practices an ethical approach to the collection and use of observational products, you will want to be aware of some of these limitations.

Limitations of the Observational Method

Appropriate use of observational methods depends on skillful, knowledgeable teachers. Teachers must know and understand child development milestones. They must be sensitive to cultural, individual, and situational variations for the attainment of these milestones. Teachers must know curriculum and instruction principles. That is, they must know how children learn and how subject matter is organized. Teachers must also avoid the following observer traps:

- Overinterpretation of behavior

  During an hour visit in a child-care home, Otto cried the entire time. He cried when the caregiver held him.

  Interpretation: Otto is ill.

  You do not have enough information to sustain this interpretation. If the observer considers other factors (too many children in this facility, five infants and one caregiver, length of time in the setting, and other unknown factors), Otto may be behaving appropriately for a stressful situation.

- Making inferences from global behavioral descriptions

  While the children were reviewing their Japanese words, Barbara was excited to answer the questions, but during free play when she was playing in the doll corner, she wanted to play alone.

  Interpretation: Barbara seems to be an outgoing person when it is necessary, but when she has more of a choice, she prefers to be by herself.

  Answering questions in large group is not necessarily "outgoing"; nor is playing alone a reflection of isolation. There is no information about antecedent events. Did Barbara fight with friends? Do her classmates function cognitively at a different level? Is this behavior a regular occurrence?

- Observer's personal bias

  Maria, age 4, chatted with friends at the kitchen table in the house corner. Alicia suggested that the table become a diner. Maria, "No, I was here first and I want it to be my home."

  Interpretation: Maria sure is bossy. Alicia is much more cooperative.

  It sounds like this observer expects girls not to be assertive. The observer may not like Maria as much as Alicia and thus interprets Alicia more favorably.

- Wrong focus

    David, age 3, is playing with blocks. He is talking very softly to himself. Occasionally, he directs a remark to his companion, Ari, in the block area. He has built a large structure. Now he seems to be hiding the small cars and animals in the structure. Ari asks him what he is doing. David doesn't answer.

    Interpretation: David is an isolated child who is not social.

    Other possibilities: David is absorbed in the play. He is concentrating. He doesn't hear Ari. The observer misses the cognitive sophistication of what David is doing because he is not speaking.

- Inaccurate recordings

    George ran around the room, then dumped blocks on Sally and another girl who were playing at the small-group table. He then settled to work on a puzzle.

    Interpretation: George is hyperactive and aggressive.

    Other possibilities: George is playful. Sally and Keisha dumped his puzzle immediately before. The three engage in playful teasing and cooperative assistance in picking up puzzles. The three are working on learning to cooperate.

- Failure to record times of beginning and ending of behavior
- Failure to show the names of all the children involved in a segment of behavioral observation
- Preconceived notions

    Ms. Clark is sure that Danny is hyperactive. She wants his parents to take him to the pediatrician to get a pill to calm him down.

    Interpretation: Danny is a problem.

    Ms. Clark records notes on Danny when he is very active in the room. She does not record Danny at times when he is absorbed in an activity, even while he is moving. She neglects the language and cognitive aspects. She does not look at her schedule and routines.

Planning and Scheduling Observations

"[A]ssessment and curriculum are integrated, with teachers continually engaging in observational assessment for the purpose of improving teaching and learning" (Bredekamp & Copple, 1997, p. 21). Your observations naturally include brief, casual observations of various children throughout the day. You adjust your teaching based on these casual observations. You record significant events as *anecdotal notes* on children. Periodically, you need more in-depth *running record* observations. Finally, you need a *systematic plan* for observing and recording the behavior of all children within your program.

Your assessment plan must include regularly scheduled running records so that you can plan appropriate learning activities based on the needs, strengths, and interests of the children in your program. Anecdotal notes document special events in the lives of individual children. Reflections of conversations and interactions with children allow you opportunities to think about individual strengths and interests of the children in your program. Checklists of developmental milestones help you see the progress of individual children and provide a group summary. Records of conferences with parents assist you in building a total picture of each child in the context of family.

In these ways, you are constantly gathering observational information to provide the best program possible for all of the children. This is a difficult and exhausting task, and it is not the only task that a teacher faces. You must also make, set up, and prepare materials; talk to children; help them settle into routines; and empathize with them. You must lead the group in song, story, and fun. You are a model of curiosity, good humor, and enthusiasm. You must set the tone for your assistant and parent volunteers, meet with parents, and handle crises as they emerge. Often, you are alone in the classroom, so you will need to develop a system that works for you. This may involve collaborating with a colleague during your respective planning times, if you need a second set of eyes in your room. It may mean that you plan for certain, more demanding note taking to occur while children are engaged in projects. Note taking should never preoccupy you so that chaos occurs in your class. Being alone in the room is not a reason to discard observation as an assessment method.

The Real World of Everyday Teaching

Observation is the partner of instruction. You cannot teach well without observing. For example, as you set out finger paints every day for a week, you notice that Jimmy will not touch them. Popping a Post-it note out of your pocket, you record an anecdote. Ms. Regan, a third-grade teacher, has index cards for each of the children in her class that are taped together in bunches and fastened to a clipboard (personal communication, 2005). She carries the board everywhere, making notes and jotting reminders of what to assess or teach. At quarter's end, she has anecdotes and documentation for report cards and parent conferences. This is just one way to keep track of the data that you need to teach well.

In another method, 6 weeks after the beginning of the year, you sit for one afternoon with your favorite checklist. For the next week, while the children are napping or participating in an informal group activity at lunch or recess, you reflect on each child and check the list accordingly. When you run into questions you cannot answer, you plan to find out whether a particular child "uses two or more sentences to tell me something" by engaging this child in conversation.

Using the schedule you have made for yourself, you systematically gather running records on everyone throughout the year. You file them away to use as you prepare reports and meet with parents. Obviously, when an emergency occurs and staff is short, the schedule is changed.

Foremost, you have a responsibility to plan systematic observation to answer the questions you have for each child in your program. Systematic observational plans are those that help you to be sure that you have answered all of the assessment questions about individuals and groups that must be answered so that all stakeholders know that learning is occurring, and if learning is not occurring, what some of the obstacles might be for individuals and the group. Thus, just as you plan what you teach—which activities, structure of the room, schedule for the day, and staff interactions with children in a developmentally appropriate way—you must plan how to collect observational information on each child regularly, covering all aspects of development and learning. You must write some information down. Your plan must reflect the philosophy and realities of your program. Practical suggestions for collecting the information have been included in this chapter. You must decide how many running records, anecdotes, logs, and checklists to collect on each child. You will need a balance of observations for each of the methods so that you will have the material you need to confer with parents and to write developmental reports.

SUMMARY

Keeping track of your observations on the children in your class makes it easier for you to teach them well. Recording observation notes and using checklists takes time in an already busy day, but it makes you a prepared teacher. Observations supplement standardized tests and provide the flesh for the description of complicated behaviors: language competence, social skills, and problem-solving approaches.

Observation is the tool you use to make teaching decisions, whether you write them down or not. Writing the notes, making the checks, or otherwise keeping track of your thoughts on the children in your class helps you be the best teacher for all the children in your care. In the end, you will be better organized. You will know which methods are working with which children. You will be able to answer questions about cognitive, social/emotional, motor, and language development, as well as academic progress, with precision and examples. You will feel more confident about your judgments and insights because you have organized and planned for your assessments. You have made the link from the curriculum to assessment and completed the circle—teach, evaluate, reteach.

FIELD ACTIVITIES

1. With a partner, go to a grocery store, park, fast food restaurant, or mall where you can observe children. Each of you should watch the

same action for 10 minutes at a time. Record the details. Discuss your results with your partner. What were the similarities and differences? Which presents the more accurate picture? See what you missed and try again.

2. At the local supermarket on the weekend, station yourself in the cereal aisle. Watch parent and child interactions. Record details. Develop a checklist based on your initial observations. Collect information on several children. What patterns did you observe?

3. Go to the park or other community location where you can find primary-aged children. Draw a sketch of the area. Develop a checklist of the areas: basketball, climber, swings, benches, and so on. Record the ages and sex of children who participate in the diverse areas of the playground. Use this information to make after-school teaching plans based on your observations of the usage patterns and the goals for the after-school program.

4. Interview teachers in preschool and primary settings about how they use observation and records in planning for instruction. List each specific type and the purposes related to each type. Discuss ways the materials can be used to solve teaching problems, to talk with parents, and to refer young children for any special intervention that may be necessary.

IN-CLASS ACTIVITIES

1. Using an available videotape or DVD of children playing, watch 10 minutes of the tape. Each participant should record a running record on one child or situation. Divide into pairs. Discuss the results of the observation. Examine the notes for objectivity and completeness of detail.

2. Using available state content guidelines for second grade, in groups of three, review the guidelines and develop a list of suggested artifacts to collect for the year. Describe how you will include children and parents in the collection and evaluation.

STUDY QUESTIONS

1. How can early childhood teachers recognize and utilize observation records most effectively? Why are observational records so highly regarded in early childhood settings?

2. How can early childhood teachers include observational records in class schedules? What are the assessment decisions teachers frequently make through daily observations?

3. In which situations will anecdotal notes provide a comprehensive assessment? How will the teacher use anecdotal notes?

4. Why should running records always include analysis or reflections on the observation?

5. What types of information will be gathered through running records? How can this information be used in classrooms?

6. What are the components and types of checklists? Checklists are most effective for the early childhood teacher in gathering what type of information?

7. How are event and time sampling used differently in the classroom?

8. What factors will make rating scales most effective? How do rating scales differ from checklists? Frequency records? Running records?

9. What are the components of a portfolio? How can portfolios be incorporated into the curricula?

REFLECT AND RE-READ

- I know what the role of observation is in a well-crafted early childhood program.
- I can identify some ways to record and summarize information.
- I know how observation fits into the portfolio process or other record-keeping system.
- I know why observation alone is not enough for a fully developed assessment system.

CASE VIGNETTE

My interest in Carlota, a 4-year-old enrolled in Head Start, came when I discovered that she is Argentine and speaks Spanish fluently. (I was reminded of my own childhood, growing up in an all-English speaking child-care environment and speaking my home language the rest of the time.) In the beginning I was intrigued by her shy personality, and then I noticed she was having trouble communicating with classmates and teachers. She seems to understand what is going on but seems to lack vocabulary to express feelings or wants. In one such instance, I noticed her shaking her head "no" and repeatedly saying "no" to the teacher who was asking her to "go biz." At first glance, it appears that Carlota is refusing to cooperate with the teacher in going to the washroom. Another teacher interrupted to say that Carlota had already visited the bathroom. It was clear that Carlota understood the first teacher, but faced an obstacle when having to reply in English. What are the next steps in observation/assessment for Carlota? How will you gather evidence to plan/modify instruction? How will you sort out the behavioral, personal, and academic issues?

Source: From Y. Jacome, 2002, submitted in partial fulfillment of T&L 411, Assessment in Early Childhood Education: DePaul University. Used by permission.

TECHNOLOGY LINKS

http://www.aacap.org

American Academy of Child and Adolescent Psychiatry. Public information pamphlets related to mental health and links to a wide variety of additional websites.

http://www.aap.org

American Academy of Pediatrics. Position papers and publications affecting the lives of young children.

http://www.hhs.gov/children/index.shtml

U.S. Department of Health and Human Services. Public information for families.

http://www.kidsource.com

The KidSource™. This site covers a broad spectrum of issues related to assessment, observation, and teaching.

SUGGESTED READINGS

Beaty, J. (2006). *Observing development of the young child* (6th ed.). Upper Saddle River, NJ: Merrill/Prentice Hall.

Gronlund, G., & James, M. (2005). *Focused observations: How to observe children for assessment and curriculum planning.* St. Paul, MN: Red Leaf Press.

Owocki, G., & Goodman, Y. (2002). *Kidwatching: Documenting children's literacy development.* Portsmouth, NH: Heinemann.

Pellegrini, A. D. (2004). *Observing children in their natural worlds: A methodological primer* (2nd ed.). Mahwah, NJ: Lawrence Erlbaum Associates.

Shea, M. (2000) *Taking running records: A teacher shares her experience on how to take running records and use what they tell you to assess and improve every child's reading.* New York: Scholastic.

Wurm, J. (2005). *Working in the Reggio way: A beginner's guide for American teachers.* St. Paul, MN: Red Leaf Press.

Using Basic Concepts
of Measurement

Terms to Know

- raw score
- mean
- range
- standard deviation
- normal curve
- standardized test
- norm-referenced test
- population
- normative sample
- norms
- criterion-referenced test
- derived score
- age-equivalent score
- grade-equivalent score
- interpolated score
- extrapolated score
- percentile ranks
- standard score
- scaled score

- deviation quotients
- normal-curve equivalents
- stanines
- reliability
- test-retest reliability
- interscorer reliability
- correlation coefficient
- standard error of measurement (SEM)
- validity
- face validity
- content validity
- criterion-related validity
- concurrent validity
- predictive validity
- construct validity
- convergent validity
- treatment validity
- social validity

Chapter Overview

In this chapter all the basic concepts needed to use tests and other measurement devices in a developmentally appropriate manner are fully described so that teachers and child-care workers can communicate confidently with parents, administrators, psychologists, and other professionals about all aspects of tests and other assessment tools and what they mean in the lives of young children. Most importantly, these are the concepts that you must understand to appropriately administer and interpret the standardized tests used increasingly in the primary years. Throughout the chapter, practical examples are included to demystify the statistics of testing.

Assess as You Read

- What do I already know about statistics in everyday life? How do these concepts translate to measurement?

- Why should assessment be a central focus of my instructional practice?
- How are tests developed?
- How can tests be an appropriate part of a multidimensional assessment plan? What are the limitations of these instruments?

NEW PARADIGMS IN ASSESSMENT

Assessment is a "hot topic" in education today. Some educators describe examples of holistic approaches as new paradigms. However, early childhood educators historically focused on assessment as inquiry (cf. Serafini, 2001). Yet, in the primary grades assessment as inquiry departs from assessment as measurement—comparison of children to standardized measures; assessment as procedure—using qualitative data gathering such as portfolio assessment to supplement standardized measures. Assessment as inquiry also has roots in the constructivist view of learning (cf. Goffin & Wilson, 2001), in which data on child behavior is gathered to obtain information to solve a learning or developmental issue. Regardless of the measurement paradigm—holistic or based on test instruments—early childhood teachers must understand the statistics of testing. This is so you will know the strengths, limitations, and values of all approaches to measurement. Here the focus is on the statistics that apply to tests that are widely used with young children today. Dive into this chapter without fear; though you may think of statistics as math-based, hard, dreaded, or whatever, statistics are logical concepts that will give you a new language to embrace. You will be able to understand why certain instruments are good ones and why certain ones are not so good. Think of yourself as the knowledgeable investor who will be able to invest wisely in the high-stakes measurement of young children.

IMPORTANCE OF BASIC CONCEPTS OF MEASUREMENT FOR TEACHERS

Do not join the "[m]any teachers [who] see no need for training in testing and assessment because they believe these activities are supplemental or peripheral to the instructional process . . . [because] it is frequently the classroom teacher who must administer and then organize and interpret high-stakes and teacher-constructed test and assessment data, including performance and portfolio data, to curious and sometimes hostile parents and other concerned parties" (Kubiszyn & Borich, 2003, 13–14). Fundamental to understanding tests is the understanding of measurement and all of its components. However, what exactly is *measurement*? According to Linn and Miller (2005) it is "the assigning of numbers to the results of a test or other type of assessment according to a specific rule (e.g., in original counting correct answers or awarding points for particular aspects of an essay or writing sample)" (p. 26). In order for you, as a teacher, to understand how to evaluate tests, interpret test results adequately, and make appropriate use of other types of assessment (inventories, observation techniques, functional assessment, portfolio, authentic assessment, and so on), you should be familiar with some concepts and terms of measurement. Some of them will already be familiar to you from other contexts; others are more specific to tests. You will need to understand this vocabulary to be a good consumer of tests. By understanding tests and their properties, you will know when it is appropriate to use one and whether you have found a good one. As you read this chapter, keep in mind the five core concepts for understanding testing:

1. Tests facilitate understanding of students' behavior and learning.
2. Tests cover specified samples of behavior and knowledge.
3. Test validity is the premier important variable among test properties.
4. Test reliability is essential for appropriate use and understanding of tests.
5. Test bias is a factor that influences interpretation and use of tests. (Popham, 2000)

According to the National Association for the Education of Young Children (NAEYC, 2003), program stakeholders are responsible for assessment that "make[s] ethical, appropriate, valid, and reliable assessment a central part of all early childhood programs . . . making sound decisions about teaching and learning, identifying significant concerns that may require focused intervention for individual children, helping programs improve their educational and developmental interventions." Tests are only one part of a multiple-measures system. But, because they are widely used, teachers must understand the purpose, characteristics, interpretations, and appropriate application of the measures. To assist you in understanding the complexity of tests, you will need to be familiar and comfortable with the technical vocabulary explained in this chapter.

TERMINOLOGY

In the following pages, you will review the definitions of terms commonly used to describe the properties of tests. It is important to develop a working understanding of these terms so you will know the strengths and limitations of the tests that you develop or use. Knowledge of assessment and appropriate uses of tests is part of an ethical commitment to young children and their families (NAEYC, 2005). The first term is one most familiar to you—how many right answers?

Raw Score

The first score you obtain on either a published test or a teacher-made
test is the **raw score,** the number of items that the child answered correctly. Knowing each child's raw score is the first step in changing the
child's score to a standardized score. However, raw scores provide little information about a child's performance in comparison with other
children. These scores are not in a form that allows comparison between
performances of children. Therefore, if Paul has a score of 10 and Nell
has a score of 15, you do not know that Paul is less successful on the
tested concept. So that you can make comparisons between Paul, Nell,
and the other children in your class, the scores are standardized. This
part of the standardization process is most important—turning scores
into numbers for comparison. One of the first standardized scores that
you need to tell you more about your class is the average score—the
average number of right answers for most of the children in your room.

Mean

Everyone is familiar with the word *average*, which is the **mean**, the arithmetic average of a group of scores. To calculate the mean age of one of
your reading groups in which the children are 70, 72, 73, 76, 78, and 81
months old:

1. add all the ages (450)
2. divide by the number of children (6)

Thus, the mean of these numbers is 75.

$$70 + 72 + 73 + 76 + 78 + 81 = 450/6 = 75$$

Let's say that you want to check the understanding that your second
graders have of subtraction facts. Over a number of days, you establish
how many of the facts each child knows. You record their names and total facts known, as shown in Figure 4.1. You add their total scores (624)
and divide by the number of children in your class (24). Now you know

Figure 4.1
The number of
subtraction facts known
by children in Miss
Take's class.

Child's name	# of facts	Child's name	# of facts
Alex	25	Lola	19
Ben	27	Maria	15
Christina	20	Martin	30
David	29	Norris	18
Dina	29	Paul	22
Ilana	31	Peter	12
Jerry	28	Ruth	28
Josiah	32	Sam	33
Juan	36	Sarah	11
Katie	30	Tara	17
Kim	40	Winston	29
Liz	23	Yolanda	40

each child's score as well as the mean for the group (26). You can also see if each child is above or below the mean. Besides knowing where most children are achieving, you will want to know if the learners in your room are very far apart in their scores—how many scored very low and how many scored very high?

Range

When you are dealing with the scores of your class, the next measure you want to determine is the variability of the scores, or how different they are from each other. The **range** is the "spread" of the scores or the difference between the top score and the bottom score. In the example where we calculated the mean chronological age of the reading group, the range is 11. This is the difference—or distribution of scores—between the lowest number (70) and the highest number (81) in the group (81 − 70 = 11). The range is not a very sensitive measure because it is dependent on only two scores in the distribution, the highest and lowest. It merely tells you how far apart the achievement of your lowest- and highest-ability students was on a particular test. For more precision, you can statistically determine the variability of scores: Is a 29 different from a 42? Maybe, maybe not. The statistical determination tells the story for each test. So, to know whether 29 is different than 42, you must find out how far each score is from the mean by calculating the standard deviation.

range the spread of the scores or the difference between the top score and the bottom score on a test.

Standard Deviation

A very important measure that helps us quantify the "spread" of the distribution is the **standard deviation.** It measures the distance scores depart from the mean. If a distribution of scores is large enough, the scores will usually form a bell-shaped curve, known as a normal distribution (Figure 4.2). This bell-shaped or **normal curve** represents the distribution of a large number of human attributes including height, weight, and for our purposes, test scores. A normal distribution is hypothetically the way scores on a test would cluster if you gave the particular test to every single child of the same age or grade in the populations for whom the test was designed. The pattern shows that most children are about average, a few are slightly above or below average, and even fewer have extremely high or low scores. The mean score, by definition, is in the middle of this hypothetical normal distribution so that half of the scores will be higher than the mean and half will be lower. The standard deviation is a unit of measurement that represents the typical amount that a score can be expected to vary from the mean in a given set of data or on a particular test.

standard deviation the distance scores depart from the mean.

normal curve bell-shaped curve representing the usual distribution of human attributes.

Looking at Figure 4.2, we can see that a large number of the scores fall near the mean or the "hump" part of the curve. Approximately 34 percent of the scores fall between the mean and one standard deviation above

Figure 4.2
Different types of
standard scores on the
normal curve.

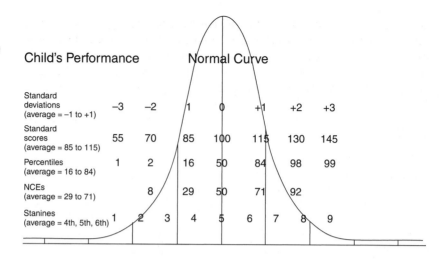

the mean; approximately 34 percent of the scores fall between the mean and one standard deviation below the mean. Thus, two-thirds of the scores (68 percent) fall between one standard deviation above the mean and one standard deviation below the mean. This means that two out of every three scores are within this range; this is certainly the "average" or, to use another term frequently applied in early child-hood education, the "normal" range. Approximately 14 percent of the scores fall between one and two standard deviations above the mean and another 14 percent fall between one and two standard deviations below the mean. If we go from two standard deviations below the mean to two standard deviations above the mean, we have taken into account approximately 96 percent of all scores (14 + 34 + 34 + 14). That leaves only 2 percent at the low end and 2 percent at the high end of the distribution.

Later in this chapter, you will apply your understanding of these terms, and their importance will become even clearer. For the moment, keep in mind that the bell-shaped curve applies only to standardized in-struments and is not a concept that you can apply directly to your class-room. Now that you have a basic overview of important statistical terms used in describing tests, let's turn to the description of how tests are created and standardized.

STANDARDIZATION AND NORMS

standardized test (norm-referenced test) test that interprets a child's performance in comparison to the performance of other children with similar characteristics.

Unlike teacher-made tests, most published tests are **standardized tests** or **norm-referenced tests.** Such measures have undergone a lengthy and often costly process in their development. Standardized tests are indispensable for clinical and psychoeducational assessment (Urbina, 2004), and increasingly these instruments play a more definitive role in most early childhood and primary-grade settings. Thus, early childhood educators should understand how such tests are developed and what the scores mean. When developers design tests appropriately and educators use them properly, standardized tests eliminate bias in the assessment of individual children as well as provide data to combine, allowing comparisons of groups to a standard (Hills, 1992; Linn & Miller, 2005). Using standardized tests requires that you adhere to the following principles (Airasian, 2005; Goodwin & Goodwin, 1997):

- Match the test to the question you want to answer.

  If you are teaching children about the difference between fruits and vegetables, you want to ask children to identify, recognize, or name fruits and vegetables. The presentation of the standardized measure should correlate with the age of the child—writing for 8-year-olds, identifying plastic objects for 3-year-olds. The level of comprehension or skill development should match the curriculum. If it is the end of the first week or a pretest, the expectations are different than end-of-year or other summative points.

- Use standardized measures according to the designed purpose.

  Suppose you want to know whether your second graders are creative thinkers. Asking these kids to take a reading test will show you who knows reading skills and comprehension, but these tests will not give you information about creative thinking.

- Choose tests that are valid and reliable.

  If the math test you choose reports a reliability score of .40, it means that the test is inconsistent enough that you cannot trust the results. While this may seem obvious, establishing reliability and validity statistics with young children is difficult because young children grow and develop so quickly.

- You must follow the directions of standardized tests exactly.

  If the test directions say that you may repeat a dictated word only once, you can only repeat the word once. This is really hard for teachers who usually respond to children's questions, even the 25th time they are asked.

- Be sure you understand what the test reports and the statistics generated.

  If you do not know what a stanine is, you cannot explain it to a parent.

- Use multiple assessment methods to evaluate children and programs.

  If you check achievement of third graders with an achievement test and you still want to know about social/emotional adjustment, creativity, and problem-solving ability because these items are part of your third-grade curriculum, you will need to choose some performance measures to supplement your assessment program.

Following these principles when choosing standardized tests assures good practice. What, then, is a standardized test?

According to Green (1981, p. 1001), a *standardized test* is a task or a set of tasks given under prescribed conditions and designed to assess some aspect of a person's knowledge, skill, or personality. A test provides a scale of measurement for consistent individual differences regarding some psychological concept and serves to line up people according to a concept. Think of tests as yardsticks, but remember that they are less efficient and reliable than yardsticks. A test yields one or more objectively obtained quantitative scores, so that, as nearly as possible, each person is assessed in the same way to provide a fair and equitable comparison among test takers. Thus, a standardized (norm-referenced) test interprets a child's performance in comparison to the performance of other children with similar characteristics. The key to the use of these instruments is being sure that the child assessed is similar to those who comprised the samples when the instrument was developed. This factor is at the heart of the debate regarding the extent of the use of these materials with young children. Thus, how do these instruments come about; what is the process that produces standardized tests?

In designing a standardized test, test developers must first determine its rationale and purpose. Second, they must explain what the test will measure (there are many types of standardized tests, such as achievement tests, readiness tests, developmental screening tests, diagnostic tests, and intelligence tests), whom the test will be given to, and how the test results will be used. Test developers try to adhere to the standards jointly developed by the American Educational Research Association, the American Psychological Association, and the National Council on Measurement in Education (1999), which sets standards for test users as well as test developers. According to the National Association for the Education of Young Children (2003) "assessments [used in programs] are valid and reliable. [As well,] accepted professional standards of quality are the basis for selection, use, and interpretation of assessment instruments, including screening tools . . . and adhere to the measurement standards published by AERA in 1999." In following these professional and ethical principles, one of the first important considerations in choosing a test is determining whether the test developer included children similar to your class members, so you need to know about the norming sample.

population group of individuals on which a standardized test is normed.

The **population,** or group of individuals, on whom the test is normed is of utmost importance. Even if it were possible, it is not necessary to test everyone in a particular population to make the norms applicable. The characteristics of a population can be accurately estimated from the characteristics of a subset of the population as long as the subset closely resembles the population in terms of specific characteristics. These characteristics must also be present in the subset in the same proportion that they are present in the population for this subset to be representative. Such a subset is the **normative sample.** Inferences based on what the developers

Population

Sample

Figure 4.3
Relationship between a population and a sample.

learn from the sample (subset) can be extended to the population at large so that inferences can be made about the population (Salvia & Ysseldyke, 2004).

Figure 4.3 illustrates the relationship between a population and a sample. Frequently, test developers use U.S. Census figures for determining the percentages of children by age and ethnicity in planning a sample to generalize to a population. Therefore, in a sample of 1,000 6-year-olds, in the development of the Shoe-Tying Test, the developer will want to be sure that there are appropriate numbers of African American, Asian, Caucasian, Latino, and Native American 6-year-olds so that when the test is published, the results can be a good predictor of where children in Mississippi, Boston, and Idaho will function in comparison to the national norm, which is representative of the population of 6-year-olds across the country. Before publishing the Shoe-Tying Test, the developers will try it out on the 1,000 children and determine the scores for describing variations in performance for 6-year-olds. This is the phase of development called norming.

Norming is the process of finding out what score most children of a given age will earn on a particular test. Take, for example, the Shoe-Tying Test, where the results might be as follows:

- Most 4-year-olds cannot tie their own shoes.
- Some 5-year-olds can tie their own shoes.
- Most 6-year-olds can tie their own shoes.

By testing 1,000 children in a systematic and consistent way, the developers obtained these results. The 1,000 children were a representative sample of those who would likely take the test once it is developed. The norming process shows whether there is any regional, gender, racial, or other salient variables that might affect results. **Norms** are the scores obtained from testing the normative sample (Urbina, 2004). The adequacy of these norms, according to Salvia and Ysseldyke (2004), is dependent on three factors: the representativeness of the norm sample, the number of children in the sample, and the relevance of the norms in terms of the test's purpose.

When looking at the representativeness of the norm sample, it is common to look at the following factors: age, grade (for children in kindergarten or above), gender, geographic regions, socioeconomic status (a factor that shows a consistent relationship to how children perform on intellectual and academic tests), and racial or ethnic cultural

normative sample
subset of a population that is tested for a standardized test.

norms scores obtained from the testing of a normative sample for a standardized test.

differences. The importance of this last factor cannot be overemphasized. "Assessment strategies that are not sensitive to cultural differences in learning style and rate and those that are not designed for children from linguistically diverse backgrounds cannot provide an accurate picture of children's strengths and needs" (Hills, 1992, p. 48; see also, Rhodes, Ochoa, & Ortiz, 2005). The Individuals with Disabilities Act (IDEA) of 2004 mandates nondiscriminatory assessment; this requires fair and objective testing practices for students from all cultural and linguistic backgrounds. The number of children in the normative sample is also important. One hundred subjects per age or grade is the minimum acceptable size.

You, as the test user, must be prepared to determine the relevance of the norms for the child or group of children you intend to test with the instrument. Generally speaking, for early childhood educators working with children in regular classrooms, nursery schools, or child-care settings, national norms would be the most appropriate. However, states and school districts are creating local norms, particularly for primary grades.

The date of the norms is also significant because we live in a rapidly changing society. For a norm sample to be appropriate, it must also be current. Norms that are more than 15 years old are out of date (Salvia & Ysseldyke, 2004).

criterion-referenced test
a standardized test that compares a child's performance to his or her own progress in a certain skill or behavior.

There is another category of standardized tests, **criterion-referenced tests,** which compare a child's performance to individual progress in learning a set of skills or behaviors arranged according to difficulty level. Such a test does not need to be normed. These are measures that contain a list of developmental or academic skills that a teacher must either observe or assess to see whether a child has obtained the concept, skill, disposition, or attitude. The results of the inventory are used to plan further instruction.

Now that you have an understanding of the process of test development and some information about basic kinds of tests, what about the all-important test score? How are test scores developed and expressed? Which are good ones to use? These topics will be covered in the next section.

DIFFERENT TYPES OF TEST SCORES

It is relatively simple to determine if a child has learned all the addition facts of single-digit numbers through direct assessment in the classroom, because there are a finite number of these facts. However, most information that we wish to assess is not finite, even for young children, so we ask a few questions and base our decisions on the assumption that what we learn from assessing a sample of behavior will give us an accurate picture of performance for the entire topic. As well, test developers strive to discriminate the performance of children with these instruments. The differentiations are the demigods of developers (Popham, 2005). With a few items, the standardized test needs to demonstrate clear differences in performance across children. When you choose standardized tests (see Appendix C for guidelines to choosing tests) to use, you will want to be sure that the test matches your purpose for assessment and that a test is the most efficient and effective way to gather the information you need.

The most important reason for assessing a child's performance or behavior is to enable the teacher to develop appropriate lessons based on what the child can and cannot do. Because you need to know if the learning activity is suitable for a child of a particular age, test scores enable the teacher to determine the amount of difference that the child exhibits in a particular area from the expected level for his or her age or grade. In addition, you must understand how to use information provided in test manuals. Thus, before using a test with a child, you must be thoroughly familiar with the manual. You must know how to give the directions and how to score the measure.

Remember, the first score obtained from a test is the raw score, the number of items on either a published test or a teacher-made test that the child answered correctly. When you are using a standardized test, this score is compared with the performance of a group of children of known characteristics (age, gender, grade, and ethnicity) that are described in the test manual. These comparison scores are **derived scores** and you obtain them by using the raw scores along with tables in the manual. The three types of derived scores frequently used with young children are developmental scores (age-equivalent and grade-equivalent scores), percentiles, and standard scores. The first derived score, developmental scores, seems user-friendly but has the most limitations.

derived score score obtained by comparing the raw score with the performance of children of known characteristics on a standardized test.

Developmental Scores

age-equivalent score
derived score giving a
child's performance as that
which is normal for a
certain age.

grade-equivalent score
derived score giving a
child's performance as that
which is normal for a
certain grade.

Developmental scores—**age-equivalent scores** and **grade-equivalent scores**—have been widely used in the past and are reported in test manuals mainly because they enjoy a false reputation of being easily understood and useful scores (McLean, Worley, & Bailey, 2004; Urbina, 2004). Currently grade-level equivalents are used by school districts and states to determine whether children in third grade have made adequate yearly progress according to the requirements of the No Child Left Behind Act (NCLB) of 2001. These scores may or may not relate to the curriculum in particular school districts or child-care programs, although increasingly school districts modify the curriculum to align it with achievement measures used. As well, grade-equivalent scores do not mean that a first grader who has a score of 3.9—third grade, ninth month—should be moved forthwith to third grade. The score only means that achievement is well above the average for first graders. An example of a developmental age-equivalent score is 3–2. This score means that the child's performance on the test is considered to be the same as an average child who is 3 years, 2 months old. This score would then be compared with the child's actual chronological age. An example of a developmental grade-equivalent score is 3.2 (the same numerals as the previous example but separated by a decimal point instead of a hyphen). This score means that the child's performance on the test is considered the same as an average child who is in the second month of the third grade. This score would then have to be compared with the child's actual grade placement. Developmental scores are obtained by computing the mean raw score made by children of a given age or grade. That point is recorded on a graph that has raw scores along one axis and age or grade levels on the other axis. Points are plotted for the scores obtained at different ages or grades and a line is drawn to connect these points so that one can easily determine what age or grade corresponds to each raw score. Figure 4.4 shows a graph for assigning raw scores to children in kindergarten, grade 1, and grade 2 on the fictitious Amerikan Reeding Test.

The graph in Figure 4.4 indicates that only children at the beginning of the school year, 3 months into the school year, and 6 months into the school year participated in the norming. The squares indicate the mean score of the children in the normative sample. This information is found in a table in the manual so you would know, for instance, that the derived grade-equivalent score for a raw score of 11 is 1.4. Such scores obviously are not based directly on evidence collected for children of a particular chronological age or grade but are estimated—interpolated or extrapolated. An example of an **interpolated score** would be if we tested a child whose derived score is between two points where data were actually collected, as in the previous example. The derived score in the manual is interpolated because no children at that grade placement (1.4) were actually tested to establish that score. An example of an

interpolated score
derived score estimated
from norm scores because
no one with that particular
score was actually part of
the normative sample.

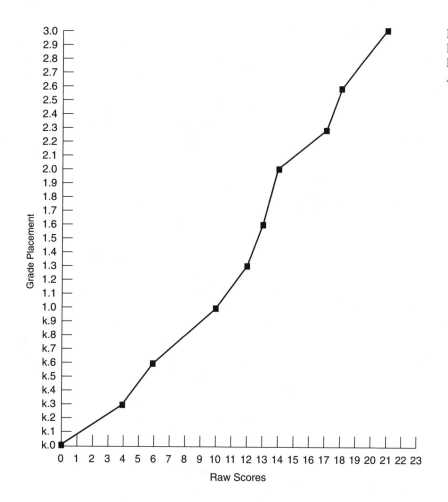

Figure 4.4
Raw scores earned by K–2 samples on the Amerikan Reeding Test.

extrapolated score would be if we used this test with a child whose raw score was beyond 21. We would have to extend the hypothetical line to determine the grade placement. Thus, we are estimating scores in both cases based on the hypothetical line of scores. These grade-equivalent scores seem to be useful, but do we really know what reading at 1.4 means for teaching on Tuesday?

According to Salvia and Ysseldyke (2004), there are at least four other types of problems with using developmental scores. For example, there is no such entity as an average 3–0 child (a child 3 years old) or an average 3.0 child (a child entering third grade), just as there is no such entity as an average family of 1.2 children. They are merely statistical abstractions and should be dealt with as such. In fact, both the International Reading Association (1980) and the Committee to Develop Standards for Educational and Psychological Testing (American Educational Research Association, American Psychological Association, & the National Council on Measurement in Education, 1999)

extrapolated score
derived score estimated from norm scores because the raw score is either less than or greater than anyone in the normative sample.

recommend that developmental scores be abandoned. However, if you are going to deal with developmental scores, remember that age-equivalent results are written with hyphens (2–3, 4–11, 6–9, and so on) to represent the number of months in a year whereas grade-equivalent results are written with decimal points (K.7, 2.3, 3.5, and so on) to represent months in a grade, which assumes that the school term is 10 months long. Thus, the developmental standard score may not be the one that will give you the best information. A more useful standard score is the percentile rank.

Percentile Ranks

percentile ranks derived scores indicating the percentage of individuals in the normative group whose test scores fall at or below a given raw score.

Percentile ranks are more useful as scores. They are derived scores that indicate the percentage of individuals in the normative group whose test scores fall at or below a given raw score. The percentile rank is not the same as percentages; it is not the percentage of correct answers. Rather, it is the percent of people who obtained the same number of correct answers. For example, if a child in your class receives a percentile rank of 84 on a particular test, it does not mean that she knew the answers to 84 percent of the problems on that test; it means that she scored as well as or better than 84 percent of the children in the sample for that test. Looking at Figure 4.2, you can see that the 84th percentile is at the top end of the average range.

Percentile ranks are not equal distances from each other. If we were to draw 100 vertical lines through the normal curve, with each line representing a percentile rank, the lines would be very close to each other near the center of the curve and get progressively farther apart from each other as they moved to either end. Thus, there is a big difference between being in the 98th percentile as opposed to the 99th percentile while there is a very small difference between the 50th percentile and the 51st percentile. In addition, because they do not represent equal differences, you cannot add, subtract, multiply, or divide them. To overcome the limitations of these derived scores, statisticians and test developers create scores to compare across the nation or other normed population. These scores are called *standard scores*.

Standard Scores

standard score is created statistically. This process converts raw scores to numbers that can be used to compare child progress on a particular dimension.

scaled score statistically determined scores that are used to derive total scores or that refer to results on subtests of an instrument.

A **standard score** is the general name for any derived score that is transformed or changed in some way so that the mean and standard deviation have predetermined values. These are sometimes called **scaled scores**; they are used to derive other scores and for statistical analyses. Unlike percentiles, these derived scores are separated by equal distances on the normal curve. Although there are five commonly used standard score distributions—z-scores, T-scores, deviation IQs, normal-curve equivalents, and stanines—only the last three will be discussed as these are the three most commonly needed by early childhood educators.

A deviation IQ is a misnomer because it is a derived score obtained from many different types of tests, not just an IQ or intelligence test. It has this name merely because it was first transformed for this type of test. More recently, this type of score is termed a *deviation quotient*. **Deviation quotients** are standard scores with a mean of 100 and a standard deviation of 15, usually. This type of score is widely used on *individually* administered tests of all types—intelligence, achievement, motor, language, and so on.

Normal-curve equivalents (NCEs) are standard scores generally found on *group* tests. Unlike percentiles, this scale divides the normal curve into 100 equal intervals with a mean equal to 50 and a standard deviation equal to 21.06. Figure 4.2 indicates that NCEs within the average zone range from 29 to 71.

Stanines are also standard scores that are less precise than the other two standard scores just described. The word "stanine" is a blend of *standard* and *nine*. Stanines divide the distribution into nine parts or bands. The middle stanine, the fifth, is .25 standard deviations above the mean and .25 standard deviations below the mean. The second, third, and fourth stanines are each .5 standard deviations in width below the mean, respectively, and the sixth, seventh, and eighth stanines are each .5 standard deviations in width above the mean, respectively. Finally, the first and ninth stanines are each 1.75 standard deviations or more below and above the mean, respectively. As a rule of thumb, the first, second, and third stanines represent below-average performance (23 percent); the fourth, fifth, and sixth stanines are average performance (54 percent); and the seventh, eighth, and ninth stanines represent above-average performance (23 percent). These percentages must be applied cautiously because children with scores near the borders of stanines may be more alike than different. With a score of 29 and stanine 6, Sally may be very much like Suzy who has a score of 30 and is in stanine 7. Parents may understand stanines easier than any other type of standard score, if they have some knowledge of the broad concepts associated with this standard score. Thus, although it is not as precise as other standard scores, the usefulness of the stanine lies in the fact that it is a single-digit score and easily understood by parents. Besides knowing about the scores, you will want to know whether the test works consistently. This, too, can be determined statistically.

deviation quotients standard scores with a mean of 100 and a standard deviation of usually 15.

normal-curve equivalents standard scores for group tests; scale has 100 equal parts, mean is usually 50, and standard deviation is usually 21.06.

stanines standard scores with nine unequal bands; bands four, five, and six represent average performance.

RELIABILITY

Reliability refers to consistency, dependability, or stability. A test needs to be reliable so that teachers and others can generalize from the current test results to other times and circumstances. If a test can generalize to different times, it has **test-retest reliability**. We can assume that we would get the same results tomorrow or next week. The typical length of time between the first test administration and the second is 2 weeks.

reliability consistency, dependability, or stability of test results.

test-retest reliability ability to get the same results from a test taken twice within two weeks.

If a test can generalize to other similar test items, it has *internal consistency*, *split-half* or *alternate form* reliability. We can assume that different test items would give us similar results. If a test can generalize to other testers who administer the test, it has interrater or **interscorer reliability**. We can assume that if other testers would administer the test, they would obtain the same results. Box 4.1 shows examples of test-retest reliability and interscorer reliability as you see them in the classroom.

Test manuals report these different types of reliability as **correlation coefficients,** so you need to know what a correlation coefficient is. Without knowing how to compute it, it is still possible to understand it. A correlation is simply a measure of how things are related to one another; it is a measure of whether there is an association between two variables and if so, how much. The degree of relationship between two variables is a correlation coefficient that can range from $+1.00$ to -1.00; no relationship at all is in the middle or .00. The number of the correlation coefficient tells us the strength of the relationship (the closer it is to one, the stronger it is) and the sign ($+$ or $-$) tells us the direction of the relationship. If the relationship is positive ($+$), as one variable goes up, so does the other. However, if the relationship is negative ($-$), as one variable goes up, the other goes down. An example of a positive relationship is the age of a child and his or her height. Generally speaking,

interscorer reliability
ability of a test to produce the same results regardless of who administers it.

correlation coefficient
degree of relationship between two variables.

Box 4.1	*Reliability*
Test-retest	When Charles takes the test today and in 2 weeks, he will have similar scores, assuming no instructional intervention.
Interscorer	Ms. Keno and Ms. Hausman give the Apple Test to Bonnie, and each gets similar scores.

as the child gets older, the child gets taller. An example of a negative relationship is the distance between the source of a sound and the ability to hear it. As the distance you are from a ringing phone increases, the ability to hear it decreases. An example of no correlation is the number of permanent teeth a child has and readiness to read, as reported by Gredler (1992). Most correlation coefficients reported in test manuals are positive.

When considering correlations, remember that correlations do not indicate causality. Just because two variables correlate, it does not mean that one has caused the other. For example, it is possible to correlate the sale of boxes of margarine with the purchase of motor scooters, but few of us would assume a relationship between the two variables. In an educational context, scores on intelligence tests and scores on achievement tests usually correlate. However, in this case, one cannot say that high intelligence scores cause high achievement scores or that high achievement scores cause high intelligence scores. Another variable may cause either or both of these results. As there are at least three possible interpretations, we should never draw causality conclusions from such data. Figure 4.5 shows correlations of subtests on the Ever-Read Test for Ms. Columbo's first grade. Besides knowing whether a test is reliable, based on the reporting of correlation coefficients, we will want to know what the error factor is.

Child	Subtest	Score	Correlation of subtest scores	Teaching implication
Ragnar	Phonemic Vocabulary	10 10	1.0	Balanced development; test is not challenging
Glenn	Phonemic Vocabulary	10 5	.5	Vocabulary development needed
John	Phonemic Vocabulary	7 10	.7	Work with rhyming and other phonemic awareness activities
Matt	Phonemic Vocabulary	0 10	0	Investigate auditory perceptional skills
Lisa	Phonemic Vocabulary	10 9	.9	Balanced development; needs attention in challenging
Erika	Phonemic Vocabulary	5 5	1.0	Balanced development; needs attention in both areas
Katie	Phonemic Vocabulary	3 6	.5	Needs skill development in both areas
Alissa	Phonemic Vocabulary	9 9	1.0	Balanced development; test is not challenging

What have you learned by reviewing the scores and correlations for the Ever-Read Test? Would you use it with your first-grade class? What additional information would you need to decide?

Figure 4.5
Reading subtest report for the Ever-Read Test for Ms. Columbo's first-grade class.

standard error of measurement (SEM)
estimate of the amount of variation that can be expected in test scores as a result of reliability correlations.

The error factor statistic that tells about the score that may occur due to chance is the **standard error of measurement (SEM)**. Commonly, developers acknowledge that no test, no matter how well designed, is free from error. The reliability of a test depends on the size of the SEM. The larger the SEM, the less reliable the test—this is true because the SEM is the estimate of the amount of variation that can be expected in test scores as a result of reliability correlations. Let's say a child in your class took an individual intelligence test that yielded a standard score of 88. The mean of this test is 100 and the standard deviation is 15. At first glance, this score suggests that the child is in the average range of 85 to 115, where 68 percent of the normative population would score. However, the SEM for this particular test is 10. That means the confidence band for this score is that two out of three times, this child's true score will be between 78 and 98 (88+ or −10); one out of three times, it will be above or below this band. If the SEM for this test was 3 instead of 10, you would have more confidence in the results because then the confidence band would be 88 (+ or −3) and the true score would fall between 85 and 91 two out of three times. The smaller the SEM, the more reliable the test is because the scores fluctuate less. Thus, you can have more confidence in its stability. Figure 4.6 illustrates this example with the two confidence bands.

The top line shows the derived standard score of 88 on the normal curve without considering any standard error of measurement (SEM). Above the second line, you can see the range where the child's true score would fall two out of three times if the SEM is 10. Below the second line, you can see the range where the child's true score would fall two out of three times if the SEM is 3. Besides the SEM, there are other factors that affect the reliability of tests—test length, time interval between testing, and size of the norming sample.

All of these variables affect reliability, and thus can inflate or deflate the reliability coefficients. The longer the test, meaning that it has more test items, the more reliable it will be. This is one of the main reasons diagnostic tests are more reliable than screening tests. Screening tests, by their very definition and purpose, are shorter tests with fewer items.

Figure 4.6
The influence of confidence bands (SEM) on the interpretation of a score.

55	70	85	×100	115	130	145
−3	−2	−1	0	+1	+2	+3

SEM = 10
88 (+ or − 10)

78 79 80 81 82 83 84 85 86 87 ×88 89 90 91 92 93 94 95 96 97 98 99

SEM = 3
88 (+ or −3)

Another factor that is very relevant to early childhood tests and test length is the fact that many tests for young children do not have enough items at the lowest age levels so that the child has fewer opportunities to demonstrate ability (Bracken, 1987a). In other words, the difficulty level at the beginning of the test is too steep, which affects its reliability. When standard scores increase or decrease as a function of a child's success or failure on a single test item, the test is less sensitive to small differences in the child's abilities. Thus, a test should have enough easy items to discriminate properly at the lower end of the range (Bracken, 1987b).

The shorter the time interval between two administrations of the same test, the higher the reliability coefficient. Thus, when looking at this statistic in a test manual, the amount of time between the two test administrations must be stated and taken into account.

The larger the norming sample, the more reliable the test will be, and this is a good reason for adhering to the minimum recommended size of the normative sample. Finally, the range of test scores obtained from the normative sample can also affect the test's reliability. The wider the spread, the more reliably the test can distinguish between them. In this way, you are sure that the test is reliable. You will also want to be sure that the test measures what it says it will measure, as discussed in the next section.

VALIDITY

Validity refers to the extent to which a test measures what it is supposed to measure. It tells how meaningful the test results really are. Developers do not measure the validity of a test per se; rather, they judge the test by its reliability and the adequacy of its norms. There are descriptions of a great many types of validity; however, validity "integrates various strands of evidence into a coherent account of the degree to which existing evidence and theory support the intended interpretation of scores for specific uses" (AERA, 1999). Developers try to determine whether they are measuring what they think they are measuring. Depending on a person's knowledge of research and reason for administering the test, an individual can consider various aspects of validity.

validity the extent to which a test measures what it is supposed to measure.

Face validity is whether the test looks as if it is testing what it is supposed to be testing. This type of validity is very superficial; yet, it is important to both the child taking the test and the person selecting the test. For example, if a mathematics test did not have addition, subtraction, multiplication, and division problems, it would not have face validity even if it were a very valid mathematics test based on other types of validity.

face validity whether a test looks as if it is testing what it is supposed to be testing.

Content validity is established by evaluating three factors: how appropriate the items are, how complete the item samples are, and the way in which the items assess the content (Salvia & Ysseldyke, 2004).

content validity extent of how well a test tests the subject matter it is supposed to test.

117

criterion-related validity
relationship between the scores on a test and another criterion measure.

concurrent validity
relationship between a test and another criterion when both are obtained at about the same time.

predictive validity how accurately a test score can be used to estimate performance on some variable or criterion in the future.

construct validity the extent to which a test measures a theoretical characteristic or trait.

convergent validity is demonstrated when similar instruments measuring similar constructs yield comparable results.

treatment validity the usefulness of test results for planning intervention.

social validity describes the usefulness of assessment information for the teacher in the educational setting.

This type of validity is especially important for achievement and adaptive behavior tests. When utilizing this type of validity, the user must keep in mind the appropriate use of the test. For example, one would not use a mathematics test for determining reading ability.

Criterion-related validity is the relationship between the scores on a test and another criterion measure. Of course, this criterion must itself be valid if it establishes the validity of a test. This type of validity is usually expressed as a correlation coefficient between the test and the criterion. The criterion does not have to be a test but often is.

Concurrent validity is the relationship between a test and the criterion when the evidence is obtained at approximately the same time. During the development of the Kaufman Assessment Battery for Children (K–ABC), children in the sample were administered the Wechsler Intelligence Scales for Children–Revised (WISC–R), a well-established intelligence test for children. If the scores on the new test correlate highly with the scores on the well-established test, then the new test has concurrent validity. The concurrent validity of a screening test is usually judged by the amount of agreement the scores have when a sample of children are given an intelligence test.

Predictive validity refers to how accurately the child's current test score can be used to estimate performance on some variable or criterion in the future. For example, you administer a reading–readiness test to your kindergartners. The test should have established predictive validity when designed so that you know, by means of a correlation coefficient, the relationship of your children's scores to reading scores at the end of first grade or second grade on a specific reading achievement test (the criterion). Predictive validity strongly suggests that if a child currently has a score that indicates a developmental delay, the likelihood is that the child is at risk of future school failure.

Construct validity refers to the extent to which a test measures a theoretical characteristic or trait such as personality, intelligence, or creativity. These traits are theoretical because they are not observable behaviors that can be seen or measured directly. As such, this may be the most difficult type of validity to establish.

Convergent validity connotes whether the information from the instrument is of a quality to be helpful to plan an intervention (Bagnato, Neisworth, & Munson, 1997, p. 11). Shoe size, weight, and height do not provide much guidance for planning intervention. However, performance scores on language scales or motor development scales that can translate to the development of activities are useful to practitioners.

Treatment validity indicates the degree to which the instrument provides information that can lead to the development of intervention strategies, including developing goals and objectives, determining methods, and detecting progress (Bagnato et al., 1997, p. 12).

Social validity represents the value and use of the information obtained from the instrument (McLean et al., 2004). IQ scores and other developmental scores are often available, but these provide limited information for what to do in the classroom or in treatment interventions

Box 4.2   *In the Real World*

Validity

Face	When Ms. Zelitski examines the Apple Test, she determines that the items seem to represent the ones she includes in her curriculum.
Content	The Second-Grade Science Wizards Test seems to have the concepts that the State of Missouri requires for second graders.
Criterion	The New Test of Reading uses (similar items at similar levels as the well-established Amerikan Reeding Test).
Concurrent	The San Francisco Test of Reading compares favorably to the Woodcock-Johnson Reading inventory.
Predictive	The History in America Test shows which third graders will be successful in the third-grade social studies curriculum.
Construct	The Whole-Child Screening Inventory for 3- to 5-Year-Olds contains items that represent the best practices articulated by professional associations such as the National Association for Education of Young Children and the National Center for Infants, Toddlers, and Families.
Convergent	The scores on the Infant Aptitude Test help Mr. Miller plan activities for Mr. and Mrs. Krasnow to try with their baby, Paul, who shows some delay in language development.
Treatment	The Second-Grade Soccer Test gives scores that show coaches how to help Carlota run more effectively, kick goals, and pass the ball to teammates.
Social	The Wheat State Achievement Test provides information that will help third-grade teachers plan effective curriculum. While the Test of Flower Knowledge gives interesting information, it is not useful in planning what to do on Thursday

for children with disabilities. In addition, these tests have been widely misused in the past to stigmatize young children.

All of these different kinds of validity are useful constructs for understanding whether tests measure what they say they are measuring. Each kind of validity is more important depending on the purpose of the test and the planned administration. The chart in Box 4.2 gives practical examples of each of the defined validities.

Just as there are factors that affect reliability, there are factors that affect validity of the experience for a given individual. First, there are test-related factors such as anxiety, motivation, understanding of instructions, rapport between the examiner and the examinee, degree of bilingualism, unfamiliarity with the test material, and differences in other experiences from the norm of the standardization group. Obviously, the test is not valid for children who are uncooperative, highly distractible, or who fail to understand the test instructions. Other moderator variables for test validity applied to the individual include interest, gender, and the social values of the child being examined (Urbina, 2004). Finally, the reliability of the test affects validity. A test cannot be valid unless it is reliable, so reliability is a necessary, but not the only, condition for validity.

A standardized test that covers a good sample of a subject, but not the subject or course as taught in a particular school, would have content validity, but not curricular validity. A test that reflects the knowledge and skills presented in a particular school's curriculum has curricular validity. In such a test, the items adequately sample the content of the curriculum the students have been studying. In recent years the consideration of the consequences of the use of standardized tests has suggested that the validity of the assessment relates to the way it is used (Linn & Miller, 2005). Popham (1997, p. 9) argues that this approach to the consideration of validity is counterproductive: "It will deflect educators from the clarity they need when judging tests *and* the consequences of test use."

In sum, validity is a unitary concept and the most important consideration when choosing a standardized test (AERA, 1999, p. 17) Curricular validity is more appropriately termed *alignment*. That is, the test aligns or matches the curriculum. Further, the use of the test should not exceed its developed purpose. In this regard, validity is a joint responsibility of the developer and the test user—choosing a test for its intended purpose (AERA, 1999). In the high-stakes, No Child Left Behind environment that you are entering as a teacher, the validity of tests relates to whether tests used are appropriate for the purposes originally intended.

With all of this technical information in your mind and in the test manuals available, how do you decide which is the best test for your purpose? How will you know whether your program or school district chooses appropriate measures to answer questions about the children in your program? First, you will want to know where to get more information beyond the publishers' claims.

GUIDELINES FOR TEST EVALUATION

Thus, when you are expected to serve on committees for the purpose of selecting a standardized test, particularly a developmental screening test or a group achievement test, you will need to be knowledgeable about where to find reviews and what to look for in such reviews. Early childhood teachers should be able to evaluate standardized tests, both in terms of their technical adequacy (norms, reliability, and validity) and their appropriateness for a particular group of children. The principles followed in the evaluation of a test should always be in congruence with the NAEYC position on *Early Childhood Curriculum,*

Assessment, and Program Evaluation (2003), the NAEYC *Code of Ethical Conduct and Statement of Commitment* (2005), and the Interdisciplinary Council on Developmental and Learning Disabilities (ICLD) *ICLD Clinical Practice Guidelines* (2000).

Evaluating tests is not a simple proposition. Even though there are standards developed by a joint committee of three prestigious and knowledgeable organizations—the American Educational Research Association, the American Psychological Association, and the National Council on Measurement in Education (1999)—not all standards will be uniformly applicable across the wide range of instruments and uses that currently exist. However, just as test developers have a responsibility to provide adequate information in the test manual, test users who need the scores for some decision-making purpose, such as teachers and administrators, have an ethical responsibility in selecting appropriate tests that meet the necessary standards for making decisions about children.

Using the previous standards as a guide and recommendations from other sources (cf. Salvia & Ysseldyke, 2004) for quantifying the standards, criteria for evaluating the technical adequacy of norms, reliability, and validity are shown in Box 4.3, 4.4, and 4.5.

Other criteria include an adequate description of test procedures in sufficient detail to enable test users to duplicate the administration and scoring procedures used during test standardization and a full description of tester qualifications. The skills specific to a particular test should be enumerated. Finally, evidence showing the appropriateness of the test for children of different racial, ethnic, or linguistic backgrounds who are likely to be tested must be stated. Due to the multicultural attributes of American schools, this is not easy. However, test developers

---

Box 4.3 *Techincal Adequacy of Norms*

1. Norms should be available in the manual or in an accompanying technical publication in the form of standard scores.

2. The test manual needs to define the standardization of the normative sample clearly so that the test user can determine the suitability for a particular population. Such defining characteristics should include five or more of the following variables: ages, grade levels, gender, geographic areas, race, socioeconomic status, ethnicity, parental education, or other relevant variables.

3. The norm-sampling method should be well defined. If the norm sample is based on convenience or readily available populations, it is not acceptable.

4. For each subgroup examined, an adequate sample size should be used, with 100 subjects per age or grade considered the lower limit. In addition, there should be 1,000 or more subjects in the total sample.

5. The test's norms should not be more than 15 years old.

Box 4.4   *Criteria for Evaluating the Realibility of a Standardized Test*

1. The test manual should supply an estimate of test-retest reliability for relevant subgroups. A correlation coefficient of 60, 80, or 90 or better for group tests, screening tests, and diagnostic tests, respectively, is a current best practice criterion.

2. The test manual should report empirical evidence of internal consistency with a correlation coefficient of 90 or better.

3. Reliability coefficients as well as standard errors of measurement (SEMs) should be presented in a tabular format.

4. Reliability procedures and samples of at least 25 subjects should be described.

5. Quantitative methods used to study and control item difficulty and other systematic item analyses should be reported in the manual.

6. Measures of central tendency and variability (means and standard deviations for the total raw scores) should be reported for relevant subgroups during the norming procedures.

7. Empirical evidence interrater reliability at .85 or better should be reported in the manual.

8. The steepness of the test items should be controlled by having a minimum of three raw score items per standard deviation. The range of items for the youngest children should span two or more standard deviations below the mean score for each subtest and for the total score of the test.

must make every effort to avoid scores that vary as a function of race, ethnicity, gender, or language.

In addition to using these criteria, formal evaluations of tests, written by experts, are found in the *Mental Measurements Yearbooks*. The most recent yearbook (Plake & Impara, 2003) is available on CD-ROM and online. For many early childhood tests, the best sources of information are the journal articles that report the research associated with the development and use of the tests. See also the *ICLD Clinical Practices Guidelines* (2000) for the birth–3 population.

The importance of using only technically adequate tests cannot be overemphasized. In many places, tests control what we teach, what children learn, and what their future holds. These high-stakes tests have assumed almost biblical powers. They determine who will fail and who will be promoted; who will graduate and who will be prevented from graduating; who will attend summer school and who will be able to make choices for themselves. The outcomes influence which teachers will be rewarded or punished; which principals will be commended or punished; which families will be disappointed or be proud; which children will feel intact or feel deficient (Meisels, 2000, p.16).

Box 4.5   *Criteria for Evaluating the Validity of a Standardized Test*

1. The test manual must define what the test measures and what the test should be used for.

2. Evidence of at least one type of validity should be provided for the major types of inferences for which the use of a test is recommended (i.e., content, criterion-related concurrent, or predictive construct).

3. For content validity, the manual should define the content area(s) and explain how the content and skills to be tested were selected. Tests that are based on content validity should update content on revised forms.

4. For both types of criterion-related validity, that is, concurrent and predictive, (a) the criteria should be clearly defined; (b) validity of the criteria should be reported; (c) samples should be completely described; (d) correlation coefficients with other tests should be reported and (e) for predictive validity, a statement concerning the length of time for which predictions can be made should be included.

5. For construct validity, the manual should clearly define the ability or aptitude measured. For tests for which there is a time limit, the manual should state how speed affects scores.

Thus, if a standardized test is not technically adequate, it should not be used no matter how well it meets the needs of your testing program from a nontechnical standpoint. You may think that using a poorly normed test is better than making a decision without any comparative data. However, once it is deemed technically adequate, other considerations are appropriate before making a decision between one or more technically adequate standardized tests. Now is the time to consider administration and scoring characteristics such as time required to administer and score the test; age and/or grade range; ease of administration; the match between the content on the test and the content in your curriculum; examiner qualifications; and the appropriateness of the test format, how the items are presented and how the children are to respond, for your population.

According to the *Standards for Educational and Psychological Testing* (AERA, 1999), test users should select tests that meet the purpose for which they are to be used and that are appropriate for the intended test-taking populations. It is the responsibility of the test user to read the test manual, examine specimen sets, become familiar with how and when the test was developed and tried out, read independent evaluations of a test, ascertain if the test content and norm groups are appropriate, and select and use only those tests for which the skills needed to administer the test and interpret scores correctly are available.

Information on specific standardized screening and diagnostic tests used with young children is located in Appendix C.

SUMMARY

This chapter emphasizes the importance of basic concepts of measurement for the competency of the professional working with young children. In order to increase that competency, basic terms are defined and examples are provided. Then more involved terms such as *standardization*, *norms*, *validity*, and *reliability* are fully discussed. These terms are then applied to evaluating tests. Guidelines are listed so that teachers may determine the technical adequacy of the norms, reliability, and validity of any given standardized test.

FIELD ACTIVITIES

1. Turn to Appendix C, which describes specific tests, at the end of this text. Select two tests from any of the categories (e.g., screening, reading, giftedness). If possible, select two tests used in your school or community so that you can borrow the actual test and manual. Evaluate each test's technical adequacy following the guidelines in this chapter. Determine which of the two tests is more technically adequate. Check your decision with expert opinions from the most recent *Mental Measurements Yearbook* or journal articles in your university library.

2. Interview two experienced teachers working with young children of different ages who use tests for making decisions about children. Ask them which tests they use, which they like best, and why. Later, determine the technical adequacy of their choices.

3. Choose a test. Review it according to the principles suggested in this chapter and with the guidelines given in Appendix C. Explain the test to a colleague or teacher in one paragraph.

IN-CLASS ACTIVITIES

1. Pretend that you are teaching a group of children in which a small subgroup consists of children who speak Spanish both at home and with each other. Your administrator wants to use a standardized test with them that is not available in Spanish. Develop a list of arguments indicating that such a test would not be appropriate for these children and a list of possible solutions to resolve this problem.

2. Bring a test to class, and then in pairs, role-play the administration of the test to a child. After that, shift gears and role-play interpreting results to a child's family.

STUDY QUESTIONS

1. What does NAEYC hold as an early childhood teacher's responsibility in the assessment process?

2. How can teachers assist parents in understanding means, averages, and ranges for their child's test scores?

3. What information will a grade-equivalent score or age-equivalent score provide? How do they differ?

4. When will early childhood teachers need developmental scores?

5. How do percentile scores and standardized scores differ? Suppose a child scores a standardized score of 50 (mean 100, standard deviation 10) and a percentile score of 60. What does this tell the teacher?

16-84 % ile
: is average

6. How do interpolated and extrapolated scores differ in classroom use?

7. Why is it important for teachers to examine correlation coefficients when reviewing assessment tools?

8. What factors will influence test reliability? What are the types of reliability in assessment? What types of reliability are teachers most concerned with?

9. How can teachers help parents understand and grasp the concept of stanine scores?

10. Why can't teachers conclude causality in the relationship between high intellect and high standardized achievement test scores?

11. Name the different types of validity. How is each type used in the early childhood classroom assessment program?

12. What factors will influence validity?

13. List the qualities that make a test technically efficient. What issues will need to be evaluated beyond technical efficiency?

REFLECT AND RE-READ

- I can define the important measurement terms and know what they mean in practice.

- I know how to explain the role of tests to parents and others, including strengths and limitations.

- I can outline a multidisciplinary approach to assessment that includes the appropriate use of tests for each of the following: infants, toddlers, preschoolers, and primary-age children.

- I am familiar with the ethical and social issues that apply to the development and use of tests with young children and their families.

CASE VIGNETTE

Makalo is a second grader in your class. He is 7.9 years old. It is November and the two of you have had many discussions about math; Makalo maintains that he doesn't like it! You administer the Key Math, Revised (Connolly, 1988) to see if Makalo has any particular strengths or weaknesses. The test has three subsets. Makalo's scores are as follows:

	Basic Concepts*	Operations†	Applications‡
Raw Score	23	19	30
Standard Score	101	102	107
Percentile Rank	53	55	68
Grade/Age Equivalent	7-11	7-8	8-3

As a mathematician skilled in interpreting statistics, what do you now know about Makalo? What else do you need to know to be able to understand these assessment results? What are the next steps in teaching Makalo?

* Numeration, rational numbers, geometry
† Addition, subtraction, multiplication, division, mental computation
‡ Measurement, time and money, estimation, interpreting data, problem solving

Source: From N. Roberts, 2003, submitted in partial fulfillment of T&L 411, Assessment in Early Childhood Education: DePaul University. Used by permission.

TECHNOLOGY LINKS

http://www.unl.edu/buros

Buros Institute on Mental Measurements. This site is the online link to the series of *Mental Measurements Yearbooks*. It is the place to find reviews of published tests.

http://www.ctb.com

CTB-McGraw-Hill. A corporate site related to standardized tests. It contains a glossary and position papers as well as test descriptions.

http://www.ets.org

Educational Testing Service. In addition to test descriptions, this site has position papers and research related to tests and testing.

http://www.aera.net

American Educational Research Association. Policy linked to research and practice issues.

SUGGESTED READINGS

McLean, M., Worley, M., & Bailey, D. B. (2004). *Assessing infants and preschoolers with special needs.* (3rd ed). Upper Saddle River, NJ: Merrill/Prentice Hall.
Popham, W. J. (2000). *Testing! Testing! What every parent should know about school tests.* Boston: Allyn & Bacon.

Popham, W. J. (2005). *Classroom assessment: What teachers need to know* (4th ed.). Boston: Allyn & Bacon.

Salvia, J., & Ysseldyke, J. (2004). *Assessment* (9th ed.). Boston: Houghton Mifflin.

Tuckman, B. (1988). *Testing for teachers*. San Diego: Harcourt.

Valencia, R. R., & Suzuki, L. A. (2001). *Intelligence testing and minority students: Foundations, performance factors and assessment issues*. Thousand Oaks, CA: Sage.

5

Testing: Choosing the Right Measure

Terms to Know

- tests
- norm-based instruments
- criterion-based instruments
- screening tests
- inventory
- diagnostic measures
- curriculum-based measures
- diagnostic tests
- criterion-referenced measures
- performance assessment
- formative assessment
- mastery learning
- portfolio
- artifacts
- performance
- IEP goals
- IDEA
- technical issues
- rubric
- interrater reliability
- authentic assessment

Chapter Overview

This chapter begins with a discussion of the role that tests play in early childhood education. Appropriate uses of tests for accountability, screening, diagnosis, and Individualized Education Plans follow. Next, using performance-based measures to answer some important assessment questions is discussed, as well as technical issues regarding the use of performance measures. Coordination of testing programs with instruction and cautions conclude the chapter.

Assess as You Read

- When is a good time to use a test?
- In addition to achievement tests, what are some other instruments for teacher use?
- What can I learn from the diagnostic process that will help me individualize instruction?
- Why bother with tests, now that we have performance-based assessment?
- How do I choose the right test for a child or a class? How do I know if the test is appropriate?
- What state and federal laws regarding assessment will affect my classroom practice?

TESTS IN THE ASSESSMENT SYSTEM

test instrument for measuring skills, knowledge, development, aptitudes, and so on.

Tests serve an important function in early childhood programs when used for a specific, suitable purpose. When you are choosing tests, examine them for their technical qualities. In addition, be sure that they are appropriate for the children you serve. Finally, be prepared to follow the directions established in test manuals carefully. Given these prerequisites, when is it okay to use tests? What are some of the problems associated with testing young children? In the following sections these issues will be addressed.

Responsible Use of Tests

Reeves (2000) suggests four straightforward questions that answer the needs of parents and policy-makers. Parents and policy-makers want to know:

1. How's my kid doing?
2. Are the schools (or early childhood programs) succeeding or failing?
3. What works best to help students learn?
4. Do test scores prove the effectiveness of educational programs?

Reeves then delineates the elements of an accountability system that will answer such questions: congruence with curriculum, respect for diversity, accuracy, specificity, feedback for continuous improvement, universality, and fairness. As you read more about assessment and the limitations of various strategies, these principles will come into play. You will need to think about the classroom level—can I answer all these questions? What data do I need to make an informed decision? When should I use a test to help me gather the information?

The term *standardized test* describes the fact that test administration, scoring of results, and interpretations follow specific standards and are referenced to a concept of *normal*. Everybody who administers a particular test is supposed to do it the same way.

When using standardized tests, you must present the instructions in a specified way, according to the manual. You must record and score the child's responses to test items according to standards described in the test manual. The directions in the manual guide the method for interpreting the results. In the same way, you derive scores and statistics from the procedures outlined in the test manual. Good tests include cautions and limitations for using the particular instrument in the manual. Accordingly, before administering any standardized test, you must be thoroughly familiar with the procedures required for administration.

Errors in Testing That Influence Results

Inexperienced examiners often commit two types of *leniency* errors: (1) coaching—assisting the child beyond that permitted by the instructions; and (2) giving the child a break on the scoring when the child seems to know an answer but cannot provide a creditable response. If teachers take liberties with administration and scoring procedures, the testing situation is no longer standard for each child and results are no longer comparable across children. Leniency errors in assessments may result in the failure to refer children who are in need of special help. Young children thus lose an opportunity for enhanced development.

To be effective, fair, and efficient, teachers must devote time to learning the administration and scoring rules for specific instruments they choose. Directions in the manual tell teachers to read instructions, word for word, but there are various other aspects of test administration—arranging materials, doing demonstrations, applying scoring rules, and so on—that must become second nature to the examiner. You must practice doing the test before administering it to children so that you can administer it smoothly and correctly.

While following standardized testing procedures, the examiner—you—must also ensure that you elicit the child's optimal performance. Unless the examiner maintains the child's cooperation, a test will not yield a valid measure of performance. Goodenough (1949) notes that this will sometimes be the case "even under the best conditions and with the most skillful examiner" and proposes, "the safest procedure to follow is not to give any test at all, rather than to give a poor test." She suggests that the child return at a later occasion if the child doesn't cooperate. Of course, then, you document the "failed" experience as part of the assessment process.

Using Test Scores

Test scores act to supplement information known about children. Tests are not infallible. Scores require interpretation in the context of the child's life. This is why the requirements for standardized achievement testing should not be applied to individual children for high-stakes decisions—promotion, retention, enrollment eligibility—but rather such measures, if used, should be applied to curricular evaluation and program adjustment. The contextual review of test scores includes awareness of the individual child's personal, cultural, social, and emotional context, as well as the school context. Information gathered from a parent interview and teacher observation is the lodestone; test scores are the glittery specks. Unfortunately, teachers sometimes pay more attention to the glitter, particularly in these days of high-stakes testing decisions made in public education. A child is not a score on a test or a level of performance. A child is an individual: Lisa, Larissa, Peter, Jose, or Stephen, each with a particular family, a culture, and a personality, who uses diverse strategies to cope with the social-emotional and cognitive demands of the school setting.

EARLY CHILDHOOD TESTS AND THEIR USE

norm-based instruments tests that compare children to others of similar age, grade level, or other important characteristics.

criterion-based instruments are those based on a learning goal or standard. Finite steps in the learning of particular concepts are measured.

Early childhood tests vary in many ways. The most important issues are their *content relevance* and *practical utility* to early childhood teachers. Some tests are *comprehensive*, covering all the major developmental domains including gross motor skills, fine-motor skills, language, and cognition. Others are limited to one or only a few domains, such as tests of language development or understanding of concepts. Some educational tests are curricular content measures used to assess the child's understanding. Educational tests are *norm-based* or *criterion-based*. **Norm-based instruments** (Box 5.1 describes one such instrument) compare children to others of similar age, grade level, or other important characteristics, whereas **criterion-based instruments** identify the list of skills or milestone markers that *all* children will presumably pass on their way to successful mastery of the developmental stage or academic subject. Such tests evaluate a child's performance on a specific standard. A teacher checks to see whether a child can count to five, hop on one

Box 5.1 *Norm-Based Test*

The Iowa Test of Basic Skills (ITBS) (Hoover, Hieronymous, Frisble, & Dunbar, 1996) is an achievement test that compares children on a number of academic tasks. At the primary level this test yields information about vocabulary, word analysis, reading, listening, language, math concepts, math problems, and math computation. At the upper levels of the primary battery, the test yields information about social studies, science, and using information. It takes about 2 hours over several days to administer the complete battery. Results can be used to plan the program and to monitor individual progress. Various standard scores are available.

foot, and so on. Some tests cover a broad age range; others target a specific age group, such as infants or pre-kindergarten children. Tests vary greatly in length, as well as in the time and skill it takes to administer, score, and interpret them.

At issue is the use of these instruments for high-stakes decisions (Box 5.1) and other similar standardized achievement tests.

Four Purposes of Tests

It is useful to think of tests as serving four purposes: (1) accountability reporting; (2) screening; (3) diagnosis; and (4) educational planning. State and federal legislation usually prescribe accountability-testing requirements. One such measure that requires links to curriculum, standards, and multiple measures is the No Child Left Behind Act of 2001 (P.L. 107–110). The passage of this legislation draws attention to the development of approaches to assessing young children for reading and mathematic achievement at third grade. Thus, early childhood teachers will need to be aware of state and local approaches toward assessment of this achievement and will need to be thoroughly familiar with the multiple ways for documenting academic progress prior to third grade. In addition, teachers must be vigilant at the local and state level to ensure that third-grade achievement measures do not become high-stakes assessment, relying on one measure for individual child enrollment or placement. Advocacy action on the part of early childhood educators is effective. One example is when the developmental screening tests initially were misused for the identification of children for special programs, a practice now prohibited in publicly funded programs.

Measures that are intentionally brief and provide a global index of developmental delay or normality are appropriate for developmental screening tests. These measures should be play-based when used for babies, toddlers, and preschoolers. At the primary level, these are the informal reading or mathematics assessments conducted by teachers. Diagnostic-level measures are more in-depth and time-consuming assessments that provide more specific information about an individual child's profile of abilities and disabilities, as well as contribute to developmental diagnosis and identification of educational disabilities. The most in-depth measures are those instruments intended to provide specific education-related information tied to curriculum goals and individual educational planning. Psychologists, special education teachers, speech therapists, and others who must identify children with disabilities most often use diagnostic instruments. However, there are diagnostic instruments that early childhood teachers may find useful in planning for instruction. As you choose appropriate diagnostic instruments to use with your students, you will want to remember the fundamental aspects of choosing the right tools.

The cornerstone of test standardization is validity. The question is "How well does the test do the job it claims to do?" For a developmental screening test, "How accurate are screening test results when compared to the results of more in-depth developmental testing?" For diagnostic measures, "How well do they relate to results of other test measures, to evaluation based on professional observation, parental reports, and school performance? Have trustworthy studies been done to decide these relationships?" Most detailed curriculum-based measures lack research evidence of validity. The presumption is that they are valid because educational specialists design them in detail. This assumption could cause problems, particularly when you choose such instruments without consideration about whether they match the philosophy, curricular goals, and developmental levels of the children in your program.

Choosing Tests

To learn the relevance and utility of various measures for the children you work with, start by listing the characteristics of these children. Include age, sex, social/economic background, cultural and language backgrounds, and any other factors you consider relevant. Are these children assumed to be normal or are they "at risk" by virtue of environmental factors, developmental delay, or identified special disability? Next, why are you searching for a test? To help identify young children who may be in need of/entitled to early childhood special education services? To monitor the developmental progress of presumably normal children? To further assess children with identified developmental problems? Then ask, "Is this test designed to serve the purpose I need to accomplish?" At the most basic level, "Is the item content of this instrument addressing the developmental or academic issues that are appropriate for my program and the children who I serve? Are there sufficient numbers of items (e.g., questions, tasks) to adequately screen or assess these areas of development?" See the Test Evaluation Guidelines in the Appendix D for a complete format to use in evaluating particular instruments. Box 5.2 illustrates teacher assessment decision-making in action.

Box 5.2 *Choosing Test for Purpose*

Ms. Wynette needs to find out which of the 10 3-year-olds in her room know colors and numbers, geometric shapes, basic direction words—*over, under, above, below*. She can, of course, observe carefully, but she will need to make sure that she checks everyone. It may be easier to choose a criterion-based curriculum instrument to assess the knowledge of the 3-year-olds because there are so many. It seems efficient to use a prepared instrument.

Mr. Nelson needs to know whether the third graders can multiply numbers from 1 to 10 in problems that are single-digit. He could, of course, administer a test that would answer this question and probably identify many other mathematical skills. It seems more efficient to use a worksheet or other classroom-based activity to assess the third graders.

Using Screening Tests

Screening tests are efficient for surveying large numbers of children. In a screening situation, you are trying to take a quick look at many children. You do not know these children or their parents very well (or at all). You choose a technically sound test designed for screening. Most of the children you see will pass through the screen to the other side.

The following two example scenarios highlight issues that often arise during a screening process. Specialists conduct these screenings in consultation with early childhood teachers.

screening test test used to identify children who may be in need of special services, as a first step in identifying children in need of further diagnosis; focuses on the child's ability to acquire skills.

Routine Vision Screening

You want to know how many children in your class need glasses. A nurse asks all the 4-year-olds in your class to identify letters or bunny rabbits, according to the directions she gives. Steven fails the screening. Before you ask Mr. and Mrs. Green to run out to get glasses for Steven, you consider whether Steven seemed to follow directions given by the nurse. If he did not follow directions easily, you might suggest a rescreening in 6 weeks. If he followed directions and his parents are concerned about his vision, you could recommend that an optometrist or ophthalmologist see him for a diagnostic assessment.

Routine Speech and Language Screening

At first-grade level, a speech therapist comes to your class to screen children for articulation or other speech impairments. You schedule this evaluation to ensure that all children will have every available chance to continue early literacy development. You are concerned about Carter, who does not always speak clearly. Following the screening, you learn how to help Carter with articulation errors he makes.

135

The speech therapist also decides, based on the results of the screening, to come to your room Thursday afternoons to interact with Gregory, Laura, and Stephan to help them with articulation. She will see them in her office on Tuesdays.

Child-Find Screening

You conduct educational screening the same way, using a technically sound instrument. You plan a day or more to screen 3- and 4-year-old children to find those children who may need a special service or to find out how the children in your community compare to the established standards. After screening 200 children, you find that 10 fall into the category of "risk" and 15 fall into the category of "watch." You let the parents of the 175 children who passed through the screen know that, currently, readiness for learning seems to be in place for their children.

For the 15 children in the "watch" category, you look at the results of screening to see if there is one area of concern or low-performance areas across all the parts of the test, and compare the information that you have about each of the individual children and their families. You share the results of the screening with the parents personally and show that they can bring Robbin, Gloria, Constance, or Larry back for screening or seek diagnostic assistance if they are still worried about progress in a few months.

For the 10 children who fell into the "risk" category, you look at all available materials and discuss the next step with each child's parents. For instance, you might refer Mr. and Mrs. Whitewater to Easter Seals for a diagnostic assessment for Ashley, since you are worried about Ashley's gross- and fine-motor performance. You may suggest to Luz-marie's mother a bilingual preschool program, since you believe she may not understand all of the English directions. Mitchell Oxford appears to be quite isolated in a world of his own. You refer Ms. Oxford

to a mental health or child guidance clinic. Erick was a terror in the screening situation; Mrs. Ross, his mother, seemed frustrated and embarrassed that she could not calm him down. You refer her to a special education diagnostic team.

If 100 of the 200 children screened fail the test or otherwise show up as "at risk of academic failure," you *change the curriculum*. Although such an event is unlikely, the point is that screening instruments catch the few who need special assistance. If the screening net is catching many children, then plan educational interventions or programs according to the needs of the children. Tests used in this way inform teachers as they make teaching decisions about how to carry out the curriculum. Screening should occur responsibly at all age levels. In addition to developmental and preschool curriculum screening, there are opportunities for screening at the primary level as well. For example, the teachers may wish to know the achievement level of a given grade level in math or reading. These teachers would conduct an inventory.

Reading Comprehension Inventory

Third graders in your school might complete a reading comprehension **inventory** conducted by the reading specialist or by the third-grade teachers. Those who score below the school cutoff points are involved in special reading tutorials planned to bridge the reading gap so that they will be successful in the independent work required in fourth grade. If only two or three in each class are eligible for this special assistance, the program is working well for most children. If half the class needs remediation, the teachers will change the curriculum by examining the results of the test; that is, they will look at the failure patterns and plan teaching strategies to help the children be successful.

inventory test to assess overall ability in a given area.

These are screening situations in action. In these examples, tests are appropriate. The tests are gathering information quickly and in a standardized manner. The test score is only part of the data used to make a decision. Teachers must responsibly make decisions that affect the educational lives of children.

DIAGNOSTIC TESTING

Qualified professionals administer individualized intelligence tests, speech and language tests, and other specialized instruments based on a referral question from a parent, teacher, physician, or other person concerned with the developmental or learning progress of a particular child. **Diagnostic measures** provide an in-depth examination of a child's performance in cognition, language, hearing, and so on. The psychologist, psychiatrist, speech therapist, physical therapist, or neurologist tries to answer the questions that lead parents, teachers, and others to seek further information to optimize child growth.

diagnostic measures tests used to identify a child's specific areas of strength and weakness, determine the nature of the problems, and suggest the cause of the problems and possible remediation strategies.

Teacher's Responsibility on Multidisciplinary Team

The *teacher's responsibility* related to these tests is as a *multidisciplinary team participant*. Following the regular screening, a diagnostic evaluation, or watching the participation of children in their classes, teachers raise questions about those children who seem to be significantly different in their functioning than other children. When such an identification is made, you make a plan for further evaluation and appropriate experts conduct the diagnostic assessment. In this process, teachers report observations, impressions, and use academic checklists, and academic test scores as the occasion demands.

After consulting the family and reviewing the tests administered, the experts, the family, and you, the teacher, meet to make a plan to serve the child and family. The models of service delivery include (McWilliam, Wolery, & Odom, 2001) the specialist—speech therapist, occupational therapist, or other—who

- takes one child out of the room for 15 to 30 minutes or so.
- takes a small group of children out of the room for a short period.
- comes into the class and works with an identified child for a short period.
- teaches the whole class or a group of children.
- participates in class routines with the target child and others.
- consults only.

To make these models successful in meeting the needs of young children, the team considers both classroom environment and specialized procedures as instructional intervention strategies (McWilliam et al., 2001; Widerstrom, 2005). When developing IFSPs and IEPs, be sure that the outcomes are broad, propose teaching skills in logical order and with appropriate intensity, be sure that instruction includes data collection

(e.g. charts, graphs of progress), and consider involving peers in instructional intervention. Finally, think about important intervention strategies beyond the classroom that might include mental health professionals, medical personnel, and parents (Hooper & Umansky, 2004; McLean, Wolery & Bailey, 2004; McWilliam, et al., 2001).

Teachers serve as informed observers prior to individualized diagnostic assessment. Afterward, teachers bear the responsibility for carrying out the specialists' individualized recommendations for service to the child and the family. Teachers can use diagnostic procedures as an outgrowth of the IFSP and IEP process or in preparation for it.

Diagnostic Curricular Measures

Teachers in early childhood use individualized diagnostic procedures to solve teaching problems. Such instruments are generally individualized **curriculum-based measures**. For example, if Sally seems to read with great difficulty, Mrs. George, the third-grade teacher, may use an individualized reading test to supplement her observations about the progress that Sally is making. She can then change her teaching approach. On the other hand, if Ms. Maloy wonders whether 18-month-old Mateo is making appropriate social progress, she can refer to a list of social skills for the age range of birth to age 2 and see how his skills compare to the progression on this list. This comparison will supplement and complement the observational data she collects.

curriculum-based measures diagnostic tests for specific subjects.

Diagnostic tests help answer questions about children. Sometimes, they entitle children to services. For example, only children with the diagnosis of a particular condition, such as learning disabilities, are entitled to receive special assistance from the teacher of the children with learning disabilities. Although the teacher of the children with learning disabilities might consult with other teachers about issues relating to learning, only diagnosed children are entitled to be included in the regular caseload.

diagnostic tests tests used to identify a child's specific areas of strength and weakness, determine the nature of the problems, and suggest the cause of the problems and possible remediation strategies.

Individualized Educational Planning

Traditional academic achievement tests are the forerunners of curriculum-based assessment. Curriculum-based assessments arose from the recognition that diagnostic measures, such as intelligence tests, were too general and not closely related to children's development and learning or to their learning-related abilities and problems. What was needed, then, were clearly defined educational outcomes (goals and specific behavioral objectives) so that teachers could measure each child's progress toward those specific objectives to evaluate both children's progress and the program's effectiveness; in other words, individual learner outcomes and general program outcomes (Deno, 1985). Box 5.3 shows a teacher's planning for individualized. This is similar to the more formal IEP process.

Curriculum-Based Assessment

Over the years, Deno and his colleagues incorporated two key assessment features in curriculum-based assessment: (1) "measurement methods are standardized; that is both the critical behaviors to be measured and the procedures for measuring those behaviors are prescribed" and (2) "the focus of the measurement is long term: the testing methods and content remain constant across relatively long time periods, such as one year" (Fuchs, 1993, p. 15). Curriculum-based measurement breaks the demands of the curriculum into measurable pieces so that appropriate requirements for learners are developed. An example of a published version of such a measure is the *Brigance Comprehensive Inventory of Basic Skills–Revised* (see Appendix C for publication details) that can be used to assess basic reading, writing, listening, and mathematics skills. You can use the instrument to assess one skill or all. Electronic support for this instrument is available. This curriculum-based assessment instrument is a form of criterion-referenced assessment. Often the approach requires special record keeping, commonly enhanced by technology. New technology, especially the computer or personal digital assistant (PDA), permits the teacher to track the students' progress and allows the teacher detailed diagnostic data. This data can provide a wealth of information to help personalize and customize teaching and learning. These instruments are particularly useful in linking assessment to instruction.

When the curriculum-based instruments are organized by developmental domain—cognitive, social-emotional, gross- and fine-motor skills—the profile for particular children may assist in picking IFSP or IEP goals (Bricker, 1989). An example of such a system is *Assessment, Evaluation, and Programming System (AEPS®) for Infants and Children, Second Edition* (Bricker, 2002), which assesses six key developmental areas in young children: fine motor, gross motor, cognitive, adaptive, social-communication, and social. The system is available for ages birth to 6. Today many published curricular programs also include itemized checklists for use in assessing goal accomplishment. An example is *The Creative Curriculum® for Infants & Toddlers* (Dombro, Colker, & Dodge, 1997). This program guide is also available in Spanish. With the conscious link of tests to curricula and curricula to assessment, the teaching-learning-assessment process is in harmony and in action, just like the babies and young children you serve.

As used in special education, the curriculum-based approach handles those situations in the primary years where teachers have specific academic goals that can be specified clearly, analyzed in component parts, and assessed. Such measures are similar in philosophy to performance measures. That is, the goal is to find a "test" that is "the same" as the "task." This is so that you treat the learner fairly and so the teacher will have concrete information about how to teach on any given day. The crucial difference between curriculum-based assessment and performance-based assessment is the underlying theoretical approach of the methods. Curriculum-based measures depend philosophically on the view of behavioral science as applied in observable, measurable terms. Consider this: Ms. Mountain wants to know how Robert is progressing through the second-grade reading program. The second-grade program specifies many word attack and comprehension skills. Children work in workbooks and read with the teacher to develop these skills. Robert gets most of the pages wrong. Ms. Mountain chooses a curriculum-based reading test that evaluates the skills taught in the second grade. She gives the test to Robert, reviews the results, and revises her teaching strategies.

Thus, curriculum-based assessment can be of value to young children, and in particular to young children with special needs who require more specific individual educational planning. If such an approach could truly bridge early developmental milestones and educational benchmarks and provide for instruction helpfully informed by relevant assessment/progress information, young children could benefit greatly. The danger in this approach is that the child and the broad understanding of how children develop might get lost in all the specifics and particulars and that teachers could be overwhelmed in the process. A comprehensive developmental perspective is basic to planning and implementing sound assessment and intervention strategies.

Without this general knowledge, the specifics of any assessment or intervention plan are meaningless.

Curriculum-based assessment traces a child's achievement along a continuum of objectives within a developmentally sequenced curriculum. In curriculum-based assessment, assessment and instruction link closely, both initially and over time, to find progress, or the lack of it, and to plan for appropriate educational help. The process is very useful as part of the assessment that seeks to entitle young children for special education, particularly when comparative data is available about the performance of peers in the context from which the child is referred. For example, if Mr. Spring refers Catherine, a second grader, because she lacks writing skills—cannot make a diagram, write a sentence, or outline a story—it is important to compare Catherine's skills to the other second graders in the school before deciding whether her performance is atypical. Mr. Spring could make this comparison by reviewing the aggregate scores for second graders at the McCoy School.

The foundation of curriculum-based assessment is a sequence of developmental objectives, sometimes called learner outcomes, that constitutes a program's curriculum. An objective may vary from landmark goals in a developmental domain (e.g., walks independently) to finely graded sequences of skills that lead to the achievement of the end goal. Such in-depth measures go beyond assessment for the diagnosis of some type of disability. They can pinpoint individual strengths and weaknesses and specific teaching objectives. Also, they provide for close monitoring of the child's progress and the program's effectiveness.

McTighe and Wiggins (2005) outline ways to incorporate curriculum-based assessment through a process called backward design process. The process includes three stages:

- Stage 1: Identify Desired Results
  - enduring understandings
  - essential questions
  - knowledge and skills
- Stage 2: Determine acceptable evidence
  - performance tasks
  - quizzes, tests, prompts
  - unprompted evidence
  - self-assessment
- Stage 3: Plan learning experiences and instruction
  - sequence of activities

Thinking through the elements in each stage ensures that assessment and instruction match. In this plan, curriculum-based assessment is formative, integral, and organized. Applied with care, backward design assures that learning goals, instructional activities, and assessment practices will be inclusive and substantive.

In defining the curriculum, schools and programs identify certain skills to master. In determining whether mastery has occurred, you compare each child to the yardstick that your philosophy deems important. You set absolute standards that everyone must meet. Examples of these **criterion-referenced measures** in action include:

- Kindergarten teachers specify self-help, beginning literacy, problem-solving skills, and social skills as the curriculum goals. They choose a published criterion-referenced instrument that provides a record-keeping system that matches these goals for quarterly recording of child progress.

- Third-grade teachers choose a reading skills inventory that matches their goals for literacy instruction. The inventory includes a list of word-attack skills, writing practice, and comprehension skills. They record child progress in 6-week increments and teach accordingly.

These measures answer specific questions: Does Harold solve the problem 2 + 2 correctly? Does Bruce know which part of the book is the title page? Can Rita count to 10? An example of one widely used published instrument of this kind is the *Learning Accomplishment Profile–Revised* (Sanford & Zelman, 1981), which assesses across the domains of cognition, language, fine- and gross-motor skills, self-help skills, and personal-social skills. It assesses children functioning in the 36- to 72-month age range and is available in English and Spanish. Another example is the BRIGANCE® Inventory of Early Development–II (IED–II) (Brigance, 2004). This instrument includes curricular skills and developmental functions and is designed for children age birth to 7.

Sometimes school districts develop criterion-referenced procedures in district-wide curriculum committees. A committee establishes overall goals by reviewing the literature on the subject. Then, the committee identifies the component skills. This creates a criterion reference against which to compare each individual child's progress. It serves both as record keeper and standards list.

criterion-referenced measures tests that compare performance in certain skills to accepted levels.

COORDINATION OF TESTING PROGRAMS

When using tests responsibly, make a plan. Choose tests to match the purpose and to match the population. Consider the tests from the point of view of usability for the faculty and staff. Such consideration includes factors such as special training required, possibility for breaking the procedure into several days, hand scoring, and so on. Make distinctions regarding screening, diagnosis, instructional, and accountability uses of measures chosen.

Factor teacher-observation and parent-interview sources into the plan. Include performance-based measures. Link to curriculum, institutional, local, and state mandates. The results of this coordination avoid both undertesting children—relying on one high-stakes measure for decision-making—and overtesting—so many assessments that teachers and children feel that they can't engage in the learning activities. Choose electronic assessment records with care so that they reflect the program's philosophy and instructional approach.

PERFORMANCE ASSESSMENT

A developmentally-based view of the educational needs of young children does not lend itself to the formation of finite lists of skills for mechanistic assessment. You may ask, How will I know whether Pauline can read, compute, solve problems, and think creatively? How will I know whether Jeff can work cooperatively in a group? How will I know whether he can work independently? How will I involve Therese in the assessment of her own learning?

You can answer these questions based on observations of children in the classroom situation. In addition, you can plan special problems or situations that will tell you the answers to these and other important developmental questions. This approach to assessment is termed *authentic*, *direct*, *alternative*, or *performance* because the child's "test" closely resembles the classroom situation (cf. Eisner, 2002; Kohn, 2004; Popham, 2003). **Performance assessment** seems to be the broadest and most descriptive term. Performance-based measures depend philosophically on the view of a constructionist approach to education. An example of a performance-based measure follows: Ms. Knapp wants to know if Paul can complete a third-grade project on pioneers. The project in part requires that each child read various materials and write a report at the end of 2 months. Ms. Knapp pulls a book from the third-grade shelf, asks Paul to read a chapter, and then to write a summary. She observes how he handles the process and revises her subsequent teaching plan accordingly.

A key aspect of performance assessment is defining ahead of time what to assess. So, Ms. Knapp will use definitions for successful comprehension of third-grade material as well as key components of summary writing in judging Paul's performance. Ms. Knapp is practicing formative assessment to adjust the intervention necessary for Paul.

Formative Assessment

Formative assessment is the concept of providing feedback to students who are working toward **mastery learning**—the implementation of a curriculum that requires the specification of goals, developing formative assessments, organization of corrective activities, planning enrichment

performance assessment determining developmenal progress of children through a variety of means, including observations and special problems or situations.

formative assessment an approach to examining young children that holds assessment is an ongoing process. It is similar to the scientific approach where a query is generated, validated or not, and then another query is formed.

mastery learning the philosophy that promotes the idea that everyone should learn particular concepts or skills and that teachers are responsible for teaching toward this level of accomplishment for all children.

activities, and developing summative assessments (Guskey, 2001). Characteristics of good formative assessment are that the tasks should have (Guskey, 2001)

- clear information, and if written, be legible for all students.
- precise directions in clear and simple language.
- minimal amount of class time—a snapshot, not a retouched photo.
- spiraling possibilities—referring back to previous learning—linking to future learning.
- clear match with curricular outcomes.

Thus, formative assessment that utilizes curriculum-based, criterion-referenced methodology as well as other holistic approaches is congruent with the early childhood ideal of good practice that uses a constructivist approach to education. In this approach, assessment—not just tests, but a multiple-measures approach—is at the center of instruction, and you view the classroom as having these characteristics:

- A learning culture with instruction, learning, and assessment integrated to serve particular student needs.
- A place with dynamic, ongoing assessment, with assessment feeding back to the teaching-learning process regularly and routinely.

- A place to start teaching by assessing student's prior knowledge. For example, what does my class of 4-year-olds know already about turtles and frogs? Do the third graders know what a "paragraph" is?

- A place that gives feedback on errors to scaffold the learning rather than paying attention to the mistakes for the virtue of identifying these alone. This includes ignoring minor mistakes that do not interfere with the result, as well as giving hints to the learner so that learner avoids mistakes.

- A curriculum that uses explicit criteria for the evaluation of assignments. For example, "When you go to your seat, each of you must finish reading the story and prepare to discuss it with a partner. The partners will decide how to demonstrate their knowledge. Each demonstration must include the main idea and new vocabulary words."

- A place that involves students in self-assessment to help students assume responsibility for their own learning and demystify the assessment process.

- Utilization of self-evaluation and peer evaluation of teaching to help all keep the focus sharp and on target. (Shepard, 2000)

Across the country, states and school districts are employing the holistic approach to assessment and reducing reliance on high-stakes measures. For example, Vermont uses portfolio assessment as well as multiple-choice measures for accountability measurement (Sacks, 1999; Vermont Department of Education, 2005). A suburban Chicago district reports the process of philosophical commitment to implementation of multiple measures (Schroeder & Pryor, 2001). The process was a multiyear project and required parent and school board education. Inspired by Rothstein's (2000) description of a composite index of school performance, the district changed focus. With these examples of good practice in action, we can keep in mind the call to action by Popham (2001, p. 12) who says that "U.S. educators have been thrown into a score-boosting game they cannot win. More accurately, the score-boosting game cannot be won without doing educational damage to the children in our public schools. The negative consequences flowing from a national enshrinement of increased test scores are both widespread and serious." Though we must be accountable, we must have the courage to collect information systematically and with multiple data sources. Finally, any single measure—including criterion-referenced or performance task—can become high stakes if status-changing educational decisions (e.g., retention in grade, eligibility for gifted program, enrollment in remedial program) are made on the basis of one single measure. The key to authentic assessment is regular, formative assessment with multiple measures leading to any summative decisions. Box 5.4 shows examples of performance-based measures.

Box 5.4 *Performance-Based Measures*

1. To assess early literacy development you might examine the way that children use written materials related to themes in the housekeeping corner. For example, you turn the housekeeping corner into a travel agency, bringing in travel posters, tickets, appointment books, and so on. You observe how much written material each child incorporates into dramatic play. This tells you the child's understanding of the functions and uses of written language. Another place to observe early literacy is at the writing table. By looking at the child's drawings and stories, you assess each child's familiarity with the features of written language (e.g., vocabulary, devices, rhythm, and intonation), spelling and decoding strategies and composing strategies. When you are reading stories to children one on one, you see which children have the concept of a story and individual progress toward sound/symbol relationship and so on (Teale, 1990, pp. 53-55).

2. To assess the mathematical understanding of young children you might observe them during routines such as setting the table for snacks. When a child must be sure that there is a cookie for everyone he is showing you whether he has developed the concept of one-to-one correspondence. You could also introduce group games involving logical-mathematical thinking. For example, young children love to play card games such as War (who has more cards), Go Fish, Old Maid, and so on. You could watch them at play to assess math concepts. In discussions of numbers, you have a chance to see which children have developed some ideas about numbers. Examples of these opportunities include judging how many marbles are in a jar, graphing which children prefer red jelly beans, and recording how many people are in each child's family (Kamil & Rosenblum, 1990, pp. 146-162).

3. Examples of science problems for primary grades include activities called Whirlybird and Sugar Cube (Educational Testing Service, 1993). In the Whirlybird activity, students watch an administrator's demonstration of centrifugal force and then respond to written questions about what occurred in the demonstration. Students need to make careful observations about what happens as the administrator puts the steel balls in different holes on the Whirlybird arms, and then infer the relationship between the position of the steel balls and the speed at which the arm rotates.

In the Sugar Cube experiment, students observe the effect of warm water on different states of sugar cubes, raw sugar, and fine granules.

Systematic Collection of Information

The teacher's responsibility as an educator then, is not to just say no to testing and accountability requirements, but to develop measures that reflect and affirm an understanding of children and a philosophy of education. As a teacher, you do this through the systematic collection of information on each child in your care. You record using checklists and interviews: child interests, thinking, conversations, children at play, children following routines, and otherwise showing developmental progress. You keep anecdotal notes, logs, diaries, and samples of children's work.

Portfolios

portfolios places, such as folders, boxes, or baskets, for keeping all the information known about the children in a class.

artifacts the materials that children produce to demonstrate knowledge, skills, or dispositions.

You can combine these collected materials into comprehensive portfolios. A **portfolio** is a folder, box, basket, or other container that serves to collect work samples from children throughout the year. You collect a wide variety of materials, or **artifacts**—pieces of child's work—to document child progress. Portfolios are " . . . the best vehicle to show us what a child learns and how schoolwork fits into that child's personal universe of knowledge" (Hebert, 2001, xiii). As well, there are commercially available electronic portfolios that you may wish to consider for compatibility with your curriculum. One example is ClassLink Portfolio System™. "The ClassLink Portfolio System provides every student with an electronic collection of their achievements, assessment, and feedback. Teachers, administrators, and parents can review a student's portfolio and determine how to better support their learning. Tied to rubrics and standards, the portfolio identifies student skills, subject area proficiencies, and achievement of state and national standards" (URLhttp://www.classlink2000.com//URL). In addition, some school districts and child-care programs develop electronic portfolios using the administrative data systems (or open-code source ware) already in place for monitoring attendance and other demographic information.

Performance Problems as Measures

performance refers to actions on the part of learners that can be assessed through observation, review of child-produced documents or other learning products.

Thus, portfolios are systematic collections that document the **performance** of the children. Because young children think differently than adults, you must watch them to see how they solve problems and set up assessment situations for them to display such skills. Examples of ways to assess naturally and to pose problems for assessment purposes are discussed in the following section. Seven common forms of performance assessment are (Feuer & Fulton, 1993):

1. constructed-response items that require children to develop answers rather than to choose "the right one"
2. essays that show analysis, synthesis, and critical thinking
3. writing that displays composition skills
4. oral discourse that includes interviews and recitations
5. exhibitions that require students to demonstrate skills
6. experiments that include the demonstration of hypothesis testing, experimenting, and writing up findings
7. portfolios that demonstrate student progress over time

Technology has a role to play as well. Computer simulations offer the opportunity for multiple hypotheses testing, and for teachers to monitor the work via printout. Increasingly, commercially available electronic performance assessments, portfolio, and work sample systems are available for classroom use. Often these materials are available on

CD-ROMs or on the World Wide Web, and most are tied to outcomes or standards. As such, these assessment materials can be a valuable link to curriculum and instruction if they match curriculum goals and instruction proceeds in a developmentally suitable approach.

Link to Curriculum

Performance assessment definitely links to curriculum. That is, the kinds of activities in assessment problems are similar to what children are already doing in the classroom. For example, to assess third graders in science, present the children with a problem of a drop of water placed on different types of building materials. Ask children to tell what will happen. The examiner observes and records each child's ability to observe, infer, and formulate hypotheses (Educational Testing Service, 1990; Lantz, 2004). This is the same kind of activity that might occur in any classroom. For example, a teacher brings into a kindergarten class a piece of wool from a sheep, as part of a follow-up of a story read about sheep. She places the wool on a science table. Children examine the wool and discuss the properties between themselves and with the teacher. The teacher poses "what if," "why," and other stimulating questions. Children explain their thinking and enlarge their concept of wool. The regular class activity and the experiment with the drop of water are similar activities. Children have an opportunity in both cases to think and express their ideas.

"The more we help children to have their wonderful ideas and to feel good about themselves for having them, the more likely it is that they will some day happen upon wonderful ideas that no one else has happened upon before" (Duckworth, 1987, p. 14).

Link to Individualized Education Plan

In the past, much of the discussion at multidisciplinary staffings related to presenting symptoms, norm-based test results, and the development of **IEP goals.** Often, there was limited information about performance on standardized high-stakes achievement tests because school districts frequently excluded special education students from the district's testing program. Since the reauthorization of **IDEA** in 1997 (and continuing with the reauthorization of IDEA 2004), such exclusion is no longer possible; districts are required to include students with disabilities in high-stakes testing programs. The issues related to this requirement are complex. How should children with disabilities be accommodated? Do we overprescribe accommodation? How are district-wide and statewide results influenced (Thurlow, 2001; Thurlow, Elliott, & Ysseldyke, 2003)? Of particular interest to early childhood teachers and constructivists is the increased use of alternative assessments in the statewide plans (Elliot & Thurlow, 2005;

IEP goals the specified learning goals for children with disabilities. These are established by a multidisciplinary team that includes the child's parents.

IDEA federal law that governs the practices for delivery of educational services to all children with disabilities.

149

Thompson & Quenemoen, 2001). This approach to accountability links testing, instruction, and the IEP process more directly to the curriculum and learning. That is, what are we going to do on Monday to help Bill in the classroom?

Technical Issues

Technical issues regarding this kind of assessment are emerging. Just because performance assessment seems user-friendly and connected to a holistic philosophy of curriculum and assessment, are the measures necessarily benign when used for accountability purposes? Probably not! The variables of task, learner, and context are each multidimensional. The consequences of errors in the interpretation of results are thus geometric rather than linear in proportion. For example, if 4-year-old Matilde fails to give each child a napkin at snack time, does her teacher, Ms. Stone, assume because of this one observation that Matilde has not accomplished one-to-one correspondence? Most early childhood teachers would consider such an interpretation an overinterpretation and come up with several alternative reasons for the omission on Matilde's part. This example is obvious and simple. In other instances, the accountability stakes are high and children may pass or fail based on the accumulation of evidence.

For example, when developing local standards or outcomes for children to meet, consider whether teachers share similar definitions for the items to be used.

- Do kindergarten teachers agree on the definition of "conversational skills" as expected?
- Do third-grade teachers know what "addition skills" are for the 7/8-year-olds in their charge?
- Are expected self-help skills for 3-year-olds uniform across cultural/family groups?

The point is that these items require operational definitions. Teachers need to train on agreement for the definitions. To do less risks the repetition of the well-known abuses of standardized assessments in the performance arena. Consider the following analogy of two gardens. One garden has wildflowers with no path. There are also many weeds. The second garden shows paths along defined schemes with small stones to set off the flowers. There are no weeds. Which garden is beautiful? What definitions of *garden* and *beautiful* are used? Which garden should "flunk"?

Rubrics

One way to address the issue of operational definition is to create scoring criteria to use with the performance tasks. These scoring criteria are **rubrics.** Teachers and others who develop performance tasks create standards and rules for judging the performance. In some cases, the criteria are points along a scale so that the criteria guide the teacher and the student in the teaching and learning process (Marzano, Pickering, & McTighe, 1993). The best rubrics give the steps in the assignment or task in explicit language for the learner, identify the process that the learner must use, and describe what the final product or performance will look like (Taylor & Nolan, 2005). Thus, the rubric guides the learner in the acquisition of the skill, process, or knowledge required. Often, rubrics include gradations of quality—excellent, adequate, and below par (Strickland & Strickland, 2000)—or gradations showing approximation toward mastery such as novice, intermediate, advanced, and superior (Airasian, 2005).

Stiggins (2005, pp. 150–158) suggests the following steps for rubric development:

- Discover—that is, watch children at work on the learning task and identify distinctive characteristics of the work that meets the learning objective.
- Condense all of the ideas into key attributes of success.
- Define simple definitions for success and the continuum leading there.
- Apply the rubric several times so that you can be consistent when it counts.
- Refine the rubric as necessary.

In this way, Stiggins (2005) argues that you will create rubrics that specify important content with sharp clarity and that are fair as well as practical. Groups of teachers best carry out rubric development for performance assessment because the work is time-consuming, important, and vital to linking assessment to curriculum and instruction.

Small school districts may decide to examine the way they teach and assess math in the primary grades. After reviewing curricula, consulting the learner outcomes for their state, and considering the National Council of Teachers of Mathematics standards, the teachers choose a sequence of instruction for K–3. They match activities to the goals. As the teachers work, they choose tasks that they believe are checkpoints along the continuum of problem solving. These will be the performance tests. When they choose the performance tasks as tests, they must identify clear criteria for judging performance and progress toward the "ultimate" or top performance.

To ignore the rubric development or to adopt haphazardly a task outside the philosophy–curriculum–assessment system offers a serious opportunity for disaster. Vague, subjective, and unspecified criteria for evaluation result in unfair practices for children. Boxes 5.5 through 5.10 show sample rubrics. In addition to clear, defined, and operationalized criteria, other technical issues face teachers when using performance assessment.

Additional important technical issues include reliability, consistency of the application of standards, and intrarater and interrater reliability.

Box 5.5 *Book Report Rubric for Second Grade*

	Yes	No
• I read the whole book.		
• The report tells:		
• Title of the book.		
• Author of the book.		
• I wrote two or three paragraphs about the book.		
• The paragraphs tell:		
• What the book is about.		
• Who the main characters are.		
• What I liked about the book.		
• I checked the writing according to the class editing guidelines.		

Box 5.6 *Class Discussion Rubric for First Grade*

	Very Well	Most of the Time	Need to Work on This
• I can sit and listen to my classmates.			
• I can wait for my turn when I am eager to add a comment.			
• I can say something related to the topic.			
• I can speak up loud enough to be heard by everyone.			
• I can appreciate the comments of my classmates even when I think that they are silly or not related to the topic.			

Box 5.7 *Science Drawing Rubric for Kindergarten*

	Yes	No
• I drew the picture to represent the item viewed (e.g. leaf, rock, bug).		
• I used realistic colors for the drawing.		
• I labeled the drawing.		

Box 5.8   *Class Presentation Rubric for Third Grade*

	Yes	No	Superb	Ok	Needs Some Improvement...
• I made a graphic organizer to show the main points.					
• The organizer is neat.					
• Spelling is final-draft accurate.					
• There are details to support the main idea.					
• I made pictures to illustrate my topic					
• The pictures are neat.					
• They are related to the topic.					
• I thought about questions that my classmates might ask.					
• I practiced my presentation.					
• I am ready for my classmates to judge my work.					

Box 5.9   *Oral Presentation Rubric*

Name: _____   Date: _____

Attribute	Evident	Not Evident	Emerging
On topic			
Organized			
Creative			
Transitions			
Eye contact			
Loud enough			
Involved audience			
Visual aids			

Comments: _____

_____

_____

Box 5.10 *Group Skills*

Name: _____ Date: _____

	Exemplary	Adequate	Needs Improvement
Uses quiet voice			
Takes turns			
Shares decision-making			
Respects others			
Contributes to conflict resolution			
Follows directions			

Listens	Often	Sometimes	Never
Helps others understand peer's ideas			
Asks questions to help group understand			
Shows interest in other ideas			

interrater reliability
ability of a test to produce the same results regardless of who administers it.

When using performance assessment for accountability purposes, it is critical to establish standards such as **interrater reliability**—statistically determined agreement of multiple raters observing the same task performance by a number of children. If the procedures are used simply to guide teaching, there is little question of validity. Questions of validity and reliability emerge when using the measures for high-stakes decisions. Such high-stakes decisions are those regarding promotion, placement in special programs, and identification as a special learner. This is due to the complexity of establishing reliability regarding these assessments.

Currently, there is limited research on high-stakes performance measures that include questions of individual differences, task specificity, and the level of difficulty of the task (Elliott, 1993; Thurlow et al., 2003). While these issues affect formally identified children with special needs, they are important considerations for all children. Whenever you make important decisions about children, you must be sure that every effort protects the rights, the best interests, and the integrity of the individual child. The tests must match the purpose of assessment, no matter what the form. A performance measure is not inherently better if the items are not congruent with the curriculum, if the child does not understand the directions, if the time limits are too rigid, or if bias exists in the material.

"When used for accountability purposes, the assessments must be conducted with many students, there must be consistency in the domains of knowledge being assessed, and the assessments must yield adequate samples of student performance within those domains. Costs and time associated with administration of the assessments to numerous students are also major considerations" (McLaughlin & Warren, 1994, p. 7). Performance assessment tasks must meet the same demands for efficiency, effectiveness, and fairness as other conventional testing approaches (cf Popham, 2005).

Some practical guidelines for school districts using performance assessment include:

- Use the standards of NAEYC (National Association for the Education of Young Children) and applicable professional associations for defining expected performance at different age levels.
- Gather some definitions or descriptions of expected performance.
- Gather samples of children's work that illustrate varying quality.
- Discuss the work with colleagues.
- Write your own descriptions.
- Gather another set of student work samples.
- Discuss with colleagues and revise criteria for judging performance. (Herman, Aschbacher, & Winters, 1992)

Authentic assessment, when compared to conventional testing, makes far greater demands on both students and teachers. Some critics believe that it takes so much time that instruction is short-changed. However, this point of view misses the symbiotic relation between instruction and assessment. Within the best models of authentic assessment, teaching and evaluation become virtually indistinguishable: an assessment that teaches students how to monitor their work is a vital form of instruction (Inger, 1993, p. 4; see also Stiggins, 2005).

The use of **authentic assessment** and a holistic approach to teaching and assessment considers the teaching-learning process as one that proceeds through the following steps:

authentic assessment
determining developmental progress of children through a variety of means, including observations and special problems or situations.

- Learner outcomes—what do I want my students to know and be able to do?
- Outcome indicators—how will I know that the learner has achieved the outcome?
- Learning opportunities—what activities will support the learner and facilitate learning?
- Assessment tasks—what documentation of learning must I collect?
- Performance criteria and scoring rubrics—how will the learning be documented and evaluated? (Martin-Kniep, 1998, p. 27)

These steps are consistent with the National Association for the Education of Young Children (NAEYC) and National Association of Early childhood Specialists in State Departments of Education (NAECS/SDE) *Position Statement on Early Childhood Curriculum, Assessment, and*

155

Program Evaluation (NAEYC & NAECS/SDE, 2003). The profession and its stakeholders:

make ethical, appropriate, valid, and reliable assessment . . . [a] central part [of programming] assess[ing] young children's strengths, progress, and needs; use assessment methods that are developmentally appropriate, culturally and linguistically responsive, tied to children's daily activities, supported by professional development, inclusive of families; connected to specific, beneficial purposes; (1) making sound decisions about teaching and learning, (2) identifying significant concerns that may require focused intervention for individual children, and (3) helping programs improve their educational and developmental interventions.

Accordingly, all assessment plans are treated systematically, seriously, and ethically, no matter how "teacher-friendly" the performance assessment measures, screening measures, or curriculum-based measures may look.

SUMMARY

Consider these final comments about testing in early childhood education. Ask yourself, "Why am I doing this?" Remind yourself of the uses and limitations of standardized tests and of their possible misuses and abuses. One common abuse is the misuse of a developmental screening test as a basis, by itself, for making placement decisions concerning educational programs. Remember that testing definitely does not equal assessment. Developmental assessment is a *process* for detecting the developmental progress of a child that may include testing. The child's parents know more about the child's development and functioning than any single test will ever reveal, and so do you as the child's teacher. Use the observations well in the service of both the child and the child's parents.

Tests are efficient and important tools used in the service of young children to provide educational opportunity (entitlement for service), instructional enrichment (diagnosis of special educational needs), and accountability (documentation of program outcome achievement). Misuse occurs when teachers and others pick the wrong tool or use one tool for everything. There is no one "food processor" that fits all of the required assessment tasks of the classroom.

FIELD ACTIVITIES

1. Visit a child-care center near you. Ask teachers at the center how they screen young children. Match their procedures to the practices described in this chapter. Are there any missing pieces?

2. Interview the special education coordinator in your area. Ask how the community uses tests.

3. Examine the contents of screening batteries. Try one or more of the measures on your classmates and on volunteer children. Discuss the

problems you had in administering the measures and compare them with your classmates' experiences.

4. Interview a primary-grade teacher about achievement testing in your state or school district. Find out what is required at each grade level. Look at the instruments at the school or in the library.

5. Visit a school or center that uses a portfolio assessment system. Ask what material the teachers collect and how they use the portfolio, plus what role, if any, the child plays in the process. Discuss with classmates whether you found any potential technical problems in the system and whether the school makes high-stakes decisions using the portfolios.

6. Interview one or two parents of young children. What are their experiences with assessment? What do they know about the instruments and tasks used to evaluate their children? What is their understanding of the scores or reports?

IN-CLASS ACTIVITIES

1. With a partner, outline a complete yearly assessment plan for a preschool program. Then, plan an assessment program for second grade using copies of your state's standards for instructional outcomes.

2. Think about a child you know (or remember from childhood or field experiences). Describe this child to a partner. Identify any particular learning or developmental concerns. Plan a way to document this child's learning. For any questions that you cannot answer about the child's development, make a diagnostic testing agenda to carry forward.

STUDY QUESTIONS

1. What role do tests play in the assessment process?

2. How can teachers avoid stigmatizing children in the assessment process?

3. Why is it important for teachers to become skilled at the administration and scoring of each assessment tool they use?

4. How do norm-based instruments and criterion-based instruments compare? In which situations will the teacher use each?

5. What information do screening tests provide?

6. What role will the teacher play in the multidisciplinary conference?

7. Diagnostic tests answer questions about children. Why are these tests useful for specific stakeholders?

REFLECT AND RE-READ

- I know what tests can do to make planning for students more efficient.
- I know about the limitations and potential biases of performance-based assessment.
- I can plan some informal assessment strategies for use in my classroom.
- I know the key ingredients for developing rubrics.

CASE VIGNETTE

Sharlene is a bright, happy, enthusiastic 4-year-old (3.11 actual age) who moved to Denver recently from Provence, France. She has a 2-year-old sister, Shanae. Sharlene's parents are Mrs. Pierre, who describes herself as German American, and Mr. Pierre, who is French. The family speaks French at home; books and movies are available for both children in French and English. Sharlene attends an after-school French Academy. Until 6 months ago, if asked a question in English, Sharlene responded in French. To determine Sharlene's English progress, her teacher, Ms. Shea, administered the Preschool Language Scale–3rd edition (Zimmerman, Steiner, & Pond, 1992). The scores* for Sharlene follow.

	Raw Score	Standard Score	Percentile Rank	Age Equivalent
Auditory Comprehension	41	86	18	4.6
Expressive Language	44	98	45	5.6
Total Language Score	184	91	27	5.0

What did Ms. Shea learn about Sharlene from this assessment conducted in English? What are the next steps for kindergarten instruction for Sharlene?

* Only the scores described in Chapter 4 are shown. The assessment instrument yields additional statistics.

Source: From J. Shea, 2003, submitted in partial fulfillment of T&L 411, Assessment in Early Childhood Education: DePaul University. Used by permission.

TECHNOLOGY LINKS

http://www.ctb.com

CTB-McGraw-Hill. This corporate website publishes excerpts from achievement tests, a test glossary, and white papers on assessment issues.

http://www.rand.org

RAND® is a nonprofit institution that helps improve policy and decision-making through research and analysis.

http://www.riverpub.com

Riverside Publishing. The publisher of the Iowa Test of Basic Skills. The website includes information about testing and reports on testing.

http://www.agsnet.com

American Guidance Services. Publishes curriculum-based and other instruments used in early childhood.

http://www.naeyc.org

National Association for the Education of Young Children. The website regularly presents position statements and links to policy related to the assessment of young children.

http://www.ed.gov

The Department of Education. Posts highlights of legislation so that you can read firsthand about assessment requirements.

SUGGESTED READINGS

Gullo, D. F. (2005). *Understanding assessment and evaluation in early childhood education* (2nd ed.). New York: Teachers College Press.

Meisels, S. J. (2005). *Developmental screening in early childhood: A guide* (2nd ed.). Washington, DC: National Association for the Education of Young Children.

National Association for the Education of Young Children (NAEYC) & National Association of Early Childhood Specialists in State Departments of Education (NAECS/SDE). (2003). *Position statement on early childhood curriculum, assessment, and program evaluation.* Washington, DC: Author. Available online at http://www.naeyc.org.

Salvia, J., & Ysseldyke, J. E. (2004). *Assessment* (9th ed.). Boston: Houghton Mifflin.

Widerstrom, A. (2005). *Achieving learning goals through play: Teaching young children with special needs* (2nd ed.). Baltimore: Paul H. Brookes.

Wiggins, G., & McTighe, J. (2005). *Understanding by design* (2nd ed.). Alexandria, VA: Association for Supervision and Curriculum Development.

Using Alternative
Assessment Strategies

Chapter Overview

This chapter surveys a variety of alternative assessment strategies employed by early childhood teachers. The use of each strategy is dependent on the particular skill or skills that you wish to assess, as well as a number of other variables such as the age of the child, the amount of time you can invest in the assessment, and the number of children assigned to your class who may have special needs.

Assess as You Read

- What assessment methods can I use when I am worried about a child's social behavior?
- What can I do when a child is not responding to the usual methods of instruction?
- What can I learn from watching children play?
- What are some practical implications of multiple intelligences for the assessment system?

ROLE OF ALTERNATIVE ASSESSMENT STRATEGIES IN THE CLASSROOM

There are a number of reasons for considering the use of alternative assessment strategies. First, norm-referenced tests often have little direct overlap between skills and knowledge assessed and the curriculum in the typical classroom. Second, published norm-referenced tests measure relative standing, how a child compares to other children. This is different from measuring change, how a child develops over time. Teachers usually are more interested in the changes children demonstrate. Third, there is wide variability in how children perform on published norm-referenced tests, depending upon the specific test used. For example, if a child has a chronological age of 6-0 and labels letters correctly but reads no words, the child's standard score can vary from one test to another. As a result, there is a high likelihood that intervention teams and teachers will disregard the data collected from published norm-referenced tests in educational planning. Yet educational planning is the ultimate reason for conducting an assessment. Often, there are limited resources of time and specialized personnel in most schools and child-care centers. Finally, more children with disabilities are now included in the mainstream of early childhood classes. Each teacher must individualize instruction and behavioral management for these children with identified disabilities as well as other children who may require special diagnosis from time to time. Thus, early childhood teachers must have strategies for teaching a variety of particular children. Some of the special techniques that teachers must know about and be able to use include those discussed in the following pages. The first of these is at the heart of early childhood education—play and its interpretive properties.

PLAY-BASED ASSESSMENT

Most teachers believe that they can recognize play when they see it. However, play is easier to recognize than it is to define (cf. Fromberg, 2002). Often theorists describe play as the natural learning medium of the child. From a competence perspective, play is defined as a complex process that involves social, cognitive, emotional and physical elements and relates to an aspect of reality as not "serious" or "real." For the child this characterization makes it possible to relate to things that might otherwise be confusing, frightening, mysterious, strange, risky, or forbidden and to develop appropriate competencies and defenses. The active solution of developmental conflicts through play thus enables the young child to demonstrate and feel . . . competence (Mindes, 1982, p. 40). Through play, children develop many capabilities. Examples of child accomplishments include improvements in communication skills, physical agility, independence, social judgment, cooperation, impulse control, and so on. Play activities must be voluntary and **intrinsically motivating** to the child; otherwise, they are not play. By watching children at play, teachers can gain insight into the developmental competencies of infants, toddlers, and young children. Play is systematically related to areas of development and learning (Linder, 1993; Widerstrom, 2005). Play influences language usage, cognitive understanding, social/emotional development, and physical and motor development. Because children's play is rooted in cultural understandings and beliefs, teachers must be sensitive and

intrinsically motivating causing a child to do something or continue doing something because of the nature of the thing or activity itself.

knowledgeable about the cultural meanings attached to toys, appropriate play activities, themes, and adult-child interactions during play when teaching and assessing young children so that bias does not enter the process (Gil & Drewes, 2005).

Intervention programs and child-care settings serving infants, toddlers, and preschoolers frequently describe programs as play-based. Thus, play is the curriculum in these child-constructed, teacher-enhanced adventures in learning. In such programs, children play and teachers facilitate learning by judging when to intervene. The teacher's role in play-based early childhood classrooms is complex. The teacher is a watcher, observer, and assessor, as well as a stage setter, stage manager, mediator, player, scribe, and planner (Jones & Reynolds, 1992). The assessor role is the one that makes the approach work. It separates the benign, neglectful— "let the children play" —classrooms from the ones where children learn, grow, and develop. In the assessor role, the skillful early childhood teacher makes numerous decisions, such as when to change the props, when to add stimulation to the theme, when to mediate between and among children, when to "play with" the children, and when to call time outs. Effective early childhood teachers are enacting this assessor role routinely and regularly. By watching the children play, you can learn about social skills, cognitive and language skills, motor skills, and beginning academic competence. Therefore, if you teach babies or 2-, 3-, and 4-year-olds, you will need to know about play, its developmental sequence, and how to intervene to facilitate development. In Table 6.1, examine some of the developmental (cf. Fewell & Glick, 1998; Johnson, 2005) and academic variables that you can document while children are playing.

Using play as an assessment tool is not a new concept, but what is new is that play scales are now refined enough that they have practical applications for young children (McLean, Worley, & Bailey, 2004; Weber, Behl, & Summers, 1994). However, the best approach for regular early childhood educators would be informal assessment of play that is appropriate for the entire age range and utilizes ordinary but interesting and age-appropriate toys to assess general aspects of a child's development through direct observation. In addition, the detailed analysis of older children's conversations as they engage in collaborative make-believe can reveal information about interactive skills, social cognition in action, and the knowledge of practical language use that young children bring to their play (Garvey, 1993; Pellegrini, 2004).

One of the easiest ways for early childhood teachers to begin assessing play behavior is to use lists of critical skills and to match these to the curricular plan. Van Hoorn, Nourot, Scales, and Alward (2003) provide several examples of these matches: (a) keep a play observation diary keyed to learning contexts and social contexts. That is, where is a particular child playing in the classroom? In each area where the child plays, is he alone, with one friend, or with several friends? Over time, examine the charts for patterns. (b) List block play stages (Chalufour & Worth, 2001;

TABLE 6.1 Play skills in active classroom life

Skills	Interactions	Potential Assessment Question
Social	Parents	Compatible, reciprocal relationship
	Siblings	Cooperative, age-appropriate
	Classmates	Leader, follower, collaborator, timid
	Isolate	
Cognitive		Problem solver
		Persistent in the face of difficulties
		Engaged and focused
		Classifies and organizes
		Sequences
Creativity		Ideational fluency
		Music or artistic accomplishment
Language		Eye contact
		Use of gestures
		Vocabulary and grammar
Motor		Grasp of objects
		Crayon and market use
		Capacity to use scissors, hammer, stapler
		Climbing, running, jumping, hopping
		Balance
		Throwing and catching ball
Academic	Interested in	Writing and drawing, labeling
		Spelling, stories, and books
		Numbers
		One-to-one correspondence
	Aware of	Geometric figures and spatial concepts
	Curious about	Natural world of plants and animals
		Approaches materials appropriately
Emotional		Self-regulated
		Appropriate affect for the situation
		Resilient
		Responsive
		Reflective

Hirsch, 1984; MacDonald, 2001) on a table with each child's name. Keep track of whether a particular stage is emerging or is at mastery level for each child in the program. (c) Chart role-play activities, including the use of props, make-believe, interaction, and verbal communication to keep track of child developmental progress through the stages of sociodramatic play. For toddlers, consider documenting explorations with clay showing their work as mathematicians and collaborators with others (Smith & Goldhaber, 2004). These charts (an example is given in Box 6.1) assist you in focusing observations, planning curriculum, and documenting child and program progress.

Box 6.1 *Role-Playing Checklist*

Role-Playing Checklist	Frequency		
Uses props in traditional ways (i.e., an apple is an apple; a car is a car; a block is a block)	Sometimes	Always	Never
Uses props in creative ways (i.e., a block is a hamburger; a scarf is a cape)	Sometimes	Always	Never
Pretend play follows script of story or family scene: Three Billy Goats Gruff, dinner at home	Sometimes	Always	Never
Pretend play shows creativity (e.g., Snow White goes to space)	Sometimes	Always	Never
Plays alone	Sometimes	Always	Never
Gives and takes in pretend roles with others	Sometimes	Always	Never
Uses gestures to communicate	Sometimes	Always	Never
Uses only a few words to move the play along	Sometimes	Always	Never
Uses four- to five-word sentences to communicate with appropriate vocabulary for the scene	Sometimes	Always	Never
Varies linguistic expression with the mood of the play	Sometimes	Always	Never

Based on a Vygotskian approach to the interpretation of play, Bodrova and Leong (1996; see also Van Hoorn et al., 2003) outline a way to gather observational information about spatial perceptions of young children using construction paper and blocks. The activity involves the development of classroom maps. Asking children to use the blocks to represent people and things in a specific environment offers rich possibilities for ongoing documentation of problem-solving strategies, perceptions of space, and perceptions of personal interactions. Repeat this activity throughout the year—say, in October, February, and June—forming a record of growth for each child. Mapping offers a window into each child's understanding of accuracy in spatial relationships, ability to use symbols to communicate to others, and understanding of the formal structure of maps and charts.

Similar approaches for charts are useful for individualizing instruction for infants and toddlers with special needs. Chart categories suggested include fine motor, gross motor, self-care, cognitive, social communication, and social (Bricker, Pretti-Frontczak, and McComas 1998; Widerstrom, 2005). A numerical rating adds the potential to assess progress of individual children on very specific aspects of the target behavior. In this way, play-based assessment becomes an integral part of the planned learning activities. Planned activities meet individualized goals for particular children. Teachers employing this approach can document individual progress, select children appropriately for group intervention, and simplify record keeping by using the chart as a combination curricular/assessment tool.

In addition to these curricular approaches, play scales are commercially available for infants, toddlers, and young children throughout the early childhood age span. Teachers can selectively match these to the population of children they serve and to their curriculum. The use of these instruments may assist in program planning and in the documentation of child progress. The key in picking these scales is "do they answer the questions you need to ask?" (See Box 6.2 for an example).

STRUCTURED QUESTIONS TO IDENTIFY STUDENT-LEARNING PROCESSES

Before turning to prepared instruments and scales to identify student-learning problems, you want to be sure that you are making the most of the instructional process by developing and using questions to "see" inside the child's learning strategies. For example, suppose you wonder why Lisa hates math and makes many mistakes. Over a week or so, you may wish to ask Lisa some questions while she is working on math problems. One area that you may wish to examine is problem comprehension. So, you may ask Lisa:

- What is the problem about? What can you tell me about it?
- How would you interpret that?
- Would you please explain that in your own words?
- What do you know about this part? Do you need to define or set limits for the problem?
- Is there something that you can eliminate or that is missing?
- What assumptions do you make (Stenmark, 1991, p. 31)?
- What do you think you should do first?
- Please tell me more about that.
- Show me how you got your answer.
- Tell me why you think that is the answer.
- Was there a rule you were following when you did that? Tell me which rule.
- Can you do that another way? What would that be?
- Draw a picture that shows that idea.
- What do you do when you run into a problem you can't solve?
- What do you do when you run into a word you don't know? (Kuhs, Johnson, Arguso, & Monrad, 2001, pp. 150–151)

Other areas of potential learning difficulties that you may choose to explore in solving Lisa's problems with math include approaches and strategies, relationships, flexibility, communication, curiosity and hypotheses, self-assessment, equality and equity, solutions, examining

Box 6.2 *Checklist for Play Assessment*

1. Choose a relevant variable: a cognitive play stage, a social play stage, or activity variable—block building, clay exploration, or drawing.

2. List the relevant stages at the top of the page.

3. Leave a space to document the evidence for your assessment of each child.

A sample template for a play assessment is provided below.

Cognitive Play Stages

1. **Functional.** Simple muscular activities and repetitive muscular movement with or without objects are used. The child repeats actions or initiates actions.

2. **Constructive.** The child learns use of play materials, manipulation of objects to construct something or create something (e.g., drawing a person, building a play dough house, measuring with beakers).

3. **Dramatic.** The child takes a role; pretends to be someone else, initiating another person in actions and speech with the aid of real or imagined objects.

4. **Games with rules.** The child accepts prearranged rules and adjusts to them, controlling actions and reactions within given limits.

Social Play Stages

1. **Solitary.** The child plays alone with toys different from those used by other children; although the child may be within speaking distance, there is no attempt at verbal communication with the peer group. The child is center of his or her own activity.

2. **Parallel.** The child plays independently but among other children. The child plays with toys that are similar to those the other children are using. In short, the child plays beside rather than with other children.

3. **Group.** The child plays with other children. The children are borrowing, following each other with play things. All engage in similar if not identical activity. For *cooperative play*, the child plays in a group that is organized for making some material product, striving to attain some competitive goal, dramatizing situations of adult or group life, or playing formal games. There is a division of labor, a sense of belonging, and an organization in which the efforts of one child are supplemented by those of another.

Not Play

1. **Unoccupied.** The child is not playing in the usual sense but watches activities of momentary interest, plays with his or her own body, gets on and off chairs, follows the teacher, or merely glances around the room.

2. **Onlooker.** The child watches the others play and may talk, ask questions, or offer suggestions to the children playing but does not enter into the activity.

continued

Box 6.2 *continued*

Checklist for Play Assessment

Name: <u>Peter</u>   Date: <u>2/28/06</u>   Time: <u>11:00 to 11:20</u>

	Solitary	Parallel	Group	Context or materials.*
Functional				
Constructive				
Dramatic			With Mallory Quintin	Block corner to building airport with starbucks, ticket counter, shoe shine stand, etc.
Games with rules				
Not play: onlooker or unoccupied				

Note date and duration of time

*Note here relevant details to support creative or other significant observation

Source: Adapted from G. Mindes, "Social and Cognitive Play of Young Handicapped Children in a Special Education Preschool Center," unpublished doctoral dissertation, Loyola University, 1979.

results, and mathematical learning (National Council for Teachers of Mathematics, 2005; Stenmark, 1991). Questions related to each of these areas correspond to the National Council of Teachers of Mathematics (NCTM) Standards. You can use prepared questions from the NCTM's *Illuminations* lessons on the Web or develop your own for this curricular area or others to focus your attention and your students' attention on identifying learning strengths and problems. To assist in understanding whether young children have developed the concept of a story, you may wish to use a sequence organizer. In a conversation, you ask the child to tell you the story, filling in the blanks as you go. See Figure 6.1 for an illustration of this technique. You can also learn about children's problem-solving skills and strategies by observing them with the task.

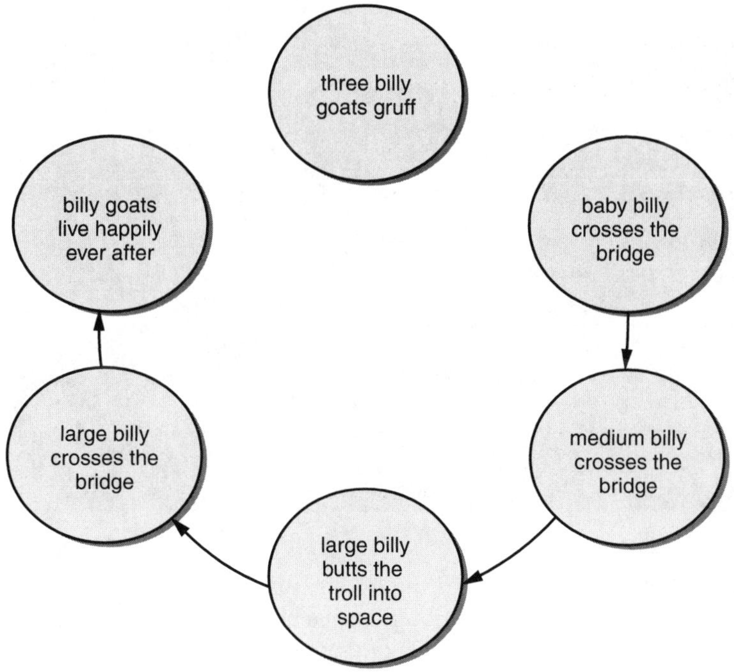

Figure 6.1
Sequence organizer.

TASK ANALYSIS

Task analysis is a process in which large goals are broken down into smaller objectives or parts and sequenced for instruction. Task analysis is the process of developing a training sequence by breaking down a task into small steps that a child can master more easily. Tasks, skills, assignments, or jobs in the classroom become manageable for particular children in ways that more generalized instruction may be missing their individual needs.

Often, task analysis is informal. Jorge, a 6-year-old who is having trouble buttoning his shirt, may be unsuccessful because, you notice informally, he usually wears T-shirts and sweatshirts. Thus, he lacks experience with buttons. Task analysis may be a more explicit and detailed process that you use with 7-year-old Brenda, who is showing limited writing fluency. The teaching question is *What can you do to facilitate Brenda's writing?* To answer this question, you list all of the steps in writing a story. For example, sitting in a quiet place with writing materials, paper, and some stimulus (picture, discussion, or thought-provoking questions); grasping pen or pencil; applying appropriate pressure to create legible marks on the paper and writing letters together to form words; grouping the words together in sentences; organizing the sentences to convey a story idea; and so on. After you list the component parts of the task, you watch Brenda at work. You see what parts of the

task analysis process in which large goals are broken down into smaller objectives or parts and sequenced for instruction.

169

presentation mode
way the task or learning
situation is presented to a
child as part of instruction.

response mode   how
a child responds to a
direction or instruction.

task she can't do—maybe it's writing letters, maybe it's organizing her thoughts, or maybe it's leaving enough space between words to make it possible to figure out what she's trying to say. At any rate, once you have identified the problem, you can decide what to do to help Brenda in your class. You may also have enough information to refer Brenda for a more specialized assessment.

One way of conducting a task analysis is to examine both the **presentation mode** and the **response mode** of any given task. You know that some children require you to tell directions; some to show directions; some to write directions; and some to tell, show, and write directions. Even if you habitually use multiple demonstration modes for tasks, skills, assignments, and jobs, you may find that a few children still do not understand what to do. In that case, through a task analysis of the presentation mode, you can decide why Joey is not singing at circle time. You may find that he requires more than multiple presentation modes (tell, show, or write). Maybe you have to repeat yourself several times or say it louder, more slowly, or using different words. You may find that Alexandra requires dual methods of presentation—for jumping rope, you must show her and tell her—but after several weeks of jumping rope with her, the skill becomes automatic. Alexandra can now show and tell Mimi how to be an Olympic jump-roper. Task analysis of the presentation mode focuses on why children are not doing what you require by looking at how you tell them to do it.

When you task analyze the response mode, you look at what you expect Jerome to do, say, write, or show to you. What you see may show that Jerome cannot tell you about the trip to the pumpkin farm but that he can show you what he enjoyed most, may be able to demonstrate how to pick pumpkins, or may be able to draw a picture about the trip. Agatha, by contrast, can't stop talking about the trip. When asked to draw a picture about the trip, she scowls and hastily scrawls a thin

orange line around the edges of the paper, then scratches across a few lines to fill in the circle and dumps her work in her cubby. By knowing how Jerome and Agatha are comfortable in responding, letting you know that they have the skill, know the concept, and so on, you can set goals that will be appropriate for each of them. That is, you can let Jerome demonstrate what he knows by showing you, while working with him to describe verbally his experiences, knowledge, and attitudes. Thus, Jerome feels successful while moving forward in your program. Agatha can dictate a long tape to you to describe her experiences. You may sit beside her while she draws; she may need just the tiny bit of reassurance that her pumpkins can be interpretations of pumpkins rather than the true representation of the pumpkin of her mind's eye.

In addition to these informal uses, task analysis is a technique for determining the steps in accomplishing a goal on a child's IEP or IFSP. One way to use this approach is to use the process of forward chaining or backward chaining through a task *Chaining* means identifying the first step in a process (or the last) and all subsequent steps that are each based on successful accomplishment of the one before. An example may be putting on a cardigan sweater, which requires a series of steps— taking out the sweater, identifying the front with the buttons or zipper, sticking one arm in one sleeve, then sticking the other arm in the other sleeve, and finally buttoning or zipping it closed. This task analysis method is useful in naturalistic early childhood settings for both assessment and for planning subsequent instruction of complex self-help skills or other complicated concepts (Cook, Klein, Tessier, 2004; Noonan & McCormick,1993). Chaining through a task means starting with an activity that a child has failed. Think about what happens before or what should happen afterward to determine where the failure occurs. Consider the following analogy: Mr. College Freshman is always getting overdraft notices from the bank. He must review the steps of checking

BOX 6.3 *Selected Steps for Teeth Brushing*

1. Locate the toothbrush, toothpaste, and water source. These may be three steps, if necessary.

2. Apply the paste to the brush.

3. Brush the teeth in sequential order, front, sides, backs, and so on. These may be listed as more steps, if necessary.

4. Rinse the mouth.

5. Rinse the toothbrush.

6. Dry mouth and hands.

7. Return the materials to storage.

account operation to ascertain the key to the task failure. Does he enter all the checks he writes in the ledger? Does he enter bank charges? Does he add and subtract regularly? Does he write numbers clearly? Does he follow the steps that the bank outlines for balancing? Once he has identified the break in the chain of steps to successful bank account management, he can make a plan to avoid overdrafts.

In early childhood settings, teachers focus task analysis on activities necessary for successful participation in the setting. For example, in many early childhood centers, children must brush their teeth after lunch. If Javier is not successful with this task, you can review the steps to success and figure out how to help him be a champion brusher. What you need to do is watch him closely, see which step or steps he cannot do, and then offer prompts or coaching until he can do the task by himself. See Box 6.3 as an example of this type of task analysis.

Four ways to develop the particular steps for a task analysis include watching a master, self-monitoring, brainstorming, and goal analysis (Cegelka & Berdine 1995; see also Mercer & Mercer, 2005). Early childhood teachers can use each of these approaches to identify and record the incremental steps, as follows:

- Watching a master: To know how to help children walk the balance beam, watch someone who is doing this task well.

- Self-monitoring: To know how to help children make a papier-mâché turkey, review the steps that you follow in accomplishing the task.

- Brainstorming: To know how to help children plant a garden in a school plot, ask all the children to give you ideas.

- Goal analysis: To know how to help children develop conflict resolution strategies, review the observable and nonobservable aspects of this task and identify ways to see how it is accomplished.

All approaches to task analysis link assessment to instruction and involve step-by-step breaking down of tasks into teachable increments.

If a task analysis was successful with one child, it may well apply to another (McLean et al., 2004). Hence, teachers should compile a *task analysis bank*. Over time, teachers may find that their task analyses fall into certain patterns related to the children they typically teach or the particular curriculum they are using. When teachers are aware of these task-analysis patterns, it is easier to write new task analyses.

Not only do you need to analyze the task, but also you need to observe the child who is to learn the task in terms of what he or she can and cannot do. The number of steps in a task analysis depends upon the functioning level of the child as well as the nature of the task. There are a number of questions to answer about the child that enable the teacher to determine the functioning level (Lerner, Lowenthal, & Egan, 1998; see also Mc Loughlin & Lewis, 2005; Mercer & Mercer, 2005). How does the child receive, store, and retrieve information? Which avenue of learning does the child seem to prefer: visual, auditory, or tactile? Does the child avoid certain pathways of learning? Does the child do better if more than one pathway is used simultaneously in the teaching process? Is intrusion necessary? How much assistance does the child require to master the step? Are scope and sequence lists available for academic subjects to use as hypothetical sequences for tasks? Answers to these questions will enable the teacher to blend the task analysis of the skill or behavior to be mastered to the current capabilities of the target child. In addition to task analysis, another teaching-related assessment activity that is gaining popularity in classroom use is dynamic assessment, discussed next.

DYNAMIC ASSESSMENT

Dynamic assessment is an approach that combines formal testing and teaching. Conduct a one-to-one interview with an individual child to learn more about that particular child as well as what the formal test may be missing. This method is particularly helpful for learners with diverse cultural backgrounds because the formal test may contain biases or language and concepts that are unfamiliar (Sternberg & Grigorenko, 2002). In this approach, the teacher uses available assessment information and tries to teach a specific skill. The available test data serve as the foundation of a task analysis for the skill or competency. The theoretical work of Vygotsky (1978, 1986) and Feuerstein (1979) are the underpinnings for this method. Quite often speech and language therapists use dynamic assessment in their work with children who have communication disabilities (cf. Otto, 2006). In implementation of the technique, the therapist or teacher uses intuitive reasoning as well as conventional thinking in ferreting out why the young child is not successful with a particular skill or competency. The teacher observes as the teaching occurs and modifies the task in the process, so that the child can be successful.

dynamic assessment
one-to-one interview approach between teacher and student using available assessment information for teaching a specific skill.

mediated learning experience (MLE)
teaching approach in which the teacher uses questions, suggestions, and cues to prompt the child to think more consciously about the task and to expand learner expertise.

How does a teacher proceed with this technique? First, give or acquire test information about the skill or competency in question. Next, try to teach the child the missing pieces, according to the task analysis (or test data), observing and modifying during the teaching process. Finally, retest to document progress. This process of teaching is the mediated learning experience (Lidz, 2003). The **mediated learning experience (MLE)** involves the teacher's use of questions, suggestions, and cues to prompt the child to think more consciously about the task and to expand learner expertise.

For example, you may wish to encourage Morgan to elaborate her concept of stories. The available data shows that Morgan knows that stories have beginnings and endings. Your objective is for Morgan to know that stories have action that moves the story from the beginning to the end and that by changing these actions the story changes. At a quiet time, you sit with Morgan and read a short, unfamiliar story to her. Then, through a process of questions and answers, you help Morgan understand what you mean about action as part of the story concept. Later, you assess whether Morgan has maintained the skill or whether she needs reteaching.

This avenue of assessment is promising for teachers who wish to link instruction to learner outcomes for early childhood settings. The approach links test results to task analysis to teaching to individualization of instruction. It is an opportunity for making the learning process apparent to those children who may need special assistance in linking thinking to academic requirements, whether these requirements are preschool or primary. Sometimes you need to consider not only the learner and the task, but also the environment. Then, you engage in a process called ecological assessment.

ECOLOGICAL ASSESSMENT

ecological assessment
an approach that includes the classroom environment, personal interactions, and the learning tasks as variables in the collection of evidence for the measure of learning for individuals.

Ecological assessment is a tactic that utilizes focused observations of young children at home, in the center, in the community, or at school. As an assessment approach, variables such as culture and beliefs of the child and family; teaching style; time allocations for activities in the classroom; academic, behavioral, and social expectations; as well as class tone become important features to observe *in situo* (Bigge & Stump, 1999; see also Brown-Chidsey, 2005). Such observation enables the teacher to assess what social/emotional variables influence successful completion of learning tasks in a particular situation. For example, sitting in a circle to listen to a story is a frequently planned early childhood activity. So, if Dana cannot listen quietly to stories, you observe what she does in the situation—interrupts to ask questions, pokes the children next to her, and shows great interest in the pictures for the story, often elbowing her way forward to look. After several days of observation at story time, you develop instructional supports that will help her sit quietly. Instructional strategies that support young children with special needs in the classroom include modeling, prompting, error correction, as well as repeated practice and incentive strategies. However, the critical variable for any instructional intervention is individualization for a particular child. For Dana, the solution might be a conversation before story time about the expectations for listening. For Ryan, the solution might be the opportunity to sit next to his best friend, Horace.

The roots of this assessment process come from Bronfenbrenner's (1979) view that various issues within and across the child's social contexts influence learning. The child-care setting and school are particularly important contexts that influence child learning and development. "Classrooms that benefit children and enhance academic performance share similar characteristics such as positive approaches to instructional planning, management, and delivery" (Sheridan & McCurdy, 2005). An additional critical aspect of this view of assessment that supports young children's development in context is that the observation is ongoing rather than a one-time event (cf. McLean et al., 2004). Thus, the method connects to curricular planning and intervention as individual children progress in a situation with appropriate developmental and instructional support. Pierangelo and Guiliani (2006, p. 39) offer questions to consider in the social context of school that may be particularly useful to teachers in the primary grades when children must move from class to class, or to preschool teachers concerned with supporting young children during "choice time" or free play:

- In which environments does the child show difficulty with the expectations?
- Are there instances where the child is successful?
- What are the behavioral and academic expectations in each situation?
- What are the differences between or among the situations?
- How can instructional planning support the child in the different situations?

Ecological assessment is dynamic, not static in nature. The focus is on the child, the situation, and the interaction between the context and the child. Thus, a number of variables are considered when reflecting on best approaches, including resources and materials, child behaviors, social relationships, and family/adult behaviors in relationship to the individual (cf. Howard, Williams, & Lepper, 2005). The process often assists in bridging home and center/school relations when observations of both situations are available. Thus, the ecological procedure creates an opportunity for home–school collaboration and definition of IFSP goals (cf. Cook et al., 2004). The approach, in sum, considers the whole child and the needs of the whole child—academic, social/emotional, and behavioral. There are situations that may require a focus on behavioral issues in particular. In these situations, you will want to be aware of ways to assess and facilitate social/emotional behavior so that young children with challenging behaviors can participate in the group life of the classroom setting. One specialized approach that serves this purpose is functional assessment.

FUNCTIONAL ASSESSMENT

functional assessment focused observational method that links individual assessment to curricular intervention for one student.

Functional assessment is a focused observational method that links individual assessment to behavioral intervention for one student. The method is most appropriate to use when you are concerned about a young child with a serious problem that interferes with successful experiences in the regular classroom. "This model does not focus on typical sequential development but rather on age-appropriate expectations for functioning as independently as possible in specific environments. A functional model of assessment requires that both the individual's skill and the environment be evaluated. Because people function in several environments, each one must be evaluated" (Hoy & Gregg, 1994, p. 240).

The method requires careful observation of small pieces of behavioral interludes. Divide the observation sequence into an ABC order—antecedent, behavior, and consequence. Thus, you observe the problem behavior (B) and then look more carefully to see what precipitates the event, the antecedent (A), and note the consequence (C). Before the careful observation, usually you have noticed either the problem behavior or the naturally occurring consequence. As a teacher, you seek to intervene or change the behavior by manipulating the antecedent or the consequence that in turn diminishes or extinguishes the targeted inappropriate behavior. The method comes from the behavioral analysis tradition of assessment and intervention (cf. Chandler & Dahlquist, 2006). Although historically the method was used in situations where children showed many problem behaviors that prohibited or limited their participation in mainstream or inclusion settings, the method has broader applicability. It is potentially quite useful as a tool to use in situations that require intervention, such as kicking, screaming, pinching, biting, cursing, or other behaviors that present group management and social acceptance concerns. The most important caveat for the method is to understand the meaning of the behavior for the child, that is, what need the child meets by employing the challenging behavior.

For example, suppose that when Martha, a 3-year-old, approaches the children in your class, they run away from her. You do not understand why this is occurring. You are concerned that it may be because Martha doesn't talk, because she walks with an uneven gait, or because she frequently arrives at school with her hair in a mess. Your tentative conclusion is that the children are fearful of Martha because they have limited experience with nonverbal children, that perhaps they are intolerant of her physical limitations, or that they are judging her on her messy appearance. You want to help the children in your class to be accepting of differences.

You want to assure them that even though Martha doesn't talk, she is a worthy playmate. You plan a time to observe, so that you can learn what will help Martha approach children confidently and/or what will help the children in your group include Martha in their play.

You watch Martha. You see that she approaches Everett, gets very close to him, then puts her hand palm down on his cheek and pats it. Everett looks at her warily, but continues to mold with play dough while Martha leaves the area. Why, you ask yourself, did Everett look at Martha warily? Why do the children sometimes run and scream when Martha pats their cheeks? If you stop the assessment at this point, you may never know, or you may conclude that it is Martha's appearance or some other historical experience that the children have had with Martha that creates this reaction on the part of her classmates. In fact, you may talk to Everett and say, "Martha is your friend. She wants to use the play dough. You, Everett, should invite her to join you." However, you continue your assessment before planning an intervention.

You continue to watch Martha. She approaches Kenneth, moving close with her open palm to his cheek. All of a sudden, instead of patting his cheek, Martha reaches with her nails and scratches a deep gouge in Kenneth's cheek. He screams in rage; Martha tries to pat his cheek; he runs away. You handle the crisis and later plan an intervention to stop the inappropriate social behavior of cheek scratching. An intervention strategy will not be easy to develop because Martha sometimes pats and sometimes scratches. It is also difficult to develop an intervention that will be meaningful to Martha. Martha is "coping" (cf. Sandall & Schwartz, 2002); she is showing behavior to affect her environment. The fact that the teachers and peers do not perceive it as effective is not apparent to her. She is doing the best she can, even though it seems erratic to others. She is not learning from the typical techniques of modeling, rule reminding, and so on. You, her teacher, must intervene so that she no longer harms the children in her class and so that she may develop a more adaptive behavior style that will serve her in inclusive environments.

To use this approach, you must observe carefully to see what happens first—the *antecedent*; what she does next—the *behavior*; and then develop a suitable intervention—the *consequence*. In Martha's case, the *antecedent* is an open palm to the cheek of a classmate; the *behavior* is a pat or a scratch; and the *consequence* is currently that children stare warily, run away, or scream.

You wish to improve Martha's functioning in class, so you must develop an intervention to change the consequence and extinguish the patting and scratching behavior. You must stop Martha from touching children's cheeks. With your colleagues you plan an intervention strategy, keep records about how the strategy works, and continue through a process until you find a strategy that stops Martha from patting or scratching the cheeks of classmates. You may need to be by her side for several weeks to prevent this behavior. You may choose to reinforce Martha's keeping her hand at her side with a positive consequence.

Or you may choose a negative reinforcer when she sticks her hand toward a child. You may also help the other children learn cues to steer Martha to a more appropriate path (e.g., "NO, Martha, you can't touch me. You can play here."). The key is that all the children use a consistent phrase.

McLean et al. (2004) discuss this assessment/intervention approach in the context of form and function. Form refers to the behaviors of children—self-injurious, aggression, tantrums, property destruction, social avoidance, and self-stimulatory behaviors—and function refers to the effects of those behaviors for the child—obtain desired outcome (teacher attention) or escape undesired outcomes (leaving favorite activity to transition to another one). This analytic approach to assessment and instruction is quite useful when teachers cannot always easily judge what the behavior, or form, is trying to effect. That is, what is the young child trying to do? What does he want? For example, Kevin, an 8-year-old whose speech is difficult to understand, says in an agitated and excited fashion, "Mumble, mumble, mumble, mumble" (to your ears) at show and tell. You respond, "That's nice," because you are reluctant to embarrass him in front of the group. He then says, "NO, THEY STOLE!" You adjust your teaching strategy (in private) so that Kevin comes to show and tell with shorter sentences, pictures, or pantomime. As his speech becomes more articulate, you encourage him to use longer sentences.

Howard, a 6-year-old, goes to the chalkboard at playtime. He picks up an eraser and runs the eraser up and down the chalk tray. He does this every day for the whole play period. What does this behavior mean to Howard? What can you do to change it so that he plays with other children, or so that he uses toys? It will not be easy to intervene. Howard doesn't talk and he screams if you try to take away the eraser. You must plan an intervention that will expand Howard's repertoire in small steps.

When using this assessment approach, you must consider both the child and the behavior, as well as the environment, schedule, routines, rules, personal interactions, and materials—the "baseline of the program" (Berry & Mindes, 1993). You examine the antecedents to see whether some aspect of the baseline of your program can change to support the behavior that you want to increase. For example, suppose your routine is that everyone must sit in a circle for large group time. Katie, a 3-year-old in your class, does not want to sit in the circle. She resists when the teacher assistant tries to hold her. She gets up and runs away. She doesn't participate. What if you change the routine so that Katie can come to the circle when she wants to and when she is ready? If she does not come to circle, she must play quietly with her doll or play dough or whatever. You have prevented a disruption to circle, and Katie can come to circle when she feels comfortable.

Or suppose Marc, a 7-year-old, cannot sit for a half hour in the discussion period. You change the rule that desks must be clear for discussion. Marc pays attention to discussion while drawing pictures.

What you have do in these situations is manipulate or change the baseline so that problem behaviors of children do not interfere with their social experiences (function) in the classroom. These changes are not always straightforward. Think about a dieter who knows that chocolate donuts should not be in the house (antecedent). The ingredients for brownies are in the cupboard. The dieter makes the brownies and eats them. The diet suffers! The dieter must develop other strategies for overcoming the weight gains by examining all of the variables that influence eating patterns, and choose behaviors and consequences accordingly. In the case of young children, the teacher or parent must choose the behavior to change so that the young child can function as well as possible in inclusive situations.

In summary, consider this assessment technique for situations where individual children show annoying behavior, yet conventional methods of observation and interventions have not been effective. It is important to remember that this assessment technique is for use with troublesome social behaviors that interfere with a young child's ability to cope or *function* in the classroom. To be effective, apply this technique to particular situations for individuals. It is a precision teaching tool to assess, intervene, and reassess. It is a tool to find the meaning for behaviors that initially are hard to figure out. By using this system of microscopic observation and personalized intervention, children can adapt more effectively to inclusive situations. The approach is often the first step in a **behavioral intervention plan** for a child who is or will be identified as one with special needs. Another approach to the ongoing assessment of children with special needs shifts the focus from deficit to strength.

behavioral intervention plans plans made based on assessment of young children who present troubling behavior. Modifications to the regular program are made and monitored.

STRENGTH-BASED ASSESSMENT AND INTERVENTION

Often, teachers and others focus on the troubling and dysfunctional deficits of children with disabilities. For example, IEP language, multidisciplinary staffings, and classroom modifications of lessons focus on Eric's inability to sit for long periods and his poor reading and writing skills. **Strength-based assessment** shifts the focus to the abilities, talents, and skills of the child with disabilities. This assessment/intervention focuses on developing **resiliency**— "the ability to emerge as a highly functioning adult despite growing up in extremely stressful circumstances—through relationship building and by developing resiliency traits such as problem solving, conflict resolution, and communication skills" (Turnbull, Turnbull, Shank, & Smith, 2004, p. 132). When you look at Eric again, you notice or assessment results document that he has a large oral vocabulary, draws imaginative pictures, and responds to teacher nonverbal cues. Which Eric do you want in your classroom? The core beliefs of this assessment method include:

strength-based assessment requires the assessor to focus on a child's capacities to plan intervention.

resiliency ability to cope in challenging environment.

- All children and families have strengths.
- Child and family motivation is higher when strengths are the focus.

- Failure of a child or family to demonstrate strength reveals absence of an opportunity for practice rather than a deficit.
- IEPs must be based on strengths. (Epstein, 1998, p. 25)

All of the special assessment methods discussed in this chapter lend themselves to application when you are trying to solve a classroom problem with a particular child. To solve the problem effectively, follow the principles and avoid common pitfalls (Kerr & Nelson, 2006):

- Pinpoint the behavior that is most important to monitor or that is the most disturbing to the class.
  - Is the behavior running around the room? Getting up to sharpen one's pencil without permission? Punching the kid next in the line?
- Don't collect answers to questions that don't apply to the problem.
  - If everyone is experiencing difficulty with sitting still for a half hour, why single out this fact for the records that you are keeping on Vince?
- Count observable behavior; note the results of the behavior for more accurate information.
  - Count the minutes of in-seat behavior rather than the stars awarded for 5-minute increments.
- Collect and organize data to use to affect the modification of a child's environment.
  - If the problem behavior is talking out, a chart summarizing this will be useful. Collecting information about roaming around the room and storing this data in a file won't help.

In addition to social/emotional issues and curricular adjustment issues, teachers are often concerned about the functional language of particular children. In these cases, the approach of curriculum-based language assessment may be quite useful.

CURRICULUM-BASED LANGUAGE ASSESSMENT

curriculum-based language assessment
a process for determining a child's functional language skills and vocabulary related to the subject matter being studied.

Curriculum-based language assessment is a special technique to use when you are not sure that a child has the linguistic capacity to understand the curriculum. With this assessment, you can plan to bridge the gap between the child's capacity and the demands of the curriculum. Suppose Henrika, a 5-year-old native Polish speaker, does not seem to follow directions well. Through a series of special steps, you can find out if her problems are linguistic rather than behavioral. Aspects of linguistic functioning to investigate by observation and interview include (Losardo & Notari-Syverson, 2001; see also Baca & Cervantes, 2004):

- Does Henrika know how to match objects with words (blocks, crayons, chalk, pencils, and so on), identify objects by sound or touch, label and describe objects, and remember objects and information about them?

- Can Henrika use categorization skills to group objects, describe their characteristics, and see similarities and differences?

- Is she able to reorder information, such as what happened before and what may happen next?

- Can she draw conclusions based on inferences from previous learning and experiences? For example, What does it mean to be "afraid"?

- Are there differences that you see when Henrika is functioning in context—with objects and pictures? Or when she is asked to imagine or recall experiences with objects?

As you think about Henrika's difficulties and explore these and other questions, you will want to keep in mind the curriculum's specific vocabulary and experiences that she has had with English and school. Learn about her culture and the ways that language is typically used at home as well as "traditional" expectations for language in "school" settings. Keep in mind that cultures vary in the ways that communication is used orally and nonverbally. "Manners" and ways to address teachers, parents, and other children vary by culture. Rules for the ways that children communicate and interact with adults vary by culture. Conversational roles for children vary by culture (American Speech & Hearing Association, 2005). Compare what you discover to your own expectations and routines. Gather data on Henrika's performance in various academic situations—small group, large group, individual activities. While becoming aware of Henrika's language issues vis-á-vis curriculum, you may wish to be sure that your teaching approaches contain a wide variety of instructional strategies and ways to view learning. Ask yourself if words and sentences are the best way to tell whether Henrika can identify shapes and concepts in science. Could she select answers from an array of objects or pictures (Sadowski, 2004)?

In addition, be sure that your academic English instruction includes vocabulary and the argument structures required for justifying answers (Bielenberg & Fillmore, 2005). See Box 6.4 for a starting point checklist for English language learners. This brief chart draws attention to the complexity of language learning by separating as much as possible the language processes of listening, speaking, writing, and reading. It offers three categories for rating performance in each of these areas. An important paradigm used by several states preparing for large-scale assessment is the one developed by the WIDA Consortium.

WIDA's English Language Proficiency Standards for English Language Learners in Kindergarten Through Grade 12: Frameworks for Large-Scale State and Classroom Assessment is the first published product of an enhanced assessment system being developed and implemented by a consortium of states. Federal grant monies available under the No Child Left Behind Act of 2001 were awarded to Wisconsin (the lead state), Delaware, and Arkansas (WIDA), the original

Box 6.4 **Checklist for English Language Learners**

For each of the language process areas, rank each child separately on the variables listed.

Name: _____   Date: _____

listening	speaking	writing	reading	English	emerging	functional	proficient
				Social vocabulary			
				Informational vocabulary			
				Academic vocabulary			
				Fluency			
				Grammar			

partners, in early 2003. Within the first half-year of the project, the District of Columbia, Maine, New Hampshire, Rhode Island, and Vermont joined the team, followed by Illinois in October 2003 (Illinois State Board of Education [ISBE], 2005).

The WIDA Consortium proposed five levels of language proficiency: entering, beginning, developing, expanding, and bridging (ISBE, 2005). Box 6.5 shows a checklist to consider when planning for the instruction and assessment of English language learners in your classroom. One useful approach for this focus is the applied aspects of multiple intelligences. This view of learning and teaching grows from the theories describing intelligence and the testing of intelligence.

MULTIPLE INTELLIGENCES

Gardner (2004, pp. 60–61) describes ". . . human intellectual competence . . . [as] a set of skills of problem solving—enabling the individual *to resolve genuine problems or difficulties* that he or she encounters and, when appropriate, to create an effective product—and must also entail the potential for *finding or creating problems*—thereby laying the groundwork for the acquisition of new knowledge . . . [in a] cultural context." Gardner cautions that the intelligences he delineates do not "exist as physically verifiable entities but only as potentially useful scientific constructs" (2004, p. 70). The multiple intelligences perspective enhances teaching by

- providing powerful points of entry to student learning—catching multiple ways to introduce and begin the study of a topic.
- offering apt analogies derived from different dimensions and appealing to various intelligences.
- providing multiple representations of the central or core ideas of the topic of study. (Gardner 1999, pp. 186–187)

In practice, Gardner (1999) suggests that teachers must provide various ways for students to become engaged in a topic, provide multiple opportunities for developing understanding, and permit diverse products and processes for assessment and documentation of work. This does not mean that you need to represent all the intelligences all the time, but that you provide diverse learning assignments and measures so that you tap the best in each child.

Gardner has attempted to do just that by developing a comprehensive framework based on his theory of **multiple intelligences** (MI). He posits that the areas of intellectual competence (intelligences) are relatively independent of each other. The intelligences are linguistic intelligence, musical intelligence, logical-mathematical intelligence, spatial intelligence, bodily kinesthetic intelligence, and personal intelligences (Gardner, 2004). It is possible to provide classroom learning centers for each of the different abilities (language center, math and science center, music center, movement center, art center, working together center, personal work center) that would help children learn subject matter content while utilizing their own relative strengths. However, you

multiple intelligence theory theory that children have seven areas of intellectual competence that are relatively independent of each other.

183

should not assume that the centers are promoting learning in a direct way; the intellectual process is much more complicated.

An example of a research and practice project based on MI theory is Project Zero, implemented at a center where Howard Gardner serves as one of the principal researchers. "Project Zero's mission is to understand and enhance learning, thinking, and creativity in the arts, as well as humanistic and scientific disciplines, at the individual and institutional levels." The center's principal researchers are involved in a variety of projects. Two projects of interest for early childhood educators involve the "creative learning" project that seeks to promote creative thinking in classrooms and the "making learning visible" project that links the practices of Reggio Emilia to MI theory and practice (Project Zero, 2005). These projects promote holistic views of children and an integrated assessment/teaching approach. For the purposes of thinking about assessment issues in the classroom, MI theory offers support for the notion of the complexity of learning/thinking. MI theory does not provide support for assessment of particular intelligences—only the notion that problem solving in all its permutations is complicated. In addition to assessing children for instruction, teachers are responsible for referring those who may be at risk or those who may have disabilities.

PREREFERRAL SCREENING

Child Find federal requirement for teachers (and others working with young children) to identify young children with disabilities so they may receive appropriate services and interventions to ameliorate such disabilities.

This referral process is **Child Find** (U.S. Department of Education, 2004). Child Find is the process of identifying young children who may be at risk for disability, previously unknown to the parents or to the school. As you carry forward your responsibility in this endeavor, you want to keep careful records of your concerns about the problems or limited progress of the few children in your room who may need the skilled diagnosis of a psychologist or other member of the multidisciplinary team member that serves your school or program. As part of this record-keeping procedure, you may find that a checklist of student classroom behaviors will be an efficient way to check your judgment of need for intervention (Busse, 2005; Schmid, 1999). For example, your impression is that Josefina has difficulty with the social routines of first grade. As a result, you might list the behaviors that you expect on a checklist, then observe Josefina for a week or so and complete your checklist on her comparison to school standards. Ms. Firestorm developed the list shown in Box 6.6 for her class.

When you are watching a young child whose first language is not English, you will want to be extra careful as you try to decide if Sofia is presenting a behavior problem or if she is still in the midst of learning English while maintaining her first language. So you will need to look at all areas of development, find a speaker of her language to assess Sofia's abilities in her first language, as well as note her capabilities in English-

Box 6.6

Kindergarten Classroom Behavior	1 (not at all) to 5 (most of the time)				
Raises hand for class discussion	1	2	3	4	5
Stays in line in the hall	1	2	3	4	5
Works on seat assignments with minimal assistance	1	2	3	4	5
Sits in the circle story time and so on	1	2	3	4	5

based tasks. If Sofia is beginning to learn English, she may show behaviors that you think are problem—nonverbal, difficulty in following directions, difficulty in expressing ideas and feelings, and difficulty in responding to questions consistently. Thus, what looks like a problem may merely be a child who needs time to learn English (Santos & Ostrosky, 2005).

Again, you have applied **functional assessment** or other individualized assessment appropriate for the problem evidenced in the classroom, as part of the referral process of young children who may be eligible for services to ameliorate their cognitive, emotional, or behavioral disorders. The identification of these young children is complex due to issues of definitions of the disorders, issues related to cultural norms, effect of poverty on learning opportunity, and the problems related to the role of norm-based assessment in identifying children who experience these disorders (cf. Howard et al., 2005). As the lines of regular and special education continue to blur and teachers assume increased responsibility for supporting young children while individualizing behavioral expectations for success in the regular classroom, functional assessment continues to be a useful tool.

functional assessment
focused observational method that links individual assessment to curricular intervention for one student.

SUMMARY

This chapter describes the most common alternative assessment strategies in use today. Their use depends on a number of variables such as the age of the child, the amount of time the teacher can invest in the assessment, and the particular skill or skills you wish to assess. These measures are often play-based methods for babies, toddlers, and preschoolers. This chapter's discussion incorporated the description of seven alternative assessment strategies: play-based assessment, task analysis, dynamic assessment, functional assessment, ecological assessment, curriculum-based language assessment, and multiple intelligences as a framework for understanding the complexity of human intelligence.

FIELD ACTIVITIES

1. With a partner, go to a local park or playground. Between the two of you, see if you can find examples of solitary play, parallel play, group play, cooperative play, functional play, constructive play, socio-dramatic play, games with rules, unoccupied behavior, and onlooker behavior. Use the checklist in Box 6.2 to record your observations or take anecdotal notes. Discuss your findings with each other to see if you can reach total agreement.

2. In a child-care center, watch a child who is off-target for the social group expectations. Try out the steps of functional analysis.

3. Visit a class with children who are English language learners. Watch one child in an academic activity. Try to identify the vocabulary that may be academic and possibly unfamiliar to the child.

4. Sit with a child who has difficulty with completing a worksheet, while teaching the child, identify through reflection afterward some difficulties that might have contributed to the child's failure with this sheet. Discuss these with colleagues.

IN-CLASS ACTIVITIES

1. Select a long-term objective that you think would be worthwhile to teach to a young child. Identify the steps involved in learning the objective.

2. With a partner, pick a task that is unfamiliar to you—peeling a pineapple, putting on eye makeup, washing a car—and analyze the number of steps in the task.

STUDY QUESTIONS

1. What are some critical skills a teacher may incorporate into a curriculum plan? List strategies the teacher may implement to assess progress.

2. How will a child's play activity provide extensive information about his personal developmental level?

3. Why is it important for teachers to include alternative assessment strategies into planning for the children?

4. What are the components of a task analysis? What skills can an early childhood teacher assess with a task analysis?

5. Create a task analysis by developing a long-term goal for a preschooler. For instance, the parents and teachers would like to see a child's play include increased appropriate exploration at the art center with manipulatives such as paintbrushes and crayons. Break this goal into steps for task analysis.

6. Consider situations throughout a school day where a teacher may use mediated learned experience and functional analysis.

7. Correlate the assessment/intervention approach to form/function.

8. What are the components of functional assessment? How will the teacher use this information over time?

9. What does multiple intelligence theory contribute to your understanding of the complexity of assessment tasks?

REFLECT AND RE-READ

- I know how to structure observational questions to help solve a social or behavioral problem.
- I am familiar with the general principles of play-based assessment and its usefulness to the teacher.
- I have some strategies for solving tough teaching problems.
- I can apply multiple intelligence theory to activities for my students.

CASE VIGNETTE

Ms. Archibald, mother of Adriana, came to school one day to say that Adrianna, a 3-year-old, wished to go on a diet. Ms. Archibald was worried because Adrianna was refusing breakfast, eating only a bite or two at dinner, and refusing her favorite after-preschool snack of frozen yogurt—she even looked in a mirror and declared herself fat. This behavior occurred for about a week. Adrianna and her 5-year-old sister, Marla, are bright, energetic, active children with no previous social/emotional, cognitive, or school adjustment issues. There are no particular family stresses. Ms. Archibald wants to know what actions or behaviors the preschool teachers are seeing that relate to Adrianna and food. What do you do at school to discover why Adrianna is refusing to eat and is thinking that she is fat? How might you use play-based assessment?

TECHNOLOGY LINKS

http://www.cec.sped.org

Council for Exceptional Children. This is the ERIC Clearinghouse for information about children with disabilities. Descriptions of publications that facilitate teaching are included.

http://www.ldonline.org

LD OnLine. A site with information for teachers, parents, and other professionals.

http://pzweb.harvard.edu

Project Zero at Harvard University. The site is a source of research and information about applied multiple intelligences applications.

SUGGESTED READINGS

Frost, J., Wortham, S., & Reifel, S. (2005). *Play and child development* (2nd ed.). Upper Saddle River, NJ: Merrill/Prentice Hall.

Gardner, H. (1999). *The disciplined mind: Beyond facts and standardized tests, the K–12 education that every child deserves.* New York: Penguin Putnam.

Gould, P., & Sullivan, J. (2005). *The inclusive early childhood classroom: Easy ways to adapt learning centers for all children.* Upper Saddle River, NJ: Merrill/Prentice Hall.

Howard, V. F. (2005). *Very young children with special needs: A formative approach for today's children* (3rd ed.). Upper Saddle River, NJ: Merrill/Prentice Hall.

7

Record Keeping, Reporting, and Collaborating with Families and Others

Terms to Know

- confidentiality
- student-led conferences
- grades
- report card
- standards-based
- screening results

- initial referral conference
- Individualized Education Plan (IEP) conferences
- multidisciplinary staffing
- stakeholders
- accountability

Chapter Overview

This chapter discusses the record-keeping, collaborating, and reporting issues for the teacher role in relation to all stakeholders in the assessment system for young children. Highlighted is the importance and role of routine parent–teacher conferences as part of a comprehensive assessment system. The chapter begins with issues and suggestions surrounding recording, storing, and maintaining child files. The topics of parent permission and parent participation in the assessment process are included, as are examples and issues related to report cards and portfolio assessment reporting procedures. Special procedures for partnerships with parents as clients are a special feature. Suggestions for involving children as partners in the assessment and reporting process are included. The chapter describes the teacher's role and responsibility in multidisciplinary staffing. Finally, there is a section on issues and suggested report procedures regarding the other stakeholders in the assessment system—administrators, boards, legislators, and the public.

Assess as You Read

- What kinds of reports are useful for reporting to parents?
- What is the role of report cards?
- Where do children and parents fit in the portfolio process?
- How should I prepare for a multidisciplinary staffing?
- What do principals and other stakeholders want to know?

RECORD KEEPING AND REPORTING IN THE ASSESSMENT SYSTEM

Collaboration and communication between parents and teachers begins at enrollment. If parents view the entrance of their child to the care and education system positively, then subsequent contacts at conference and report card times will start favorably. Parents will enter the conference with the expectation of respect, cooperation, and mutual discussion about the best interests of their child. Engagement of families in the process improves student achievement as well, according to a review of 50 studies on parent, family, and community connections (Mapp & Henderson, 2005). The National Association for Elementary School Principals (2005, p. 24) affirms this research with the expectations that effective principals for young children and their families adopt the following principles:

- Acknowledge and support families as children's first and most influential teachers.
- Provide early education experiences that are informed by young children's cultural and community experiences.
- Act as a bridge between schools and community-based supports for young children and their families.
- Build coalitions with community organizations to strengthen learning for children from birth to the start of fourth grade.

This "best practice" statement gives teachers and families support for placing families at the center for decision making about their young children. Thus, as teachers, you need to establish the first conferences and reports—whether in child-care or school settings—as the best experiences for all stakeholders.

Conference and report card periods are the summative opportunities for parent–teacher communication. It is a time when all parties in the assessment system—parents, child, teacher, and other professionals—share information from their diverse perspectives. It is a time to reflect on the past and to prepare appropriate intervention, teaching, and learning goals for the future.

In preparation for these times, teachers must formally reflect about each child in the program, collect records, and prepare for the conference or translate the material to a child-study or report-card format. These efforts must match the philosophy, curriculum, and parent program.

MAINTAINING CONFIDENTIALITY OF ASSESSMENT INFORMATION

confidentiality allowing a childs's assessment and other records to be available only to school personnel, agency officials, and parents.

As teachers prepare written records for these conference intervals, careful attention is required for the ethical and legal responsibilities for confidential child progress records. Teachers maintain **confidentiality** by treating assessment and other child records as private documents. Only authorized school or agency officials and the child's parents know the contents of these materials. Official school or agency records should be stored in only one place (P.L. 93–380, the Family Educational and Privacy Rights Act [FERPA], 20 U.S.C. § 1232g; 34 CFR Part 99). This includes demographic information, family and social history, academic history, attendance records, medical data, test scores, anecdotal notes, and report cards (narrative or checklist). Schools and centers house these records in a locked file. Authorized school personnel (principal, teacher, specialists) may view the records; these personnel maintain the records. Parents may see the records by appointment within 45 days of the parent-initiated request.

In the classroom, before records become *official*, teachers must safeguard notes, scores, and drafts of reports. Teachers must also choose with care the words that they use in recording notes and progress. Describe behavior of note or concern, specifically. Label judgments, opinions, and hypotheses clearly as such. Avoid broad, sweeping generalizations and value judgments. Teachers and other professionals may only write about observations and experiences that they have the credentials to assess; for example, teachers are not qualified to judge mental health and intelligence. However, teachers may appropriately discuss observable concerns and problems in performance. Box 7.1 shows illustrations of appropriate and inappropriate practices.

Teachers prepared the notes shown in Box 7.1 prior to parent conference time. The notes represent the reflections of the teachers. Parents can be similarly involved by asking them to bring notes or observations of their children doing particular activities at home.

INVOLVING PARENTS IN ASSESSMENT

Before parents come to school to hear the report at the conference, teachers can suggest real assessment partnerships for parents:

1. Ask parents for their goals for their children. This will provide an opportunity for you to talk with parents about the curriculum and their child.

   Ms. Berkeley, the parent of a kindergartner, believes that her son, Seth, is gifted. She bases her assessment on Seth's early talking. Ms. Berkeley wants Seth to read at the end of the first quarter of kindergarten. Ms. Myers, the kindergarten teacher, explains the developmental stages of literacy to Ms. Berkeley. She shows Ms. Berkeley evidence of Seth's progress and invites Ms. Berkeley to keep a log of stories and other literacy activities that occur at home over the first quarter of the year.

2. Ask parents for their opinion about homework assignments. Ms. Donohue asks children in her third-grade class to interview a senior citizen, relative, or friend. Children must be prepared to summarize their interviews in a paragraph. The Robins moved from Houston; they know no one in the neighborhood. Their daughter, Sylvia, is distraught that she will fail the assignment. Sylvia has attended a developmentally inappropriate second

Box 7.1 *Teacher Comments on Report Cards*

Inappropriate

- Garfield has caused me a lot of concern.

- *Very hyperactive and immature.* He needs a medical exam and perhaps something to calm him down!

Appropriate Practice

- Ms. Taylor collects notes and checklists that she developed for use with the kindergarten. At report time, Ms. Taylor notices as she reviews her notes that Garfield spends an average of 5 minutes on drawing, painting, and puzzle activities. He spends an average of about 10 minutes in the block corner. At the circle times, Garfield wiggles, but listens attentively to the stories. In writing, Ms. Taylor can report the facts of her observations and notes. She may then interpret the facts with a sentence or two. Garfield prefers block play. This activity seems to hold his interest more than other available areas in our room. He seems to enjoy story time. He follows the story line well. Whether Ms. Taylor initiates a discussion about unusual activity level will depend on additional information available (e.g., family has new baby, Garfield responds to structure and limits offered). Garfield is probably functioning within typical limits for 4 1/2-year-olds.

Inappropriate

- Patty is lazy and shirks responsibility for getting work done. She must be prodded to do neater work.

Appropriate Practice

- Patty is a third grader in Mr. Merrill's class. Mr. Merrill assigns work at the beginning of the week. Each third grader is responsible for personal time management. Assignments include small group project work, individual worksheets for math, and reading books by interest and level. Science, art, music, drama, and physical education are separate subjects taught by subject area specialists. Students who do not finish assignments at school must take them home. Mr. Merrill notices near the end for the quarter that Patty has many worksheets that are incomplete. He notices that the ones that require writing are written in a haphazard fashion. Stories prepared by Patty are short, one or two sentences. Mr. Merrill reflects that this behavior is new for Patty. In second grade, she completed assignments and seemed enthusiastic about school. Mr. Merrill plans an open-ended parent conference, rather than a narrative report summarizing his findings. He plans to ask Patty's mother, Ms. Jones, questions about school from Patty's perspective and from Ms. Jones' perspective. Then he will ask Ms. Jones if there are unusual stresses at home. Following this discussion Mr. Merrill will make a teaching plan to assist Patty.

  If required to write a narrative report for the quarter, Mr. Merrill can state the following: Patty has not finished assigned work at school. She has written very short essays. This approach to school work is very different than her approach in second grade. Ms. Jones, let's meet to discuss how we can assist Patty in becoming a successful third-grade learner.

Box 7.1 *continued*

Inappropriate

- Alan doesn't copy from other children anymore, but he lacks original ideas. Goes home for lunch and forgets to come back from the playground.

Appropriate Practice

- Alan, a first grader, seems to like to work with friends. He thrives on their simulation. He likes active play. Lunchtime is his favorite time of the day. He needs some assistance in remembering to return to the room after lunch. We are developing a plan with Alan.

grade with stress placed on completion of assignments according to exacting directions. Ms. Donohue learns of Sylvia's distress through the return of the parent questionnaire about homework and can reassure Sylvia before the problem casts itself into a concrete mountain. Ms. Donohue suggests, for example, that Sylvia can interview Ms. Donohue's mother, who is a school volunteer, as well as the chief engineer, the security guard, or other friendly adults around the school.

3. Provide checklists or open-ended question sheets for parents to record their own experiences with their children's progress in a subject area.

    Mr. Lester, the science teacher, suggests several take-home science experiments for young children attending Bowman Early Childhood Center, which serves children birth to age 8. Parents and children are encouraged to try the experiments at home. Parents, with their child's help, record the experiment results. They are encouraged to keep a notebook of experiments, results, any problems, and a record of concepts. At conference time, parents share with teachers the observations and solicit suggestions for associated readings. Teachers can comment on the observations from school. Thus, the partnership becomes solid.

4. Use the written parent comments at conference time: My child . . .

    a. understands more of what he/she reads.
    b. enjoys being read to by family members.
    c. finds quiet time at home to read.
    d. sometimes guesses at words but they usually make sense.
    e. can provide summaries of stories read.
    f. has a good attitude about reading.

g. enjoys reading to family members.

h. would like to get more books from the library.

i. chooses to write about stories read.

j. is able to complete homework assignments. (Fredericks & Rasinski, 1990)

You can develop similar questionnaires for any subject or developmental area. These items serve as suggested activities for parents and involve parents in the assessment process. Ms. Jewel can develop a list of questions for parents of the 3-year-olds in her program about favorite play activities. For example, my child . . .

- enjoys pretend play with dolls and small figures, cars, spaceships.
- enjoys water play at bath time or in kitchen sink with parent or responsible older sibling.
- likes to go to the park to run and chase friends.
- loves to act out favorite stories.
- sings songs from school.

All of these procedures provide meaningful, personalized opportunities to involve parents in the regular child-care and educational lives of their children. Sometimes the results of these regular contacts, or initial contacts, will require specialized assessment to develop appropriate planning for children with special needs. In those cases, parent involvement is not only recommended but also required.

Parent permission is required for any specialized assessment of children. This includes any measure beyond the usual and customary actions of teachers and caregivers—for example, a speech therapist screening Lori for a lisp, an in-depth assessment by a school psychologist on Bartholomew, or a physical-therapist review of Daniel. Obtain permission as an outgrowth of a routine or special conference with parents.

CONFERENCING WITH PARENTS

Preparing Parents for the Experience

Preparing parents for conferences is an important teacher role. Use many approaches to communication of expectations due to the diverse needs of parents. Parents themselves may have ideas about good preparation strategies. The parent community may be especially helpful in those situations where cultural and linguistic differences between teachers and parents affect basic communication. Eggers-Pierola (2005, p. 43) suggests bringing pairs of parents to class to observe the activities. As the parents watch the activities and observe the environment, they will focus on any number of program variables that you identify. Then, you can discuss with individuals or in small groups such issues as:

- What behaviors, activities, or practices do you encourage at home that you see (or don't see) here?

- What did you notice about the personal interactions here—among children, between teacher and child? Were they respectful?

- Did you notice something new about your child?

- What is missing from our program that might assist your child?

This preobservational procedure serves to identify potential value conflicts that influence parent perceptions of child progress and program effectiveness, and is one of many techniques to consider for diverse settings. Therefore, in preparation for conferences, teachers continue their parent communication through various formats, including casual conversations, telephone calls, and e-mail contacts (Box 7.2 shows some guidelines for communicating by e-mail).

Box 7.2 *Communicating by E-mail*

When using e-mail with parents, think about the following:

- Remember that email is very *public* and can be deceptively friendly.

- Be concise and to the point when you send notes. Use correct spelling, grammar, and punctuation so that you will appear professional.

- Write personally to parents, using the "Dear all" only if the message applies to everyone (e.g., write only to the parents who did not send in a permission form rather than to everyone). Blanket messages such as ". . . for those of you who haven't," etc., lead parents not to read any—blanket or individually specific.

- If parents write to you, decide whether e-mail is the best way to discuss the question or comment. Do not, for example, e-mail test results or concerns about child behavior and learning. Invite the parent to schedule a phone or in-person appointment about serious issues. You might ask yourself: Is this a message I would like to receive by e-mail (or voicemail)?

- Develop templates for regular items.

- Let parents know when you will respond—perhaps once per day and not all day because you are teaching their children.

- Avoid using "high priority" indicators and never write in all capitals.

- Use carbon copies sparingly.

- Be sure to include a relevant message heading so that you don't wind up in the spam drawer.

- Be sure to proofread before sending.

Teachers create a welcoming environment by being available to parents before and after school. During these informal chats, a comfort level is established. Teachers can also set times to be available by phone. They communicate with parents by notes and in newsletters or on websites; increasingly school districts have customized websites for parent–teacher and teacher–student communication. At conference time, teachers may make suggestions in the newsletter concerning effective conference participation. Dietel (2001) offers specific suggestions from the parent perspective:

- Know what is expected in the school or center for the age of your child.
- Know how well your child is reading or what interest your child has in books and stories.
- Understand test scores (see Teachers and Families First for a Primer for Parents at http://www.teachersandfamilies.com/open/parent/scores1.cfm) or be prepared to ask.
- Ask the teacher for information and opinions on your child's progress.
- Know about your child's homework and work products sent home.
- Be aware of your child's social skills in other group situations.
- Ask your child about school perceptions and listen to responses.

When meeting parents from cultures different from your own, prepare ahead to be sure that you know about the cultural concepts of family and family roles, expectations for behavior and academic performance, and important customs and traditions (Jordan, Reyes-Blanes, Peel, Peel, & Lane, 1998).

Regular—weekly or monthly—newsletters (cf. Berger, 2004) to parents often contain information about class activities, wishes for volunteers, and recyclable material, as well as parent-education pieces such as those shown in Box 7.3.

Preconference Survey to Parents

Child-care programs and public schools may wish to develop a survey to send to parents. This may be particularly useful when parents are entering a program. A survey gives parents time to clarify their goals for their children and an opportunity to solidify their knowledge. It may serve to prepare them for the world of child care or school. This also may help a teacher guide the discussion. Parents feel empowered because they have had an opportunity to prepare for their first encounter with the school.

Primary teachers may survey parents about experiences with school, using open-ended questions such as the following:

- When you think about it, what excited Willard most about second grade? Were there assignments or activities that he

Box 7.3 *Newsletter Suggestions to Parents*

- Think about your child before meeting with the teacher. What do you know about the school schedule, routine, and curriculum? What do you want to know more about? Jot down a couple of notes. Identify any particular developmental issues that you think the teacher may have suggestions for.

- Think about what your child tells you about school. If your child is old enough, ask what the child expects to happen at the conference. Ask if there are any problems with the curriculum or peers.

- Come prepared to learn about ways to help your child at home. Besides supervising any homework, find out what you can do to further the school objectives. Listen to suggestions about ways to volunteer at the school. If you are not free during school hours, find out what you might do in the evening or on weekends. Remember that parents who participate in schools show their children that school is important. The children respond by achieving.

seemed excited to do and couldn't wait to go to school for that day?

- Which projects seemed most difficult for Willard?
- Did Willard enjoy cooperative assignments with classmates?
- Are there some children that Willard has difficulty working with?
- How do you describe Willard as a learner? Worker?
- What are the most important learning goals for third graders from your perspective?

Teachers will want to develop the questions so that they focus and relate to their school goals. Writing style and language should be suited to the school community. (See Box 7.4 for a suggested form to use as a preconference survey.)

When developing guidelines for parents, you will want to pay attention to the developmental issues that may concern the parents in your community. Useful materials include suggestions for health and nutrition, television management, story reading, and sleep routines. You may want to illustrate academic skills used at home, such as locating information, organizing information, recalling information, adjusting reading rate, formalizing study methods, using graphic aids, and following directions. It is useful to include age-appropriate expectations with illustrations for preschool and primary ages. Skills included in checklists, posters, or newsletters serve to help parents invest in a partnership with the school. Progress on home activities shared with teachers assists teachers in responsive programming for individual children and families. Such materials also serve to empower parents as experts in the lives of their children. This may be

Box 7.4 *Preconference Survey*

Child's name: _____ Date: _____
Parents/guardians: _____

	Most of the Time	Sometimes	Rarely
My child loves to come to school			
He/she feels that the activities support his/her learning			
He/she understands "school"			
Homework is easy for him/her			

Other things to think about before our conference

_____
_____
_____
_____
_____
_____

See you on October 15 at 4:30 as planned.

particularly important in situations where parents are uncertain or insecure about their own levels of educational attainment (Maxwell & Clifford, 2004; Ohio Department of Education, 1990a, 1990b; See also *Beyond the Journal, Young Children on the Web* at http://www.naeyc.org for topics on readiness and parent communication).

Staging Effective Conferences

The seating and room arrangement will influence the success of a conference. For the first conference of an academic year, it is helpful to hold the conference in the classroom so that you can show the living walls of your room. Be sure that your classroom has enough adult-sized chairs so that parents and teachers sit equally. Late in the year or for problem situations, if possible, choose a small conference room for the conversation so that quiet may be preserved. Be sure everyone can see each other at the conference and that there is appropriate space. Too much open space may be intimidating. Constant brushing against participants may also be disconcerting. At the end of the conference held elsewhere, be sure to invite parents to visit the room to see displayed work, bulletin boards, and other important environmental supports to instruction.

Greet parents at the door and introduce yourself by first and last name or by following the conventions of the community for formality. It is inappropriate to call parents by their first names and to call yourself Ms. Teacher. Some parents prefer the formality of the address of Mr. and Mrs. Parent and are comfortable if you introduce yourself as Ms. Teacher. Others will prefer first names on all sides—parents and teacher. In addition to following conventions regarding addressing parents, you will want to respect parent norms regarding time and formality of dress.

Observe appropriate time-keeping customs for the community in scheduling and holding conferences. Hold conferences when parents can come to school conveniently. Provide child care, if necessary. If parents view the starting time as a target time to arrive at the meeting, then allow appropriate latitude in keeping with the cultural community perspective.

Provide opportunities for parents to participate in decision-making about their child's educational plan. Some parents will come with questions and suggestions. Others will have limited information about school. Some will remember with horror their own negative experiences. The structure of the meeting may intimidate some; that is, the number of professionals may threaten parents who are insecure with their own development or educational attainment.

Suggestions for effective parent–teacher conferences are as follows:

- Notify (or invite) parents about the purpose, place, date, and length of time.
- Offer a flexible conferencing schedule.
- Allow enough time and be sure to schedule at least 10 minutes between appointments.

- Provide a welcoming atmosphere.
- Identify any parent concerns.
- Start with descriptions of the child's strengths, interests, or abilities, and be personal.
- Concentrate on priorities.
- Be honest in your descriptions of learning and behavioral progress.
- Show that you care.
- Use parent-friendly language (i.e., "Michael shows strong ability to put objects together by group" rather than "Michael has great classification skills").
- Help children understand that conferences are routine.
- Collect relevant materials.
- Use examples of children's work to support your points.
- Listen carefully and be tactful in presenting information that parents may regard as threatening or may respond to with distress. For example, Mrs. Lawyer may not be delighted to hear that her daughter has failed the second-grade math test.
- Watch the time so you give time for everyone; schedule an extra conference if necessary.
- Don't respond to seemingly hostile or threatening comments.
- Make notes of relevant information after the conference is over or secure parent permission to make notes.
- With the parents' assistance, summarize the conference. If the conference plans a discussion of written reports, test scores, and grades, share a copy of these materials.
- Seek parent input for any next steps.
- Plan follow-up activities, interventions, and conferences with parents.
- Suggest simple activities for at-home educational enrichment (e.g., arranging socks in pairs and counting them by twos). (Bell, 1989; Million, 2005, Potter & Bulach, 2001; Seplocha, 2004)

These suggestions apply to preparation for conferences with all parents.

In addition, teachers must be sensitive to the individual needs of parents. For example, a sit-down conference may be difficult for a young mother who has a new baby and a preschooler in your program. She may prefer to visit by phone. She may likewise invite you to her home. Teachers, however, must be sensitive to parent preference about the location of the conference. Some parents may prefer not to have the privacy of their home invaded by the school. Others may feel that it is their responsibility as a parent to go to the school. It is a demonstration of their perception of the *good* parent. For example, Mrs. Cobb, a mother of 10 children who did not have a car, categorically refused to have her youngest child's teacher come to the home, in spite of the 1-hour bus trip necessary for Mrs. Cobb to arrive at the school. She cared for her children, and going to school was a demonstration of care.

Survey parents to obtain suggested procedures for further individualization of conferences to determine their preferred level of participation.

- How much time do you spend at night discussing your child's day at school? (de Bettencourt, 1987, p. 26)

- How many hours a day do you work? (de Bettencourt, 1987, p. 26)

- Do you find it stressful to help your child at home with school-assigned tasks?

- What do you do with your child that is fun?

- Which other family members are available to help your child with school-related activities?

Seligman (2000) suggests that teachers work at establishing rapport with parents, or be aware of why the rapport is difficult; for example, if you are preoccupied with your own personal crisis, very fatigued, or if there is a reason that you may not respect a parent who may have a history with drug addiction, child abuse, or whatever. If there are cultural differences between you and the family, Seligman (2000) suggests that you inform yourself of special terminology of other languages and speak in straightforward English, avoiding the use of slang and jargon. In addition, be aware of the role that nonverbal behavior plays cross-culturally so that you are not inadvertently offensive to families. Finally, know when to be supportive—for example, with the young mother who is exhausted with the care of three children and a new baby—and when to be firm—for example, telling a parent that he or she must be sure that George comes to school on time with his homework completed. At the end of a conference held about an achievement issue or a behavioral problem, consider creating a summary form. (Box 7.5 shows an example.) In addition to the parents, another key stakeholder in the reporting process is the child. More and more, as an outgrowth of authentic assessment in the classroom, children can be involved in the parent–teacher conference process.

Involving Young Children in Student-Led Conferences

As part of a schoolwide emphasis on student responsibility for authentic learning and assessment, you may wish to explore the development of **student-led conferences** (cf. Bailey & Guskey, 2001; Shores & Grace, 2005). This approach leads to the possibility of following the 3 Rs of assessment—relevance, responsibility, and reliability—for you are helping children see the link from learning to evaluation to communication to others, and therefore you are removing some of the mystery of the

student-led conferences are those meetings between teacher and child where the learner holds the responsibility for reviewing and judging self-progress in relationship to class standards and teacher judgment. May include parents.

BOX 7.5 *Example of a Parent Conference Summary Form*

Parent Conference Summary Form

Date of conference:

Name of child:

Parent/guardian name:

Purpose of conference (e.g., regular, special problem, parent request):

Documents related to the conference (portfolio, work samples, screening results, checklists, parent questionnaire, etc.):

Significant input from parents:

Summary of the conference:

Plans, next steps:

Parent signature: _____   Teacher signature: _____

accountability process. In addition, students learn at an early age to assume responsibility for their own progress and the display of it. Of course, you must help children organize their work for presentation. It is easy to accomplish in programs where you are using portfolios and holistic approaches to instruction; for example, if children are accustomed to preparing for class presentations including evaluation: "This story about my camping trip works well, but it might have more details to support the moves from the campsite to the water hole and back. I know this because my classmates asked so many questions—showing that I was not clear."

Then, they can begin to learn to organize a presentation for families reporting their personal learning progress: "I want my parents to know these things about my progress in _____. They need to know that I can now work in a group cooperatively. I can document this by including evidence of _____."

A good place to begin thinking about student-led conferences is in the portfolio display process. Even if the child's responsibility for the conference is minimal, the portfolios allow a beginning step toward this authentic assessment approach. Besides academic performance, you will want to help children report on social/emotional behavior. To help children report on social/emotional, character, or other student traits in this process, Austin (1994) suggests the use of concept maps.

- Pick a value, such as cooperation, then ask children to give examples of how they fulfill this goal; or
- Ask each child to rate personal performance in "collaboration" and illustrate the rating.

This focus builds on reflective learning for all aspects of being a student and gives voice to student accomplishment. The portfolio can be a useful adjunct to this process.

Using Portfolios Effectively at Conferences

Prior to the first set of parent conferences, think about the way you use portfolios in your program. Define for yourself or in consultation with others the purpose of portfolio assessment. Is this the only information collected? What other sources of information are available? How are students and parents involved in deciding what stays in the portfolio?

One possibility for younger children is to share portfolios with parents biweekly (Hill, Kamber, & Norwick, 1994). Children look through the collection of their own work. Then they dictate or write a letter to their parents about what they have studied. As well, children might choose samples of work to go home. In Hill's suggested format, parents review the work over the weekend. Then, they send comments to their child and teacher about their impressions. Donovan (1995) developed a two-way form for the Chicago Public Schools Project of Erikson

Institute, as shown in Figure 7.1. Gronlund and Engel (2001, p. 194) describe a systematic reflection for teachers using portfolios with parent conferences that suggests a number of questions for consideration:

- What do I know about the interests, accomplishments, progress, and challenges for each of the children in my care?

- How can I encourage family members to share important information about their child's development with me?

- How will the conversation affect my planning and teaching strategy choices after our conference?

Using these questions as a focus assures that you approach conferences and reporting as formative steps in the assessment process. The reflection also offers you the opportunity to think about children holistically and your program organically. You can engage in this thinking even if you are required to give grades to young children in the primary years.

Shores and Grace (2005, pp. 129–130) suggest that a conference with portfolios takes at least 30 minutes per family. In addition to sharing school or center information from both the child and teacher's perspective, you may invite parents to contribute written home information. Writing prompts for families include "tell me about your child's favorite game"; "tell about times when your child enjoys talking with one or more family members"; "tell about chores your child does"; and "tell me about a favorite book that you read or a favorite TV program that you watch together." Though sharing portfolios supports a holistic approach to care and education, some systems are requiring grades or summary evaluation as part of the drive toward accountability, with the idea that grades are somehow more objective and concrete.

Parent Response Form			Teacher Reply Needed?	
Date	Intials	Comments from Teacher	Yes	No
		Comments from Parent		

Figure 7.1
Parent response form.
Source: Donovan, M. (1995). *Parent response form for The Chicago Public Schools Project.* Chicago: Erikson Institute on Early Education. Used by permission.

GRADING IN THE EARLY YEARS

Progressively more school districts require letter **grades** for the K–3 years. If this is happening in your area, you will want to advocate for change. Young children do not understand marks for academic accomplishments and grades act to summarize work that is complex and evolving. Nevertheless, if you are required to use them, try to help parents and children see that the scales report to other stakeholders and that these simplify very complex accomplishments for a point in time. This kind of reporting is clearly out of alignment with a holistic approach to instruction and highlights the need for a report card that matches the program philosophy. In addition, schools use grades for a variety of purposes that create a validity problem. Various purposes include ranking of children, reporting academic progress, and motivating children to try harder (Brookhart, 2004). None of these purposes are particularly useful in developmentally appropriate practice.

grades letters or numbers ascribed to child-performance, based on a summative judgment by the teacher regarding child accomplishment of a task, a course, or a marking period—quarter, semester, year.

PREPARING REPORT CARDS

The form of a report card must match the philosophy and educational approach of the school or program. That is, in developmentally appropriate preschool and primary settings, parent conferences, narrative reports, and checklists are appropriate. Letter grades and arbitrary rankings are not appropriate for young children. If school districts move toward the philosophy of holistic instruction and performance assessment, new report processes must be developed. **Report cards** are formal, written documents that form a legal academic history for each child in your program. In modern public schools, report cards are often **standards-based**. Standards-based reporting involves using local, state, or national standards as outcome statements. The standards may be content standards that describe the knowledge and skills expectations for a given grade, or performance standards that identify a level of proficiency that a student must obtain (Popham, 2005, p. 106). Teachers compare performance of children to both the content and performance standards, noting accomplishments or absence of progress toward meeting the standard. In preparing report cards as part of a reporting system addressing standards, Carr and Harris (2001, p. 106) suggest that report cards answer the following questions for parents:

report card formal, written documents that form a legal academic history for a child.

standards-based teaching an approach to teaching that requires teachers to coordinate instruction to specified standards or goals.

- What is my child doing at school—activities, units?
- What standards—knowledge and skills—is my child learning?
- What evidence—products or performance—is available to show my child's learning?
- How is my child's behavior in class?

- Is my child making progress or is assistance needed?
- What can the family do to support my child's progress?

Regularly, parents pick up report cards, receive a mailed copy, or perhaps view them on the web. One system is MarkBook® 2004 (http://www.asyluminc.com); the system automatically calculates summaries for attendance and grades, if necessary. The system includes options to enter comments on student progress. Other companies with similar products include Thinkwave (http://www.thinkwave.com), Filemaker (http://www.filemaker.com), and Rediker Software, Inc., School Administrative Software (http://www.rediker.com). Often the electronic report card is part of a larger administrative management information system adopted by child-care centers or school districts. Renzulli (2005) describes the accomplishments of a Philadelphia program in providing administrators and teachers with one-stop access to student demographic and assessment data linked to the district's core standards-based curriculum. Parent and child access to the Web-based system begins in Autumn 2005. If your center or school does not have a system-wide electronic report card and you want to use one, there are some packages available or you can create useful forms using Adobe Acrobat®. San Bernadino City Unified School District (http://www.sbcusd.k12.ca.us/) developed and uses e-cards as part of the reporting system for families.

Whether you use paper forms or electronic ones, teachers and schools must be clear about the criteria and choose criteria according to the evidence available for report cards. Kovas (1993) describes the following three categories:

1. **Product criteria:** What can the child produce at a particular point in time? Does the product match expected developmental or academic progress?
2. **Process criteria:** How does the child function as a learner? Is his or her progress appropriate for age, stage, or grade?
3. **Progress criteria:** What gain has the child made in relation to his or her previous performance at a point in time? Individual evaluation is key. Comparison to the group is not a part of this approach.
4. **Standards-based:** How do the child's knowledge and skills compare to the expected outcomes of local, state, or national standards? (cf. Carr & Harris, 2001)

Many districts use a combined method. The combination yields a fuller picture and provides opportunities for a description of special needs and social context in relation to the criteria. A combined method follows the principles of multiple data collection to give a more accurate portrait of child progress. A complete system might include the following: report cards, notes attached to report cards, assessment reports, phone calls to parents, regular progress reports, open house, newsletters, personal letters to parents, comments written to students/parents about projects completed, portfolios exhibited, homework assignments and hotlines, school Web pages, and conferences (Guskey & Bailey, 2001).

It is possible to key modern report cards to standards with performance-based descriptors that include both achievement descriptors and behavioral descriptors. Some categories used in Kentucky include *distinguished, proficient, apprentice,* and *novice.* Nebraska uses *advanced, proficient, progressing,* and *beginning* (Guskey & Bailey, 2001). When choosing the descriptors, it is important to choose words that the parent population understands and that are clear to the teachers who must interpret the distinctions to parents. An example of such a procedure is the one used by the Tucson Unified School District (http://instech. tusd.k12.az.us/Progress_Report_Web/download.htm). In this program, teachers use academic state standards to report performance in learning. For each grade, there is a checklist in Microsoft Excel format for teachers to download. In a Microsoft Word document there are phrases that teachers can use to report on learner qualities such as *demonstrates perseverance, shows initiative, communicates effectively, takes responsibility, contributes to group effort, uses conflict-resolution techniques,* and so on. Further, the district advises teachers "non-achievement factors such as effort, participation, and the number of assignments completed, cooperation, etc., are reported in learner qualities. They should not be used as criteria for academic grades."

Ann Arbor Public Schools use the following reporting categories for social behavior, writing, and reading: Secure (S), Progress (P), and Needs Improvement (I) for social behavior. In grades K–2, teachers report progress on a continuum of skills for the year. Teachers mark the quarter (fall, winter, spring) that students meet the standard. Teachers identify reading progress as "on target," "below target," or "above target" (http://www.aaps.k12.mi.us/aaps.schools). Box 7.6 shows examples of outcomes and report card entries.

Whichever report card you use as part of a reporting system, each requires a four-step process to preparation. Gather the evidence needed to support that the child is accomplishing the outcomes you are reporting. Store the information in a grade book, folder, secure computer disk, or other suitable locked storage. Summarize the information that you have. Then report the information clearly and fairly (Stiggins, 2005). Report cards are powerful communicators with parents. They are familiar; most parents received them when they were students. In the primary years, they are ever-more complex as school districts strive to create standards-based reporting systems. As new systems fall into place, teachers do not want to repeat the errors of the past that sometimes served to stifle self-esteem and promote child/parent/teacher conflict due to the ambiguity or inappropriate yardstick measure applied.

- Suzy was an A student in all subjects—reading, science, math, and social studies—when she was 8 years old. Nevertheless, no matter how hard she tried, she could not produce uniformly round, slanted, and looped handwriting as required by the teacher. The teacher gave her an F in handwriting. Thirty years later, as her child enters third grade, she shudders about this nightmare.

- Leroy remembers whippings for low marks in "effort." At age 7, he could read and compute well. However, he did not choose to do all the worksheets required by the teacher. The worksheets seemed boring to him.

- Mrs. Stewart comes to school at the end of the year for a final conference. She wonders why her son, Everett, received a D in math. The teacher, Mrs. Packard, had sent home papers with shiny faces and stars all year. At the midyear conference, Mrs. Packard assured Mrs. Stewart that Everett performed in math in accordance with expectations. The fact that Mrs. Packard thought Everett was "a bit slow" never entered the conversation.

Communicating Fairly

As report cards and reporting systems evolve, educators must communicate in fair ways with parents. Report cards should clearly indicate

- how a child's performance compares to local and national norms.
- child progress toward learner outcomes.

- child progress compared to previous achievement level.
- progression of learner goals from grades K–3 so parents have a perspective of the big picture.
- enough subdivisions of learner outcomes so that parents can clearly see the scoring or evaluation criteria.
- descriptions of learner development that include quality of work and comparisons to expectations for long-term goals. (Wiggins, 1994)

Whenever teachers report to parents in conferences, in report cards, or casually at the drop-off/pick-up time, goals for the report should be clear. Keep the frame of reference in mind. Parents want to know the following:

- What is my child's present achievement level?
- Is my child functioning at average, above-average, or below-average level for his or her developmental age or grade level?
- How do my child's work samples compare to his or her previous work and to those of other children?
- What can I do as a parent to help my child be a better student?
- Are you, as a teacher, doing everything you can to assist, challenge, and encourage my child?
- Does my child get along with friends and peers in the setting?
- Is my child making progress (i.e., does my child have weaknesses? What strengths does my child have)?

In addition, at report time invite parents to analyze their own efforts and to seek suggestions for ways that they can meaningfully provide help to their child.

As teachers prepare for reports to parents, reflective questions include:

Are you confident about the reliability of the data that you plan to report to the parent?

Did you use an appropriate method to gather the data?

Is the material stated in objective or appropriately qualified terms?

Is the information appropriate for the problem?

Is there evidence to support the interpretation of the data?

Do the data provide new information?

Do the data fairly represent the child as a learner or as an achiever in a content area?

Are there any circumstances that would cast doubt on the accuracy of the information? (Guerin and Maier, 1983, p. 139).

In addition, Brookhart (2004, pp. 123–124) suggests that you examine the format of the report card. Are the instructional targets traditional subjects: reading, math, and so on, or lists of performance criteria, such as "can complete one-to-one correspondence tasks"? The form of the report card influences the value and kind of information that the school district or agency wishes to communicate. If locked into a system that communicates letter grades, you may wish to supplement the communication with a parent letter.

Common Errors

Teachers should also check that their reports do not make the common types of errors—computation or recording errors—and do not overlook important developmental information and situational factors (Guerin & Maier, 1983, p. 142). For example, Victor, a 2-year-old, has difficulty holding a crayon. He was a premature baby who is small, but is making good progress in language and other cognitive and social/emotional areas. Allow developmental latitude for Victor in acquiring fine-motor skills. Also, Aretha, a 5-year-old, is the only survivor of a house fire. She doesn't talk to the teacher and begins to suck her thumb. It is not an appropriate time to interpret this behavior as socially immature.

Writing Notes on Report Cards

Lee and McDougal (2000) suggest general rules of thumb to be sure that the written communication you send to parents preserves the partnership that you seek to foster. These principles include:

- Be personal. "Dear Parent" implies that you don't have a relationship with a child's family.
- Be sure to use the actual names of the parents or foster parents. For a widow, getting a letter addressed to Mr. and Mrs. Calvin is not only rude, but also painful.
- Personalize the report so that you are talking about Katie, not the generic "your child."
- Sign the note or letter with your first and last name, not "Mrs. Wishe."
- Be sure to type or write neatly, proofread, and re-read, particularly before hitting the send button on e-mail. Review to see if you have been tactful.
- Think about whether writing is the best way to deliver the message, particularly when the parent may perceive the information as threatening. That is, if you see a serious problem, and did not discuss it with the parents, a conference is probably a better venue.

These rules of thumb remind you of the weight of your words. Of course, you have to follow ethical principles as well as program and school district policies when writing notes. For example, if there is a possibility that a second grader will be retained and you've tried unsuccessfully to reach his or her parents, a tactful note may not only be necessary, but required.

WHEN FAMILIES ARE CLIENTS

Sometimes parents seek early intervention or education experiences that involve the whole family. These situations include the times when there is an at-risk birth of an infant, when parents are concerned about the development of their child, and when others recommend to parents that an educational experience may assist the family. When the family is the client, the family must be involved in assessing priorities and planning interventions (cf. Turnbull, Turnbull, Erwin, & Soodak, 2006). Sometimes it may be useful to involve the family in record keeping. Family record-keeping involvement offers the potential to educate parents as well as involve and inform them about progress in the program.

Early Head Start, a program to serve infants and toddlers, generated increased research related to working with the hard-to-reach family. When mothers have their own histories of abuse, trauma, loss, and current family violence, they are at-risk as first-time mothers. That is, they need special help with mothering and child care. Home visiting is a promising method of support for these families (Spieker, Solchany, McKenna, DeKlyen, & Barnard, 2000; see also Shonkoff & Meisels, 2000). As teachers, focus on helping families play with their children in a way that will facilitate development and that will be comfortable for the parents. These plans grow from a collaborative partnership and can include such programs as toy lending, book sharing, or other clearly academically focused ventures.

Family literacy projects are one such venture. For example, collect portfolio material reflecting parent and child growth. Examples of the portfolio contents include a page of the storybook that the parent and child are writing; a photo of holiday activities, such as stuffing a turkey, and a written paragraph about it; drawings illustrating a parent reading a story; songs written by parents and the child; photos of activities that the parent and child enjoy; and videos and audiotapes of activities. Parents and the teacher can review these items to develop plans for future program participation (Popp 1992; see also http://www.famlit.org/, the website the National Center for Family Literacy, for other ideas for your community).

To the extent possible, in situations where the teacher is part of a team working with a multiproblem family, the parent should be part of the assessment process. Sometimes, parents may be involved with a social worker or psychologist to assist with parenting or personal issues. Part of that process will include parent self-assessment. Teachers will be responsible for communicating and eliciting appropriate cooperation in

the assessment of children involved at the level of readiness that the parents possess.

In the Women's Treatment Center in Chicago, a state preschool program involves parent participation in the classroom. Women in the program are concentrating on rehabilitation of their lives dominated by substance abuse. Some of the women have a history of child abuse and neglect. Teachers work carefully with the therapeutic staff to pick a good time for moms to participate in the classroom. The assessment aspect involves teachers pointing out to mom the appropriate play of the young child. As time goes by, mom can recognize appropriate limits and play activities. She can then be involved more concretely in the assessment of her child.

In this scenario, parents are involved in assessment of themselves as well as their children. This can demystify the assessment process for them and provide positive empowering opportunities that can counter any previous negative experiences that they may have had.

MULTIDISCIPLINARY STAFFING

Staffing conferences are potentially stressful times for parents. The conference thrusts parents into the school or agency turf and frequently outnumbers them with an array of experts who have evaluated their child and who have begun to make preliminary plans for services for the child. The most stressful times are those when the parents have just completed an initial evaluation. Each of the professionals who participate in this meeting must prepare to report assessment results in a way that will honestly describe the scores and impressions, but each must sensitively recognize the parents' perspective. This requires judgment of the social, educational, emotional, and economic context of the family. It requires empathy. Often, teachers are the people that parents are most comfortable talking with about the results of assessments. Therefore, you need to become familiar with the ways that you may be involved.

Teacher Role

As a teacher, you report **screening results** because these instruments assess developmental and educational territory that you know. In addition, if you notice an issue or problem and need to work with the parents to solve it, you will need to schedule an **initial referral conference.** Depending on the nature of the referral planned, you may call upon the principal, a social worker, or other professional to assist you with this conference. Finally, you have a responsibility for preparing written and oral reports for annual **Individualized Educational Plan (IEP) conferences** that summarize the classroom interventions and outcomes accomplished in your work with individual children with disabilities. These roles are described in the following sections.

Reporting Screening Results

Teachers are responsible for knowing the technical characteristics of the measures that they are administering. They must then explain the process and the results of the assessment to parents. Teachers must understand the process of typical child development and variations due to social, cultural, and economic conditions.

For example: Mrs. Jenkins is a member of the Child Find team in Local School District, New York. Local uses the DIAL3 to screen children in the spring and in the fall. Mrs. Bond brought Carrie to the spring screening. Carrie is 3. She is the third child in the Bond family; her siblings are 10 and 6. Mrs. Bond is concerned that Carrie doesn't talk very much at home.

Mrs. Jenkins reviews the procedures and limitations of the DIAL3. Mrs. Bond was an observer and participant in the process, so this review is by way of a refresher. Then, Mrs. Jenkins interprets the results of the screening.

Carrie's performance is within developmental limits. Mrs. Jenkins and Mrs. Bond examine opportunities for Carrie to talk. Maybe older siblings are talking for her. Mrs. Jenkins tells Mrs. Bond about a weekend program for parents and tots. They agree to meet in 3 months or sooner if Mrs. Bond is still worried.

Initial Conference or Referral Conference

At an initial or referral conference, early childhood teachers appropriately listen to evaluation results presented by professionals who have assessed the child. Teachers also listen to parent perceptions and concerns. In addition, teachers must be prepared to describe their program.

screening results documentation of broad-based, quick overview of child's developmental or educational progress on a set of objectives/milestones.

initial referral conference the meeting where teachers and parents meet to share concerns about a child's progress in the learning situation.

Individualized Educational Plan (IEP) conference the multidisciplinary meeting where parents and those involved in intervention with a young child with disabilities meet to assess progress, or review initial assessment results, and plan educational interventions to support the child's learning.

Each must identify modifications to incorporate easily for an optimum inclusion experience. Teachers are responsible for identifying necessary support services for the program.

For example: Ms. Seefeldt has 25 kindergartners in a developmentally appropriate play-based kindergarten class in Baltimore. She needs to be able to describe her program. What are the routines and schedule? How does she plan? What modifications does she make for the three children with special needs in her room now? For example, Betty has a diagnosis of spina bifida with some cognitive delays. What assistance will Ms. Seefeldt need to provide so that Betty receives a developmentally appropriate program, yet Ms. Seefeldt is allowed to continue her fine work with the 24 other kindergartners? Ms. Seefeldt may appropriately request a teacher assistant to care for Betty's medical needs. She will be able to describe the justification for this request.

Ms. Seefeldt will listen to the psychologist's suggestions about appropriate cognitive intervention. The speech therapist will schedule regular visits to the classroom. Ms. Seefeldt will implement suggestions for follow-through into her regular curriculum.

Ms. Seefeldt will express a welcoming attitude toward Betty's parents. She will assure Mr. and Mrs. Columbus that kindergartners will treat Betty fairly and kindly. She will invite them to visit the room before enrollment and during the first weeks of school.

Annual Individual Education Plan Conference

At annual IEP conferences, teachers are responsible for reporting progress on the annual goals derived for every child with special needs. This conference is a **multidisciplinary staffing** that includes all of the professionals involved and the parents of children with special needs. They must state and justify deviations from the plans that have occurred through the year at the classroom level. Teachers must report progress in all the ways that they have gathered the information. Progress data may include observations, checklists, screening results, achievement scores, curriculum progress, and diagnostic assessment test scores. Teachers must listen to the concerns and issues raised by parents and other professionals at this conference. In addition, they must have thought through the next steps for the children in their care. What are appropriate educational goals? Where do these goals fit in the normalized environment and routine? Does an effective program plan require additional assessment information?

For example: Baby Stacie, the firstborn daughter of Mr. and Mrs. Hewlett, is 18 months old. She and Mrs. Hewlett have regularly attended the infant-stimulation program for children with cognitive delays and Down syndrome. The facilitator–teacher of the program is Mrs. Meadows. The program meets weekly for 1 hour. During the program, Mrs. Meadows plans gross-motor activities, songs, and exploration of infant toys. Parents assist their own children throughout the morning. Mrs. Meadows, her assistant, the physical therapist, the

multidisciplinary staffing group of professionals involved in the assessment of children with special needs, the teaching of these children, and the evaluation of their progress.

occupational therapist, and the speech therapist join in the play as individual demand dictates.

At the multidisciplinary conference, Mrs. Meadows reports that Mrs. Hewlett and Stacie have attended regularly. Mrs. Hewlett has learned the songs. Stacie smiles and laughs when she sings the familiar songs. Stacie is following along with the circle activities, happily ensconced in Mrs. Meadows' lap. Preferred toys for Stacie are foam blocks and water toys.

Mrs. Meadows suggests that Stacie seems to be making fine-motor progress—her grasp is improving. She is prepared to state that Stacie should participate in the program for another year. She will listen to suggestions from the physical therapist, occupational therapist, and language therapist. Otherwise, she has no strong recommendations for a program change.

Another example is as follows: Kevin, a 3-year-old in the Mother Goose Child-Care Center, has finished his first year of inclusion placement. Mrs. Gardner, the head teacher for the 3- and 4-year-olds, presents his progress. Kevin's mother, Ms. Wood, who is 18 and enrolled in a work-study program, the district mainstream coordinator, and the child-care center director attend the multidisciplinary staffing.

Goals for Kevin for the year include:

1. Following the center's routines with support.
2. Beginning to use words to express needs.
3. With support, using words to solve disputes.

Mrs. Gardner reports with the assistance of checklists and anecdotal notes that Kevin does not follow the center's routines. He wanders from the group at circle time and from the playground. Kevin does not speak in intelligible language to the staff. Kevin continues to take toys away from peers and hits children when they will not give them up.

Mrs. Gardner reports that Ms. Wood has regularly volunteered with the program. She has taken a leadership role in identifying speakers and parent needs.

Mrs. Gardner likes Kevin. He is warm and affectionate in her one-on-one contacts with him. She wants to keep him at Mother Goose, but she is worried that other children and parents are beginning to complain about his combative behavior. Mrs. Gardner asks whether the mainstream coordinator can give additional specific suggestions for modifying the structure for Kevin. She asks whether there are ways that Ms. Wood and she can work together to maintain Kevin's enrollment in the Mother Goose Child-Care Center.

Also consider this final example: Jose, a second grader with a learning disability, lives in a school district that plans to move from self-contained special education to inclusion. Mr. Decker is Jose's second-grade teacher. The resource LD teacher, the inclusion administrator, the school psychologist, the speech therapist, and Mr. and Mrs. Castillo, Jose's parents, attend a multidisciplinary staffing conference.

Mr. Decker reports that Jose is cooperative and well liked by his peers. He seems to pay attention in small-group activities. When working with a partner, Jose completes written assignments quite well. In large-group discussions, Jose frequently stares out the window, fidgets, looks into his desk, and sometimes rolls his pencil on the desk. Mr. Decker and the children have learned to ignore this distracting behavior. Mr. Decker prepares written notes for Jose when necessary. Jose pays close attention when he knows something about the subject at hand.

Mr. Decker and the team make plans for third grade. They identify goals for developing and enhancing note taking and other supports for large-group discussions. Mr. Decker knows that Jose will be fine in Ms. Heather's third grade. He will talk with her about the cuing and mediation strategies that he has developed with Jose.

Mr. and Mrs. Castillo will help Jose with organizational skills in the summer, including color-coding notebooks, folders, and a planning calendar for third grade. They will send him to an art program for part of the summer. Part of the program will help Jose enhance fine-motor skills and develop his interest and skill in art.

The preceding examples show the teacher's role in the assessment system with children and parents. Another important role for teachers is reporting to additional stakeholders in the educational lives of children and families. These include administrators, boards, school councils, legislators, and the public at large. (See Box 7.7 for an example of an IEP conference summary form).

REPORTING TO OTHER STAKEHOLDERS

stakeholders people important in the lives of children, especially regarding the assessment of children.

The importance of reporting to other **stakeholders** has acquired new urgency as teachers seek to preserve the child's best interests in the face of greater demands for high-stakes performance results—No Child Left Behind and Head Start Outcomes Report, for example. Teachers must assume responsibility for reflecting, recording, and reporting group assessment results according to their holistic philosophical beliefs regarding developmentally appropriate practice. Otherwise, measuring the progress of young children may continue according to test scores and test reports alone.

One method for reporting results to these other stakeholders is to use illustrations of the progress of individual children to validate the method of teaching that you are using. For example, if your goal for first grade is to show that the children in your program can write a simple story, review individual child reports and tally how many children can write a story. Then, use samples from the reports on individual children to illustrate the different levels of sophistication of stories written by the children in your program. Thus, you have shown that children are reading and writing and that they have achieved these skills without the use of workbooks.

Box 7.7 *IEP Team Meeting*

Date_____

Child's name_____

Parents_____

Team members present

Purpose of the meeting (initial placement, ongoing planning, transitional to different program)

Meeting notes

Next steps

Lesson adaptations required

Expected learner outcomes

Products or processes that show competence

Modifications
    Presentation of tasks
    Time for completion
    Support strategies

Another method for demonstrating child accomplishment with assessment information is to use displays of work samples. Show the graphs that children are making. Display the write-ups of scientific experiments conducted by children. Show the solutions generated for performance-based tasks in social studies.

The most comprehensive way to demonstrate child and class accomplishment to other stakeholders through assessment information is to be able to describe the assessment system. You should be able to address thoughtfully the following issues in nontechnical language:

- philosophy of the program
- program goals
- teaching methods
- ways that child progress is monitored
- how adjustments are made to accomplish child goals
- ways to see the precursors of reading, writing, math, and other learnings

These are, after all, the questions that you answer in collaboration with parents. The difference in the two reports—parents/others—is the emphasis shift from an individual and particular child to a group of children. The process for preparation of an **accountability** report is the same as that illustrated in Figure 7.2. Recording and reporting assessment results to parents and others is one of the integral roles of the teacher.

accountability being responsible for the proper education of all children.

Figure 7.2
Accountability through reflection on goals and practices resulting in changes.

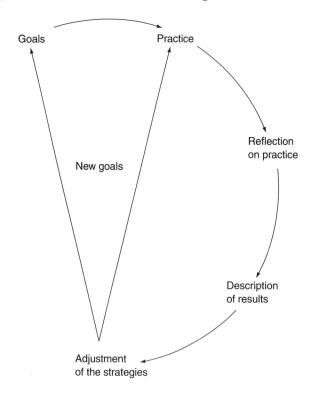

Goals

Practice

Reflection on practice

New goals

Description of results

Adjustment of the strategies

SUMMARY

Reporting assessment and progress to parents and other stakeholders is a key part of the educational process. The technique for reporting must match the purpose. Each teacher must have a repertoire of methods. At the beginning of programs, teachers describe the philosophy and curriculum to parents. Teachers report casually to parents in daily chats, telephone visits, or e-mail conversations. Teachers report at regularly scheduled times through conferences and report cards. Teachers report when problems arise. On each of these occasions, the teacher must be sensitive to the emotional and social context of the child and his or her family. Teachers must respect parents individuality. Teachers must be prepared to articulate clearly and concisely orally, in writing, and on websites. Finally, teachers must understand the role and limitations of the diverse assessment methods that are included in their program. Assessment procedures and reporting must match the philosophy and the curriculum. This includes the use of any software or Web-based programs.

FIELD ACTIVITIES

1. For a grade level of your choice, develop a performance task to address one of the required reporting areas. If possible, try the task on a child. Report and discuss your results with colleagues.

2. With permission, interview parents about their experiences in receiving information from child-care centers and schools. Discuss your experiences with colleagues. Are there any improvements that you might suggest?

3. With permission, sit in on a parent conference. After the conference discuss your observations with the teacher who conducted it. Ask any questions that may have concerned you about the proceedings.

4. With a classmate, visit a school board or local school council meeting. Observe the proceedings. Pay particular attention to issues of accountability that arise in the meeting. With a classmate, plan how you might address the requests for information that might arise if you were teaching in the school.

IN-CLASS ACTIVITIES

1. Using collected sample report cards from the communities in your area, or from the Web, examine the criteria that teachers must address. Develop an assessment plan to help you answer the questions.

2. Develop a timeline for holistic reporting system for preschool and for primary grades. Include the relevant standards addressed. Identify what information to collect as well as when to collect. Identify

summary points and procedures. Specify regular conference times for all stakeholders.

3. Design a developmentally appropriate report card for an age level of your choice.

4. Brainstorm comments that teachers or parents might make in conferences. Design a way to counter or respond to these comments in a conference (e.g., "I don't know if I should tell you this, but my wife is a meth addict." "What's the best way to get my kid to eat broccoli?" "Do you think Spruce will ever learn to add numbers? I know I hate math.").

STUDY QUESTIONS

1. What are the steps teachers must take to ensure confidentiality in the classroom?

2. How can teachers and school professionals ensure parent involvement in assessment and diagnosis? How can teachers ensure parents will feel comfortable and confident in advocating in the interests of their children?

3. What strategies will help teachers prepare for conferences with parents? How do you integrate portfolios into the parent–teacher conferences?

4. How can teachers lessen the ambiguity of report cards? How do report cards stifle the self-esteem of children? How can teachers circumvent this potential downfall?

5. What are some situation factors not reflected on report cards? How can teachers include these in the child's assessment?

6. How can you link curriculum, assessment, and reporting through the use of standards?

7. Why is it useful for teachers to consider families as "clients"?

8. How can teachers prepare for a multidisciplinary conference? What role does the teacher play in the Individualized Education Plan?

9. What are the methods teachers utilize to report results to stakeholders? How can these be included in accountability reports?

REFLECT AND RE-READ

- I know several ways to report to parents and how to involve them in the process.
- I can prepare my students for the reporting process.
- I know how to be a responsible team participant in the multidisciplinary staffing.
- I can design a report card to match my teaching philosophy.

CASE VIGNETTE

The following is an excerpt from the June report card for Mina, a first grader:

Work Habits	First Marking	Second Marking	Third Marking
Follows directions	N	N	S−
Works in a group	N	N	N
Works independently	U	N	S
Listens attentively	U	U	N
Organizes time, area, and materials	U	U	N
Works to ability	U	N	N
Demonstrates effort	N	N	N
Completes class work	U	N	S
Completes homework	U	U	N

Mina continues to be unfocused and careless in her schoolwork and when it comes to homework, forget it. She needs to improve her behavior.

Code: Unsatisfactory; Needs Improvement; Satisfactory; Excellent

What do you know about Mina's experience in first grade based on this report card excerpt? What do you imagine her achievement is like? As you prepare to welcome Mina to your second-grade class, what will you do? What assessment plan will you make?

TECHNOLOGY LINKS

http://www.aasa.org

American Association of School Administrators. Short articles that examine current trends from the administrative perspective with links to relevant websites.

http://www.ascd.org

Association for Supervision and Curriculum Development. Searchable database on topics such as report cards and other instructional issues.

http://dadsdivorce.com/

Dad's Divorce. Resources for dads including a chat opportunity.

http://kidsturn.org/

Kid's Turn is a not-for-profit organization with links for children, parents, and "others."

http://www.marchofdimes.com/

March of Dimes. Public interest information on babies and children with disabilities.

http://www.naesp.org

National Association for Elementary School Principals. Reproducible bulletins on current topics to share with parents. Some are translated into Spanish.

http://www.psparents.net/

Public School Parents Network. Resources for issues that affect parents in public schools.

http://singlemothers.org

National Organization of Single Mothers. Discusses all of the issues facing the single mother; includes a chat room.

8

Building a Child Study

- Apgar Rating Scale
- child study
- primary responsibility
- Child Find team
- diagnostic evaluation
- referral questions
- typical development
- atypical development

Chapter Overview

This chapter shows how a child study serves as a summary point in a comprehensive assessment system. The first part of the chapter identifies the purposes of child studies. Then, the discussion delineates the elements of child studies and gives suggestions for writing child studies. Finally, there are examples of child studies with analyses and issues to ponder.

Assess as You Read

- What can I use, in addition to tests, to create a child study?
- When will I need to conduct a child study?
- What are some important elements of a child study?
- When I write my report, what are some limitations that I must keep in mind?

CHILD STUDIES IN THE ASSESSMENT SYSTEM

A **child study** is an in-depth look at a particular child at a specific point in time. A study summarizes the information available from all sources: child, parent, teacher, and specialist. In addition, the study raises and answers questions through the process of gathering the material for the report of the child study. Some studies are brief and geared to one developmental or teaching issue. Other studies are complex and include formal assessment.

PURPOSES OF CHILD STUDIES

Child studies serve diverse purposes. A study summarizes available knowledge about a child at a moment in time. In early childhood, different professionals may assume **primary responsibility** for the preparation

of this summary report, depending on the age of the child and any questions about learning, behavior, or development.

Apgar Rating Scale
screening test given to
newborn infants 1 minute
and 5 minutes after birth.

- *At birth*, Sheila—who shows a low on the **Apgar Rating Scale** score—will have a case study summarizing available medical and social history information. Plans derived from the known information delineate the proposed medical intervention. The physicians plan diagnostic tests. If necessary, social workers gather further family history and plan social service intervention.

Child Find team   group
of professionals whose
responsibility it is to
determine children with
special needs.

diagnostic evaluation
see diagnostic tests.

primary responsibility
the person expected to
perform a certain task.

- *At preschool*, the **Child Find team** summarizes screening results on Oswald. Oswald shows no difficulties. Thus, the child study ends.

- Ricardo displays speech and language problems. After screening results substantiate the teacher's perception, the Child Find team refers Ricardo and his family to a speech therapist for **diagnostic evaluation**—an in-depth, specialist-conducted assessment related to the developmental or learning aspect in question. The child study then evolves. First, the Child Find team assumes **primary responsibility** for summarizing Ricardo's available history and screening results. Then, the speech therapist adds diagnostic assessment results and addresses any questions that may occur during the assessment process. If the speech therapist questions Ricardo's intellectual capacity, then a referral to a psychologist occurs. The evolution of the study continues. At any point in the process, the Child Find team members discuss a summary of the available information and results with Ricardo's parents so that permission for diagnostic assessment can be obtained and so that plans for Ricardo can be made.

The following are examples of the different situations in which a **child study** might evolve:

child study   in-depth
look at a particular child at
a specific point in time.

- Ms. Hayes, who teaches at Merry Mack Preschool, meets twice a year with parents. She collects observational material and samples of each child's work and writes a narrative report to share with parents. There is a child study of progress at Merry Mack for each child in the program.

- Mr. Anastasiow worries about Albert, a second grader. Albert seems sad. He has no friends at school. He watches everything and seems to know answers when called upon, but does not complete any projects or write in his journal. Mr. Anastasiow gathers any available achievement test scores and his own observations and contacts Albert's parents to share his concerns. He summarizes the material. A child study evolves.

- Ms. Zecker visits a first-grade class to observe the dual-language learners. She spots Sarah, whose first language is English. In conversation with Sarah, conducted in Spanish, Ms. Zecker concludes that Sarah will require tutoring in Spanish vocabulary related to school topics. She wonders if this vocabulary limitation relates to other learning problems and suggests that the school conduct a bilingual learning disabilities assessment. A diagnostic child study evolves.

In each of these examples, the reasons for developing the child study are different. The procedures are the same: summarizing and organizing information for effective screening, assessment, and intervention planning for children.

ELEMENTS OF A CHILD STUDY

Items to consider in answering questions about a child's development include those listed in the following section. Whichever professional is initiating the study or whoever is the case manager should comment on known information in these areas. When information is unknown or when there are different perceptions about available facts, summaries

referral questions
questions posed in a child study to aid in the determination of the specific problems and needs of a child and the assessing of the developmental progress of the child.

serve to identify questions for further investigation. What are the **referral questions**—the questions from various stakeholders about problems or learning and developmental progress? A child study is a dynamic process. The process begins with basic demographic information that is pertinent to the questions at the time. As available and for serving the child and family, items to consider include the following:

- Identifying information: name, age, sex, birth date
- Description of the child: appearance, general physical characteristics, personality, position in the family
- Questions, concerns, problems
- Family background: siblings, family's social/economic status, known family problems, concerns, family crises or tragedies, parental attitudes, separation issues, home, neighborhood
- Medical history: circumstances of child's birth
- Early developmental milestones
- Current functioning: self-help and daily living skills; handling of body functions; body movement and use of body (motility, energy); facial expressions; speech and language; emotional reactions (expression and control of emotions and feelings, imagination and fantasy, self-concept, self-management skills); reaction to other children; reaction to adults; play or school activities; thinking and reasoning; problem-solving skills; health; developmental progress for social, emotional, cognitive, and physical skills; communication skills; school adjustment (attendance and arrival, reaction to routines, following directions, taking turns, response to support and individualization)

When a child study or summary is prepared because there is an educational or group care issue or concern, the child study may include items and descriptions related to a child's adjustment to this group setting. In addition, an observer may record, suggest, or include any ideas about any changes that may assist teachers in preparing a more suitable environment.

CONDUCTING A CHILD STUDY TO DETERMINE TEACHING OR INTERVENTION STRATEGIES

When a child study is prepared because there is a question about learning or socializing in a child-care or educational setting, consider the following factors:

- physical environment of the group setting
- snack, lunch, naps, toileting, routines
- scheduling and planning
- individualization

230

- Check accuracy of information for all the details.
- Sequence the events correctly.
- Outline the information.
- Prepare neatly and proofread.
- Check clarity of expression.
- Check to see that there is specific and descriptive information.
- Differentiate fact from impression.
  - Give test scores.
  - Include as available.
  - Interpret according to directions and limitations.
  - Watch technical aspects of the test—validity and reliability.
  - Watch age of child at administration—infant scores should be used and interpreted in preschool children only when these are a part of a trend.

- activities
- record keeping
- teacher style and interactions
- parent communication and activities

Once all the material for a child study is gathered, the teacher or other professional writes a summary report. The first step before writing the report is becoming familiar with the information available. Next, organize it to address the purpose of the study—report, referral, or summarization of a year. A checklist for preparing the report is given in Box 8.1.

EXAMPLES OF CHILD STUDIES

In the following sections, child studies are presented as examples for discussion. These case studies were submitted by students at DePaul University as a requirement for the course "Assessment in Early Childhood." The selected case studies were edited and indentities of the children were changed. Notes about the progress and limitations of the studies follow.

CHILD STUDY 1: *Bradley Howshaw, 4 years 11 months, Home-Schooled*

Background Information: Bradley is a 4-year-old Caucasian child of average height and weight. He is fair in complexion with blond hair. There is no history of medical problems, and from observation it seems that he is at expected levels for physical and cognitive development. The observer finds that he has an outgoing and pleasant personality. Bradley is the oldest of three children, with two sisters, ages 3 and 12 months. Bradley lives in an apartment in a middle-class Chicago neighborhood with his father and mother. Mr. Howshaw works full-time while Mrs. Howshaw is a homemaker. Bradley is home-schooled, but will be attending kindergarten next year. Mrs. Howshaw works with Bradley daily and says she reads frequently to him, and has done so since birth. Mr. Howshaw plays with him after work. Mrs. Howshaw tells the observer that she is looking forward to her son starting school because she feels he is bored at home. She feels that being in a classroom will keep him more structured and appropriately motivated. Bradley's parents expect him to go to college; thus, the family engages in many mentally and physically stimulating activities together. They visit the zoo and museums, and go to plays and parks often. The family's apartment is also well suited for his appropriate development. Bradley has a large collection of books, many developmentally appropriate toys such as blocks, Lincoln logs, Legos, an easel and paint, and play dough. From all appearances Bradley seems to have a happy home life. Mrs. Howshaw says Bradley has friends in the neighborhood who will be attending his school, so she imagines that separation anxiety upon entering kindergarten will not be an issue with Bradley.

Question for This Study: The central question is whether or not Bradley is developmentally equipped to succeed in a kindergarten program. Because Bradley is home-schooled, the assessor was interested in determining whether he would be ready and well-enough equipped to achieve success.

Formal Assessment: The assessor administered the Woodcock-McGrew-Werder Mini Battery of Achievement (MBA) to Bradley one afternoon before his dinner. Bradley was excited to take the test because his mother told him he would be looking at pictures and numbers. The MBA is a brief, wide-range test of basic skills—reading, writing and mathematics—and knowledge designed for use with children and adults ages 4 through 90+. Factual knowledge is also tested. On the basic skills portion of the test Bradley scored within the high average range of scores obtained by others at his age level. His writing and mathematics scores were within the very superior range of others at his age level. His reading scores were within the high average range. The factual knowledge portion of the test is a measure of science, social studies, and the humanities (art, music, and literature). Bradley's performance on this section of the test placed him in the high average range compared to others his age who took the test. Bradley was very strong in the factual knowledge portion of the test. He named the pictures and symbols before the assessor could finish reading the question.

Bradley performed well in the identification section of the reading test, identifying correctly all letters, both upper- and lowercase. During the dictation portion of the writing section Bradley was able to print all upper- and lowercase letters asked of him. In the comprehension section of the reading test Bradley did not answer any questions correctly because he cannot read; Mrs. Howshaw told the assessor this prior to the administration of the test. Bradley does possess some decoding skills, as demonstrated by his determined efforts to sound out all the words he saw. He struggled to identify the letters *b* and the cursive *u* in the identification section. It is developmentally appropriate for him to be struggling in these areas.

In the mathematics section, reasoning and concepts, Bradley really surprised the observer with his ability to tell time by looking at a clock. Mrs. Howshaw claims he can't really tell time but is able to recognize the hour hand on the appropriate number. He failed to read the correct time on a digital clock. Bradley failed to name the days of the week, although he was able to recite correctly up to Thursday. Bradley is able to identify and print all numbers up to 10 and do basic single-digit addition. He doesn't know how to subtract. Bradley showed no problems discriminating between largest/smallest, last/middle and most/least.

Bradley separated easily from his mother for this assessment, not bothering to notice his mother watching from across the hall. He enjoyed the test, and told the assessor that some of the questions were way too easy for him. At one point when he was puzzled, he tried to stump the observer by asking a random riddle. Bradley was extremely determined and performed with complete attention with only minimal squirming during the approximately 35 minutes of assessment.

Informal Assessment: The informal assessment of Bradley is based on an interview conducted with him on a previous visit a week prior to the formal assessment. During the conversation, Bradley said he liked being read to and is learning how to play the guitar with his uncle. He stated that he is looking forward to starting school so he can learn how to read to himself and his two sisters. He also said he wants to join the school band and play guitar. When asked what he likes to do, he said watching television, playing outside, and going on walks to the park. His favorite color is blue and his current favorite book is *Squarehead.* He stated that he knows how to write his name and all the letters in the alphabet. He was very talkative during the interview, easily volunteering information and skills he has learned and things he has heard, such as songs and jokes.

Summary of the Child Study: Bradley is on-level developmentally across every area based on formal and informal observational assessments. Mrs. Howshaw's only concerns are that recently he has become very disruptive around the house. She hopes this is because he is bored from not being challenged enough socially and somewhat academically. Mrs. Howshaw says she runs a very structured and routine-based schedule with their daily instruction. She feels this will help him adapt to the regular routine of a classroom next year. Bradley performed in the high average range on the Woodcock-McGrew-Werder battery and has demonstrated normal social skills in all meetings. Based on these assessment measures, Bradley will succeed wonderfully in kindergarten.

Comments on the Child Study: This study of a typical 4-year-old boy shows that he is academically and developmentally on-target for kindergarten in the autumn. What suggestions would you make for Mr. and Mrs. Howshaw to begin the partnership with his kindergarten teacher? If they plan to home-school the sisters until kindergarten age, what, if any, suggestions would you make for modification in Mrs. Howshaw's approach?

CHILD STUDY 2: *Connie Morgan—A Family in Transition*

Connie Morgan is five and a half years old; she is the oldest of three children (Connie has one younger sister, Quinn—age 2 years—and one younger brother, Max, who is less than 1 month old). Connie is petite with a delicate bone structure, light skin tone, and strawberry blond hair. She is articulate and conveys her feelings with words that are appropriate to the situation. Connie's mother, Hazel, had a normal pregnancy and delivered at term (38 weeks). One month after Connie's birth, Hazel suffered from gallstones and was hospitalized for 1 week. Subsequent pregnancies have been without incidence. Since birth, Connie has suffered from constipation that made using the bathroom a difficult and time-consuming process, which involved crying and refusal to sit on the toilet during the toilet training years. The Morgans worked with Connie's pediatrician to find reasons for the constipation and therefore have altered her diet to aid in the process. She has not experienced the severe constipation in the last 2 years.

The Morgans are of upper-middle-class status and have the opportunity to have one parent in the home at all times. Fred Morgan is a stay-at-home father while Hazel Morgan is a software developer. The parents met and started dating in high school, married in their 20s, and waited until their early 30s to have children. Both Fred and Hazel have suffered family tragedies: when Fred was 17, his younger brother was killed in an accident while driving. Fred was the first person notified and had the responsibility of telling the rest of the family. Hazel had three family elders die in a carbon monoxide poisoning accident when she was 10. Currently, Fred is dealing with his father having lung cancer. His father is in Michigan, so Fred has gone several times in the last 3 months to visit for extended periods of time. Beyond trips to Michigan, Fred refuses to drive on the interstate within the city of Chicago. Therefore, it is rare that Connie and her siblings leave the home during the day when Hazel is at work.

Before becoming a stay-at-home father, Fred was unable to hold a job for more than 1 year. Interviews with acquaintances and personal observation lead me to describe Fred as a social person who can often be found out late on weekends around the neighborhood. As well, he often seems intoxicated early in the day. Fred has been known to be verbally abusive to his wife, many times in front of neighbors and children. I have observed occasional derogatory comments, such as "you're an idiot," directed toward Connie but never toward the younger siblings. Hazel has told me on several occasions that when she is home the children are her responsibility, as is the care of the home even if Fred is home. The Morgans currently live in a town home complex on Chicago's northwest side but are moving to Schaumburg this

fall. The new home in Schaumburg will be a large single-family home on a cul-de-sac. Their current home is a three-bedroom town home that backs up to a busy city street. Within the town home complex, many of the families are young with at least one parent staying home with the children. There are 40 children under the age of 8 living in the complex and this provides opportunity for social interaction on a daily basis. For the past 2 years, Connie has attended a local parochial preschool on a half-day basis. Because of the pending move, Connie did not return to her school for kindergarten, but will start in a public school in early November in their new community.

Connie, as described in interviews with Fred and Hazel, was on the early side of the developmental curve in comparison to other children in their social circle, but they could not come up with firm answers for dates when she first spoke, crawled, and walked. My observations show Connie to be a child who functions in a developmentally appropriate manner with abilities that include two-wheeled bike riding, scooter riding, jumping rope, skipping and running. When in a preschool program, Fred described her separation as being smooth and willing.

My observations from watching her on the playground over an extended period of days are that socially, she is often the one in control and instigates plans to exclude other children from play. Based on early childhood screening assessments I performed, I know Connie is capable of following multistep directions; however, on numerous occasions I have witnessed her refusal to follow directions given by Fred or Hazel.

She often lashes out at Fred with bouts of screaming and quick comments about his abilities as well as her thoughts about him. Comments that I have heard over the course of several years include, "you are an idiot," and "you are the meanest father in the world, I hate you." As a parent of a child who plays with Connie, on numerous occasions I have had to explain to my child that her behavior toward Fred is not acceptable. However, I have never felt it appropriate, nor, I assume, has my child felt comfortable stepping in during her bouts of screaming and saying, "Hey, don't talk to each other like that." Perhaps my child has simply come to accept this as the way Connie and her father interact.

The purpose of this child study is to assess the possible effects of Connie not having the opportunity to begin kindergarten with her peers. While it is not possible to predict success in a child, it is necessary to watch carefully as the child goes through a series of life changes. With this child study, I am asking: Has she obtained and is she retaining the skills necessary for kindergarten and is she receiving the stimulation necessary to bridge the gap between June and November? I am asking this question while bearing in mind that within the period of 3 months, there is significant change happening in Connie's life:

1. All of her neighborhood friends, her daily playmates during the summer, are back in school for a good part of each day.
2. Connie must adjust to the addition of a new sibling.
3. The family is starting to pack for their upcoming move.
4. Connie will have to say goodbye to friends she has grown up with in her old neighborhood.
5. Connie will have to go through the process of being the new kid in the class, at a time in the school year when relationships have already been formed within the classroom environment.

To address the purpose of this child study, I utilized two assessment methods: a Kindergarten Screening assessment tool, and social interaction observations of Connie as an individual with friends and Connie with her family in social situations. In an ideal world, I would have the opportunity to follow Connie to her new school and community and see how her social behavior is affected by the move and all of the changes she is experiencing. It will be the role of the new teacher to take this information provided and build on it based on observations post-move.

To measure the academic progress of Connie, I used the Brigance K–1 Screen. This screening tool gave me the opportunity to observe Connie's cognitive abilities and retention of skills learned in preschool. The screening was performed in my home at the kitchen table during the early afternoon. This is a location that Connie has visited on a number of occasions so she is familiar with the setup and the environment. Connie was inquisitive during the screening procedure and at times she offered alternative answers to questions she could not answer in the manner required. I was intrigued that Connie insisted that we call the Brigance K–1 Screen an interview rather than a test. In response to the information learned through the Brigance screening, the following report will be submitted to Hazel and Fred Morgan:

Parent Report: Brigance K–1 Screening: Connie was successful in her completion of the Brigance K–1 Screen. The Brigance Screen is set up to measure a wide representation of skills. She has retained critical knowledge from preschool, which suggests successful performance in kindergarten. It appears that Connie understood the idea of doing a screening because several times she suggested we refer to it as an interview instead of a test.

In reviewing the test protocol, you will find that Connie successfully answered most questions and scored 97/100 points. Some areas that I would like to point out to you include:

- Personal Data Response: In this section, you will see that though Connie could not give her address, she voluntarily supplemented with her home phone number. Her responses were without pause and appeared confident.
- In the rote-counting category, she successfully counted through 10 and continued up to 38 without error.
- In the category titled "Number Comprehension," Connie successfully made correspondences between objects and numbers. She completed this category utilizing groups of pencils and later by drawing the number of objects given.
- In the gross-motor-skills category, she successfully completed all tasks and supplemented with a high kick after standing on the left foot for an extended period of time, suggesting that she has good coordination.
- In the recommendations section, you will notice that according to the score given upon completion of the screening and observations regarding her expansion of the responses, I conclude that Connie may qualify for a gifted and talented program. However, bear in mind that the purpose of the Brigance K–1 Screen is to measure abilities and what is known by the child. A decision regarding gifted and talented abilities should be made by someone qualified to screen for gifted and talented students while utilizing an appropriate diagnostic tool.

To aid in Connie's assimilation into the new kindergarten, being that she will start mid-year, it would be valuable to contact the new teacher and request information and available materials about units being studied in the classroom in the months of September and October. As a parent, you can help Connie by addressing some of the ideas being studied in the units so that she has the same base knowledge as the other students when topics are revisited later in the year. Also, request information about what Connie can do at home to supplement the work that is being done at various learning centers within the classroom.

Comments on the Chid Study: In this study we have rich detail about the family life and Connie's social interactions with peers in a neighborhood setting. If you were the Schaumburg kindergarten teacher who will receive Connie in November, what would you do to welcome her? What further assessments might you conduct? What problems might you anticipate?

CHILD STUDY 3: *Beatrice Jewel, an Adopted Toddler*

Beatrice is a 5.2-year-old African American child who was adopted at 18 months by Mr. and Mrs. Jewel (also African American). She currently attends kindergarten at the neighborhood public school. Prior to entering kindergarten this fall, she was in a preschool program at a for-profit commercial child-care center. She was the youngest child in the family until the birth of her little brother in 2002. She has an older brother who is 9 years old. She lives with her mother, father, and brothers in an affluent suburban community. Not much is known about Beatrice's biological parents or health and family history, but Beatrice's adopted parents are both college-educated, having attained master's degrees in their fields of study. English is the only language spoken at home. Mrs. Jewel is a stay-at-home mom, having elected to do so after the birth of her son in 2002. She values the importance of schooling, and thus is very involved in her children's education and facilitates literacy activities in the home at every opportunity. She loved to read as a child and into adulthood, and subsequently obtained a B.A. and M.A. in English. Prior to electing to stay at home, she was employed as a technical writer.

Beatrice is very sociable, talkative, inquisitive, and accommodating, as noted in my various interactions with her. She is confident and secure in her role and position in the family. Her hygiene is well maintained, and she is always dressed cleanly in conservative clothing. She possesses typically described normal self-help and daily living skills. Her emotional status appears to be intact and normal (appropriate affect, happy, playful, etc.). Her overall health and development appears to be normal as observed via sentence structure and language skills, conversational skills, listening skills, and math one-to-one correspondence skills. Mr. and Mrs. Jewel believe that Beatrice is developing normally and have even been told that Beatrice is above average for her age, as documented on numerous teacher assessments from the preschool. Mr. and Mrs. Jewel are somewhat curious about this, and thus supported the idea of doing an assessment, specifically in reading skills or reading ability.

The Test of Early Reading Ability—Third Edition (TERA-3) was chosen for three reasons: one, appropriateness for the type of assessment to be done; two, ease of administration; and three, quickness of administration—Beatrice is 5.2 years old and generally cannot sit still for long periods of time. Form B of the TERA-3 was administered to Beatrice at her home, 20 minutes after arriving from school at 3:40 P.M. She had been told by her mother 2 days before that I would be coming over to administer the test. Beatrice was excited and eager to take the test. The test was conducted in the well-lit kitchenette area at the family dining table. The testing area was free from distractions because her older brother and mother were in another part of the house working quietly, her younger brother was at child care, and her father was at work. In addition the ringers on the phones were turned off. The total test time was 30 minutes. Beatrice began to drift toward the end of testing, specifically toward the end of the third subtest, which assessed meaning. Beatrice was praised and encouraged throughout the testing period per the guidelines set forth in the TERA-3 Examiner's Manual.

Beatrice scored equally well in Conventions and Meaning, receiving a standard score of 10 in each section. This translates to average for both subtests. Thus 50 percent of the standardization sample scored the same or below Beatrice in each of these two sections. Alphabet was Beatrice's strength, as evident from a standard score of 15, which was superior. Thus,

95 percent of the standardization sample scored the same or below Beatrice in this section. Her Composite Quotient was above average at 111.

Based on Beatrice's test results and the interpretation guidelines of the TERA-3, she appears to be good at phonics and decoding words in print. She generally understands how to hold a book and where to start reading. She exhibits some difficulty in knowing when to turn a page at times, and appears to not have a clear understanding of different parts of a book or different functions of punctuation marks. She exhibits difficulty in recognizing signs and knowing their meaning, but appears to grasp logos and their meanings.

It seems that Beatrice has benefited from an aggressive in-home literacy program along with her natural abilities. A continuation of emphasis on literacy will continuously propel Beatrice forward and enhance learning potential and skills in all developmental domains (language arts, math, science, art, music, physical/motor, social/emotional). Suggested activities might include reading stories aloud and having her summarize them; choosing books that have numbers corresponding to pictures, books with science themes, and books with heart themes; visiting the American Heart Association's website; and singing nursery rhyme songs.

Case Comments on the Child Study: Beatrice seems to be a typical first grader in terms of overall development and progress in reading. It is November, what should her first-grade teacher do to support Beatrice's growth? What recommendations do you have for Mr. and Mrs. Jewel?

CHILD STUDY 4: *Angela, a Second Grader*

Angela has been observed three times and interviewed once by an outside consultant to her second-grade classroom. Ms. Kim describes Angela as a friendly, sensitive, and shy 7-year-old. Angela attends an urban public school in a predominantly Puerto Rican neighborhood. The school divides students into classrooms based on English-language strength in four levels and by parent request. Angela's home language is Spanish; she is in the English-only second grade by parent request. Angela, her mother, her older 8-year-old brother, and her mother's boyfriend, Jose, live in the home. Jose works as a janitor and her mother stays home with the children. Angela has no contact with her biological father. Angela's mother uses an authoritarian discipline style with her children. Angela has no history of medical problems and seems to be at expected developmental levels for physical and cognitive development. She seems shy in large-group classroom situations, but is comfortable in small-group activities. Her mother comes to school daily to drop off and pick up her children and asks about Angela's progress; communication with the second-grade teacher is limited by her mother's English fluency issues and the second-grade teacher's limited Spanish vocabulary.

Ms. Kim wanted to see what progress Angela was making in language arts. She describes the classroom as a literacy-rich one where there are many opportunities for all language arts, with many books available and accessible to students.

In the first observation, Ms. Kim spent the morning observing Angela using the four language processes: reading, writing, listening, and speaking. She showed no difficulty with reading, speaking, and listening. The writing assignment required children to write three things that go together; the class was studying comma usage. Angela had difficulty with this assignment. Ms. Kim asked her the following questions: What are three things that you like to eat? What are your favorite zoo animals? What are your favorite things to do at school or home? Angela wrote: I live at home with my mother, Jose, and my brother.

For observation two, Ms. Kim observed Angela in a class discussion activity. The teacher would read a page on animal tracks, and all of the other children tried to guess the animal. Angela tried to hide behind other students to avoid answering the questions raised by the teacher about a story on animal tracks.

During the last observation, Ms. Kim led a small group of children in a guided reading activity that included Angela. First, the children took a picture walk through the story. Angela was able to describe pictures in detail. Page reading by each child in the group followed. Then shared reading occurred. Angela performed successfully in both situations, reading with enthusiasm and confidence.

Ms. Kim administered the Developmental Reading Assessment (DRA) (1994), using the story *The Wagon*. Angela's running record shows 98.5 percent accuracy. She was able to determine story meaning from the context. She used sight word recognition strategies. She replaced sight words with other high-frequency words when she made errors. She tried to use pictures for clues in these situations and used pictures as a problem-solving strategy. In the retelling analysis, Angela was able to tell the story in her own words, including characters, important details, special phrases from the story, the setting, and the major events in the correct sequence. Angela enjoys reading before she goes to sleep, and when she has difficulty sleeping she reads to her stuffed animals. Her favorite books are the Arthur series by Marc Brown.

Ms. Kim recommends that Angela continue to read. She further suggests that the third-grade teacher promote and encourage Angela to speak Spanish with her peers who also speak her first language.

Reflections: Ms. Kim finds this performance assessment effective and efficient. It is not an in-depth measure, and Ms. Kim thinks another measure that focuses on language development would be a wise next step.

Comments on the Child Study: Ms. Kim is very concerned about the language development of young children. She wants to be assured that a child's culture and language is respected. As well, she wants to be sure that an English-only situation supports Angela's learning. Do you think she is justified in her perception that Angela is well served in this program? Why do you think Ms. Kim and Angela's mother have different opinions about English-only education?

CHILD STUDY 5: *Marlene*

Marlene is a 4.2-year-old who lives in an upper-class suburb of a major city. Her father works full-time and her mother works 3 to 4 days per week; both hold professional positions. A nanny cares for Marlene when her parents are not at home. At home, Marlene helps her sister, who is in kindergarten, with her homework, loves being read to, and listens to her oldest sister, who is in third grade, read the Harry Potter books. The central question chosen by the observer, Ms. Katz, is: Is Marlene developmentally equipped to succeed in a preschool program? Currently, Marlene attends a park-district preschool program where screening occurs only when teachers think there is a developmental delay. Marlene was observed twice in the preschool setting and once at home. Her mother was interviewed as well.

Marlene is very small (25th height/weight percentile at her recent physical; 10th percentile in prior years) and very quiet in the preschool setting. She speaks only when called on in the circle activities. She seems to engage mostly in parallel play. She seems to have one friend in the class who is also a small girl. When Ms. Katz approached her, she engaged easily, but became shy when other children approached her.

DIAL3: Developmental Indicators for the Assessment of Learning (1998) was administered at Marlene's home after lunch at a child-sized table. She performed all of the gross-motor tasks with ease. Fine-motor tasks were completed easily, as well. She drew six out of eight shapes and started writing her name, but drifted at the end.

In the concepts area, Marlene knew 8 out of 10 body parts, 7 out of 7 colors, and could name 23 out of 25 colors in 30 seconds. She mixed up some of her number sequences, but she soared in the concept of position and description, scoring 6 out of 6 and 12 out of 12, respectively.

For the language area, Marlene supplied personal data. Articulation errors occurred with *s, sh*, and *th*. She named objects and supplied appropriate actions. Marlene can sing the alphabet song, but can only identify (by sound) one out of seven letters in print. She has a perfect score on rhyming and zero on "I spy." Marlene performed well on the problem-solving game; she understands the basics of problem solving.

Marlene separated easily from her mother for this assessment; her mother went grocery shopping. She enjoyed the games, but told Ms. Katz that she was too smart for some of the questions. Marlene was persistent and performed with absolute attention, with only some wiggling. The assessment experience lasted 30 minutes; both Marlene and Ms. Katz felt energized at the end.

Summary Scores for Marlene:

Area	Scale Score Total	Percentile Rank
Motor	17	92
Concepts	21	90
Language	19	90
Total	57	94

Ms. Katz wonders if Marlene is understimulated in class; is this why she is silent? Her teachers might try asking her more difficult questions. She recommends that more writing activities be promoted for Marlene and the other children as well.

Reflections by Ms. Katz: This experience helped Ms. Katz to understand more concretely what is "normal" for children ages 3 to 6. Ms. Katz says: "I may have underestimated preschoolers in the past." Before she assessed her, Ms. Katz thought that Marlene was not prepared for a 4-year-old preschool experience, so her eyes are open now! Ms. Katz reports that the DIAL3 is easy to administer, but requires a couple of run-throughs before administering because it has so many parts.

Comments on the Child Study: Marlene is new to this preschool program. She relates easily to adults. Are there experiences in her home life that might contribute to her being somewhat quiet? Do you share Ms. Katz's perspective on the need to encourage Marlene to be more vocal? What academic interventions are indicated for this preschool program?

CHILD STUDY 6: *Jacob, a First Grader*

Ms. Russo became concerned about the developmental and learning progress of Jacob during the first 2 months of first grade. She planned a special assessment using anecdotal notes, running records, functional assessment, a rating scale, the Peabody Individualized Achievement Test-Revised (PIAT-R) (1993), and formal and informal reading, writing, and math assessments. In addition, she will analyze the daily reflections that she has been keeping on Jacob.

Background Information: Jacob's first experience with school began in kindergarten; he attends the same school for first grade in a suburban public school near a large urban area. Jacob is of average height and is overweight for a 6.11-year-old. Jacob is losing baby teeth, as are his classmates. He is sent to school dressed neatly and casually. He doesn't mind getting dirty at recess.

Jacob lives with his mother and 10-year-old brother. Jacob's parents are divorced; he has regular contact with his father. His mother is critical of his father's living environment and the absence of structure, as well as the activities that some of the adults engage in around the children when they visit. Jacob's paternal grandfather cares for him regularly; Jacob's mother approves of this relationship. Jacob calls his mother's boyfriend his uncle-dad. The boyfriend helps him with homework, reads to him, and plays with him. His mother recently rearranged her work schedule to be home after school, and reports that Jacob is affectionate and that he enjoys playing video games—an activity that he will continue until redirected.

Fine-Motor Development

Jacob uses his right hand to print, color, and cut. He holds pencils with an appropriate grip. Though Jacob is capable of providing neat work, he performs inconsistently.

Both the physical education teacher and Ms. Russo report some delay in development here. Jacob seems to lack bodily kinesthetic awareness. For example, Jacob rarely sits on his bottom on a chair. He sits a variety of ways, including on his knees; he stands; he lies across the table. Ms. Russo tried a functional analysis to improve his sitting behavior, but she was unable to identify a consistent antecedent behavior.

When walking in the hall and at transition times, Jacob frequently hops, skips, jumps, spins around, walks in baby steps, walks with feet spread wide apart, or walks backward. He will do this until redirected. Sometimes, he merely shifts the alternative walking style. These behaviors often make him tarry behind his classmates. Jacob never has an explanation for walking differently. Although this walking pattern has a strong behavioral component, Ms. Russo feels that he does not have a sense of where his body is in relation to others.

Social Development

Jacob is very kind and helpful to others. He will push in the chairs of others, bring lost items from the playground to children who leave their coats, and pick up dropped items. He shares materials and will readily volunteer a crayon for someone who doesn't have the right color.

In all social situations—individual, small group, and large group—Jacob has a short attention span. For example, during a 30-minute lesson that included discussion, then a story, then more discussion, Jacob made eye contact with the teacher conducting the lesson only three times. He looked in every other direction including left, right, up, down, and backward. His hands were busily playing with his ears, nose, and lips during the lesson.

Jacob often talks while other students are talking, Ms. Russo is talking, or during quiet activity periods. His peers are upset and frustrated with him.

When called on in a large-group discussion—Jacob volunteers frequently—he hides his face, starts to blush, or mumbles: "I don't know" or "I forgot."

Ms. Russo completed an Attention Deficit Disorders Evaluation Scale that is available from the school counselor. The counselor will score the scale and return it to Ms. Russo. Although Ms. Russo does not have the results, on the 60-item 5-point Likert scale, Jacob scores in the range that she believes will show ADD of some type.

Emotional Development

Jacob generally seems happy. He acts proud of stories that he writes in writer's workshop, and looks content during reading time. He is easily frustrated when confronted with difficulties in reading at the instructional level. He gives up and wants to read materials that he can manage at an independent level.

When children try to cue him to be quiet with the agreed-upon class signal, he becomes annoyed and shouts at them to leave him alone.

Language Development

Jacob lacks confidence in speaking in class. In reading he scored at the 30th percentile on the PIAT-R and scored 59 out of 331 on a district-wide reading assessment given to all first graders in August. He is a beginning writer; his writing conveys meaning. He can read his writing and sometimes others can read it. He has difficulty listening to and following directions.

Cognitive Development

Jacob has a good concept of number and is developing a strong concept of addition. In problem-solving situations, Jacob has difficulty in moving beyond literal levels.

Overall PIAT-R results show Jacob to be in the 42nd percentile. Working with his parents, the school is starting an investigation to support Ms. Russo's hypothesis of ADD. The Child Find team will be involved in supporting Ms. Russo as she tries to scaffold learning for Jacob.

Comments on the Child Study: Ms. Russo has developed a comprehensive portrait of Jacob, a young boy with limited school experience, obesity, and a budding reputation as a "social" problem in the classroom. Though some of the development areas reflect material that might be construed as academic in nature, the picture of the overlap of behavioral issues as they interface with academics seems clearly drawn. What special modifications might you think about to assist Jacob as you wait for the completion of the referral process?

CHILD STUDY 7: *Matilde*

Ms. Wolf conducted an evaluation of Matilde, a 6-year-old, in her home setting. She administered the Stanford Early School Achievement Test (SESAT) (1989).

Background Information: Matilde attended half-day preschool programs from the time she was 3. She began all-day kindergarten in a suburban private school, where she continues in first grade. Matilde has one older brother in fourth grade and a younger brother in kindergarten. She is fluent in Spanish and English, although she reads and writes in English only.

The SESAT was administered after dinner at the kitchen table in Matilde's home, while her mother and brothers were occupied in another room. The test took some time to administer and toward the end, Matilde tired. She also did not like doing the silent reading portion.

Matilde's performance is summarized as follows:

- She did well on the sounds of letters portion, matching correctly the sounds of letters to pictures and words. She used picture clues to help.
- She did have some difficulty in putting letters together to form words, after sounding them out.
- She seems to have a short attention span related to reading.

- She did not remember the minor details from stories, although she could tell me the main ideas.
- In math, Matilde understands one-to-one correspondence, number sense, shapes, and patterns. She enjoyed the nonroutine math problems.
- She has good initial understanding of time and currency.

Reflections by Ms. Wolf: "I felt comfortable with the test and chose it because the norms are based on a diverse population. The directions were clear and precise; I felt prepared after running through it three or four times, before administering the test."

Comments on the Child Study: This report contains no standard scores, so we must rely on Ms. Wolf's interpretation of the strength of Matilde's performance. What would the next assessment step be for this first grader who, according to Ms. Wolf, is on-target? Does she have the requisite skills for the first-grade curriculum in your district/state?

CHILD STUDY 8: *Baby Ralph*

Ralph is a 12-month-old who receives monthly early intervention sessions to monitor his development in all areas. He lives with his mother, father, and 7-year-old sister, Tracey. Services were initiated following the death of his 3-year-old brother, Michael, in a home accident. Michael was involved in a preschool special education program before his death. Tracey had been scheduled to be screened by the school district to determine if she had special education needs before Michael's death and her own injuries in the home accident.

Ralph's mother, Connie, is 21 years old. She received special education services for the mildly mentally retarded from elementary school through the beginning of high school. She quit high school in her first year due to an unplanned pregnancy. Connie is quiet, often looks depressed, and holds her head down when spoken to. She makes little eye contact. She says that Ralph is smarter than Michael was and she is not sure why Ralph needs this program, yet she comes each month and calls if she has to miss. She loves her children. She does make eye contact with them and provides them with food and clothing. She does not talk to them very much.

Ralph's father, Arthur, age 29, has a high school diploma and works seasonal jobs. Ralph's parents do not view him as having any special needs. Child assessment revealed that Ralph is approximately 6 months delayed in personal, social, and communication development. Qualitative concerns exist with fine- and gross-motor development.

Ralph receives health care through the County Hospital Medicaid Program. Extended family members assist with financial needs. Tracey receives treatments for her burns in a large Los Angeles hospital 35 miles from home. Prior to Michael's death, Connie received birth control services and counseling from a California Public Health Program, but services were discontinued due to funding cuts. Connie pursued her GED but discontinued the program due to learning difficulties. Homemaker services were also being investigated but were discontinued at the parent's request. Connie has expressed an interest in obtaining a job.

Parent Requests

A job for mother; a second-grade program for Tracey.

Providers' Assessment of Need

Parenting skills; parent-child interactions; homemaker skills; financial planning assistance; special education screening for Tracey; tutoring for GED courses, vocational assessment, assistance in placement; and health care management.

Comments on the Child Study: The writer is an early intervention specialist who has summarized notes of an initial conference with Connie, Ralph's mother. She has identified the problems that the family presents, both from the record and from the interview. She has made notes of what the family wants in further early intervention service. In addition, she has prepared her own list of suggested services. At a multidisciplinary staffing, she will choose which of the suggestions to share immediately and relate those to parent goals. The effectiveness of future collaboration will depend on the sensitivity of the specialist in weaving the different agendas—parent and early intervention—together.

CHILD STUDY 9: *Ted*

A physician who, along with Mr. and Mrs. Miller, was concerned about a possible language delay and the quality of Ted's walking had referred Ted, a 21-month-old and his mother, Mrs. Miller, for assessment. The doctor's report stated that Ted had been suffering from upper respiratory problems and ear infections since 1 month of age. Ted's mother filled out a family form that stated that the oldest sibling, now 10 years old, was an apnea baby. The 5-year-old sibling has no hearing in one ear, and the 3-year-old sibling is in an early intervention program due to a developmental speech delay. Mrs. Miller drives the 3-year-old to therapy appointments three times per week.

Developmental History: The Shaker Heights Child Find program was responsible for screening Ted a day after his first birthday. At that time, the Denver Developmental Screening Test results indicated a slight language delay. All other areas were scored within normal limits. However, during this time frame Ted had eye surgery due to one eye turning inward. He is to wear prescription lenses with bifocals. Mrs. Miller reported that she has been busy with her other children and cannot buy the glasses until next month.

The Battelle Development Inventory was used to determine if Ted was eligible for services 6 months ago when he was 15 months old. At that time, Ted performed well in the cognitive domain and passed in the area of gross-motor skills. He passed, even though he could walk only 2 feet before falling down, as reported by the nurse. The occupational therapist explained that the quality of the walking is not a consideration with this test. Ted scored at 11 months in expressive communication and at 9 months in receptive communication. Once again a discrepancy seemed to exist since Ted used no speech imitations, no word sounds, and could not follow any directions. However, at the same time, Mrs. Miller reported that Ted said a few words. The developmental specialist who did the testing was confused by the results and recommended an arena assessment, so that other specialists might contribute insights.

Mrs. Miller scheduled an appointment within a month but did not keep the appointment. Mrs. Miller reported that her mother was ill and that she had assumed care of her. This care included having her mother move to the family home. For the next 5 months, all attempts to reach her were unsuccessful. Finally, Mrs. Miller initiated contact with the center and reported that in the interim her husband had walked out on her, the four children, and her mother. At this point she had contacted a lawyer to file for maintenance support.

Arena Assessment: Ted, on the day of the arena assessment, was wearing his shoes on the wrong feet to correct a "toeing in" problem. Mrs. Miller also had not bought the corrective shoes that were prescribed months ago.

Ted held up well throughout the 1-hour session. The occupational therapist used a fine-motor adaptive checklist that combined items from the Bayley Scales of Infant Development, the Revised Gesell Developmental Schedules, and the Denver Developmental Screening Tests—Revised. At 21 months, Ted vocalizes but does not talk. He does a lot of "mouthing" of objects. He enjoys putting objects into a container and taking them at. He turned his head to sounds made behind and to each side of him but he did not seem to comprehend the words. Sometimes he responded to gestures or demonstration. He did not respond to a loud, firm "no" from the therapist who tried to get him to stop an activity. There was no eye contact made and Ted appeared to have difficulty focusing on objects.

The physical therapist concluded that Ted is unstable when walking, has difficulty getting into and out of a chair, trips himself when attempting to run, cannot step on an object on the floor, cannot shift the weight of his feet, and cannot climb stairs. According to the physical therapist, Ted's problem seems to be solely in his feet: "His hips are in place and structurally he looks good."

The speech therapist seemed to feel that the inside of Ted's mouth looked intact, but she could not continue her assessment because Ted was ready for a nap and began to cry.

Discussion: The members of the team met for an hour after the assessment session. They completed a checklist and summarized as follows: Ted was content throughout the session. Although unaware of the situation, he was friendly, cooperative, and moderately active. He adapted to the tasks required. He was tolerant of handling. Socially, Ted showed poor responses to interaction and initiated no interaction. He was not distracted by visual or auditory stimuli. Even though he did not understand the tasks presented, he was not easily frustrated. The reliability of the test results were judged to be "average."

Comments on the Child Study: This team is just beginning to work with the family. They have identified a number of problems through observation during the arena assessment. In addition to the developmental problem, they have a record of the family emotional problems, based on the interview with Mrs. Miller. They have a history of the Millers' previous involvement with the agency. The next step will be the development of a plan that addresses the mother's emotional needs as well as Ted's early intervention needs. They have the basis of referral for social services and interagency collaboration.

CHILD STUDY 10: *Jorge, a Kindergartner*

Background Information: Jorge is a 5-year-old child enrolled in a full-day kindergarten class at an urban public school. Jorge is of average height and weight for his age. His has a medium-to-dark complexion and dark hair. Jorge's parents were born and raised in Mexico. They moved to the United States 3 years before Jorge was born. Jorge is an only child. Jorge's parents mainly speak English at home but do speak Spanish with other family members occasionally. Jorge learned both languages simultaneously as he grew up. He speaks English slightly better than Spanish due to the fact that he uses English more often. Each summer the family returns to Mexico for a few weeks, during which Jorge speaks only Spanish.

Jorge has been enrolled at the school since he was in the state prekindergarten program at age 4. I have numerous opportunities to meet with and observe Jorge because his mother is my classroom assistant. Jorge helps his mother every morning and afternoon with cleaning and preparing my classroom. He often talks to me about his school day or what books he read. Jorge willingly helps his mom with any task but especially loves putting the books away. Jorge and I talk often about books and his schoolwork. Every day at 2:30 he comes down to my classroom to meet his mom and announces that he received a 100 percent on his test or homework. He also pulls all his papers out and displays them to his mom and me. Jorge obviously takes great pride in his work. Jorge recently received an award for reading the most Accelerated Reader books in the kindergarten!

Jorge's mother is very involved in her son's education. She speaks with his teachers every day and often requests extra work for him at home. Jorge's parents have limited formal education—the equivalent of a high school diploma. However, they would like to see Jorge go to college. Jorge and his parents engage in many stimulating activities together as a family. They often go to the zoo, museums, and parks. Jorge replays these events for me each morning while preparing the classroom. Jorge's home environment is also very suitable for his development. He has a large library of books, numerous appropriate and open-ended toys such as blocks and Legos®, and a wide array of art supplies and play dough. Jorge is very well spoken for his age. I observed his vocabulary to be well above that of most of his peers. I have often observed Jorge to initiate conversations with adults in topics ranging from his school day to his most recent outing to the zoo. His extended family includes numerous cousins his age whom he frequently spends time with. There are also a few families with children his age living on his block. This allows Jorge frequent opportunities to socialize outside of school with children close to his age.

Developmental History: Jorge's mother reports typical development throughout infancy and toddlerhood. He was walking by 12 months and talking in sentences by age 2. Characteristic of boys, his toilet training began at age 2 but he was not fully trained until he was 30 months old. She reports that he has always been especially interested in animals and clearly spoke words such as *cow* and *dog* by age 1!

Jorge's mother is concerned because his teacher, Ms. Swenson, is reporting that Jorge is talking too often and at inappropriate times during class. Mrs. Sanchez is concerned that Jorge needs some extra attention or maybe more playtimes with children his own age at home. Ms. Swenson has observed that Jorge disrupts students working around him to talk to or laugh with. Mrs. Sanchez also thinks that maybe Jorge is too bored in school and possibly needs to be in the next grade or needs more advanced work.

Mr. Sanchez expressed the opinion that Jorge is functioning at a higher cognitive level than the rest of the children in the kindergarten. Both parents reported that he is reading books at home with very little adult assistance. He also adds money and counts change for his piggy bank at home. If Ms. Swenson continues to have difficulty with Jorge, they do not want to transfer him to the half-day kindergarten because they have very limited resources for child care for him. Mr. and Mrs. Sanchez feel that Jorge is more advanced than the rest of the children in the class and this is causing his disruptive behavior. They feel that putting him in a first-grade classroom will keep him more focused and attentive to his more-challenging work.

When questioned about his behavior, Jorge stated he spoke to the other children because he was finished with his work. His parents have also talked to him about this and expressed to him that this may be the cause. Jorge responded that he normally talked to two specific friends about schoolwork or other people in the room. He also said he thought the work was really easy.

Question for This Study: Based on Mr. and Mrs. Sanchez's concern, the basis of this clinical study is to determine the readiness of Jorge for first grade at this November date. The results of the study are intended to assure the parents that Jorge is in the most appropriate class. The study will include interviews with teachers, interviews with the parents, interviews with Jorge, informal assessments, and the results of the Metropolitan Performance Assessment.

School History and Academic Progress: Jorge attended the prekindergarten class at our school last year in the mornings. Ms. Cooper, his previous teacher, reported that Jorge's play and social behaviors were all appropriate for his age. She noted his exceptional language and cognitive development. Jorge loved reading about animals he had seen at the zoo such as lions and flamingos. His knowledge about specific zoo animals was more extensive than she had ever seen from a child at his age. He appropriately labeled all animals in her books. He had also learned to spell certain animal names, such as bear, lion, flamingo, turtle, snake, and so on. Ms. Cooper informed me that Jorge often played with other children in associative or cooperative play without teacher direction. He had two specific male friends and they would play together most days. Their favorite activity was building a tent in the block area. They told the teacher they were sleeping in the tent in their backyards! Jorge often led these boys around the class and chose what activities to engage in during center time. Jorge spent most of center time playing with other children. He rarely painted or went to the art table independently. The teacher often prompted him to make pictures or go to the art table because he would not choose them otherwise. He did enjoy painting and coloring but usually would complete one picture then go to the blocks or truck area. Occasionally Jorge would sit in the book area and ask the teacher to read books with him. Jorge was "reading" his favorite books through memorization. He used no decoding skills. Ms. Cooper reported that he was able to dictate the sounds of specific letters, displaying emerging phonetic awareness. He was still at the prereading level. He was writing all uppercase letters and random lowercase letters.

At kindergarten, Ms. Swenson asserts that Jorge is on-level developmentally across every area based on informal observational assessments. Ms. Swenson's only concerns are Jorge's frequent disruptive talking behaviors during class. She expects most children to need time to adjust to a full-day kindergarten. Ms. Swenson's class follows a clear visual schedule that is reviewed each day. The school day is structured based on specific routines. The children have certain specific times when they are allowed to talk to the people at their tables. During other times the children are required to sit quietly and listen to the teacher. However, Jorge seems to be having more trouble adjusting than the rest of the students. Ms. Swenson notes that he is often the first to finish his work. He will talk to other children or get up from his seat and walk around the room without permission. Typically Jorge will finish his seatwork, stand up from the table, and walk around the room to the other areas even when instructed to sit in his seat. Ms. Swenson believes that Jorge's phonemic awareness skills are developing on-level according to the kindergarten guidelines for classroom work. Jorge often requests reading books and asks to go to the listening center to listen to books on tape during free time.

I observed Ms. Swenson's interactions with the children at different points throughout the day. She spoke with them during center times. She listened to their stories and concerns attentively. Most interactions involved Ms. Swenson "talking at" the students. Ms. Swenson's style of teaching is very structured and teacher-directed. The children are expected to sit quietly and follow her commands frequently throughout the day.

Interview of Jorge: Jorge said he liked to read and he wanted to be in the first grade so he could read better. I asked him what he liked about school and he responded that he liked playing with his friends, reading books, and the listening center. His current favorite book is Dr. Seuss' *ABC* and his favorite animals are baby lions. One day Jorge plans to be a veterinarian or work at a zoo.

Formal Assessment: The formal assessment used in this child study was the Metropolitan Readiness Test MRT (1995). I administered the Performance Assessment for Level 2. The test assesses objectives taught at the end of kindergarten or early in first grade. The test gives a holistic score for the child along with scores in the areas of Language/Literacy and Quantitative/Mathematics. This is a performance-based assessment that will give a measure of Jorge's readiness for first grade. The tasks are integrated within a specific theme. I decided to use both the "Pizza Party" and "Birthday Surprise" for greater reliability in results. I also wanted to have numerous documents to show his parents the results of the examination. The validity of the test is reported to be high across all measures. The author of the scoring booklet also notes that the Metropolitan Readiness Test (MRT) is an authentic measurement. The test measures the ability of the child to independently perform tasks introduced in the classroom. The behaviors necessary for the completion of each task are seen in the regular classroom. Predictive validity is not relevant in the MRT because it measures the developing concepts and strategies used by the children. The test can be administered to a group. The teacher and children are expected to interact throughout the test with the teacher observing the children to see what they are answering and how they answer. The MRT is designed to help the teacher understand what strategies and concepts the child has mastered thus far.

I completed the examination over four sessions. Jorge was very compliant and eager to finish the work with me. He insisted on taking the work home with him, so we made a copy of it together. Jorge takes great pride in his work. The most interesting aspect of the interview was watching the strategies he employed to solve the problems. Because this is a performance-based assessment I was able to observe how he processed the problem more than I was able to do with other assessments in the past. Jorge is very strong in the areas of computation. He solved the fractions problems without waiting for me to finish the explanation in the manual. He easily worked through the patterns and addition problems. The first page shows he is not wasteful with the pizza! He obviously did not fully understand the concept of splitting the pizza into four separate slices.

Jorge completed the addition problems quickly and easily. The subtraction problem took more time but he finished successfully. He finished the pattern problems with no trouble. The only area of concern was the story writing. Jorge was hesitant to even begin writing the story. He stated, "I do not know how to write." I urged him to do his best and he sounded out "pepperoni" and copied "pizza party" from the book cover. He shows phonemic awareness of a kindergarten level with only the beginning and ending syllables represented in the invented spelling of pepperoni. Overall this assessment clearly places Jorge at the kindergarten level for reading and writing but at the beginning first-grade level for math.

I also administered the "Birthday Surprise" edition of the Metropolitan Performance Test. He did very well with the patterns but had some problems with the story writing, as in the "Pizza Party" test. This shows the reliability of the test. Jorge again proved very efficient in math. His reading and writing skills place him on-level for his age. He clearly falls above average in math for a kindergartner. His reading and writing skills are average. I have a feeling Jorge has more math experience throughout his day than writing. He seemed very unsure of his abilities in reading and writing. He hesitated and wanted assistance with each reading and writing problem. His reading comprehension was shown to be higher than writing, delineating the fact that Jorge needs more writing opportunities.

Jorge has very clear strengths and weaknesses as previously discussed. Through the observations and testing procedures I have determined Jorge to be a very gregarious, communicative 5-year-old. He enjoys school and especially enjoys math. It is not atypical for a child to perform better on math than reading. Frequently, this may be the sign of a learning disability in children. Jorge, however, performs average for his age in writing and slightly higher in reading comprehension. Thus, Jorge does not need further testing. He will succeed fabulously in kindergarten proceeding with the curriculum in place. Ms. Swenson may consider providing more writing opportunities and integrating reading with math. Jorge will benefit from more proactive writing. This will give him more confidence to attempt this skill.

Jorge displays greater strength in math than reading. He has practiced at home using a number line for addition and used a number line during this test. He has not had any experience with money and values in school, but uses money at home. His reading skills are at level for a kindergartner. He had some problems with sequencing and story comprehension. He is not yet able to write word sentences, although he had no problem writing the math sentences! He was not yet able to sequence the "Birthday Surprise" story with pictures after listening to part of it. This is a first-grade skill. Additionally, he had difficulty answering the questions with pictures on the third page of "Birthday Surprise." Overall he had more difficulty with the "Birthday Surprise" than the "Pizza Party." Both are Level 2 assessments, meaning they are meant for the end of kindergarten or the beginning of first grade. Interestingly, he had no problems with the phonemic awareness skill of matching initial sounds on the first page. I am certain he performs numerous tasks similar to this each day in school, thus explaining his ease with this task. He demonstrates definite skills in identifying the initial sounds of words as evidenced through his invented spelling of *pepperoni*: "Pronee." Overall Jorge exhibits clear cognitive strengths. He is an exceptional student; however, Jorge would not benefit from skipping kindergarten for first grade. Kindergarten will provide him with the social and language-enriched base to help him move successfully through school. Jorge's parents are aware of a gifted program at a school in the district. They would like him to remain at his current school due to proximity and the fact that his mother works there. They do not want to pursue this school at this time.

Recommendations for Mr. and Mrs. Sanchez: Jorge's parents can encourage Jorge to write stories about their trips through pictures or words. Jorge should keep a journal of his trips with his family and even present them to the class. This would provide a great learning experience for Jorge and his peers. Ms. Swenson might also include journaling in the daily routines. Jorge is progressing well in his current placement and should do the same next year. Mr. and Mrs. Sanchez should be encouraged to allow Jorge to use invented spelling and pictures through his journals. They may even begin their own, as a model for Jorge.

Recommendations for Ms. Swenson: Jorge will need ample opportunities to write and share his writings. He excels at math and may be useful as a peer tutor for children struggling through math. Jorge enjoys helping others and often finishes his work quickly. This may provide time for Jorge to help around the classroom in such tasks as cleaning the fish bowl, organizing the library, or providing journaling time. Ms. Swenson can work with the fact that Jorge loves helping adults and peers. He takes every job his mother or I give to him with great seriousness and diligence. I am confident this will transfer into the classroom. At this point I do not feel that Jorge is academically ready for first grade, especially having missed the first quarter. I feel both Jorge and Ms. Swenson will benefit from thinking creatively and working together to help Jorge continue developing into a productive, successful student. Mr. and Mrs. Sanchez should be part of the process and remain the teacher's best resource for working with Jorge's strengths.

Jorge's parents agree that journaling is a fabulous idea for him. They would like to work with Ms. Swenson to see if he can work on a journal after finishing his class work. Jorge agrees that he can do this. Jorge feels he will not talk as much if he has more to do!

Comments on the Child Study: This study shows the interaction of formal knowledge with informal assessment. It also raises some issues regarding peer-teacher review. How can teachers work together in Jorge's interest? What additional curricular or instructional suggestions might you have for Ms. Swenson? Are there cues that you might suggest for Jorge, so he can perform well in a teacher-directed classroom? Do you have any other ideas about how Mr. and Mrs. Sanchez might support their son in school?

SUMMARY

Each of these examples of a child study shows a summary point in the assessment process. Teachers and others conduct child studies so that all the information on a particular child is gathered in one place. Usually this summarization occurs when there are developmental or educational questions to be answered. Then, a team of parents, teachers, and other professionals will review the available material and plan the next steps in the process.

In each of these vignettes, the reader is allowed to see the dynamic process of child-study development. The observers report progress from their vantage points. Available history and school progress are included.

typical development
the usual or expected developmental pattern of children.

atypical development
unusual developmental pattern of children.

A diverse group of studies is presented—children in various settings, of various ages, ranging from **typical** to **atypical development**, in the sophistication of the reports—to help guide you in preparing your own reports and in reading those of others.

The notes following the child studies raise questions for further consideration and elaboration of the issues and concerns. The teaching-assessment-reteaching process continues.

FIELD ACTIVITIES

1. Observe a child in school or child care. Summarize your information in a child study in as much detail as available. Outline your next teaching, intervention, or assessment steps.

2. With permission, review a child study for a child in a center or school. Outline the next steps in teaching, intervention, or assessment.

3. Plan a parent interview for a child you are studying. What additional information will assist in the teaching, intervention, or assessment of the child? Compare your notes with colleagues.

IN-CLASS ACTIVITIES

1. Pick one of the child studies presented in this chapter for further consideration. Plan the next steps in assessment, intervention, or teaching. Compare your notes with a colleague.

2. Examine one of the child studies presented in this chapter with a classmate. If the child was in your class, what would you do differently at the outset? Compare your thoughts with those of your classmate.

STUDY QUESTIONS

1. What are the purposes of a child study for early childhood teachers? Who are the key people involved in executing and evaluating the child study? What elements of a child study are most important for teachers?

2. What role does the early childhood teacher play in the Child Find team?

3. What role do child studies play in the assessment process? How does the Child Find team use child studies?

4. Why must early childhood teachers have a clear understanding of child development before completing a child study?

5. Review the examples of child studies presented in this chapter. What are the strengths and weaknesses of each? Do they include all of the components necessary for child studies? Identify the extent to which each focuses on typical and atypical child development theory.

REFLECT AND RE-READ

- I can describe the important elements of a child study.

- I know how to use a child study to answer a behavioral or academic question.

- After reading the sample case studies, I can think of ways to teach the involved children.

- I can identify more questions to ask about the children described and have some strategies for gathering more information.

TECHNOLOGY LINKS

http://www.ed.gov/policy/speced/guid/idea/idea2004.html

The U.S. Department of Education. Contains a website link to the Individuals with Disabilities Act.

http://www.zerotothree.org

Zero to Three. This site is concerned with assessment and intervention for infants and toddlers.

http://www.naeyc.org

National Association for Education of Young Children. This site covers topics related to the education and assessment of young children.

CONTRIBUTORS TO THE CHILD STUDIES[1]

Barton, E. (2001). Submitted in partial fulfillment of T&L 411, Assessment in Early Childhood Education: DePaul University.

Boneck, D. (2000). Submitted in partial fulfillment of T&L 411, Assessment in Early Childhood Education: DePaul University.

Fantroy, L. (2004) Submitted in partial fulfillment of T&L 411, Assessment in Early Childhood Education: DePaul University.

Finlay, J. (2004) Submitted in partial fulfillment of T&L 411, Assessment in Early Childhood Education: DePaul University.

Foxgrover, G. (2000). Submitted in partial fulfillment of ECE 375, Early Childhood Assessment: DePaul University.

Grasso, M. (2000). Submitted in partial fulfillment of T&L 411, Assessment in Early Childhood Education: DePaul University.

Lee, L. (2001). Submitted in partial fulfillment of T&L 411, Assessment in Early Childhood Education: DePaul University.

Ose, P. C. (2004). Submitted in partial fulfillment of T&L 411, Assessment in Early Childhood Education: DePaul University.

---

[1]These case studies were submitted by students at DePaul University as a requirement for the course: Assessment in Early Childhood. The selected case studies have been edited and identities have been changed. Recognition is given here to those whose work was selected.

Ull, J. (2001). Submitted in partial fulfillment of T&L 411, Assessment in Early Childhood Education: DePaul University.

Zeller, H. (2001). Submitted in partial fulfillment of T&L 411, Assessment in Early Childhood Education: DePaul University.

SUGGESTED READINGS

Almy, M., & Genishi, C. (1979). *Ways of studying children*. New York: Teachers College Press.

Borich, G. D. (2003). *Observation skills for effective teaching* (4th ed.). Upper Saddle River, NJ: Merrill/Prentice Hall.

Deater-Deckard, K. (2004). *Parenting stress*. New Haven, CT: Yale.

McWilliams, P. J. (2000). *Lives in progress: Case stories in early intervention*. Baltimore: Paul H. Brookes.

Pellegrini, A. D. (2004). *Observing children in their natural worlds: A methodological primer* (2nd ed.). Mahwah, NJ: Lawrence Erlbaum.

Sharman, C., Cross, W., & Vennis, D. (2004). *Observing children: A practical guide* (3rd ed.). New York: Continuum.

Suárez-Orozco, C., & Suárez-Orozco, M. M. (2001). *Children of immigration*. Cambridge, MA: Harvard.

9 Special Issues in Infant and Toddler Assessment

Terms to Know

- functional assessment
- prenatal testing
- amniocentesis
- ultrasound
- chorionic villus biopsy (CVS)
- precutaneous umbilical blood sampling (PUBS or cordocentesis)
- gestational age
- developmental delay
- established risk
- biological risk
- environmental risk
- Individualized Family Service Plan (IFSP)
- family involvement
- fetal alcohol syndrome (FAS)
- outcomes

Chapter Overview

This chapter covers special issues in infant and toddler assessment, those aspects of assessment that are unique to the population of birth to age 3 (or even prior to birth). Some of the assessment methods used for preschool- and primary-age children also apply to this discussion. In order to identify problems in the development of infants and toddlers, it is especially important to understand the meaning of development, recognize developmental milestones, and grasp the factors that affect developmental change in the first 3 years of life. An especially critical component of infant/toddler assessment is family collaboration.

Assess as You Read

- How do you assess babies? Why is this assessment important?
- How are parents and others involved in the assessment of babies and toddlers?
- How does assessment lead to intervention?
- What should I know about infant/toddler assessment if I am working in a child-care setting that serves typical children?

THE TOTAL ASSESSMENT PROCESS OF INFANTS AND TODDLERS

More and more infants are in child-care situations, because many women with young children are now working. In addition, with the new requirement for services to infants, toddlers, and pregnant women

through Early Head Start beginning in 1995, the issues related to curriculum and assessment gain increased importance. Early Head Start requires screening of infants and toddlers within 45 days of program enrollment (Head Start, 2002). The principles of appropriate practice are the same—whole child, constructivist approach, safety, cultural sensitivity, and individualization (Bredekamp & Copple, 1997; Interdisciplinary Council on Developmental and Learning Disorders [ICDL], 2000; Sandall, McLean, & Smith, 2000). Specifically, screening should follow the best practices, as follows:

1. Screening is part of intervention service, not just a means of identification and measurement.
2. Use processes, procedures, and instruments only for the specified purpose of each.
3. Incorporate multiple sources of information as part of the process.
4. Periodic screening is important because babies change developmental status rapidly.
5. Screening is only one approach to ongoing evaluation.
6. Use reliable and valid procedures when choosing approaches.
7. Conduct screening in natural, nonthreatening environments.

And, of course family partnership is the cornerstone (Head Start, 2002). Although the screening results do not provide direct links to curriculum, the observation of infants and toddlers during the process reveals trends in behavior that may allow you to choose among goals for emphasis during the coming weeks. Basic goals for teachers working in the mainstream with infants/toddlers include helping infants/toddlers to learn about

- themselves
- feelings

- others
- communicating
- moving and doing
- thinking skills

An example of such goals in a curriculum, planning, and assessment system for caregivers created by Dombro, Colker, and Dodge (1999) is the *Creative Curriculum for Infants and Toddlers®*, available in English and Spanish. The program integrates assessment and teaching/learning activities. It is vital that programs address these goals in a meaningful way because by age 3, almost 85 percent of the brain's core structure is formed (Bruner, Goldberg, & Kot, 1999). "High quality early learning experiences during the infant and toddler years are associated with early competence in language and cognitive development, cooperation with adults, and the ability to initiate and sustain positive exchanges with peers" (Zero to Three, 2005). But, before infants and toddlers are enrolled in programs, they are often assessed by other professionals.

Assessment at birth and shortly thereafter is best described as a "snapshot" that will be revised following the rapid early growth of infants (Smith, Pretzel, & Landry, 2001). Depending on the medical condition and the nature of family support needed, the assessment will focus more or less on the baby and more or less on the family. This is true particularly in the cases of HIV/AIDS or cranio-facial anomalies and other complex medical issues. That is, medical intervention occurs according to medical need, whereas assessment issues relate more to what support the family needs at birth and the first months following, rather than exclusive concentration on the baby.

Using the principles behind **functional assessment,** "contextually relevant, functionally appropriate, relationship-enhancing, observationally based" (Meisels, 2001), describes how assessment, intervention, program, and activities can be linked to serve infants and toddlers, their families, and their caregivers. Thus, practitioners situate assessment in the developmental tasks, processes, and content of appropriate educational activities. With this approach to assessment, there is minimal need for parents, caregivers, and early interventionists to extrapolate from isolated tests to learn about infant/toddler developmental progress. Following these principles, Meisels, Marsden, Dombro, Weston, and Jewkes prepared the Ounce Scale™ (2003) with the "purpose to assist families and service providers in observing, collecting, and evaluating functional information about infants' and young children's development and provide a framework that helps parents and service providers use this information to plan curriculum and engage in relationship-enhancing activities and experiences. The Ounce Scale™ provides an interactive system of documentation, monitoring, and evaluation for Early Head Start and other early care programs for infants, toddlers, and pre-schoolers" (Meisels, 2001, p. 7). The Ounce Scale™ Kit includes an Observational Record, a Family Album, and a Developmental Profile. The Ounce Scale™ answers developmental questions about personal connections, feelings about self,

functional assessment
focused observational method that links individual assessment to curricular intervention for one student.

relationships with other children, understanding and communication, exploration and problem solving, and movement and coordination (http://www.PearsonEarlyLearning.com, 2005).

Other instruments that take this approach include the DIR (Developmental, Individual-Difference, Relationship-Based), designed for use by therapists and skilled clinicians (Wieder & Greenspan, 2001). The instrument assists in understanding both current functioning and how the baby functions. These assessment approaches have evolved as programs and services to infants/toddlers and their families have become more commonplace in our world.

Contemporary research identifies the importance of timing, individualization, cultural relevance, and sustained and intense intervention for best outcomes (cf. Feldman, 2004 Maldonado-Duran, 2002; Ramey & Ramey, 2000). Interest in the prompt and accurate identification of infants and toddlers with developmental disabilities or potential learning problems has increased significantly over the years. (cf. Gargiulo & Kilgo, 2005). In addition to the influence of Early Head Start, other federal policies governing the changing nature of infant/toddler assessment are the evolving policies related to young children with disabilities.

The Individuals with Disabilities Act (IDEA, 2004) governs assessment and intervention practices for infants, toddlers, and children of all ages. Part C is the portion of this legislation that refers to early intervention. "The process involves anticipating, identifying, and responding to child and family concerns in order to minimize their potential adverse effects and maximize the healthy development of babies and toddlers. . . . Services include evaluations of a child's strengths and needs; individualized educational experiences; special therapies such as physical, occupational, and/or speech and language therapy; family supports such as home visits; service coordination; and transition to supports to facilitate a smooth change from early intervention to preschool programs" (Zero to Three, 2004). This legislation is in constant revision to ensure best program practice as practice and research influence the definition of these principles (see the U.S. Department of Education website at http://www.ed.gov or the Division of Early Childhood at http://www.dec-sped.org/ for the most current rules and regulations governing practice).

The values of best practice as outlined by Bailey (1989) (see also ICDL, 2000) and shared by professionals, families, and legislation continue for infants and toddlers:

1. Quality of infant/toddler physical and social environment significantly influences behavior and long-term development.
2. Early intervention reduces the impact of disability conditions.
3. Family partnerships are essential.
4. Interdisciplinary teams are most effective.
5. Focus on infant/toddler strengths rather than deficits.

6. Developmental and individualized goals are the means to effective intervention.

7. Effective intervention requires individualized assessment.

8. Planning is integral for generalized effects of intervention program goals.

In addition, such values are congruent with IDEA 2004 (P.L. 108–446, the Individuals with Disabilities Education Improvement Act of 2004).

This legislation continues the following priorities of previous versions of the law:

- Statewide services for all infants/toddlers with disabilities and their families are encouraged.
- Coordinated services across public and private sources, including insurance, are encouraged.
- Enhance states' intervention services capacity.
- Special efforts to serve the underserved are necessary.

Infants and toddlers must receive service or intervention if they are

- experiencing developmental delays in
  - cognitive development
  - physical development
  - communication development
  - adaptive development
- have a diagnosed physical or mental condition that has a high probability of resulting in developmental delay

States may also elect to serve babies and toddlers who are at risk of substantial developmental delays, although IDEA 2004 proposes stricter regulations regarding the definition of developmental delay. Thus, everyone involved in the lives of families—medical, educational, and child-care providers—must assume responsibility for assessing infants and toddlers who may be at risk of disabilities. The Division for Early Childhood of the Council for Exceptional Children (1998) endorsed a natural environments policy for the delivery of assessment and intervention (Sandall et al., 2000). What this means is that separation of babies and toddlers for special intervention from families and peers is inappropriate practice. Another imperative that serves families and young children is IDEA 2004 special emphasis on the underserved (U.S. Department of Education, 1991).

The 1991 reauthorization of IDEA required states and school districts to recruit underserved families from minority, low-income, inner-city, and rural areas for early intervention services that will promote learning and development. This emphasis continues with the 2004 reauthorization of IDEA. In reaching this population, intervention teams must be particularly aware of cultural and linguistic issues. Steps to developing a culturally sensitive Child Find program include:

- Promoting public awareness of early intervention services in the native language of all populations served
- Involving community members in planning early intervention services and referring families to services
- Involving the whole team—medical, child care, school—in services
- Developing conveniently located and culturally appropriate screening centers
- Recruiting and preparing professionals from the targeted population
- Developing a tracking system to monitor the progress of at-risk and identified children (Pavri, 2001, p. 5; see also Baca & Cervantes, 2004)

How do all these imperatives and best practices influence the teacher working with babies and toddlers in child-care or educational settings? First, you must be aware of the nature and types of disabilities in the birth-to-3 age range. As you may know, the first disabilities identified are usually medical or physical.

Following the identification of medical and physical disabilities that may be present at birth or shortly after, the most frequent symptom that parents and caregivers identify is difficulty with communication—talking. Communication is a complicated area to assess. It includes assessment of gestures, responsiveness, comprehension of language, and vocalization. This process view of communication assessment requires ongoing evaluation, multiple sources, sharing observations, and making interpretations to generate new hypotheses with the selective use of standardized instruments (Reed, 2005; Rossetti, 2001). Though communication may be the initial focus of assessment, the symptom may be indicative of another problem. Greenspan and Wieder (1997, p.5) identify four truths that apply to assessment and intervention with young children:

1. Every child has a profile of development and requires an individualized approach.
2. Child symptoms and problem behaviors often stem from underlying problems in sensory modulation and processing, motor planning, and affective integration.
3. All areas of development are interrelated.
4. Child interactions in relationships and family patterns are the primary vehicle for mobilizing development and growth.

These truths support the need for an integrated developmental approach in support of families. Greenspan and Wieder (1997, p. 7) use a pyramid to illustrate basic services (see Figure 9.1). Safety, protection, and security form the foundation of the pyramid, next is the formation of ongoing trusting relationships, then the implementation of relationships geared to

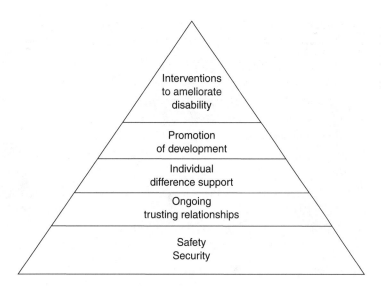

Figure 9.1
Integrated developmental services build on foundation needs.

individual differences, then, techniques to promote development, and at the top specific interventions.

The rapid growth and early nonverbal nature of infants and toddlers complicates their assessment. In addition, our dependence on talking as a measure of understanding developmental progress, the inadequacy and/or inaccuracy of many standard measures, and the inextricably linked family and cultural factors that influence development also complicate the process. To determine infant and toddler competencies fairly and for best services to infants and toddlers in their diverse learning environments, base the assessment process on an integrated developmental model and involve multiple sources of information and multiple components. An assessment should proceed in the following sequence:

1. Establish an alliance of trust with parents. Listen to their views of the baby's strengths and challenges.

2. Realize that parents may not share all of the baby's developmental history at once. They will share more as they trust.

3. Initial observation should occur in a familiar or naturalistic setting with parents or caregivers present.

4. Later observations and assessments by clinicians should offer parental opportunity for participation.

5. Utilize standard measures and tests sparingly to answer specific questions that cannot be answered in another way.

6. Interpret all of the gathered material from observations, interviews, and formal assessments in a developmental framework that incorporates knowledge of child development in a social/cultural context. (Zero to Three Work Group, 1994; see also ICDL, 2000)

265

These ideas have guided the preparation of *Diagnostic Classification: 0–3* (Zero to Three, 1995), as well as the *Clinical Practice Guidelines: Redefining the Standards of Care for Infants, Children, and Families with Special Needs* (ICDL, 2000) and *DEC Recommended Practices in Early Intervention* (Sandall et al., 2000). These manuals should serve as a reference for all who serve the birth-to-3 populations so that the assessment of infants and toddlers can be systematic, comprehensive, and inclusive of diverse settings with various caregivers. The measure of humans begins at birth or before and continues lifelong. How, then, is assessment focused in infancy? The sections that follow elaborate.

The foundation of assessment in the early years is observation by the first caregivers—parents and others in contact with infants. To help parents think of important components of development, Greenspan and Wieder (1998, pp. 3–4) identify six fundamental developmental milestones that lay the foundation for future learning and development. These include the abilities to

1. take an interest in the sights, sounds, and sensations of the world and to calm oneself down—take in and respond.
2. engage in relationships with other people.
3. engage in two-way communication.
4. create complex gestures, to string together a series of actions into an elaborate and deliberate problem-solving sequence.
5. create ideas.
6. build bridges between ideas to make them reality-based and logical.

Biological challenges—sensory, processing, creating, and sequencing planning responses—affect these functional and emotional skills. In addition, interaction patterns with others, as well as family and social patterns, influence development (Feldman, 2004; Greenspan & Wieder, 1998).

THE IMPORTANCE OF ASSESSMENT IN THE FIRST 3 YEARS

Not too long ago, when a baby was born, the primary questions asked, after determining the sex of the baby, were "How much does the baby weigh?" and "How long is the baby?" Nowadays, it is far more common to ask, "What is the baby's Apgar score?" Most hospitals across the United States use the Apgar Rating Scale (Apgar, 1953) to screen newborn infants. One minute after delivery the evaluation occurs, and then it is repeated at 5 minutes (and sometimes 10 minutes) after delivery. Five easily observed signs—heart rate, respiratory effort, muscle tone, reflex response, and color—are scored on a scale from 0 (poor) to 10 (good). Total scores in the 0 to 3 range suggest extremely poor physical condition, are very serious, and indicate an emergency concerning the infant's survival. A score of 4 to 6 indicates fair condition, and a score of 7 to 10 implies a good condition. Color is the least dependable of the signs, as pink and blue tones do not apply to all babies. For all babies physicians can see a darkening glow as oxygen flows through the baby (Berk, 2005). The purpose of this screening is to determine the developmental status of the baby at birth and to identify, as early as possible, infants who may be at risk for serious developmental problems. Most babies, (97 percent) are born without major birth defects (American College of Obstetricians and Gynecologists [ACOG], 2005). Nonetheless, for the other 3 percent, early identification, screening, and assessment are integral parts of early intervention services. Several tests before birth provide information to parents about the health and wellbeing of their expected baby.

Prenatal Testing

Prenatal diagnostic tests that identify a serious medical problem include maternal serum screening, real-time ultrasound, magnetic resonance imaging, fetal echocardiography, amniocentesis, chorionic villus sampling (CVS), diagnostic testing of fetal cells, and percutaneous umbilical blood sampling (Schonberg & Tifft, 2002, pp. 30–35).

Many parents opt for **prenatal testing** such as **amniocentesis** in which a slender needle inserted through the mother's abdomen into the embryonic sac surrounding the fetus in the womb draws a small amount of amniotic fluid for biochemical analysis (ACOG, 2005). The fluid contains fetal cells that when analyzed determine fetal maturity and chromosomal and metabolic abnormalities such as phenylketonuria (PKU) and congenital hypothyroidism, or 250 other genetic abnormalities such

prenatal testing testing done prior to the birth of a baby.

amniocentesis a prenatal test in which amniotic fluid is withdrawn from the embryonic sac of a fetus.

ultrasound a prenatal test in which sound waves are used to determine a fetus's development.

chorionic villus biopsy a prenatal test in which chorionic tissue is removed from the developing placenta.

Precutaneous umbilical blood sampling a specialized prenatal test performed during pregnancy. The test predicts the potential for biological disability.

as Down syndrome, Tay-Sachs disease, and spina bifida. Usually physicians perform this procedure during the 15th to 18th week of pregnancy for women in the at-risk category—maternal age of 35+, previous baby with chromosomal abnormality, positive carrier of known genetic defect, prediction from the maternal serum screening test, or abnormality identified by ultrasound (Schonberg & Tifft, 2002, p. 33).

Ultrasound (sonography) is another, less-intrusive screening method in which sound waves enable the technician to determine the fetus's development. In the first trimester, ultrasound can show the number of fetuses, the viability of one or more fetuses, and the placement of the placenta. During the second trimester, ultrasound images may show subtle findings associated with genetic disorders, as well as neural tube defects, facial clefts, renal anomalies, skeletal anomalies, hydrocephalus, and certain brain malformations (Schonberg & Tifft, 2002, p. 30)

Another method of prenatal testing that may eventually replace amniocentesis is **chorionic villus biopsy,** or CVS (Schonberg & Tifft, 2002, p. 33). This procedure is performed earlier than amniocentesis or ultrasound, usually in the first trimester (9th to 12th week of pregnancy), before the mother feels any movement of the fetus. The main advantage of this earlier screening is that a decision to terminate a pregnancy is usually emotionally easier and medically safer at this earlier stage. Guided by ultrasound, some chorionic tissue, which is the fetal component of the developing placenta, removed by suction is examined under a microscope. Because fetal cells exist in relatively large numbers in the chorion, they are analyzed directly, unlike the process in amniocentesis that requires 2 to 3 weeks for the fetal cells to grow in a culture medium. CVS has been used successfully to detect certain chromosomal abnormalities, measure the activity of specific enzymes, and determine the sex of the fetus.

Precutaneous umbilical blood sampling (also called **PUBS** or cordocentesis) detects intrauterine infections, evaluates fetal anemia, and checks blood type in rhesus (RH) pregnancies (Schonberg & Tifft, 2002). At the 18th week, the test is performed under ultrasound guidance.

The maternal serum screening happens at the 16th week (ACOG, 2005; Schonberg & Tifft, 2002). In this screening, blood is analyzed for alpha-fetoprotein (AFP) levels, estriol, human chrorionic gonadotropin, and inhibin A. A small amount of blood is drawn from a vein in the woman's arm during the first 15 to 18 weeks of pregnancy. The test results show if there is an increased risk for neural tube defects, Down syndrome, trisomy 18, or abdominal wall defects (ACOG, 2005). These are multiple-marker screening tests, and the physician usually will perform three or four.

Prospective parents use these tests in consultation with physicians not only to satisfy their curiosity, but also to relieve their concern and anxiety over possible difficulties and to identify any deviations prior to birth that might cause the parents to elect aborting a fetus with serious, maybe even fatal, defects. Such procedures carry with them many ethical issues that must be resolved by the individuals directly involved.

Assessment at Birth

A common measure that describes the infant's status at birth is the determination of **gestational age**, and a baby born before the 37th week is considered premature. From the 23rd week, babies are viable—capable of survival outside the uterus. Premature babies are born with underdeveloped organs. Depending on the gestational age, body systems affected are respiratory, cardiovascular, neurological, renal and gastrointestinal, muscular, skeletal, skin—in short, all of them. Babies of low birth weight and very low birth weight also are at risk of health problems and often cognitive or other disabilities (Howard, Williams, & Lepper, 2005). Thus, major prenatal hospital centers that serve high-risk infants often use infant development scales to plan intervention and family support.

gestational age how long a baby had been developing in the uterus before birth.

One of these instruments is the Brazelton Neonatal Assessment Scale (BNAS); (Brazelton & Nugent, 1995). This is a detailed examination designed to identify abnormalities in the central nervous system and sensory abilities, but it goes beyond a focus on neurological reflexes. It can describe the quality and level of the infant's behavior, detect changes in the infant's behavior, assess the impact of treatment interventions, and predict future development and function.

A screening mandated in most states before the infant leaves the hospital is a blood sample taken with a heel stick. Analysis of the blood seeks indications of metabolic diseases that may result in retarded growth and development. Among these diseases are phenylketonuria (PKU) and congenital hypothyroidism. Screening for the prediction of optimum development is not easy, for there are many developmental and social factors that contribute to a baby's welfare.

Principles of Child Development

No two babies, not even identical twins, are exactly alike. Each will develop somewhat differently based on genetic and environmental factors. Furthermore, there is no single theory of child development that all experts accept (cf. Papalia, Olds, & Feldman, 2006). However, there are a few general observations about very young children that are commonly accepted:

- Multiple factors determine development.
- Environmental influences support, facilitate, or impede developmental change.
- Parental figures mediate societal and cultural influences on the child.
- The family plays a unique role in and makes vital contributions to the child's development.
- Parenthood is a developmental and adaptive process (Meisels & Provence, 1989)

When working with infants and toddlers, it is important to recognize the early childhood milestones. Teachers can find examples of milestones in the NAEYC Position Statement on Developmentally Appropriate Practice in Early Childhood Programs (Bredekamp & Copple, 1997) and in Appendix B of this book. (See Box 9.1 for an example of a checklist to use when modifying care in infant/toddler programs.) Early Head Start publishes and distributes many materials for use in programs serving infants and toddlers (http://www.ehsnrc.org/; Website of the Early Head Start National Resource Center) that will be useful for developing curricula and assessment programs for infants and toddlers. As well, *The Creative Curriculum® for Infants & Toddlers* "is a comprehensive and easy-to-use framework for planning and implementing a quality program, one where building relationships with children is central.

The Curriculum outlines:

- what children learn during the first three years
- the experiences they need to achieve learning goals

Box 9.1 *Checklist of Developmental Considerations for Babies and Toddlers in Group Care*

Modifications Needed	Developmental Aspect
Describe briefly what modifications are needed for group care situation.	Eating
	Sleeping
	Dressing
	Communicating
	Playing
	Muscle tone
	Locomotion
	Fine motor

- what staff and parents do to help children reach these goals" (Dombro et al., 1999)

Developmental principles are embedded in this program. Also, caregivers should consult milestone lists found in theoretical discussions of issues such as attachment, perception, emotions, language, and so on (cf. Eyer & Gonzalez-Mena, 2004). By being aware of these milestones, an early childhood educator can often allay unwarranted concerns of parents.

Answers to the following questions may help determine whether to refer a child for diagnostic assessment in the first year.

- Are the child's skills consistently delayed in a *number* of areas such as motor, language, and self-help?
- Has the 1-year-old child started to *understand* some words?
- Are there any doubts about the child's hearing?
- Is the child's motor development significantly delayed in a *variety* of tasks, such as sitting, crawling, standing, and walking?

Risk Factors

Most infants and toddlers develop without developmental problems; however, several different factors put infants at risk. These factors, divided into four categories, are not mutually exclusive; thus, an infant may be at risk due to one or more of the following:

1. **Developmental delay:** Each state defines this differently, but includes significant delays in the usual developmental milestones or unusual patterns in development.

   developmental delay term used by states to entitle infants, toddlers, and young children to intervention services.

2. **Established risk:** Infants in this category possess a gene abnormality, a malformation or structural problem with the brain or central nervous system, or received alcohol or illegal drugs in utero. These factors contribute to challenges in development.

   established risk risk to infants because of gene abnormality, malformation or structural problems, or in utero drug exposure.

3. **Biological risk:** Infants in this category have a prenatal, perinatal, or neonatal difficulty, including low birth weight, respiratory distress at birth, central nervous system infection, or difficult birth process. These difficulties are associated with challenges to development.

   biological risk risk to infant because of prenatal, preinatal, or neonatal difficulty.

4. **Environmental risk:** Infants in this category may be affected by family or social stress. Factors that contribute to challenges in development include malnutrition during pregnancy or in the period immediately following birth. Additional difficulties include patterns of care by the primary caregiver that may be inadequate. Overall, family poverty contributes risk to this category.

   environmental risk risk to infants because of family or social stress.

271

These categories of risk create eligibility for service for babies, toddlers, and young children (under IDEA), although the services vary by state (McLean, Worley, & Bailey, 2004). Interactions across risk factors occur. In brief, poverty heightens the likelihood of established risk. Child abuse, malnutrition, and accidents also heighten the development of special needs identified before school entrance. Disability can range from visual and hearing impairment to complex mental and physical handicaps. Although risk conditions may create the possibility that infants, toddlers, and young children may need special intervention to foster growth and development, these factors cannot determine eligibility for early intervention services. Informed clinical opinion is the measure required for entitlement to early intervention. This clinical judgment must support the presence of a medical disability, other known disability, or a developmental delay. Definitions, by state, include percentage of chronological age demonstrated by performance, number of months of delay, score of one standard deviation below the mean on a norm-based instrument, and observed atypical behaviors. Some states have developed matrixes and charts to aid agencies, clinics, and programs in determining eligibility for early intervention (Shackelford, 2000). The thrust of best practice in all of these definitions is looking at the individual baby, toddler, or 3-year-old in the context of family and community and judging whether the individual needs early intervention. In the next section, some of the factors that affect the assessment of infants and toddlers are highlighted.

UNIQUE ASPECTS OF INFANTS AND TODDLERS

What makes assessment of infants and toddlers different from assessment of preschool and primary-age children? Some of the distinctive characteristics of infants and toddlers that affect assessment are the following:

Babies and toddlers may:
- lack expressive skills.
- struggle with separation issues.
- demonstrate a limited attention span.
- be uninfluenced by extrinsic motivation.
- adapt slowly to new surroundings.
- fatigue easily and need naps.
- refuse to cooperate.
- exhibit a wide range of normal behaviors.
- demonstrate highly variable hour-to-hour behavior, although behavior and personality are globally stable over years.
- tend to put the testing materials in their mouths.

- show the effect of developmental overlay; that is, each area is influencing the total so it's difficult to isolate particular problems.
- change rapidly.
- show cultural variations in behavior and consequent development.
- often demonstrate subtle developmental problems and require professional interruption (Head Start, 2002; McCollum, Azar-Mathis, Henderson, & Kusmierek, 1989).

Another important difference is that although the term *development* implies a high degree of continuity and stability in behavioral change across time, in general the first few years are characterized by a lack of permanence in development and lack of smoothness in behavioral change (cf. Berk, 2005). This means that the infant or toddler may demonstrate a developmental milestone one day and never perform it again for days, weeks, or months. Or, the baby may progress on a regular basis and then reach a plateau and stay at that point of development for a long time.

Thus, an early childhood educator must consider a number of issues and trends to see the overall picture of infant and toddler assessment and the requirements and principles of IDEA Part C (2004). The outcome orientation of the law states that early intervention services should

1. enhance a child's development, minimize the potential for developmental delay, and recognize the significant brain development that occurs during a child's first 3 years of life . . .

2. reduce educational costs by minimizing the need for special education and related services after infants and toddlers with disabilities reach school age;

3. maximize the potential for individuals with disabilities to live independently in society;

4. enhance families' capacity to meet the special needs of their infants and toddlers with disabilities; and

5. enhance the capacity of state and local agencies and service providers to identify, evaluate, and meet the needs of all children, particularly minority, low-income, inner city, and rural children, and infants and toddlers and in foster care (Turnbull, Huerta, & Stowe, 2006, pp. 38–39).

Fortunately, the mandate also has procedural safeguards that include frequent parent and professional review of **Individualized Family Service Plans (IFSPs)**, as well as the right to appeal, the right to confidentiality of information, the right to prior notice to parents in their native language, the assignment of surrogate parents, and the establishment of procedures to ensure that services are provided while complaints are being resolved. The 2004 IDEA ". . . proclaims the nation's goals are to preserve and strengthen the families of children with disabilities and the children themselves, while, at the same time, developing state and local capacities to serve them" (Turnbull et al., 2006, p. 39).

Individualized Family Service Plan (IFSP) specific plan for the assessing of needs and for the services needed for a child with a developmental problem.

IFSPs must be written and must contain the following:

1. Statement of child's present levels of physical development, cognitive development, communication development, social or emotional development, and adaptive development, based on objective criteria.

2. Statement of the family's resources, priorities, and concerns relating to enhancing the child's development.

3. Statement of the measurable results or outcomes expected to be achieved for the child and family, including pre-literacy and language skills as developmentally appropriate for the child; the criteria, procedures, and timelines used to determine the degree to which progress toward achieving the results or outcomes is being made; and whether modifications or revisions of the results or outcomes or services are necessary.

4. Statement of specific early intervention services based on peer-reviewed research, to the extent practicable, necessary to meet the child's and family's unique needs, including the frequency, intensity, and method of delivering services.

5. Statement of the natural environments in which early intervention services shall appropriately be provided, including a justification of the extent, if any, to which the services will not be provided in a natural environment.

6. The projected dates for initiating the services and the anticipated length, duration, and frequency of the services.

7. Identification of the service coordinator from the profession most immediately relevant to the child's or family's needs who will be responsible for implementing the plan and coordinating with other agencies and persons, including transition services.

8. The steps to be taken to support the child's transition to preschool or other appropriate services (Turnbull et al., 2006, pp. 39–41)

Multidisciplinary teams write these IFSPs in collaboration with families. Services provided include family training and counseling, special instruction, speech and language therapy, occupational or physical therapy, psychological assessment, medical services for diagnostics and evaluation, social work services, assistive technology, transportation and related costs, and service coordination. In making the plans, teams follow the best practice principles for assessment and intervention described in the following section.

PRINCIPLES THAT GUIDE INFANT AND TODDLER ASSESSMENT

Once it is determined that an infant or toddler should be referred, there are a number of principles that guide the assessment approaches with very young children. First, assessment is a continuing, evolving process rather than a discrete activity initiated and completed at a single point in time. Thus, assessment must be blended with intervention (Bagnato, Neisworth, & Munson, 1997; Feldman, 2004; Sandall et al., 2000).

Because infants display complex patterns of interaction with the world from birth, there has been a continuing movement to document their behaviors and reactions in some formal way. The most striking aspect of the evolution of infant assessment has been the logical shift from measuring what we think of as intelligence (Bagnato et al., 1997) to assessment of a number of interrelated systems in very young children combined with a move toward interdisciplinary assessment (ICDL, 2000).

As it is not possible to divide the infant's skills and activities along such lines as motor, social, and cognitive domains in the early weeks of life—and even during the first 3 years such a division remains somewhat artificial—it is necessary to assess the infant's behavior and capacity by considering the underlying internal organization that has been suggested by current developmental theory. Professionals should accomplish this with training in many diverse fields of study. Thus, assessment of very young children involves the sampling of behavior. A specific task is presented and then analyzed to determine the baby's underlying competencies and ways of organizing the world. For example, if we roll an attractively decorated ball to a baby sitting on the floor and request that the baby roll it back, we learn about the baby's interest in the object and ability to roll it back as well as how the baby relates to requests. If we see whether the toddler can lick food from around his or her mouth, we are really observing sensory awareness, voluntary control of oral structures, and body awareness. If we engage the baby in playing peek-a-boo, we can observe social awareness, turn taking, role perspective, imitation, body awareness, cooperation, and anticipation or prediction. Identifying the critical functions underlying each task enables the assessment team to use the information for program planning purposes.

To get the most reliable results, assessment should take place in multiple settings—home, child care, or school—and on multiple occasions when the baby is awake and alert and when the parents are not anxious or under stress. This reduces the pressure to finish the assessment on a particular day and reduces the parents' feeling that the child failed any particular task (Bagnato et al., 1997; McLean et al., 2004). Above all, support the family priorities when planning any potential intervention.

Family Involvement

Therefore, family priorities and information needs shape the assessment process, as well as child characteristics and diagnostic concerns (ICDL, 2000). This necessitates **family involvement**—the identification of the family's strengths and priorities, and the family's determination of which aspects of their family life are relevant to their child's development. The assessment process reflects family values and family styles

family involvement
including the parents in all phases of the assessment of a child with a developmental problem.

275

of decision-making. It is particularly important that teams consider the traditional cultural values and traditions of the families that they serve. These factors include whom the families would traditionally respect for advice and help. Particularly important is the role of elders and spirituality in the traditional culture. A plan that does not consider these issues for the family is doomed to failure if it is in conflict with the belief system. Additional factors of importance to cross-culture understanding include styles of interaction and communication, as well as the concept of cultural identity—there are many variables here regarding the perceived identity of the particular family (Hanson, 2004).

All aspects of infant evaluation should reflect interactions between the child, the family, the professional, and the setting (cf. Hooper & Umansky, 2004). Infant evaluation variables are infant endurance and states of alertness, responsiveness to new tasks and unfamiliar situations, spontaneous activity, unstructured discovery, levels of frustration and irritability, and interaction with varied objects and toys in addition to the infant's interaction with caregivers.

When assessing preschool and primary-aged children, parents may sit and observe or may not even be present. However, parents are an integral part in the assessment of infants and toddlers. Why should we involve parents in the assessment? First, it acknowledges that parents know their baby best and are their baby's most important teacher. It implies that parents are most likely to get a typical response from the baby. Family involvement provides a more complete understanding of the child—how the child fits into the family. The collaborative assessment and interview process provides opportunity for the parental perspective. Family involvement provides a basis for planning intervention that fits within everyday routines and coordinates what occurs in the group setting with what occurs at home. Parents identify goal priorities from their perspective as well as in conjunction with the developmental status of the child. In this way, parents reduce anxiety and parents learn how professionals plan learning experiences and activities for their baby. Now parents are part of a problem-solving team in which intervention solutions evolve through the collaborative assessment-intervention process. This increases the parents' involvement and likelihood that they will believe the results and work with the team for the benefit of the child.

Special At-Risk Populations

fetal alcohol syndrome
physical and mental abnormalities associated with infants born to mothers who consumed excessive amounts of alcohol during preegenancy.

Babies exposed prenatally to alcohol, drugs, cigarettes, and marijuana suffer physical or neurological harm (cf. Howard et al., 2005). One of the most common risks is **fetal alcohol syndrome (FAS)**. In this case, infants exposed to excessive amounts of alcohol during pregnancy develop the key features of growth retardation, characteristic facial features, and abnormalities of the central nervous system (Abel, 1998). Medical personnel make the diagnosis with a checklist of relevant characteristics to entitle babies and their families to intervention and possible prevention of future cases, since the syndrome implies a familial issue (Morse & Weiner, 2005). Current research suggests that the incidence is .33–.40 cases per 1,000. Blood alcohol level determines heavy drinking; however, a rule of thumb is five or more drinks per day, although even weekly binges may affect fetus development. The greatest effect to skeletal structure occurs in the first trimester, with effects on the central nervous system highest in third trimester (Morse & Weiner, 2005).

Babies exposed prenatally to drugs, such as cocaine, are at risk for environmental and biological reasons. However, recent research shows that the long-term effect of cocaine exposure is not as once imagined (Howard et al., 2005). Newborns exposed to cocaine show symptoms of irritability, restlessness, lethargy, poor feeding, abnormal sleep patterns, tremors, increased muscle tone, vomiting, and a high-pitched cry; the symptoms last for up to 48–72 hours after birth (Winch, Conlon, & Scheidt, 2002). Long-term effects are most likely due to polydrug use and environmental conditions that contribute to sustained parental drug use rather than cocaine per se (Howard et al., 2005).

"More than 10% of pregnant women smoke throughout their pregnancies . . . (leading) to an increased risk of preterm delivery, and infant death. Research also suggests that infants of mothers who smoke during and after pregnancy are 2–3 times more likely to die from SIDS than babies born to nonsmoking mothers. The risk is somewhat less for infants whose mothers stop smoking during pregnancy and resume smoking after delivery" (American Cancer Society, 2005). In addition, smoking during pregnancy contributes to the incidence of low-birth-weight babies. Smoking slows fetal growth (American Cancer Society, 2005).

There is little information about the effects of maternal marijuana use on babies prenatally. However, while there are no differences in miscarriage rate, Apgar scores, or fetal malformations in infants whose mothers smoked marijuana regularly during pregnancy and those who did not, there is an association with prematurity and decreased birth weight (Winch et al., 2002).

The best intervention in these emotional/social issues of pregnant women is substance abuse treatment during and after pregnancy. If mothers do not receive assistance during pregnancy, the problems increase with subsequent pregnancies (Winch *et al.*, 2002). As well, early childhood intervention programs often support infants/toddlers and their families who are wrestling with these complex social/environmental issues. "Effective interventions, however, increasingly require striking a fine balance among the characteristics of the participants, the characteristics of the services, and service use (especially participants' active involvement). Policy-makers, moreover, cannot expect early interventions to inoculate vulnerable infants to future difficulties. Rather, as a nation we must support multifaceted early intervention programs and evaluations that will, in turn, continue to shed light on enhancing development throughout the life span" (Berlin, Brooks-Gunn, McCarton, & McCormick, 2004, p. 147).

ECOLOGICALLY AND DEVELOPMENTALLY RELEVANT ASSESSMENT STRATEGIES

Assessment of infants and toddlers is a blend of testing, informal observation, and parental interviews over an extended period. Traditional instruments—norm-referenced and criterion-referenced measures—often have the goal of quantifying a child's abilities, which means attaching a number or score to the responses. However, they often fail to address the qualitative aspects of a child's abilities, such as appropriateness of movement patterns, social competence, and attention abilities (Barnett, Macmann, & Carey, 1992; Hauser-Cram & Shonkoff, 1988). As a result, there is a definite trend in infant and toddler assessment away from traditional instruments toward more ecologically and developmentally relevant assessment strategies that lead directly to program planning (ICDL, 2000).

The Team Approach

The fields of child development, early intervention, and mental health have a rich history of interdisciplinary work that has evolved in the last 40 years or so as the importance of early attention to developmental disabilities gained increased recognition. When assessing infants and toddlers, a set of interdisciplinary assessment principles includes the following:

- Validate scores from standardized instruments against the material gathered from naturalistic settings.

- Reevaluations should be routine, considered in context, and note that uncertainty may be an ongoing feature of the results.

- Testing should be coordinated and case histories collected to avoid redundant use of particular instruments or procedures.

- The assessment process itself is dynamic and may yield new information.

- Different disciplines bring various communication styles, protocols, and philosophies; thus, the team must operate from a perspective of respect for the diverse traditions in support of the particular infant.

- View each child in a cultural context that considers the definition of competence from the uniqueness of that culture.

- The family perspective is the central guiding force in assessing and planning for infants and toddlers.

- Include community providers in the assessment process when recommending special services and an IFSP.

- As part of assessment, inclusion and support of the family and infant are key. (Guralnick, 2000)

IDEA (2004) also mandates that professionals from several disciplines need to work cooperatively to provide services to infants and toddlers with disabilities and their families. The purpose of the team is to determine eligibility and develop the IFSP. A number of disciplines mentioned in the law are involved in the assessment and program development of an infant or toddler. These include a special educator, nurse, speech and language pathologist, audiologist, occupational therapist, physical therapist, psychologist, social worker, and nutritionist. Of course, it is unlikely that all of these disciplines would be involved in any given assessment. The background and issues surrounding the particular child would determine the exact composition of the team. Besides the parent, others who might be directly involved are the early childhood educator, the building or program administrator, the counselor, and the adapted physical education specialist. These individuals make up the early intervention team.

What may best distinguish early intervention teams from one another is neither their composition, since they are all composed of some combination of the disciplines just mentioned plus the family, nor the tasks that include assessment and intervention, but rather the structure of interaction among team members. Family members participate as full members of the team in determining assessment results and in developing the program plan. The case manager, one member of the team, writes reports separately for the team and family (Hooper & Umansky, 2004).

THE INTEGRATION OF ASSESSMENT INFORMATION INTO PROGRAMMING

Infant assessment is in actuality infant intervention, according to Bagnato et al. (1997). The continuous observation of the infant and toddler, along with talking with the parents, provides the opportunity to note the child's responses and blend the assessment into the intervention plan. As much as possible, the assessment process simultaneously serves as a guide to individual programming, program planning, and evaluation.

The assessment team needs to answer a number of questions in order to plan the most appropriate program for the child and the family (cf. McLean et al., 2004). Not only do teachers and other team members need to know *what* the child can do, but also *how* the task is performed. In addition to examining the critical functions mentioned earlier in this chapter, team members need to examine the quality of the performance. Then team members need to determine what the infant or toddler needs to learn next, what the baby is unable to do and why, and, finally, how this particular baby learns best. The answers to all of these questions will enable the assessment team and family to develop the most appropriate program for the infant or toddler, including the daily planning that integrates the goals and objectives of the IFSP into the routines of

outcomes are the specifications used by school districts, states, and professional associations to describe measurable educational goals.

the early childhood setting. Without a doubt, the most important purpose of assessment is program planning and monitoring of individual and group progress.

Some important considerations for ensuring that the assessment information translates to **outcomes** that make a difference in the lives of infants, toddlers, and their families are as follows:

- Do we know why we're writing this?
- Does this outcome mesh with activities that the family chooses to do?
- Have we explored informal, natural, and community-based supports (i.e., those that are least restrictive)?
- Who will pay for or provide services?
- Can the family understand the language of the outcome?
- Does this outcome really matter to the family and the infant/toddler/young child who will be evaluated against it? (Rosenkoetter & Squires, 2000, pp. 4–5).

The answers to these questions are critical, for the most important outcome for early intervention is school success.

The characteristics that enable children to learn in school are now: curiosity, confidence, the capacity to set a goal and work towards its accomplishment, the ability to communicate with others, and to get along with them. Children who don't have these characteristics do not perform well in school. School readiness—or un-readiness—begins in the first years of life (Zero to Three, 2004).

SUMMARY

This chapter describes the role that assessment plays in the lives of all infants, often even before they are born. After describing the total assessment process used with infants and toddlers and the importance of assessment in the first 3 years, current assessment issues and trends, such as principles that guide infant and toddler assessment and the significance of family collaboration, are discussed. Finally, the chapter ends with a short discussion on the integration of assessment information into programming because the most important purpose of assessment is program planning for individual infants and toddlers.

FIELD ACTIVITIES

1. Visit the newborn nursery in your community. Observe the infants through the window. Note the difference in size, coloring, movement, and so on. Ask the hospital administrator or head nurse if you could observe any screening (e.g., Apgar, Brazelton).

2. Visit an early intervention program in your community. Observe the children to see if you can ascertain the reason they are in the program.

Observe the speech therapist and the physical therapist as well as the early interventionist. Inquire if any of the children also spend time in another child-care program in the community.

3. Visit a neonatal intensive care unit (NICU). This facility will probably be further from home than the other two programs. Ascertain if you may observe any infant. Depending on the facility's policies and the amount of time you have to spend on this activity, there may be other roles for you to play in the NICU.

4. Identify the number and types of programs serving infants and toddlers in your community. Compare your findings to numbers of programs 10 years ago by consulting library copies of community resources for the previous decade.

IN-CLASS ACTIVITIES

1. With a partner, identify play activities for infants/toddlers at various developmental stages: 6 months, 1 year, 18 months, 2 years, and 2½ years. Describe how you might use these activities in a learning assessment.

2. In small groups, develop questions that you might use with families seeking to enroll infants and toddlers in your center. What questions would be included that might give you information about the baby's developmental state? How would you ask these questions with sensitivity?

STUDY QUESTIONS

1. Define *prenatal assessments* and list examples.

2. When and how is the Apgar Rating Scale used? What information does it provide?

3. What are five principles of child development? Why is knowledge of these necessary when thinking about infant/toddler assessment?

4. How do the three risk factors relate? Why do early childhood teachers need this information?

5. What characteristics of infants and toddlers make it imperative that specifically designed assessments be used before age 3? What principles guide these assessments?

6. How can family involvement reduce parent anxiety?

7. Why is it important to identify at-risk infants and toddlers?

8. What does IDEA state regarding early interventions and their purpose?

9. What role does intervention play in infant/toddler assessment?

REFLECT AND RE-READ

- I can list common prenatal assessment procedures.
- I know how infant/toddler assessment is unique.
- I understand the link from assessment to intervention.
- I can use developmental principles to identify at-risk babies.
- I know what is unique about the parent role in infant/toddler assessment.

CASE VIGNETTE

Setting up to assess a 28-month-old toddler, the assessor notes the following description of Deiondre and her family situation: On a bright day in November, Deiondre is wearing blue jeans with embroidered flowers, a pink long-sleeved shirt, and pink socks. Deiondre is a tall, thick caramel-colored toddler with dark curly hair braided in five French braids in back. Deiondre is the only child of Della Masters and Ronald Lark. When the observer arrived, Deiondre seemed to be a very active and energetic toddler. Ms. Masters and Mr. Lark report that they have a hard time keeping her out of things; she loves to rub on lotions and body oils. Last year she swallowed a Tylenol and her parents rushed her to the hospital for treatment.

Deiondre seems to speak very well for a toddler; she can hold a short conversation with an unfamiliar adult, using clearly understood words correctly. Occasionally, she uses swear words, a habit she picked up from family members who have since stopped swearing in front of her. Deiondre loves to mimic the activities of adults such as writing, dancing, typing on the computer, and washing the dishes. While in the kitchen with her family, Deiondre scoots a stool to the kitchen counter and stands on it to "wash the dishes." When someone takes away the stool, she simply pushes the kitchen chair to the sink and tries once again to "wash the dishes." Finally, after a lot of crying and pleading, and the help of Gerber fruit snacks, Ms. Masters gets her to stop.

If Deiondre enrolled in your infant/toddler program, what additional assessment information would you plan? What instructional plan would you make? How will you collaborate with Ms. Masters and Mr. Lark?

Source: From J. Darko, 2004, submitted in partial fulfillment of ECE 375, Early Childhood Assessment: DePaul University. Used by permission.

TECHNOLOGY LINKS

http://www.apha.org

American Public Health Association. Publishes material on mental health and health issues related to children.

http://www.aap.org

American Academy of Pediatrics. Position papers and publications affecting the lives of young children.

http://www.acog.com

American College of Obstetricians and Gynecologists. Information pamphlets on women's health and prenatal care and development.

http://www.brightfutures.org

Bright Futures at Georgetown University. Promotes health and mental health; site includes checklists and information about health assessment.

http://www.nectas.unc.edu

National Early Childhood Technical Assistance System. A clearinghouse for information on the education of young children, with technical papers and practical suggestions for programming and assessment.

http://www.pitc.org

Program for Infant/Toddler Caregivers. Resources to support a relationship curriculum for infants and toddlers.

SUGGESTED READINGS

Gonzalez-Mena, J., & Eyer, D. W. (2004). *Infants, toddlers, and caregivers: A curriculum of respectful, responsive care and education.* (6th ed.). New York: McGraw-Hill.

Kessen, W. (2006). *Infant care.* New Haven: Yale University Press.

Lynch, E. W., & Hanson, M. J. (2004). *Developing cross-cultural competence: A guide for working with children and their families* (3rd ed.). Baltimore: Paul H. Brookes.

Rochat, P. (2001). *The Infant's World.* Cambridge: Harvard.

Sandall, S., McLean, M. E., & Smith, B. J. (2000). *DEC recommended practices in early intervention/early childhood special education.* Longmont, CO: Sopris West.

Schiller, P. (2005). *The complete resource book for infants.* Beltsville, MD: Gryphon House.

Wittmer, D., & Petersen, S. (2006). *Infant/toddler development and responsive program planning: A relationship-based approach.* Upper Saddle River, NJ: Merrill/Prentice Hall.

10

Issues in Preschool Assessment

Chapter Overview

This chapter traces the use of assessment systems in preschool settings. One use of such systems is selection of children for participation in limited and competitive enrollment situations. Using screening instruments for enrollment decisions and the important limitations of such an approach is a featured debate. Next is a focus on the issues surrounding the connection from assessment to curriculum, instruction, and the return. A segment is included regarding referral to special services. Included in the discussion are links to appropriate teacher roles in the process and play-based assessment. Finally, there is a spotlight on the issues of first-grade transition.

Assess as You Read

- When and how do you assess preschoolers?
- What is the role of screening in the early childhood program? What are the limitations?
- What are the Head Start Performance Standards? Why is Head Start requiring educational outcomes assessment?
- How do I plan for outcomes assessment?
- How can I articulate with kindergarten-primary teachers?

PRESCHOOL ASSESSMENT SYSTEM ISSUES

At the preschool level, young children may attend a child-care center, family child care, a half-day nursery school, a part-time playgroup, all-day care, Head Start, or a regular or special education program. Teachers in each of these settings have similar demands for assessment measures. They plan instruction and keep track of child progress. Sometimes teachers participate in decisions that require consultation and professional assistance. The most common preschool assessment decisions include selection for the preschool program, planning for instruction, referral for special services, and transition to kindergarten/ first grade. In each of these situations, preschool teachers are problem solvers who use assessment to teach.

SELECTION FOR THE PRESCHOOL PROGRAM

Parent Convenience

Parents often choose a program close to their home and enroll their children there. These programs usually accept children on a first-come, first-served basis. These community-based programs generally select children because of age, religious affiliation, ability to pay, or other demographic characteristics. A child's ability is not usually the basis for selection decisions.

Limited Enrollment Decisions

Choosing children deemed "academically at risk" currently proceeds in a manner dictated by the restricted public funds available for screening. Selection criteria may apply to family and child characteristics. Family demographics included are poverty, limited English fluency, or teen mothers. After agencies and school districts collect a pool of demographically eligible children, they employ an efficient method to choose those most in need of the special program. School districts frequently choose screening instruments for this purpose. These measures give a general overview of a child's ability and achievement in self-help skills, cognition, language, fine- and gross-motor skills, and

social/emotional development. The opportunity for participation in screening should be open to all children to secure this developmental review.

Screening programs survey many children in a short period. Thus, most children pass through the screen and go to a regular program; they are not eligible for an at-risk program. The screening procedure acts as a selection device. Because screening procedures typically survey developmental milestones, the results have a short time of usability. The younger the child, the more limited the time frame. This is due to the rapid nature of developmental change in young children. When there is a long time delay between screening and program delivery, rescreening is necessary. The critical time delay varies with the age of the child, but a good rule of thumb is a delay of 3 to 6 months.

CHOOSING A SCREENING INSTRUMENT

When choosing a screening instrument or procedure, consider many factors. First, a developmental screening review should be comprehensive, reviewing all aspects of development: cognitive, physical, and social/emotional. Conduct activities with the children that they see as play; concrete materials ought to form the basis of the activity. The procedure must reflect the cultural diversity of a particular community. Parents should be involved in providing primary information about a child's history and perceptions of current functioning. Of course, consider technical qualities of reliability, validity, and overreferral/underreferral when choosing a screening system. The procedure or plan must be quick to administer to individual children. Young children can give limited attention to formal screening tasks. Quickly administered measures function efficiently for the screening agency.

Head Start placed increased emphasis on screening with the passage of legislation requiring attention to performance outcomes. Screening of young children is required within 45 days of enrollment in the program. The screening focuses on the whole child—health and developmental assessment. The screening process identifies child strengths and any areas of concern to follow throughout the child's enrollment in Head Start. "Through this process, [teachers and parents] come to know each child's strengths, interests, needs, and learning styles in order to individualize the curriculum, to build on each child's prior knowledge and experiences, and to provide meaningful curriculum experiences that support learning and development. In these ways, staff, parents, and programs support each child in making progress toward stated goals. [This Head Start policy supports a national concern] . . . with the whole child, [including] social competence as part of school readiness" (Head Start, 2003, p. 15).

Of particular interest is the need to screen for behavioral problems, since these problems interfere with later school adjustment and achievement. Preliminary studies (Kaiser, Cai, Hancock, & Foster, 2002; Kaiser, Hancock, Cai, Foster, & Hester, 2000; Serna, Nielsen, Mattern, & Forness, 2003) show an overlap of language problems with parent-reported behavioral problems and classroom-observed behavioral difficulties, and difficulties with social skills. Thus, screening in Head Start must find those at risk for these difficulties while remaining fully aware of the potential stigmatizing effects of early identification and labeling and the contextual differences in behavioral expectations.

Limitations of Screening Instruments

Screening procedures and instruments have limitations. These tools cannot diagnose children. They can appropriately select children who may be at risk of academic failure. However, they cannot definitively decide individual developmental profiles. Further assessment is necessary to decide eligibility for special education placement or to plan for educational intervention. This is in keeping with best practice as defined by the American Educational Research Association, the American Psychological Association, and the National Council on Measurement in Education. Their joint Standard 13.7 states: "In educational settings, a decision or characterization that will have major impact on a student should not be made on the basis of a single test score. Other relevant information should be taken into account if it will enhance the overall validity of the decision" (AERA, 1999, p. 146).

Thus, "screening programs identify those children who may need special kinds of help to function well in school. They should not exclude them from a program for which they are legally eligible. Sound, ethical practice is to accept children in all their variety, identify any special needs they have, and offer them the best possible opportunity to grow and learn" (Hills, 1987, p. 2). "When a screening tool or other assessment identifies concerns, appropriate follow-up, referral, or other intervention is used. Diagnosis or labeling is never the result of a brief screening or one-time assessment" (National Association for the Education of Young Children and National Association of Early Childhood Specialists in State Departments of Education, 2003). Finally, children who are chosen for special enrichment programs should not be labeled "at risk" or by any other label that may result in lifelong stigmatization.

SELECTION OF CHILDREN IN COMPETITIVE SITUATIONS

Highly touted programs may find parents camping in the parking lot overnight to secure applications for the few available places in the program. Often, such programs resort to paper-and-pencil instruments of various kinds in an effort to reduce the number of applicants. And, sometimes parents resort to various "high anxiety" approaches to try to manipulate a placement in an "elite" school or program. For a fictionalized account, based on the author's years of experience as an admissions counselor, see *The Ivy Chronicles* (Quinn, 2005). If child assessment measures decide eligibility for these programs, the criteria should be published for parents to review. Sometimes, these settings use individualized intelligence tests to select children (Robinson, 1988). A qualified psychologist should administer intelligence tests. Utilizing intelligence tests professionally with parent permission may be a better practice than using *homemade* tests that may have limited validity or reliability. Sometimes these homemade tests are criterion-referenced measures that are inappropriate as selection measures.

The pinch of salt to keep in mind: Whenever screening children for eligibility to participate in a program, all of the limitations and cautions for these instruments apply. The primary tenet of appropriate assessment is to match the method to the purpose. The major corollary is to use multiple measures for high-stakes decisions.

PLANNING FOR INSTRUCTION

Once children enter a program, the program philosophy guides the curriculum and instruction. Assessment links the instructional strategies to individual children. *Observation* of children forms the backbone of the preschool assessment program. This assessment method is an integral part of the play-based curriculum found in preschool settings. Play-based curricula incorporate concrete experiential activities. In this approach, you plan projects grounded on the interests and needs of the children. Commonly, the divisions for curricula are knowledge, skills, and attitudes. Knowledge is the content or subject matter for the program. Typically, curricular themes for preschool include those rooted in the immediate social world of the children—my family, my community, my friends, our garbage, and so on. The skills of the instructional process include problem solving; communicating in words, pictures, and writing; cooperating with friends; following schedules and routines; and so on. Attitudes include curiosity, risk taking, self-confidence, respect for others, and so on. Learning of knowledge, skills, and attitudes occurs in activities that tap the intellectual, creative, social/emotional, and physical domains (see Box 10.1).

Themes and projects organized around a topic provide children opportunities to develop in holistic fashion in each of the domains. Opportunities for children to experience the topics occur in small groups, at interest centers, individually, and with the whole class. The teacher provides the environment and activities for children to explore in their relationships with children, materials, and the teacher.

Teachers plan activities around themes that offer multiple outcomes, so that they serve a wide range of child abilities and interests. These complicated activities accommodate the typical range of development

Box 10.1 *Happy Valley Kindergarten Baseline Individual Profile of Progress (For Teacher Use Only) August–September*

Student: _____   Teacher: _____

NY	B	D	S	Concepts/Skills	Criteria and Notes
				1. Name eight basic colors (red, green, brown, orange, blue, black, yellow, purple)	Show marker/crayon and ask, "What color is this?" NY = 0; B = 1–5; D = 6–7, S = 8
				2. Rote count to _____	Ask, "Can you count for me? Please start." NY = 0; B = 1–9; D = 10–19; S = 20+
				3. Count backwards 10 to 0	Ask, "Can you count backwards for me? Please start." NY = Cannot; S = Can
				4. Identify numbers 0 to 20	Use sheet to record which numerals are identifiled. NY = 0 numbers identified; B = 1–9; D = 10–19; S = 20–21
				5. Rational counting to _____	Spread out 10–20 Unifix cubes on the table and ask, "Can you count these for me? Please start." If the child wants to continue, spread out another set of 10.
				6. Write first name	Use boxed signature paper for four administrations during year. NY = Cannot; S = Can

Key NY = Not Yet; B = Beginning; D = Developing; S = Secure

Letter Identification*	Notes
Uppercase _____	
Lowercase _____	

Source: Developed by Marie Ann Donovan, DePaul University. Used with permission.
*Use master sheet to record which particular letter was identified.

as well as mixed-age groups and children with special needs. Choosing activities that accommodate the diverse social experiences of children permits the enrichment of their basic understanding of their broadening social world.

By starting with their interests, knowledge, and skills, teachers create an excitement for learning. Children learn by experimenting with materials, observing their environment, conversing with others, and sharing their insights. The teacher sets the stage for the integration of learning by starting with complex topics that lead in many directions. Questions that teachers ask to assess curricular effectiveness include whether they encourage children to

1. think divergently?

2. seek alternate solutions for problems?

3. be independent?

4. develop foundational skills in literacy, numeracy?

5. see logically integrated curricular topics?

6. participate in a balance of teacher-initiated and child-initiated activities? (Cromwell, 2000, p. 160)

The child-initiated theme approach to curriculum is an example of a complex topic developed with multilevel experiences to meet the needs of the diverse group of 4-year-olds in Ms. Berg's class, as discussed in Box 10.2. Draw parents into the process as the experience evolves. The theme offers opportunities to develop knowledge, skills, and attitudes in the intellectual, social/emotional, physical, and creative domains. Experiences in this theme are concrete and active (cf. Berry & Mindes, 1993; Wortham, 2006).

An explicit outline and explanation of this approach is available in *Developmentally Appropriate Practice in Early Childhood Programs Serving Children from Birth through Age 8* (Bredekamp & Copple, 1997; see also DAP, 2005). One important principle of this approach is that process

---

Box 10.2 *Garbage in Our World*

Ms. Berg's 4-year-olds attend a school that recycles papers, magazines, glass and cans. The children see recycling efforts made by the whole school in the cafeteria that uses donated silverware and dishes to avoid paper plates. The dishes don't match. One day at lunch, Kimberly asks Ms. Berg why the dishes don't match. From this discussion, the children decide that they want to explore other ways to help the school and their families conserve and recycle. Ms. Berg prepares a number of interest centers for the children that will elaborate the theme. The children develop a compost heap, interview their families about garbage awareness and recycling habits, read books about ecology, draw pictures representing a world full of garbage, and so on. The children begin a schoolwide drive to collect cloth napkins as a further recycling effort.

and presentation—the *how* of instruction—is as important as the specific content. Complex activities that have multiple outcomes form the content. The presentation of the activity and the teacher's interaction helps and stimulates the acquisition of content and/or skills. In this curricular approach, the teacher plays a critical role as "decision-maker," motivator, model, innovator, environmental planner, and evaluator (Berry & Mindes, 1993). The teacher shifts roles based on observation of the children in action.

Teacher Instructional Role

As they observe, teachers change their roles in instruction from observer to validator, participant/converser, extender, problem initiator, model, instructor, and manager/organizer/provider (Lee-Katz, Ellis, & Jewett, 1993; see also Feeney, Christensen, & Moravcik, 2006). Teachers use role shifting based on inference through observation; teachers also ask children to describe and interpret their work. In this way, the teacher can explicitly understand a child's thinking and goals. Teachers design games, interviews, contracts for specific work, and directed assignments to gain a better understanding of children's development and to plan instruction (Hills, 1992; Yelland, 2000; see also Kostelnik, Whiren, & Soderman, 2004).

Teachers establish the baseline for the program: routines, room arrangement, rules and expectations, schedule, and interpersonal relationships (Berry & Mindes, 1993). Once the stage is set and the theme chosen, teachers assess the curriculum effectiveness for individual children and for the group by watching the children. Teachers then adjust the baseline to meet the needs of children. For example, if an objective of the program is to increase knowledge of the functional uses of print, then how does a teacher know whether Maria understands? In a dramatic play setting, she observes Maria grabbing a message pad and scribbling as she listens to the phone call. Maria shows that writing is a substitute for oral messages (Tompkins, 2006). Teachers instruct and assess simultaneously. Focus questions for this kind of integrated teaching embrace the following developmental issues:

- Are children showing progress in relationships?
- Are they expressing joy, anger, jealousy, or fear in ways that facilitate coping?
- Do they run, skip, climb, and move with greater ability?
- Can they handle scissors, pencils, and tools more efficiently?
- Do they show increased knowledge about their world?
- Are they using language effectively?
- How do they solve problems?
- What new concepts do they seem to be exhibiting? (Seefeldt & Barbour 1998, p. 328)

Teachers should adjust their interactions with children, create an environment that promotes self-discipline, and assist children in mediating their own interactions. Sensitive responses and adjustments to observed problems help children grow and succeed. Teachers can decide what to teach by watching the children. Who is interested in leaves? What do the children know about squirrels? Can they identify red, blue, or green? Checklists and discussions of materials, room arrangement, and activities are available in the child guidance and curriculum literature (cf. Beaty, 2006; Dodge & Colker, 2002; Hohmann & Weikart, 2002; Kostelnick, Stein, Whiren, Soderman, & Gregory, 2006).

Link to Philosophy

Teachers should carefully select recording methods and the particular goal for observation based on the philosophy and goals of instruction for the program. You can find examples of different assessment traditions by reading ecological studies of teaching. Teachers talk about how they have incorporated assessment in the teaching-learning process. Teachers discuss how philosophy, planning, and assessment go together. Assessment is not an extra; it's part of what a teacher does (Genishi, 1992; see also Paley, 2004).

Assessment is developmentally appropriate to the extent that the processes are

- continuous.
- directed to all developmental areas.
- sensitive to individual and cultural diversity.
- completely integrated with curriculum and instruction.
- based on a defensible theory of child development and learning.
- collaborative between teachers and parents.
- helpful to teachers in their planning to meet the needs of children and the goals of the program.
- unequivocally in the best interests of the children. (Hills, 1992, p. 61; see also Gullo, 2005)

Thus, the preschool way of teaching is active, and involves problem solving and decision-making. Teachers show children how to learn by observing, questioning, and developing interesting projects for them. Teachers establish what children can do through their interactions with them. Using their knowledge, teachers individualize instruction. This is possible in the optimum preschool setting because the activities and procedures are broad. Multiple outcomes and levels of success are possible. For example, a teacher plans a theme on *Where Do We Live? Houses and Shelter*. "This theme allows children the opportunity to develop knowledge of the physical properties of their immediate family and the home environment. In addition, the theme fosters scientific inquiry about building materials" (Berry & Mindes, 1993, p. 87). One of the activities for the theme is "4.3.6: Make House Structures—Use paste, liquid cornstarch, sticks, and so on to make buildings with paper and wallpaper samples. Glue on vinyl tiles for roofs. Discuss what makes these structures work or fall apart" (Berry & Mindes, 1993, p. 94; see also Kostelnick et al., 2004).

Every child who attempts this activity can be successful. There is no right answer to the "house" or the "apartment." Not all children are required to make a shelter. Some may choose to read about houses, some may choose to draw, or some may choose to build houses with blocks. Because you do not require that all children engage in the same activity, they can choose an activity rather than fit into a "one size fits all" activity; all can be successful. Children build confidence in themselves as learners and dare to try new things. Teachers inventory knowledge, skills, and attitudes of children in the intellectual, social/emotional, and physical domains. They search for ways to stretch and encourage children as learners and achievers. Successful preschool teachers braid assessment and teaching into a smooth coil. The Head Start Child Outcomes are a nationwide example of this approach.

"Released in 2000, the Head Start Child Outcomes Framework guides Head Start programs in their curriculum planning and ongoing assessment of the progress and accomplishments of children" (Head Start, 2003). The Head Start Child Outcomes Framework models a coordinated philosophy, holistic curriculum, and assessment framework. The framework contains 8 general domains, 27 domain elements, and 100 indicators of specific elements of child development and learning. The learning domains are language development, literacy, mathematics, science, creative arts, social and emotional development, approaches to learning, and physical health and development. By promoting growth in these areas, regularly measuring progress, and individualizing instruction, teachers can be sure that the young children in their care are ready for elementary school. While this holistic framework addresses important learning outcomes for young children, it does not specify a particular model for delivering curriculum. Many models offer a holistic approach to curriculum including High Scope, Creative Curriculum™, Montessori, and so on. Examples of curricular approaches that promote a holistic view of the integration of assessment and instruction include those based on the theory of multiple intelligences (Gardner, 2004), the project approach (Katz & Chard, 2001), and the Reggio Emilia (Edwards, Gandini, & Forman, 1998) approach.

Multiple Intelligences Curriculum

multiple intelligences theory that children have eight areas of intellectual competence that are relatively independent of each other.

There are many interpretations of the **multiple intelligences** curriculum. Gardner (2004) identified at least eight forms of intelligence—linguistic, logical/mathematical, spatial, musical, bodily/kinesthetic, interpersonal, intrapersonal, and naturalist. Some curricular manuals seek to match "an intelligence" to "an approach" to instruction. More appropriately interpreted, Gardner's (2004) theory leads teacher to develop various tactics for instruction. Thus, instruction supports learners thinking from diverse perspectives.

One of the best places to learn about such an approach is through the selection of readings from the Project Zero website. As an outgrowth of research in schools and elsewhere, Project Zero is the center at Harvard Graduate School of Education that seeks "to understand and enhance learning, thinking, and creativity in the arts, as well as humanistic and scientific disciplines, at the individual and institutional levels" (Project Zero, 2005). One product of this work is a handbook for teachers that identifies:

five 'pathways' or approaches . . . exploration, bridging, understanding, authentic problems, and talent development—represent[ing] the ways in which the multiple intelligence [techniques] can be implemented and nurtured across the elementary grades. The Pathways Model promotes and supports the development of a well-grounded understanding of multiple intelligences theory to inform goal-setting and planning for using multiple intelligences theory in the classroom. Each pathway addresses a different set of goals and provides appropriate guidelines and examples (Baum, Viens, & Slatin, 2005; see http://www.pz.harvard.edu/ for additional or current information about Project Zero).

Starting with the theory that intelligence is not "a thing" but composed of many specific "ways of knowing," a multiple intelligence curriculum intentionally links all aspects of intelligence—movement, language, mathematics, science, social, visual arts, music—and adds working styles to systematically stimulate growth and development geared to each of the ways of knowing. The resulting holistic approach to instruction links naturally to portfolios for documentation of child progress (discussed later in the chapter). Another holistic approach to curriculum and assessment is the project approach.

The Project Approach

Drawing from child curiosities and implementing with strategies that foster inquiry-based and **project-based learning**—investigation of topic from multiple perspectives (cf. Katz & Chard, 2000), teachers construct activities with children that enhance development of self-understanding, foster investigatory skills, and promote cooperative learning and enhanced appreciation of cultural diversity in the community of the classroom. One of the benefits of the approach is the promotion of communication skills as part of the small-group work that is a hallmark of the approach (Katz & Chard, 2000). The approach uses **webbing**—a graphic organizer that starts with a circle delineating a topic, say cactus; lines leading from the cactus identify what children know about cacti—plant, requires little water, grows mostly in deserts, and so on. Then, children decide what else they would like to learn about cacti—can they survive in rainy places? How big do they grow? Are they all green? Do they have flowers? Next, children investigate using resources that teachers and parents provide. Finally, children document their learning with posters, stories, constructions, and so on. Box 10.3 illustrates a possible cactus web. The web and the processes and products generated during the projects serve to document learning (cf. Helm & Beneke, 2003).

project-based learning curricula organized on the basis of child-generated curiosities.

webbing an outlining technique that shows graphically or visually the relationships among ideas.

Box 10.3 *Cactus Webbing Example*

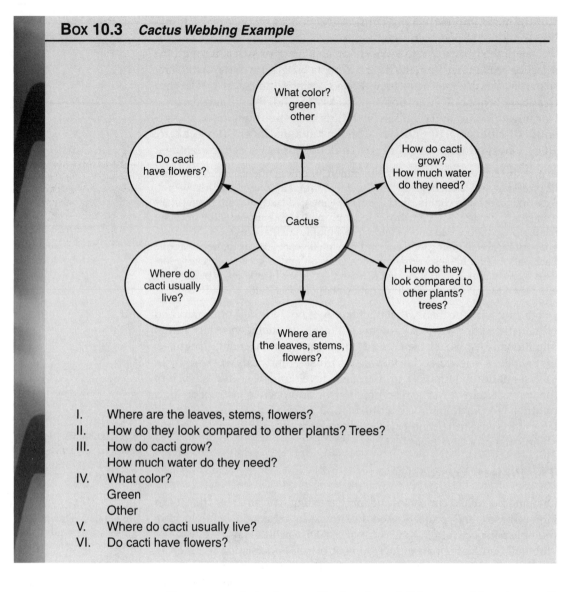

I.   Where are the leaves, stems, flowers?
II. How do they look compared to other plants? Trees?
III. How do cacti grow?
     How much water do they need?
IV. What color?
     Green
     Other
V.   Where do cacti usually live?
VI. Do cacti have flowers?

Because projects frequently involve children working in small groups to investigate questions of interest, peer collaboration is a vital part of the method. "[T]he content of the social action rules will not be the same from classroom to classroom, but the need for a social participation structure to be co-constructed, explicit, and working well before productive projects can be accomplished is essential" (Williams, 2003). Therefore, when planning a project-based approach to instruction, you will need to assess your students' developmental and functioning social skills. Then work out meaningful ways for young children to work together—maybe it is only sitting beside each other and looking at a book, or maybe it is cooperating to build a model cactus. In these situations, teachers and children need to assess whether the group works well.

A simple checklist serves as a rubric to document the way that 4-year-olds work together to solve a problem. For example, the checklist might include: listens to everyone's ideas; uses respectful words; accepts group decision without complaint; does what needs to be done (Diffily & Sassman, 2002). Another approach to project-based learning is Reggio Emilia.

Reggio Emilia

The **Reggio Emilia approach:**

fosters children's intellectual development through a systematic focus on symbolic representation. Young children . . . explore their environment and express themselves through 'expressive, communicative, and cognitive language,' whether they be words, movement, drawing, painting, building, sculpture, shadow play, collage, dramatic play, or music. . . . From the beginning, . . . explicit recognition of the . . . partnership among parents, educators, and children [is made]. Classrooms . . . support a highly collaborative problem-solving approach to learning . . . use small groups in project learning, . . . sharing of culture through joint exploration among children and adults. (Edwards et al., 1998, p. 7).

> **Reggio Emilia approach** holistic community way to develop early childhood programs that includes all stakeholders—child, parents, teachers, school leaders, and the community at large.

Child, teacher, and family interest drive the curriculum through long-term projects that promote engagement in learning and child development. School schedules are flexible so that time matches activity rather than the reverse. The approach requires "constant reflection, collaboration, and questioning" (Wurm, 2005, p. 5) by teachers who plan and implement learning with/for young children. The assessment portion of the practice is **documentation**—the "process of gathering evidence and artifacts of what happens in the classroom . . . not only the process of gathering . . . but also a physical collection . . . the reflection on and analysis of the collection . . . in a way that makes children's learning visible" (Rinaldi, 1994 in Wurm, 2005, p. 98) to all stakeholders. Documentation begins with everyday observation of child learning. It includes child products that have grown from their investigations. All the tools for recording observations—including anecdotal notes, photos, and child work samples—are available for the documentation process. In the Reggio Emilia approach, a documentation panel shows the work formatively and in summation; the panel functions to display learning and offer opportunities for reflection about its meaning. (See Box 10.4 for an example of a documentation panel.) Thus, from an early age children engage in critical analysis of their work, enhancing their understandings and development. An additional way to collect child documents and to document learning is through the portfolio.

> **documentation** collection of artifacts to support record keeping of child progress in learning.

Collecting Assessment Information in Portfolios

Portfolios serve as documentation for assessment information. For portfolios, you collect, review, and share teacher observations, informal assessments, and student work products with parents and students.

> **portfolios** places, such as folders, boxes, or baskets, for keeping all the information known about the children in a class.

Box 10.4 *Apple Picking Trip*

We saw apples grow on trees. We picked the apples from the ground and baskets.
We drank apple juice. We ate doughnuts.

Apples

We cut the apple open. The apple has small black seeds. We planted the seeds in a flower pot. We will watch the pot.

We made special apples

Ms. Eldorado brought apples to school. We used a recipe to make special apples.

Recipe

30 apples
30 sticks
Caramel sauce
Waxed paper for the drying apples

Wash the apples. Dry the apples. With teacher's help, stick the stick in the center of the apple. Pour the caramel sauce in a bowl. Dip the apples in the caramel sauce. Swirl the apples carefully in the sauce. Move the apple to the wax paper next to the bowl. Let dry.

The portfolios are a more dynamic record of child practice than records of formal screening tests and other measures. To be effective, portfolios must contain representative work samples, reflect clear rubrics or outcomes, and be relevant for the learning documented (Borich & Tombari, 2004). An accompanying reflection details why a particular product is part of the portfolio. Comments that teachers use to inspire reflection consist of the following examples:

- The process I went through to create this piece
- Who or what influenced me to create the piece
- New insights I gained about myself
- I have discovered that I am good at (Costa & Kallick, 2004, pp. 65–66)

Even young children can begin to be reflective learners (Smith, 2000) if they are given time to practice reflection. They can teach each other through sharing reflections. To become reflective learners, they need to be involved in decision-making. The reflective portfolio provides a common ground for children, teachers, and parents to think about learning holistically. "I have a picture to show you. You're a good drawer. The sun looks really good with the rays coming out" (Smith, 2000, p. 208).

One promising use of portfolios is as a parent-education piece. That is, you review the portfolio with parents. In addition to seeing child progress, parents learn about **developmentally appropriate practice**—instruction that is child-centered and holistic—in a practical, specific way. You show them examples of the way that Deidre shows that she knows story concept. Horatio is ready to go to kindergarten because, among other things, he can write his first and last name and can organize materials in space in three dimensions through construction (e.g., using Legos™), as well as solve science problems. All of this learning shows up in the portfolio work products, for example, in photos with dictated child reflection about the works. Examples of organizational categories for portfolios include products from a theme on personal growth, favorite stories, special science projects, or other materials chosen by the child and teacher to show the parent (Gelfer & Perkins, 1992; see also Shores & Grace, 2005). Portfolios are the paper or electronic storage frameworks for collected information. Regardless of the assessment measures required by the stakeholders, portfolios are appropriate even in such instances as the Head Start Outcomes requirement, where specific goals must be measured. Children produce the outcomes, but the measures and interventions show achievement in a variety of ways. (An example portfolio template is given in Appendix F.)

developmentally appropriate practice planning instruction for preschool children around topics rooted in the children's social world.

Outcomes Teaching and Performance Standards

Released in 2000, the Head Start Child Outcomes Framework is intended to guide Head Start programs in their curriculum planning and ongoing assessment of the progress and accomplishments of children. The framework also is helpful to programs in their efforts to analyze and use data on child outcomes in program self-assessment and continuous improvement. The framework is composed of 8 general domains, 27 domain elements, and numerous examples of specific indicators of children's skills, abilities, knowledge, and behaviors (Head Start, 2003).

The domains are:

- language
- literacy
- mathematics
- science
- creative arts
- social and emotional development
- approaches to learning
- physical health and development

The framework (is a foundation) of building blocks that are important for school success. The framework is not an exhaustive list of everything a child should know or be able to do by the end of Head Start or entry into kindergarten. [It is] intended to guide assessment of 3- to 5-year-old children (Head Start, 2003).

Head Start programs, then, must seek assessment materials that match the curriculum and the national framework. Common instruments used to support these efforts include the Work Sampling System™—including software options and Child Observation Record (COR)—with software support, and the Creative Curriculum® Progress and Outcomes Reporting Tool (CC-PORTTM)—a software product designed for use with the Creative Curriculum® Developmental Continuum Assessment Toolkit for Ages 3–5. In addition to routine assessment to improve the child outcomes and the program itself, sometimes you must assess and report your findings related to children who may need special services so that you can optimize an individual child's progress.

REFERRAL FOR SPECIAL SERVICES

Thus, after adjusting the baseline and the activities, teachers will find some children who need special services. These include speech and language therapy, occupational therapy, physical therapy, play therapy, and other special services to the family. In such situations, teachers need to document their observations in a child study. The child study serves as a basis for communicating with parents and other professionals. Increasingly, children who need special services receive them in the regular preschool setting. Consequently, the preschool teacher is an integral member of the team serving the child and the family. Therefore, teacher observations serve as a source of information for choosing appropriate referral starting points and for ongoing assessment of the effectiveness of the interventions planned and carried out.

Standard ingredients in a child study and questions to ask include birth history, motor development, language history, family composition and history, interpersonal relationships, and medical history. Obtain this information by interviewing the parent. A social worker, psychologist, or counselor may conduct more in-depth interviews as the diagnostic process proceeds.

Teacher Contribution to the Process

The teacher offers observations, strategies used to modify the curriculum, and modifications to the instructional process. Strategies employed may address variations in classroom organization and instructional techniques. Instructional activity individualization considers the child's particular social responsiveness, cognitive style, interactive competencies, and developmental progress (Raab, Whaley, & Cisar, 1993; see also Wood, 2006). A qualified professional should then evaluate the child depending on the complaint presented or set of symptoms of concern. Qualified professionals include speech and language clinicians, occupational therapists, physical therapists, psychologists, and social workers. Sometimes only one specialist will be necessary. For example, if a teacher observes difficulty with the form of language that a 3-year-old uses, an on-site evaluation by a speech and language therapist may be necessary. The teacher's role in this situation is to help the therapist pick a good time to visit the class to assess the target child's use of language in the play setting and to help the therapist in establishing rapport for an interview. Sometimes, the teacher may interview the child to obtain information for the therapist.

However, a social worker, psychologist, child psychiatrist, or counselor usually interviews a child with behavioral problems. The nature of the problem and the kind of services most conveniently available to the community and family will influence the choice of the mental health professional. For a child presenting severe symptoms such as hitting, kicking, screaming, or biting, a comprehensive evaluation by a team of professionals may be required.

Of course, for any evaluation, parents must give written permission. This is in keeping with good practice and federal law (e.g., IDEA 2004). Appropriate and best practice in preschool settings involves teachers in creating a regular dialogue with parents about child progress and adjustment. Thus, parents and teachers form an ongoing partnership in the best interests of the child. To begin this partnership in a play-based program, one assessment method that is used is play-based assessment (Linder, 1993).

Play-Based Assessment

play-based assessment
relies on the teachers's
knowledge of child's play
to judge the
social/emotional,
language, cognitive, and
physical development of a
young child. This can be
conducted in a natural
situation or by interview.

Play-based assessment utilizes an observation protocol with categories that include cognitive development, social/emotional development, communication and language development, and sensorimotor development. The team of professionals, including the preschool teacher, observes and records information according to a protocol. This method of assessment is best practice in infant/toddler programs serving typical children. Parents are an integral part of the process (McGonigel, Woodruff, & Roszmann-Millican, 1994). Preschool teachers must be familiar with this approach to assessment as a possibility for their programs, as well as part of their responsibility for articulation with infant/toddler programs. It is an example of holistic assessment and it embodies the principle of multiple assessments to identify young children with disabilities. In addition, assessment of an individual child's play helps teachers plan activities for children who do not at present play well, either by themselves or with others. You can observe many important characteristics that will help with program planning by watching children at play. For example, child contact with toys, toy preferences, play level (i.e., the cognitive and social sophistication that is present or not), typical ways of communicating with peers and adults, favorite activities over time, ability to sustain and engage in sociodramatic play activities, and so on (Garfinkle, 2004). As well, it offers opportunities for child-care settings to see concretely the continuum of development of young children and their special needs.

The Continuum of Referral

Referral of young children for special services operates on a continuum. At the beginning, teachers observe and interact with the children, adjusting various aspects of the program—routines, relationships, room arrangement, and activities. In these situations, the teacher seeks to individualize the preschool setting so the child can be successful.

Next in the continuum, teachers may contact parents to obtain suggestions and insights for helping a child participate successfully. Sometimes teachers will discover a family event or crisis that requires special support for the child and the family. Stressors for children include a new baby, the loss of a pet, a move, a change of child-care arrangements, an illness, a death, or a divorce. Whatever the situation, teachers and parents need to work together to support the child in adjusting. (See the National Association for Education of Young Children's website at http://www.naeyc.org for many articles on dealing with particular stressors that may affect the whole class, such as violence, turbulent times, and war.)

At the next step of the continuum, teachers and parents exhaust their ideas and resources for solutions to the child's symptoms. Then a specialist evaluates and makes suggestions for modification to the preschool program or special services. Speech therapy is a commonly required special service. It is critical that teachers and parents prepare young children for the experience of a formal assessment (diagnostic testing). Children will have many questions, such as "What will the examiner do?" "Can Mom or my teacher stay with me?" "Do I have to?" "Why me?"

Agencies and schools need to be sure that whoever conducts the examination is an experienced therapist with young children. To assist the examiner, teachers and schools must

- give a clear and specific referral question.
- supply information and materials that will help the examiner understand the history of the problem.
- identify all the relevant people to be included in the assessment.
- assist in identifying all areas that need to be emphasized.
- assist the examiner in developing an overall testing strategy. (Romero, 1999, pp. 57–58; see also, Lewis & Doorlag, 2006)

On rare occasions, teachers, parents, and specialists will decide to remove a child from the typical preschool program. In these situations, a specialized setting may be necessary to help a child. Children with profound hearing loss, for example, may profit from a class with sign language as the instructional focus.

At each point of the continuum, assessment results will suggest intervention modifications. Intervention modifications succeed or other strategies are tried. The process of intervention modification continues until something works.

Mrs. Martin cannot say, for example: "I tried seating Jerard next to me at large-group time and it doesn't work. He continues to get up and leave the group." You must try another modification. Maybe offering Jerard the opportunity to listen to the large group from the block corner, house corner, water table, or other favorite area would be more effective.

At the same time, communicate to the rest of the children that modifications made for Jerard as an individual in the group are just like modifications made for them as individuals. Mary Lou doesn't drink milk because she is allergic to milk. Muhammad doesn't eat pork because it is against his religion. Alice doesn't eat birthday cake because it is against her religion. Arnold doesn't run because he is recovering from heart surgery. Marta stays away from chalk because she is allergic to chalk dust. James doesn't have to count to 20 because he is still learning to talk.

A structured approach to curricular modification for children with special needs is an activity-based approach (Pretti-Frontczak & Bricker, 2004). In this approach, a specific analysis of child functioning matches to specific behavioral expectations for successful accomplishment of class activities. The structured activities grow from child interests and from needed skills. For example, for 4-year-old Ethyl who does not use words to communicate, the intervention team will identify word approximations for her to use in expressing her needs to the teacher, then the children. Or, Iyor may need step-by-step help for successful puzzle completion. First, make the pieces right-side up, then place the pieces, one at a time, into each space to see which fits, then try another, and so on.

The team of parent, teacher, and specialists strives to strengthen child successes in the preschool setting so that the child becomes a confident learner.

Formal Identification for Special Education

For any child identified and classified as a child with a disability, the provisions of IDEA (U.S. Department of Education, 2004) apply.

Assessment must

- be selected and administered so as not to be discriminatory on a racial or cultural basis.
- be provided and administered in the language and form most likely to yield accurate information on what the child knows and can co academically, developmentally, and functionally, unless it is not feasible to so provide or administer.
- be used for purposes for which the assessments or measures are valid and reliable.
- be administered by trained and knowledgeable personnel.
- be administered in accordance with any instructions provided by the producer of such assessments.

The evaluation process must

- include a variety of assessment tools and strategies to gather relevant functional, developmental, and academic information, including information provided by the parent, that may assist the team in making the two critical determinations: does the child have a disability? Which disability?
- not rely on any single measure or assessment as the sole criterion for determining whether the child is a child with a disability or determining an appropriate educational program for the child.
- use technically sound instruments to assess the child across four domains: cognitive, behavioral, physical, and developmental.

In conducting initial and subsequent reevaluations, the team must

- review existing evaluation data on the child, including evaluations and information provided by the parents of the child, current classroom-based local or state assessments and classroom-based observations, and observations by teachers and related service providers.

- on the basis of that review, and input from the child's parents, identify what additional data, if any, are needed to reach the required conclusions about disability and special education needs. (Turnbull, Huerta, & Stowe, 2006, pp. 20–21)

Formal Planning and Documentation

Federal law requires an Individualized Family Service Plan (IFSP) for infants and toddlers (0–3) or an Individualized Education Plan (IEP) for older children. This document serves as a record of goals, interventions, and results. The child manager or teacher convenes regular meetings with the family to review and change this planning document. All records of assessment and intervention are confidential. The Family Educational Rights and Privacy Act (FERPA) of 1974 governs access and confidentiality specifications.

The planning may include modifications to the curriculum in a typical setting. Methods for individualizing and delivering curriculum in the mainstream program include (Lieber, Schwartz, Sandall, Horn, & Wolery, 1999; see also Gould & Sullivan, 2005; Cook, Klein, Tessier, 2004):

- Environmental support

    This includes modifying the classroom baseline (Berry & Mindes, 1993)—room arrangement, personal interactions, transitions, and so on—to support a child with special needs.

- Adaptation of materials

    This includes clarifying boundaries with tape or lines, or consulting with occupational therapists to modify cutting, pasting, and other fine-motor projects, to support a particular child.

- Simplification of activities

    This includes looking at activities to remove extraneous steps, such as eliminating walking across the room to get supplies by delivering the supplies to a child who has difficulty with movement or who is easily distracted.

- Use of child preferences

    This includes knowing what will capture a child's curiosity or motive to learn and not expecting everyone to produce or be interested in the same activity.

- Adult support

    This includes modeling, giving extra cues, scaffolding the task, and stepping to ensure child success.

- Peer support

    This includes the practices of working with a collaborator and involving the classroom community in supporting each other differentially.

- Special equipment

  This includes the use of communication devices, specially modified puzzles, or other items to promote successful social and communicative integration.

- Embedded learning opportunities

  This is a more intrusive support that involves directed teaching of an individual within the mainstream, often at a time when this individual cannot participate effectively in the whole-class activity.

- Specialized instruction

  This may include Braille instruction or other support that is beyond the preschool teacher's expertise.

TRANSITION TO KINDERGARTEN OR FIRST GRADE

Leaving a comfortable early childhood setting to go to the *big school* is a major adjustment for young children. Though they may look forward to the idea of being "grown up" enough for this next step, the unknown is still scary. Preschool teachers can make the process less scary. The best way to help children and their families is to be familiar with the diverse settings where the children will be transferring. This happens through regularly scheduled meetings with kindergarten and primary teachers. Discussions can focus on curricula and transition plans.

Articulation of Preschool/Kindergarten Goals

Preschool programs need not change philosophy and goals in response to pressure from primary teachers, if such proposed practices from primary teachers seem developmentally inappropriate. Teachers should articulate child progress and the preschool program philosophy in developmentally appropriate language and function.

For example, instead of responding to the demand from school districts to interpret reading readiness as letter recognition, letter writing, and other specific skills, describe readiness to learn in broader terms with illustrations of child performance to support this broader response to literacy development. As interpreted by early childhood advocates, literacy activities support the development of children, including physical well-being, emotional maturity, social confidence, language richness, and general knowledge (cf. Morrow, 2005; Neuman, Copple, & Bredekamp, 2000). As well, you may wish to focus on school readiness more broadly when articulating with kindergarten or first-grade programs. In a comprehensive view, preschool programs prepare young children for school with foci on physical well-being and motor development, social and emotional development, children's developing approaches to learning, language development, as well as cognition and general knowledge (National Education Goals Panel, 1997; Shonkoff, 2004). Also, schools need to accept responsibility for readiness for young children. This vision is articulated by the National Association of Elementary School Principals (NAESP), which developed six leadership standards and strategies for principals:

1. Embrace high-quality early childhood programs, principles, and practices as the foundation for education throughout the school community.
2. Work with families and community organizations to support children at home, in the community, and in pre-K and kindergarten programs.
3. Provide appropriate learning environments for young children.
4. Ensure high-quality curriculum and instructional practices that foster young children's learning and development in all areas.
5. Use multiple assessments to create experiences that strengthen student learning.
6. Advocate for universal opportunity for children to attend high-quality early child education programs. (NAESP, 2005, pp. 8–9)

With this holistic approach to early childhood programs in elementary schools, articulation should proceed smoothly. Because 81 percent of young children enroll in preschool or other child-care programs before kindergarten, articulation and collaboration is critical (West, Denton, & Germino-Hausken, 2000).

Appropriately planned preschool settings can describe child progress in terms of broad developmental categories that underlie the development of academic skills and knowledge acquisition. Summative or final/cumulative reports should describe children in terms that highlight their knowledge, skills, and attitudes as problem solvers, self-confident and independent learners, cooperative group workers, and so on. This gives schools or parents the big picture about individual children. Descriptions of children as curious learners or effective group participants are the global behaviors that will serve children well in tackling learning to read, compute, and write.

Preschool programs form the foundation of exploration and socialization for children to begin the discovery of the primary-school educational agenda. By describing children in this way, you have redefined readiness in service to individual children. The list of narrowly defined concepts such as knowledge of colors and numbers, ability to write one's name and the alphabet, ability to count, and so on may cast some children in a bad light if they are missing some of these concepts or skills. To the receiving teacher, it may sound as if the absence of these items is yielding a class of slow learners when quite the contrary is true. The children in your program have learned to investigate the answers to questions of concern to them, and they are expressing their thinking in words, pictures, and invented spelling. They have learned to work together, to respect diversity, to appreciate stories, to memorize favorite songs, and so on.

Rich preschool reports describing learning style and accomplishments can go a long way to bridging the transition to primary school. In addition to being advocates for children with the primary-grade teachers, you need to help parents make the transition from preschool to the primary-grade experience—arm them with the knowledge that their children are "ready" to learn to read by showing them all the ways that this has occurred.

Teachers should equip parents with information about the appropriate use and misuse of tests. In settings where school districts have adopted screening tests as placement tests, teachers can help parents lobby for a differentiated diagnosis, if necessary. This avoids the heartache experienced by someone like Sue Long of Denver City, Texas (Atkins, 1990), who discovered that one of her twin daughters was scheduled for the developmental kindergarten and the other for the regular kindergarten, based on the results of a screening test. Screening tests are inappropriately used for this purpose.

Preschool teachers who assist parents in understanding and anticipating kindergarten issues such as screening, entrance age, extra-year kindergarten programs, and readiness as a child characteristic (Pianta & Kraft-Sayre, 2003) make the process of going to school a smooth one for children and families. Preschool teachers pave the way for continuity in education. They articulate the *real* characteristics of successful students—motivated, self-confident, curious, proud of accomplishments, knowledgeable in the process of inquiry, and capable of communicating in verbal and early writing ways.

Preschool teachers can advocate that the only true criterion for admission to kindergarten is chronological age. It is not *child readiness* that should concern teachers, schools, and parents, but broad curricula that allow the acceptance of all children (Maxwell & Clifford, 2004; NAEYC, 1995). Broadly focused teacher descriptions of children address the attention to this approach. "Early childhood education research provides for preschool teachers a clear notion of child development, an awareness of the role of play in the young child's life, and an understanding of the collaborative role of parents. Early childhood educators, as the experts, must present facts, illustrations, and a firm commitment to best practices in kindergarten" (Mindes, 1990; see also Fromberg, 2002; Johnson, Christie, & Wardle, 2005). In this way, preschool teachers serve children and families as the foundation of a rewarding trip through the educational system. We must always be on our toes and advocate for young children.

SUMMARY

The preschool teacher is a busy professional. Child assessment is a vital part of the job. Teachers share the responsibility for choosing wisely when selecting informal and formal instruments. They must serve as reflective, conscientious teachers of young children. This involves knowing the children, planning, and making changes based on children's work. Responsible and responsive teaching of children involves sensitivity. Sensitive teachers report their knowledge to parents and others, based on their observations and routinely collected, fair assessments.

FIELD ACTIVITIES

1. If possible, observe a screening session at a local child-care or school setting. Are appropriate safeguards for privacy and confidentiality in place?

2. Interview a teacher about his experiences with screening procedures. Focus some of the discussion on the way the teacher uses screening results in planning instruction.

3. With permission, observe a multidisciplinary staffing. Note the diverse ways that assessment data are included. After the meeting, plan how you would instruct the children in your class.

4. Visit some first-grade classrooms in your community. Outline an articulation procedure for a preschool of your choice.

IN-CLASS ACTIVITIES

1. Bring examples of assessment systems to class. With a classmate, compare assessment systems used by Head Start, other child-care settings, and the local school district. What are the differences and similarities? Would you make any suggestions for change in any of the three settings?

2. Develop an articulation plan for a preschool program that will graduate children for the local school district. Decide what kinds of information you will share at each quarter of the year that will show what the 4-year-olds are learning.

3. With a partner, develop a list of questions to use to help 3-year-olds critique their work.

4. Develop a symbol system that can be used to show whether skills are emerging, accomplished, or absent in 4-year-olds.

STUDY QUESTIONS

1. What role does assessment play in the enrollment of preschoolers? How are parents and children often mistreated during this process? In what ways can teachers prevent this?

2. What can the teacher do to ensure that the children in the preschool program remain intrinsically motivated to explore and learn within the classroom?

3. Why is it important for teachers to offer continually a wide range of activities and manipulatives to children within the program?

4. Teachers must establish developmentally appropriate assessment techniques. List the guidelines that will assist teachers in this endeavor. How do portfolios fit into these guidelines?

5. How can teachers introduce parents to the concept of developmentally appropriate practices in school and the home?

6. How do you integrate developmental milestones into the assessment process?

7. What steps must a teacher take in the referral process?

8. Explain the steps included in the continuum of referral for children. What role does the early childhood teacher play in this process? How can the early childhood teacher advocate for the children with special needs in the classroom?

REFLECT AND RE-READ

- I know what a comprehensive preschool assessment system looks like.
- I know how to find young children who are academically or developmentally at-risk.
- I know how to assess educational outcomes holistically.
- I have in mind the key ingredients for the successful transition from preschool to primary grades for young children and their parents.

CASE VIGNETTE

Kristal, a 5.7-year-old kindergartner, lives with her mother (her father returned to Puerto Rico when she was 4 months old and she never sees him) and grandmother. Although members of Kristal's family speak Spanish, the home language is English and Kristal knows only a few Spanish words. Kristal attends half-day kindergarten and an after-school child-care program. The observer notes that Kristal can run very fast and has strong fine-motor skills—her printing is "beautiful." On the Early Screening Inventory—Revised,[*] when asked to draw a person, she drew a girl sitting in a chair with many more details than classmates. On the Peabody Picture Vocabulary Test—III,[†] Kristal's scores are as follow:

Raw Score	Standard Score	Percentile Rank	Stanine	Age Equivalent
107	126	96	9	8-01

*Meisels, S. et al. (2001). *Early Screening Inventory—Revised (ESI-K) for Children 4.6 to 6.0.* Pearson Early Learning. http://www.pearsonearlylearning.com.
†Dunn, L. M., & Dunn, L. M. (1997). *Peabody Picture Vocabulary Test—III Form A.* Circle Pines, MN: American Guidance Services.
Source: From T. Kennedy, 2003, submitted in partial fulfillment of T&L 411, Assessment in Early Childhood Education: DePaul University.

As the kindergarten teacher preparing a report for the family and the first-grade teacher, what additional assessment information might you include? What recommendations will you make to Kristal's family for summer enrichment?

TECHNOLOGY LINKS

http://www.teachingstrategies.com
   Teaching Strategies. Curricular and assessment materials for teaching in preschool settings.

http://www2.acf.dhhs.gov/programs/hsb
   Head Start Program with performance standards.

http://www.naeyc.org/beyondthejournal
   National Association for Education of Young Children. Position papers, articles on teaching.

SUGGESTED READINGS

Cook, R. E., Klein, M. D., & Tessier, A. (2004). *Adapting early childhood curricula for children in inclusive settings* (6th ed.). Upper Saddle River, NJ: Merrill/Prentice Hall.

Gandini, L., Hill, L., Cadwell, L., & Schwall, C. (2005) *In the spirit of the studio: Learning from the Atelier of Reggio Emilia.* New York: Teachers College Press.

Gould, P., & Sullivan, J. (2005). *The inclusive early childhood classroom: Easy ways to adapt learning centers for all children.* Upper Saddle River, NJ: Merrill/Prentice Hall.

Hohman, M., & Weikart, D. P. (2002). *Educating young children* (2nd ed.). Ypsilanti, MI: High Scope Press.

Special Issues
in Primary Grades

Chapter Overview

This chapter presents special assessment issues in the primary grades. Teachers must assess a diverse population of children in these programs. Children in the primary grades have different learning styles and developmental and educational strengths. Teachers can use many informal methods to determine the learning needs of these children. A feature of the chapter is the topic of learner outcomes and accountability. The discussion incorporates the special issues of urban and nontraditional learners. Effective ways for incorporating portfolios in an assessment system is also discussed. The implications of No Child Left Behind (NCLB) for practice in the primary grades is a focus in this chapter. Finally, there is a description of textbook and individualized academic tests.

Assess as You Read

- What can I learn from preschool teachers?
- How can I use assessment to plan for instruction?
- If I teach in an urban area or work with nontraditional learners, what must I know?
- How do I prepare my students for achievement tests?
- Where do portfolios fit in the primary program?

PRIMARY ASSESSMENT SYSTEMS ISSUES

Primary teachers are responsible for formal assessment decisions for all the children they serve. In addition, teachers must prepare report cards, keep cumulative records, and use assessment to plan. Primary teachers must give standardized tests. These begin in grade 3 by federal law (P.L. 107–110) with the No Child Left Behind Act. Teachers are

learner outcomes
expectations for children's
performances.

accountable for meeting learner goals or outcomes. **Learner outcomes** are expectations for children's performances as defined by professional associations, the federal government, state legislatures, and school districts. In most cases, these various government and policy bodies are not concerned with the learner outcomes for preschool children. The notable exceptions are the Head Start Outcomes Framework with its associated assessment imperatives that began in 2000 (Head Start, 2003) and the requirements for early intervention for infants, toddlers, and preschoolers with special needs that require greater alignment with NCLB (IDEA, 2004).

Finally, the Committee for Economic Development (CED) calls for universal early childhood education for children age 3 and older. The CED issued the report *Preschool for All: Investing in a Productive and Just Society* in 2002. The report "argues for a strong federal/state partnership that expands access to high-quality learning opportunities and links providers and programs into coherent state-based early education systems. To achieve this goal, CED is calling on the business community to help build public understanding about the economic and social need for early childhood education in the United States" (CED, 2005). Thus, the broad outcome expected by the CED is social and economic in nature. Although universal preschool education is not yet available and there is limited public concern about specific outcomes for most preschool programs, early childhood educators are eager to make a difference in the lives of young children. Recently, however, there is a federal priority on preschool reading programs, with the "Early Reading First, part of the President's 'Good Start, Grow Smart' initiative (2002), designed to transform existing early education programs into centers of excellence providing high-quality, early education to young children, especially those from low-income families. The overall purpose of the Early Reading First Program is to prepare young children to enter kindergarten with the necessary language, cognitive, and early reading skills to prevent reading difficulties and ensure school success" (Good Start, Grow Smart, 2002).

Therefore, preschool children are busy learning and have already entered the assessment system in increasing numbers with the growth of Head Start, early intervention programs, and special projects of school districts and states. Yet the formal assessment experience of young children and their teachers intensifies in the primary years. As well, too often, the stakes of assessment become higher.

TRANSITION FROM PRESCHOOL

What, then, is the experience that preschool children bring to the primary grades? According to a report on the state of America's children by the Children's Defense Fund (2004), 64 percent of mothers with children under age 6 and 78 percent of mothers with children ages 6 to 17 work outside the home. Thus, their children are in out-of-home care. In the best situations, children have discovered how to learn, feel confident about themselves, enjoy their relationships with peers and teachers, possess basic self-help skills, and know some basic concepts—colors, numbers, letters, shapes, and so on. They are curious and ready to hit the big school running. Unfortunately, not all children have optimum preschool experiences. "In 48 states, the cost of center-based child care for a four-year-old is greater than tuition at a four-year public college. The number of children participating in Head Start has more than doubled during the past three decades, but currently the program only serves three out of five three- and four-year-olds" (Children's Defense Fund, 2004). Some children are coping with risk factors in their lives. "Studies repeatedly have shown that quality child care—care that provides a loving, safe, and stable environment—helps children enter school ready to succeed, improve skills, and stay safe while parents work. The positive effect of good care is even greater for low-income children" (Children's Defense Fund, 2004). Thus, you will find that not everyone is on the same developmental step. Even under the best family and social conditions, development occurs in an uneven fashion. So, a big part of a teacher's job is assessment of developmental and educational progress. This assessment is essential to appropriate planning for the individuals and group in each teacher's class.

ASSESSING TEACHING LEVEL

Therefore, in September, when children transfer schools, and throughout the year, teachers must quickly find out the instructional needs and levels of their children. Besides observation, the primary mode of assessment for young children, teachers review records of children. When records are not available, not complete, or not definitive, teachers must quickly assess children as they teach.

Informal Evaluation

Informal evaluation is comprised of techniques used in these circumstances. These techniques are task activities for the learner to solve. The activities fit into the routine of the day. They are similar to the tasks or activities that engage children in learning centers and in didactic experiences with the teacher, both solely and in small groups. The tasks specify scoring criteria or rubrics. These scoring criteria ensure **objectivity**—the same score regardless of who marks the answers. In the boxes that follow (Box 11.1, Box 11.2, Box 11.3), examples of performance tasks with rubrics are shown.

informal evaluation task activities used to assess the instructional needs and levels of children.

objectivity implies that a scoring scheme is sufficiently clear and discrete so that all those applying the criteria will obtain similar scores.

315

Box 11.1 *Math Assessment*

Teachers watch children perform classroom activities to see/assess what they are learning. Activities to observe children performing include:

- Group games involving logico-mathematical thinking (Kamii, 1985, 1989b, 2000). An example is the game "Always 12" consisting of 72 round cards bearing the numbers 0 through 6. The object of play is to make a total of 12 with 4 cards. Two to four children can play. The winner is the child with the most cards (Kamii, 1989b).

- Using computers to record data; calculators to add, subtract, multiply, divide.

- Counting and using numbers as names.

- Activities involving the demonstration of number facts, properties, procedures, algorithms, and skills (Schultz, Colarusso & Strawderman, 1989).

- Geometric analysis of characteristics and properties of two- and three-dimensional geometric shapes, including recognizing, naming, building, drawing, comparing and sorting shapes, and investigating and predicting results of putting together and taking apart geometric shapes (NCTM, 2000).

- Measurement activities including recognizing attributes of length, volume, weight, area, and time, comparing and ordering objects, and using standard and nonstandard measures as tools. (NCTM, 2000).

Examples of specific informal tasks that can be used follow.

M&M Task for Pre-K to Second Grade

Materials

Small bags of M&M's, napkins, paper, crayons, markers or other recording materials.

The Task

Conduct this task in small groups or with individual children. Give each child a bag of M&M's. Ask each child to show the color distribution in the bag. Explain that each bag will have a different amount of candy of each color, so that there is not one right answer, but multiple answers to this problem.

Allow children to express their answers in diverse ways. Children may draw circles to represent the numbers of red, green, yellow, and so on. They may summarize their count—2 green, 3 red, and so on. They may prepare a graph.

The teacher's role in this task is to observe. Ask the children to give a product showing their work. When finished, children may eat the M&M's.

Scoring the Task

    0 = unable
    1 = can sort by color, but cannot illustrate the solution
    2 = can identify same, more, less
    3 = illustrates task
    4 = makes a pictorial graph
    5 = makes a numerical or tabular graph

Box 11.1 *continued*

Pizza Party for Second Grade

Materials

A large cardboard circle resembling a pizza.

The Task

Conduct this task in small groups or with individual children. Show the cardboard pizza form to the children. Tell the children to pretend that they have two pizzas that size. The two pizzas are for a party. Seven boys and five girls will attend the party. Then say, "We want to give everyone a piece the same size. How can we do that?" Ask children to illustrate the answer to this question. Explain that each child may answer this question in different ways.

Supply paper, Crayons, markers, pencils, or other recording materials and scissors for children to show their work. Allow children to express their answers in diverse ways. Children may draw circles and divide the pizza; they may cut out paper to represent pieces and children; they may illustrate the answer with fractions, and so on.

The teacher's role in this task is to observe and ask the children to give a product showing their work.

Scoring of the Task

0 = no idea
1 = drawing stick children (or hatch marks) to decide the number of pieces needed
2 = cutting up paper to show the answer
3 = drawing fractional representations of circles
4 = showing the answer arithmetically with numbers

Box 11.2 *Informal Language Arts Assessment*

As the children move in the room around the interest centers, observe literacy development. Categories of observation and informal assessment include the following:

- *Interest in books.* Teachers can see which children are interested in books. Children and teachers can record lists of favorite books. Parents can be involved in this recording of favorites.

- *Concept of print.* Teachers can evaluate students ability to read environment print, own words as sight vocabulary, attempts to read predictable books, identification of letters of the alphabet, association of letters and sounds, and the use of story books (Morrow, 2005).

- *Story concept awareness.* Teachers observe how students attend to pictures, but not stories; attend to pictures and form oral stories; attend to a mix of pictures, reading, and storytelling; attend to pictures but form written stories, and attend to print (Sulzby, 1985). This can be evaluated by observing story retelling, attempted reading of favorite

continued

Box 11.2 *continued*

storybooks, role playing, picture sequencing, use of puppet or felt board, and questions and comments during story reading (Morrow, 2005).

- *Reading strategies.* This includes evidence of how the children approach reading. Where does each child fall in the continuum toward conventional reading?

- *Using reading.* In which ways do children use reading for pleasure, to discover information, and so on?

- *Writing strategies.* Developmentally, writing begins with scribbling and proceeds through a number of stages to conventional spelling and grammar (cf. Teale & Sulzby, 1986).

- *Handwriting mechanics.* This task includes use of pencils and markers and ability to form letters, stay on line, and so on.

- *Listening strategies.* This task includes the child's ability to grasp information in one-to-one situations, small groups, large groups, note taking, and so on.

- *Speaking strategies as evidence of language development.* This task includes phonology, syntax, and semantics (cf. Morrow, 2005).

Examples of informal performance tasks include the following:

Morris's Ten Words (Morris & Perney, 1984)

This is a means to assess invented spelling (child's creation of a word, based on his or her understanding of the sounds involved) and potential readiness for formal reading instruction. Model phonetic spelling for children by showing them how to sound out the word *mat.* Write it on the chalkboard or on chart paper as you sound out the word. Continue this process with the words *let* and *stop.* Use these words in sentences, so the children have a context.

Give the children paper and pencils. Then dictate the following 10 words and sentences.

1. *fit:* These shoes do not fit correctly.

2. *side:* I have one hand on each side of my body.

3. *dress:* Latoya's new dress is pretty.

4. *stick:* Juan found a stick under the tree.

5. *rice:* I like to have rice with dinner.

6. *beg:* The dog likes to beg at the table.

7. *seed:* The flower grew from a tiny seed.

8. *gate:* The gate on the fence was open.

9. *drop:* If you drop the plate, it will break.

10. *lake:* Jennifer is swimming in the lake.

Scoring

0 = only unrelated letters are used
1 = first or last letter of the word

Box 11.2 *continued*

2 = part of the sounds represented
3 = initial consonant, vowel, and final consonant
4 = conventional English spelling

Composition Assessment

Assign a topic. For example, "One day, I found a magic hat. . . ." Then ask the child to dictate, write, and/or illustrate the story, as age appropriate.

Scoring

0 = undecipherable or blank composition
1 = random words or child repeats prompts
2 = ideas have little or no relationship to the magic hat or simply repeats ideas from the story
3 = at least one new idea present, ideas lack development or are contradictory, writing may simply list ideas or wishes
4 = several new ideas present; ideas are not fully developed; sentence structure is repetitious; lacks structure
5 = ideas are fairly well-developed and expressed; writing has some structure (beginning, middle, end); development and organization could be improved
6 = ideas are very well-developed and expressed; fully developed structure with beginning, middle, and end; logical and well-organized; good sentences, variety, and expression

Each of these informal assessment procedures can be incorporated into the day-to-day activity of the classroom. These activities are performance-based assessments. The examples are drawn from teachers in the field. In implementing these procedures, teachers think about what they need to know about the children so they can provide the activities that lead the children to academic success. Starting from learner outcomes, specified by school districts and state legislatures, teachers plan what to teach. Using the tools of books and other materials in their classroom, they carry out the required curriculum. Knowing where the children are, developmentally speaking, is the key to creating meaningful activities and successful experiences.

Box 11.3 *Social/Emotional Assessment*

Teachers need to plan assessment to measure social/emotional adjustment to school. Zvetina and Guiterrez (1994) have described this adjustment as "the school self." It is the child's sense of oneself as a learner and as a member of the community of learners that influences behavioral adjustment to academic demands of the environment. The school self can be seen in children who participate and invest in the community of learners. Zvetina and Guiterrez suggest that such students will

• show a sense of themselves as competent learners.

• display increasing motivation manifested by their own curiosity, interest, and persistence toward school-related tasks and experiences.

continued

Box 11.3 *continued*

- initiate, participate, and connect in relationships with their peers and teachers.

- use problem-solving skills to work through and resolve problems related to tasks and interpersonal conflicts.

- draw upon a repertoire of internal and external coping strategies for controlling their impulses, modulating these affects, and effectively using time and space.

Through their work with teachers in urban classrooms, Zvetina and Guiterrez (1994) have developed this concept of the child role in behavioral adjustment. They are developing observational criteria for assessing this adjustment.

Traditionally, teachers have used categories such as self-esteem, achievement motivation peer relationships, relationships with teachers, persistence, and attention to describe social/emotional adjustment. Today's teachers must be aware of contextual and cultural factors relating to adjustment as they develop distinct specific criteria for describing the *successful*. Henning-Stout (1994) reminds us that learning is a personal process mediated by the culture of a given community as well as the community of the school. In schools where cooperative learning and child-initiated activity are valued, social/emotional assessment must include opportunities for students and teachers toward the assessment of these valued practices.

Learner Outcomes

From the perspective of educators, learner outcomes are a discrete expression of a philosophy of education. That is, what do you want children to know and be able to do or how do you want them to behave? Once you have decided the goals—learner outcomes—you can match the teaching method with the assessment method. For example, the Illinois State Goal 7 for Early Elementary is as follows:

- Estimate, make, and use measurements of objects, quantities, and relationships and determine acceptable levels of accuracy.

- Measure length, volume and weight/mass using rulers, scales and other appropriate measuring instruments in the customary and metric systems.

- Measure units of time using appropriate instruments (e.g., calendars, clocks, watches—both analog and digital).

- Identify and describe the relative values and relationships among coins and solve addition and subtraction problems using currency.

- Read temperatures to the nearest degree from Celsius and Fahrenheit thermometers.

One inappropriate way to teach this curriculum is to select workbooks containing all or most of these activities. The teacher then divides the children into groups by ability or by convenience. On day 1, children look at cardboard coins, count them, and then they go to their seats and circle the right pictures—identifying sums of pennies, nickels, dimes, quarters—in their workbooks. Everyone marches through the same pages of the workbook. The teacher plans extra sheets for those who don't grasp the particular concept being taught. He or she judges success by right answers on the workbook pages and the answers in small-group discussion.

In this scene, children are discussing the calendar every day. "Today is Tuesday, October 15. It is sunny and bright. We go to gym today. It is Audrey's birthday and she is 7 years old." In some classes, children would then copy this story from the chalkboard. This example shows inappropriate practice (Bredekamp & Copple, 1997).

Instead, you might bring in a jar of pennies and ask children to guess the number in the jar; ask children to measure the size of the shoes of the people in their families, using paper clips to graph their answers; or measure the classroom using pieces of yarn. As well, you tie the mathematics curriculum to science through an analysis of the weather trends for the month. Tie the mathematics curriculum to social studies through historical examination of money in the United States or changes in trading and currency practices around the world. And, of course, tie math to reading by using newspapers, books, and the Internet to read about data and data analysis—for example, economic trends or weather trends. These activities come from the experiences that children bring from kindergarten and first grade and coordinate with school-district goals based on state standards for learning.

Today, most states and many school districts have adopted a standards-based approach to instruction. Many of these state standards link to state-developed or other standardized tests. Most of the state and local standards are derived from the national standards of the subject areas—mathematics, reading, science, and social studies. Thus, primary-grade teachers are required to plan lessons geared toward the accomplishment of the local and state standards. Schools use standardized tests to assess children at third grade and report results to the public. You still have the choice of teaching from a **constructivist perspective**—a child-centered, holistic, problem-solving, investigatory approach to creating curriculum experiences.

One example of holistic, standards-based teaching is offered by the National Council of Teachers of Mathematics (http://www. illuminations. nctm.org). Its website lists the standards by grade level and divides them according to content and process standards. You can see both standards with explanations and lesson plans on this site. Teachers can pick activities to meet the objectives of the curriculum. For example, an algebra activity might involve classifying the animals in Old MacDonald's Farm. A data analysis activity might involve the collection of buttons with several analyses performed subsequently. In addition, the suggested activities contain links to children's literature (http:// www.illuminations.nctm.org/K-2).

Kentucky (Guskey, 1994) developed the first comprehensive system that encompasses learning goals comprised of basic skills and the core concepts of self-sufficiency, group membership, problem solving, and

constructivist perspective views teaching and learning as a process of discovery for the learner, based on the learner's prior knowledge. Teacher facilitates knowledge, skills, and attitude learning to support individual development.

integration of knowledge. There are two strands for the learner out-come assessment—continuous and accountability. Included in the ac-countability strand are

- scheduled performance events

  On demand, children are asked to complete performance tasks, including observation of experiments and recording and reporting results.

- portfolio performance tasks

  Initially, only a writing portfolio was required. The goal now includes paper products, video, and computer products.

- scheduled transitional times/tasks

At specified intervals, students complete both multiple-choice and open-ended standardized tasks.

Recently, Kentucky modified the assessment plan to comply with NCLB so that third-grade children experience a norm-referenced test in reading and math (Kentucky Department of Education, 2005); prior to this modification fourth grade was the first year for standardized assessment.

Within the continuous assessment strands there are formal proce-dures that include performance assessments, portfolio tasks, and infor-mal instructional-embedded assessments, Kentucky's system is complex but it is a good example of a comprehensive approach to school reform. All states must study the link of standards, curriculum, and as-sessment as part of the sweeping changes to accountability infused in P.L. 107–110, the No Child Left Behind Act. The Council of Chief State School Officers published *State Content Standards: A 50-State Resource* (2003) and plans updates to this publication; its website serves as a ready reference for the standards across the country. As well, state departments of education show the outcomes expected for schools in the state.

Using National Standards to Develop Checklists

With the enhanced focus on accountability as well as the emphasis on limited teacher time, a good source for developing teacher-friendly checklists is agreed-upon national and state-specific standards. All stakeholders use these—test publishers, curriculum writers, child-text producers, and teachers. Parents are reassured that their children are meeting the demands of more than local norms so that they will be prepared wherever they move in a highly mobile society. Finally, these measures remind us of research-identified behaviors that support learning and curricular development. An example of a checklist based on the International Reading Association reading standards is found in Harp and Brewer (2000, p. 159), where a reading checklist is divided into emergent reader behaviors, developing reader behaviors, and fluent reader behaviors. This developmental checklist helps focus observation and informal classroom assessment. Items on the emergent reader behaviors checklist may contain items such as "enjoys listening to stories, rhymes, songs, and poems," something that most teachers would think to observe and record. Another item that is indicative of reading progress is the item "uses pictures to help create meaning," a task that some may not readily associate with reading fluency. Taken together, the 15 items on the checklist provide the busy teacher with a focus for observation and record keeping, particularly when you format the checklist to comprise the categories of "not yet," "some of the time," and "most of the time." The use of these measures also assists with parent communication. You can say with confidence, "Our program uses national standards based on research as part of our record-keeping system." See Boxes 11.4 through 11.7 for examples of checklists that you might develop for yourself based on curricular outcome requirements. As well, there are prepared software programs to assist you in the systematic development of performance tasks associated with standards.

One of these programs is the Classroom Planner®. The software program provides features for grading, lesson plans, seating charts, calendars, budgets, attendance, state and local objectives/standards, assessment markers, medical information, IEP (Individual Education Plan), and parent/student Internet access (Innovative Education, 2005). PLATO® eduTest Assessment is a comprehensive online assessment solution that quickly identifies strengths and needs for students, classrooms, schools, or the entire district, guiding instructional decisions to improve student achievement over time. Teachers use "Strengths & Needs" reports to understand exactly how individual students and the class as a whole performed on each state standard (T.H.E. Journal, 2005). In addition, many school districts use conventional productivity software to custom-build programs to manage instructional assessment. Thus, this software can be useful as you prepare to answer the stakeholder questions of your state education department who must implement the accountability plans of state legislators and those required by NCLB.

Box 11.4 *Writing Rubric for Third Grade*

Name: _____   Date: _____

Did you write a story?

☺   ☺   ☹

Did it have a beginning, middle, and end?

☺   ☺   ☹

Did you stay on topic?

☺   ☺   ☹

Did you read your story to a classmate?

☺   ☺   ☹

Did your classmate understand the story?

☺   ☺   ☹

Did you check for spelling and punctuation errors?

☺   ☺   ☹

Did you revise?

☺   ☺   ☹

Did you illustrate or use graphic organizer?

☺   ☺   ☹

Compare this student rubric, for example, to the New Jersey Core Curriculum Standards for Language Arts at *http://www.state.njus/njded/cccs/s3_lal.htm#32* to see what information would be collected for the required outcomes. Develop modifications to this template for documenting all of the required elements.

accountability being responsible for the proper education of all children.

Outcome-based **accountability** requirements—specified learning objectives stated in broad behavioral terms, including NCLB—come from the input/output philosophy of business. The debate then becomes "What is worthwhile to know?" Currently, the definition of what is worthwhile is what is measured on standardized achievement tests. If definitions for academic success move toward more holistic definitions, then assessment must change as well. Performance on the outcomes shows success. The risks, of course, are the re-creation of another set of *high-stakes* test hurdles for children. Much of the debate about NCLB focuses not on the desire to reduce learning opportunities for children, but the current high-stakes nature of the outcomes-based assessment requirements. As states attempt to modify this requirement

Box 11.5 *Rating Scales*

Make these charts for each member of your class. Choose skills to rate that are of interest for report cards or other data collection demands.

Skill	Child's Name	All of the time	Some of the time	None of the time
Uses a variety of reading strategies				
Shows oral reading fluency				
Reads fiction and nonfiction				
Interprets pictures				
Interprets charts and graphs				
Responds orally to reading				
Responds in writing to reading				

Box 11.6 *Oral Presentation Rubric*

Name: _____   Date: _____

Attribute	Evident	Not Evident	Emerging
On topic			
Organized			
Creative			
Transitions			
Eye contact			
Loud enough			
Involved audience			
Visual aids			

Comments

Box 11.7 *Problem Solving and Reasoning*

	Accomplished	Practicing	Emerging
Organizes information			
Develops strategies			
Uses different strategies			
Keeps after the problem until solved			
Draws pictures			
Uses trial & error			
Can explain solution			

in the climate of the ongoing debate, performance assessment may become an added part of the process.

From an educational policy perspective, learner outcomes and performance assessment improve programs for all children. However, the weight of the assessment should not fall on the back of an individual child and thus deny access in an unfair way. That is, when judging a child based on performance tasks, educators must assure that prior educational experience included tasks similar to those requiring proficiency at specified age or grade levels. It is easy to see that a standardized achievement test requiring an in-depth knowledge of static electricity is not *fair* for children who have not studied electricity. Teachers must also keep well in mind that performance tasks have the capacity for bias, as well. If children have not participated in *hands-on* science, for example, they may not be able to handle problems that are presented by asking, "How many ways can you use a widget?"

Illinois Learning Standards "are content standards that describe 'what' students should know and be able to do . . . each . . . includes 5 benchmarks" in the K–12 span (Illinois State Board of Education [ISBE], 2001). Illinois, like other states, is developing performance standards that "will indicate 'how well' students are to perform to meet the standards" (ISBE, 2001). An example follows from the field-test draft of science performance descriptors for the "Standard 11A: Students who meet the standard know and apply the concepts, principles, and processes of scientific inquiry" (ISBE, 2001). The performance indicators are divided into five stages for each grade level. Thus, one aspect teachers must observe and measure is whether their kindergartners can "describe an observed event by:

- using senses to describe an event,
- observing measurements made by an event,

- listening to what might happen in an event based on previous observations,
- explaining what happened in an event,
- choosing a prediction based on observation." (ISBE, 2001)

The challenge for teachers is to take this discrete and content-free objective and turn it into part of an integrated curriculum. Because the blame for nonachievement or under achievement is usually laid at the door of the teachers and children, rather than at the door of school conditions—absence of materials, digital divide, and limited time—hundreds of discrete objectives and standards must be "taught." In addition, most often schools that do not meet state goals are beset with children who are at risk—children who are poor; who may be malnourished; who may live in violent situations; and whose schools are in disrepair, poorly equipped, and often filled with teachers who are new to the field or tired and disheartened. If you choose to dedicate your teaching career to the children in urban and nontraditional settings who need you most, you will need special skills.

Urban and Nontraditional Learner Issues

The task for the teacher in urban and nontraditional settings is to look beyond the traditional academic readiness rubric: assess the child's conformity to traditional learning settings. What bridges must you provide? Does Erica need a bit of phonics instruction because she has not heard standard English? Should you show Garth, a 7-year-old who comes to school for the first time, how to use lockers? To what extent have teachers incorporated an understanding of cultural groups in their approach to education in these urban schools?

Independence and interdependent functioning are not universally accepted values by all cultures in our society. For example, doing your own work is a traditional American value, a part of the self-actualization ethic

of America. Some cultures value teamwork more than independence. Not putting yourself forward is yet another value held by many cultures (Greenfield & Cocking, 2003; see also Spodek & Saracho, 2005). Thus, if a teacher is measuring initiative as maturity, without consideration for the traditional values of the children taught, the teacher may misjudge the child and decide that the child is lazy or dumb or mentally assign another negative characteristic. Other threats to the validity of assessment, particularly standardized assessment, include your own attitudes, values and behaviors related to racial or ethnic groups, the child's perception of meaning associated with belonging to a racial or ethnic group, and child and family experience with discrimination and prejudice. In addition, issues concerning nonequivalent community experiences due to economic circumstances, variation in acculturation to mainstream "American" values, and variation in language use affect child performance. And, sometimes individuals adopt the "inferior" stereotypes held by the majority culture or resist perceived traditional cultural expectations because family members, or they themselves, may see the demands for conformance to "values" and the consequent behavioral expectations as being one-way—from the mainstream without reciprocity and appreciation for the special racial and ethnic differences (Armour-Thomas, 2004). For these and other reasons, cultural understanding of learners and their familial experiences profoundly influence their perceptions and attitudes toward school and learning. Teachers' knowledge and skills regarding cultural expectations and experiences of the particular learners they serve also profoundly influence educational experience and learner outcomes for each of the learners in their care. All of this required sensitivity must occur in a climate of documenting child progress on multiple variables. Constructivist teachers employ performance assessment measures for this documentation.

Collecting evidence on learner outcomes with performance tasks requires a new format for record keeping. The most common method is evidence collection in a portfolio. Portfolios are dynamic and inclusive—involving the child, teacher, and parent. (See Appendix F for a sample template for portfolios.) These dynamic documents also are useful for recording the progress of students with disabilities.

Inclusion of Students with Disabilities

The portfolio reflects the learning goals for such children in the mainstream. As teachers strive to individualize instruction for all learners, including those with disabilities, there are curricular and assessment implications. These include the following principles of integrated curriculum and assessment (Pugach & Warger, 1996, 229; see also Polloway, Patten, & Serna, 2005):

- Covering less material, but covering it in-depth
- Focusing on meaning rather than rote learning of facts
- Teaching facilitates child learning

- Linking ideas across subject matter
- Constructing knowledge and building on prior knowledge
- Creating authentic activity where students work collaboratively in a community
- Embedding skill acquisition into meaningful learning activities
- Engaging children in problem solving and cooperative learning
- Closely aligning curriculum, instruction, and assessment

When you review these principles, compare them to the best practice guidelines for teaching in early childhood settings—they are remarkably similar. Examine and compare the multidisciplinary team and the interdisciplinary team recommendations. Box 11.8 shows a handy form to use to record instructional modifications for learners with special needs. Thus, including students with disabilities in the mainstream requires, and is supported by, good teaching practices.

Box 11.8   *Instructional Modifications Form for a Child with Special Needs*

Classroom Modifications for _____

Date _____

Seating
Near the teacher _____
Away from others _____
Near special friend _____

Instructional Modifications

Assessment Modifications

continued

Box 11.8 *continued*

Structural supports: calendar, assignment chart, PDA

Give directions with pictures or other clues

Special materials

PORTFOLIOS

portfolios keeping all of the information known about each child's progress and overall classroom activities.

The collection and development of **portfolios** is the most current way to link teaching and assessment. Most approaches to the collection of portfolios suggest that the process should be as important as the products stored. Teachers and students must think critically about what to include in these folders/boxes/baskets or electronic files. Parents are sometimes involved in helping teachers and children.

Portfolios serve several important purposes:

- integration of instruction and assessment,
- provide students, teachers, parents, administrators, and other decision makers with essential information about child progress and overall classroom activities,
- make it possible for children to participate in assessing their own work,
- keep track of individual child progress,
- form the basis for evaluating the quality of a child's total performance (Meisels & Steele, 1991; see also Eckert & Arbolino, 2005).

It is ideal to use portfolios according to an established purpose. Define goals and design activities to carry out the goals. Students and teachers determine the criteria for success. Students choose, under teacher guidance, examples of their work efforts for the year.

Examples of categories for math portfolios (Stenmark, 1991; see also NCTM, 2000) include:

- problem comprehension
- approaches and strategies
- relationships
- flexibility
- communication
- curiosity and hypotheses
- equality and equity
- solutions
- examining results
- mathematical learning
- self-assessment

Work samples for math include:

- Written or dictated description of the results of investigations
- Pictures: drawings, paintings, photos of the child engaged in significant activity
- Teacher or student sketches of products made with manipulatives
- Diagrams, graphs
- Excerpts from students' math journals
- Sample solutions of problems (Charlesworth, 2005, p. 53)

For early literacy documentation, work samples that might be included in a portfolio are progress in writing—for example, from scribbling to mock letters to conventional writing. For composition, elements to include are the young child's ability to develop a story from words as labels, to single statement, simple story, complex story (McGee & Morrow, 2005).

In portfolio development, students help teachers generate criteria for effective work (Hebert, 2001; Shores & Grace, 2005). Children form criteria for good and great work. They evolve clear models for the required assignments. Children refer to the criteria for success as they work. The teacher's job is to provide resources for quality work.

The *Work Sampling System*™ (Meisels, Jablon, Dichtelmiller, Dorfman, & Marsden, 2001) yields developmental guidelines and checklists as well as portfolios that include core items to show growth over time and individualized items that reflect original characteristics of learners. This research-based assessment system keys to state and national standards, as well as developmental guidelines. To guide planning and to summarize growth, teachers produce summary reports three times per year. The system separates developmental readiness and progress from academic knowledge and skills. Parents, students, and teachers are involved in creating the system. The system models a comprehensive approach for the assessment of young children. Materials included in the assessment system in addition to the guidelines and checklists are *Omnibus Guidelines* that show "how performance indicators change over time and provides examples of active learning" (Pearson Early Learning, 2005). Report formats for standards and narrative summaries are available in print and electronically.

In all of these examples of portfolio assessment, the reader gains an appreciation for the similarity of day-to-day curriculum with the periodic assessment tasks. The assessment procedure is not a "get the learner" activity, but part of the check on learning progress. Where is the learner in relation to goals? Teachers, parents, and children collaborate to address these issues. Many examples of performance tasks and portfolio examples are available in published form today. Teachers must use good judgment in choosing published tasks or portfolios. The crucial factors are the relationships of philosophy, goals, activities, and assessment strategy. There must be a match between all of these elements.

One system of assessment that meets the highest standards is the *Work Sampling System*™ (Meisels et al., 2001). This assessment system contains developmental guidelines and checklists, covers all curricular areas, and provides for the development of summary reports. The system is standards-based, can be modified for local or state needs, and includes children with special needs in its approach. Finally, it models the involvement of young children in portfolio development.

Involving Children in Portfolio Data Collection

Young children who study in schools that appreciate their problem-solving approaches and learning styles can learn early on about the link from curriculum to assessment to reporting through the modeling that teachers provide. Questions that teachers might ask include:

1. What is your work plan?
2. What difficulties are you having in accomplishing your plan?
3. Are your goals realistic for the time period?
4. What are you especially interested in?
5. What strategies have you tried? What might you try?
6. How will you know when your work is ready to turn in? (Costa & Kallick, 2003, p. 36)
7. What did I enjoy learning most this week?
8. What have I learned about _____?
9. What have I learned when trying to explain _____ to my classmate? (Martin-Kniep, 2000, p. 24)
10. How do the pieces in your collection illustrate what you can do as a reader, writer, mathematian?
11. What do you notice about your work in September and now?
12. What strategies have you learned for problem solving?
13. If you picked one thing that helped you most as a learner, what would it be?
14. What have you learned about yourself as a learner as you put together your portfolio? (Martin-Kniep, 2000, p. 71)
15. What makes this your best piece of work?
16. How does this relate to what you have learned before?

In addition, students can construct statements such as the following:

1. I still don't understand _____.
2. I didn't enjoy _____ because _____.
3. I find _____ most challenging because . . .
4. This assignment is quality work, because . . . (Benson, 2003, p. 173)

In addition to conversation geared to child's linguistic sophistication, you may consider using some paper-and-pencil methods to promote reflection. For example, teachers can develop self-evaluation forms for children to fill out. Morrow (2005) suggests one that includes items related to letters and sounds, reading, and writing. Items consist of *I know all the letters of the alphabet, the things I need to learn how to do better,* and *the things I do well.* Assessment becomes a part of the everyday classroom using these paper-and-pencil self-evaluation forms. These forms grow out of the classroom discussion with young readers and writers of kindergarten age in which teachers ask children to be involved in the planning of the evaluation of activities.

In an activity entitled *I can paint a picture,* kindergartners listen to a story and then they are asked to draw a picture about the story or to draw a picture of the new ending. Before children begin the activity, they develop a rubric for successful completion of the assignment (Mindes & Donovan, 2001, pp. 34–35; see also Strickland, 2005). Rubrics can be holistic—giving a single score or rating for a work products—or analytical—dividing a product or performance into essential elements so that the performance can be studied in its component parts. A holistic rubric is quick and easy to use, but gives less information to the learner. For example, children with identical holistic scores may have very different component skills. Children can participate in the aspects of rubric development by identifying attributes for the quality for a product or process, thinking about and drafting the weight of the attributes of the rubric, using the rubric for self-assessment, using the rubric to assess anonymous classmate's work, and using the rubric for peer assessment (Martin-Kniep, 2000, p. 54).

Another promising way to help children organize for learning and assessment is graphic organizer completion. The most familiar is the Venn diagram—two circles that overlap in the middle. This diagram is frequently used to show similarities between concepts or stories. Another familiar organizer is the web described earlier in the project approach discussion. In addition to commercially available template books (cf. Jacobson & Raymer, 1999), a popular software program called Kidspiration® (http://www.inspiration.com) provides a dynamic vehicle to organize information in all subject areas. These visual organizational cues help learners see where they are in a project or process, making it possible for them to decide how to display their knowledge and skills and what to include. Finally, some children may wish to show their learning by using Kid Pix® Deluxe 3 (published by Broderbund, http://www.broderbund.com), a presentation software package, for part or their entire portfolio.

By involving children in day-to-day assessment, testing, and reviewing, the leap to the spring achievement test program is clearly established. The classroom evaluation is a counterpoint to achievement testing.

STANDARDS-BASED TEACHING

Currently, most school districts require you to key your teaching to standards and show that you have done so on your lesson plans. More and more school districts also expect to see the link from standard to lesson to assessment. In addition to locally developed and mandated materials, technological sources of information are also helpful. Several commercial products are available now to assist busy teachers. Some products that meet the demand for comprehensive and appropriate practice that you may wish to explore include those developed by the following organizations:

- Mid-continent Research for Education and Learning
  http://www.mcrel.org
- Classwell™ Learning Group http://www.classwell.com

- Teachmaster from PLATO® http://www.plato.com
- Prosper™ Assessment System http://www.pearsonncs.com/prosper/
- Homeroom.com from Princeton Review http://www.princetonreview.com/educators/instructional/approach.asp

These are but a few of the products available to support **standards-based teaching** that connects teaching and assessment. These products are, however, among the most comprehensive and appropriate resources for use by early childhood teachers. All of the major testing companies have some products related to curriculum, standards, and assessment. No doubt, more products will explode on the Web and in software packages marketed to schools. Finally, state departments of education and school districts use conventional software to create accountability systems for particular stakeholder-driven questions.

A working example of using standards and working with accountability demands in the service of children in an urban environment is located at the DePaul University Center for Urban Education (http://teacher.depaul.edu). Under the leadership of Barbara Radner, the Center developed Teachers Toolkit. Boxes 11.9 through 11.11 show excerpts

standards-based teaching an approach to teaching that requires teachers to coordinate instruction to specified standards or goals.

Box 11.9 *Teachers Toolkit—Language Arts Strategies*

Focus ➡	Get It Clear ⇨	Think More ➡	Think It Through ⊃	Get It Together ❖	Get It Across ⤾

LANGUAGE ARTS STRATEGY DEVELOPMENT WITH ACTIVITIES/ASSESSMENTS

| WORD KNOWLEDGE STRATEGIES
1A apply word analysis and vocabulary skills to comprehend selections
> Focus on one kind of decoding/word attack strategy each week.
> Use words of the week all week.
> Use structural analysis strategies.
> Develop vocabulary in content areas.
> Display words and pictures by phonics/structural patterns and topic. | *Activities/Assessment*
❖ *Draw words or pictures to explain vocabulary.*
❖ *Chart word-picture-word.*
❖ *Chart or match word/synonym, word/antonym.*
❖ *Find word in newspaper, book.*
❖ *Write sentence with word(s).*
❖ *Make/complete grammar chart or glossary.*
❖ *Make/complete prefix-suffix chart/guide.*
❖ *Write with the "words of the week."* |
| FLUENCY STRATEGIES
Also include 4A (listen) and 4B (speak) effectively plus comprehension standards. | *Activities/Assessments*
❖ *Read aloud from texts and their own writing.*
❖ *Re-read texts individually and in groups.* |

continued

Box 11.9 *continued*

> Read aloud, think aloud. > Coach. > Model fluent reading of a variety of kinds of texts.	❖ *Partner reading* ❖ *Poetry reading across the curriculum* ❖ *Make your own read-aloud guide.*
COMPREHENSION STRATEGIES *1B Apply reading strategies to improve understanding and fluency.* *1C Comprehend a broad range of reading materials.* *2A Understand how literary elements and techniques are used to convey meaning.* *2B Read and interpret a variety of literary works.* *5A Locate, organize, and use information from various sources to answer questions, solve problems, and communicate ideas.* *5B Analyze and evaluate information acquired from various sources.* *5C Apply acquired information, concepts, and ideas to communicate in a variety of formats.* ✓ Think out loud. ✓ Read with a partner. ✓ Use a variety of strategies. ✓ Read aloud; re-read independently.	***Activities/Assessments*** ❖ *Illustrate text.* ❖ *Construct and explain graphic organizers.* ❖ *Answer questions; justify answer choice.* ❖ *Make up questions (and provide answers).* ❖ *Sequence events in pictures or words.* ❖ *Write or match sentences that describe or explain _____.* ❖ *Infer and explain basis of inference.* ❖ *Outline text.* ❖ *Outline topic with information from two or more texts.* ❖ *Identify main idea or theme and explain its basis in text.* ❖ *Write the next part.* ❖ *Write a paragraph, poem, booklet, letter about what you read.* ❖ *Make your own "How To" reader's guide.*
WRITING STRATEGIES *3A Use correct grammar, spelling, punctuation, capitalization, and structure.* *3B Compose well-organized and coherent writing for specific purposes and audiences.* *3C Communicate ideas in writing to accomplish a variety of purposes.* ✓ Incorporate writing in all subjects ✓ Model—"write aloud." ✓ Focus on one writing element weekly. ✓ Model how to write.	***Activities/Assessments*** ❖ *Write with focus, organization, support, coherence, and clarity.* ❖ *Edit writing.* ❖ *Write in a variety of formats—letters, poems, diaries, fiction, nonfiction, booklets, etc.* ❖ *Make your own Writer's Guide that explains how to write.*

Source: http://teacher.depaul.edu; Polk Bros. Foundation Teacher Leadership Network, DePaul Center for Urban Education © 2003. Used by permission.

Box 11.10   Teachers Toolkit—Reading Outcomes and Assessments

Focus ➡ Get It Clear ⇨   Think More ➡   Think It Through ⟳   Get It Together ❖   Get It Across ⇨

Reading Outcomes and Assessments

	Standards	Performance Descriptors	Assessments
Word Knowledge	*1A Can apply word analysis and vocabulary skills to comprehend selections.*	✓ Recognize literary devices in text. ✓ Use roots and affixes to figure unfamiliar words. ✓ Infer meaning from context.	✓ Make guide to using this quarter's word analysis skills. ✓ Test on unfamiliar words requiring use of roots, affixes, inference.
Reading Comprehension	*1B Can apply reading strategies to improve understanding and fluency.* *1C Can comprehend a broad range of reading materials.* *5A Locates, organizes, and uses information from various sources to answer questions, solve problems, and communicate ideas.*	✓ Apply survey strategies (e.g., use of bold print, organization of content, key words, graphics). ✓ Infer and draw conclusions about text, and explain basis. ✓ Organize and integrate information from a variety of sources.	✓ Create "my own reading strategy guide." ✓ Open-ended questions/ multiple-choice questions—students justify responses. ✓ Make Venn diagram with information from different texts.
Fluency	*4B Can speak effectively using language appropriate to the situation and audience.*	✓ Read aloud fluently (with expression, accuracy, and appropriate speed).	✓ Read aloud with appropriate rate and expression. ✓ Present poem effectively. ✓ Set and reach fluency goal— rate and comprehension levels.
Writing	*3B Can compose well-organized and coherent writing for specific purposes and audiences.* *3C Can communicate ideas in writing to accomplish a variety of purposes.*	✓ Use adjectives and other elements to enhance writing. ✓ Edit and revise content.	✓ Edit, revise paragraph, letter, or poem. ✓ Write guide to writing with this quarter's elements.

continued

Box 11.10 *continued*

Reading Outcomes and Assessments for _____ Quarter

	Standards	Performance Descriptors	Assessments
Word Knowledge	1A Can apply word analysis and vocabulary skills to comprehend selections.		✓ Make glossary. ✓ Demonstrate word attack skills of the quarter in reading aloud and/or guide.
Reading Comprehension	1B Can apply reading strategies to improve understanding and fluency. 1C Can comprehend a range of reading materials. 5A Locates, organizes, and uses information from various sources to answer questions, solve problems, and communicate ideas.		✓ Answer questions. ✓ Make graphic organizer to show relationships in text. ✓ Write about a text. ✓ Illustrate a text.
Fluency	1B Can apply reading strategies to improve understanding and fluency.		✓ Read with appropriate expression and rate. ✓ Set and reach fluency goal.
Writing	3A Can use correct grammar, spelling, punctuation, capitalization, and structure. 3B Can compose well-organized and coherent writing for specific purposes and audiences.		✓ Write a _____. ✓ Write guide to writing with this quarter's elements.

Source: http://teacher.depaul.edu; Polk Bros. Foundation Teacher Leadership Network, DePaul Center for Urban Education © 2004. Used by permission.

Box 11.11   Teachers Toolkit—Math Outcomes and Assessments

Focus ➡   Get It Clear ⇧   Think More ➡   Think It Through ➡   Get It Together ❖   Get It Across ⇨

Math Outcomes and Assessments for _____ Quarter _____ Grade: _____

Some elements of math may not be emphasized in a specific quarter. Include the performance descriptors for the math emphasized this quarter.

	Standards	Performance Descriptors	Assessments
Number Sense and Operations	6A Demonstrate knowledge and use of numbers and their many representations in a broad range of theoretical and practical settings. 6B Investigate, represent, and solve problems using number facts, operations and their properties, algorithms, and relationships. 6C Compute and estimate using mental mathematics, paper-and-pencil methods, calculators, and computers.		✓ Make glossary. ✓ Make guide to operations of the quarter. ✓ Solve problems. *Primary: Make number book.*
Measurement	7A Can measure and compare quantities using appropriate units, instruments, and methods. 7B Estimate. 7C Solve problems.		✓ Make glossary. ✓ Solve problems. ✓ Make measurement guide.
Math Patterns/ Algebra	8A Describe numerical relationships using variables and patterns.		✓ Make glossary. ✓ Make guide to algebra of the quarter.

continued

Box 11.11   continued

Focus ➡ Get It Clear ⇨   Think More ➡   Think It Through ↻   Get It Together ❖   Get It Across ↬

Reading Outcomes and Assessments for _____ Quarter

	Standards	Performance Descriptors	Assessments
	8B Describe numerical relationships using tables, graphs, and symbols. 8C Solve problems. 8D Solve algebra problems.		✓ Solve problems.
Geometry	9A Demonstrate and apply geometric concepts involving points, lines, planes, and space. 9B Identify, describe, classify, and compare relationships using points, lines, planes, and solids. 9C Construct convincing arguments and proofs to solve problems. 9D Solve problems.		✓ Make glossary. ✓ Solve problems. ✓ Make geometry guide.
Data Collection and Analysis	10A Organize, describe, and make predictions from existing data. 10B Formulate questions, design data collection methods, gather and analyze data, and communicate findings. 10C Determine, describe, and apply the probabilities of events.		✓ Make glossary. ✓ Solve problems. ✓ Make data analysis guide. ✓ Organize data project.

Source: http://teacher.depaul.edu; Polk Bros. Foundation Teacher Leadership Network, DePaul Center for Urban Education © 2004. Used by permission.

from this Teachers Toolkit. The Toolkit links to national, state, and local standards. A working document links teaching plans to assessment strategies. Many downloadable teacher materials are available on this site. The Toolkit fosters a holistic approach to learning while being mindful of real accountability demands. This Toolkit supports teachers working in a system where achievement testing is used in a high-stakes way and is applicable to similar situations across the country.

ACHIEVEMENT TESTING

Across the country, achievement tests are part of the primary program. Some districts use tests to assess readiness for reading at the kindergarten level. States and school districts may require regular achievement testing at the third grade. The federal priority for annual assessment beginning in third grade (P.L. 107–110, No Child Left Behind, 2001) requires states to develop plans for the annual assessment of children and to report the results. This is a way to check the curriculum and instruction process for children who have historically been underserved or disserved by schools. Yet, this accountability emphasis must not rely on the high-stakes use of achievement tests:

- Using tests to decide which children should fail kindergarten and other grades.
- Ignoring the limitations and technical aspects of tests (i.e., using instruments that are not matched to the curriculum).
- Placing inappropriate weight on the statistics of tests, (e.g., ignoring stanines and percentiles, but placing great faith in grade-level equivalents).
- Using closed-answer instruments to judge the effectiveness of constructionist curriculum.
- Relying on test scores to evaluate the success of students, schools, and teachers.
- Accepting without question "the science" of tests. (Kamii, 1989a; see also Popham, 2004)

One of the potentially most devastating ways that schools misuse tests with young children is in readiness testing. Administered at the beginning of a child's career in school, children are subject to failure experiences that shape their entire lives. Relying on a readiness test to determine placement in grades is inappropriate. Such measures neglect the social/cultural context and typical individual developmental deviation found in all groups of children. The National Association for Education of Young Children (1995) disseminated a position statement on readiness that is more holistic. Recently, the concept of school readiness implies that the school is ready for the child at whatever skill and knowledge level the child brings to school (cf. Maxwell & Clifford,

2004). However, reading and reading readiness are a sustained federal focus, as seen with the Reading First Initiative.

The No Child Left Behind Act signed into law by President George W. Bush on January 8, 2002, established Reading First as a new, high-quality evidence-based program for the students of America. The Reading First initiative builds on the findings of years of scientific research, which, at the request of Congress, were compiled by the National Reading Panel. Ensuring that more children receive effective reading instruction in the early grades is of critical importance to the President and the nation . . . Reading First is a focused nationwide effort to enable all students to become successful early readers. Funds are dedicated to help states and local school districts eliminate the reading deficit by establishing high-quality, comprehensive reading instruction in kindergarten through grade 3. . . . Building on a solid foundation of research, the program is designed to select, implement, and provide professional development for teachers using scientifically based reading programs, and to ensure accountability through ongoing, valid and reliable screening, diagnostic, and classroom-based assessment"(U.S. Department of Education, 2005a).

Reading readiness can be appropriately assessed by redesigning the concept of reading to include the topics thought of as emergent writing and reading (Sulzby, 1989; see also McGee & Morrow, 2005). "Children appear to add new understandings about writing, somewhat as a repertoire of understandings in the sociolinguistic sense. . . . Their development does not follow one invariant, hierarchical order. We see several patterns of development, with a general progressive track . . . to conventional writing" (Sulzby, 1989, p. 85). Sulzby defines conventional writing as "the child's production of text that another conventionally literate person can read and that the child himself or herself reads conventionally" (Sulzby, 1989, p. 88; see also McGee & Morrow, 2005).

Children simultaneously learn to read contextually and specifically. That is, young children can read the word *stop* when it appears on a sign, but not in a book or on a chalkboard (Teale, 1989, p. 49; see also McGee & Morrow, 2005). They have read the word in context. Through exposure to familiar words—*dog, pat, dinosaur, Barney*—in favorite stories, they learn the specifics. Gradually, they can form greater understandings from contextual situations. Teachers of young children must keep these academic developmental principles in mind, particularly at the kindergarten level.

In a position statement, the National Association of Early Childhood Specialists in State Government and the National Association for the Education of Young Children (2001) point to the continuing inappropriate use of assessment measures for the entry and placement of kindergartners. The call to action includes the following principles for kindergarten teachers:

- Guard the integrity of effective, developmentally appropriate programs for young children.

- Enroll children based on their legal right to enter (i.e., at age 5).

- Inform yourself about assessment strategies and techniques.

- Reject retention as a viable option for kindergartners.

- Use valid, reliable tests; align these with curriculum; involve all stakeholders.

- Welcome all children in kindergarten; avoid extra year or other special discriminatory programs. (p. 60)

When Teachers Do Use Achievement Tests

Teachers should involve the decision-makers in carrying out the testing practice in the classroom. A kindergarten teacher in a suburban school district, Ms. Green, was told that she must administer a reading readiness test to her group in November. The teacher, an experienced early childhood teacher of 3- to 5-year-olds, was hired late in August. Her assignment was to teach a group of 25 children whose parents had just registered them for school. The parents had not registered the children in the spring round-up, as many families had done. The group of children had limited experience in a formal learning situation—many were learning English. The classroom supplies given to Ms. Green were workbooks, dittos, crayons, and a limited number of table games. She immediately went to garage sales to find housekeeping center materials, borrowed big books from the library, and reorganized the room into interest centers. Ms. Green created a developmentally appropriate environment. She developed an assessment system based on district goals as stated on the kindergarten report card. She organized folders for each child, kept work samples, and made anecdotal notes. Ms. Green created partnerships with parents and children. They (teacher, children, and parents) all knew that they were:

- learning how to be students

- satisfying their curiosity

- enjoying the group experience

- discovering new information

- learning English

- writing and reading at the preliteracy level

- solving problems

- using numbers and equations

All of this information about achievement was available by teacher report. What would a reading readiness test add?

Ms. Green protested to the district test coordinator. She gave all the reasons about why not to test. She even referred to the National Association for the Education of Young Children Position Statement on Early Childhood Curriculum, Assessment, and Program Evaluation (2003; see also Copple & Brede Kamp, 2006). The test coordinator remained firm. All kindergarten children would be tested.

The teacher asked for help to administer the test. She was working alone in the room with 25 children, except for an occasional parent volunteer. Test day arrived. The children were prepared. The test director could not get the children to cooperate! Testing was abandoned. Ms. Green served as an advocate for the young children in her program. She did so at personal risk to her career in that district. When teachers choose to resist tests, they must be prepared to show why the tests are inappropriate and how the necessary progress and accountability information can be obtained in a different way.

As teachers, we need to be aware of the research that shows that teachers do not always pay attention to the learning environment by providing work that is intellectually challenging, aligned to required standards, with clear criteria and specific feedback to students on the performance of particular tasks. Often, teachers give unclear rubrics for assignments. Finally, teachers give higher ratings to students than a standards-based assessment yields (Aschbacher, 2000, pp. 6–8).

When you plan to use an achievement test, keep the following in mind:

- Help the district be aware of the limitations of testing for young children.
- Point them in the direction of some newer standardized tests that attempt to include problem solving and multiple correct answers.
- Lobby to have testing begin—at the earliest—at third grade. Then, at least, children have some capacity for sustained attention to detail, writing, and reading skills.
- Prepare the children in advance for the experience.

There are two distinct aspects of preparation: preparation for the actual administration of the test and cluing the children in to the activity. Teachers must review the test and available samples so that they know what tasks children will be required to complete. Teachers must also be thoroughly familiar with the required testing conditions. This familiarity is not *teaching to the test*, but providing appropriate experience so that children can be successful. Once teachers have completed their homework, then they may help the children in the following ways:

- Provide opportunities to mark papers in the same way required by the test.
- Provide directions as limited by the test.
- Include opportunities to work under time pressure.
- Use separate answer sheets for assignments if children will be required to juggle these.
- Use the real machine-scorable answer sheets.
- Describe and practice appropriate test behavior: do one's own work, be quiet.

- Talk about guessing.
- Identify strategies for managing the number of items (i.e., which ones to do first).
- Help children cope with the anxiety of the task through story reading.
- Incorporate test materials in the literacy or other interest centers so children can cope through play.

To be fair to children, teachers must be thoroughly familiar with the test, its components, and procedures; follow the directions explicitly; adhere strictly to the time components; note any deviations made inadvertently; record notes about any unusual circumstances that occur with individual children; and be prepared to help children live with the stress that they feel during the test administration.

Federal law (IDEA) requires the inclusion of children with disabilities in the achievement-testing program. So that these measures are fair for students with disabilities, accommodations must be made. Elliott and Braden (2000; see also Elliot & Thurlaw, 2005; Thurlow, Elliott, & Ysseldyke, 2003) list that the most common testing accommodations are:

- reading the test to the student
- allowing extra time
- breaking a test into shorter sessions
- reducing the number of students in the room to minimize distractions
- providing a quiet room for testing

Parents need to prepare for the achievement test experience as well. You don't want Greg's mother saying on the day of the test: "This is the most important thing you will do this year at school—don't mess it up." To prevent this anxiety-provoking experience or others that parents may create, prepare newsletter announcements about the role that this standardized experience will play in the total assessment plan for the year. Consider using commercial explanation materials from the publisher of the instrument you will be using. For example, "The main purposes of the ITBS are to provide the school with information to improve instruction and to help teachers make sound educational decisions about each student's learning. The scores allow teachers to check each student's year-to-year growth and to identify some of each student's strongest and weakest areas of achievement. The Iowa Tests of Basic Skills cover many of the fundamental skills your child is learning in school" (Hoover et al., 2001, p. 1). In addition to a statement of purpose, the testing booklet has examples of the kinds of items used on the test.

Once the test is over, skillful teachers go back to business-as-usual in the classroom. However, starting where children are comfortable or with favorite activities is a good way to recapture the momentum of life in the classroom. The test is just one of the cycles of student life.

Using Achievement Test Results

You gave the tests—now what? Look at the results for individual children. An example of one commonly used standardized test program—*The Iowa Tests*—makes it easy for districts to provide teachers and other stakeholders with essential information. Through *Interactive Results Manager* (http://www.riverpub.com/products/achievement.html) users can

- analyze assessment results to inform instruction and ensure that students are making progress in academic achievement.
- disaggregate data by race/ethnicity, special program involvement, and gender to effectively monitor the progress of mandated reporting groups.
- investigate student performance in comprehensive content areas or in each test within a content area—providing flexibility with the level of achievement analysis desired.
- examine group achievement data using an advanced analysis tool included with the application providing an unsurpassed level of reporting flexibility.
- control report access at three different levels—class, building, and system.
- export group level data in a variety of formats so that data may be used in other applications.

Once you receive the appropriately customized report for classroom teachers, put the scores into the context of what a teacher knows about the child. Do the scores make sense? Often the answer will be "yes." For those cases where the answer is "no"—the child's performance is higher, lower, or different—gather support for the position through observation, task analysis, or individualized academic assessment. Then document the results. When it will be in the best interest of a particular child, ask that the results be set aside, considered as a minimal estimate of performance, and supply corroborating evidence.

The next major task is to interpret the test results to parents. To do this most effectively, be thoroughly familiar with the technical terms of the test, know what the scores mean, and be able to explain the results to parents in comparison to classroom functioning.

Parents will want to understand what the test means about their child. Is it a fair assessment? Does the test measure the curriculum? Can the parents help their child to improve? Will the score influence school practices? That is, will it entitle their child to special services?

Explain the meaning of *percentile, stanine, standard scores, mean, median,* and *variance* to parents. The best preparation is a thorough understanding of the terms and the limitations of testing in the early years. In addition to achievement tests, another common form of tests used by primary-grade teachers are textbook tests.

TEXTBOOK TESTS

Publishers of textbooks publish **textbook tests.** These include sample test items, chapter reviews, and other assessment materials to go with instructional materials. Examine these materials with the same intensity that you apply to the texts. Are the materials harmonious with the philosophy of education? If teaching from a process approach, use the suggested performance tasks that can be set up for children to solve. Use the record-keeping forms that are compatible with your learner outcome requirements.

textbook tests
assessment materials published by textbook publishers to accompany their instructional materials.

Because these items say "test," do not assume that they are necessarily appropriate to use. Examine the materials as if they were tests. Are the materials valid? Do they match what you are teaching? Is there another way to gather the information that will be more efficient? Do the materials fit into the portfolio plan? See examples of textbook tests in Boxes 11.12, 11.13, and 11.14.

Box 11.12 *Textbook for Third-Grade Social Studies*

Textbook for Third-Grade Social Studies	*Teacher's Key*
Pioneers	
The pioneers lived in the time period _____	1800s
They traveled on _____	horseback
Some of the pioneers ran out of _____	food
Others did not bring enough _____	warm clothes
Many lost _____	family members

This test relies on reading and memorization. Also, it promotes one-right-answer thinking.

Box 11.13 *Pioneers in California for Third Grade*

Pioneers in California for Third Grade	*Teacher's Key*
Tell the ways pioneers came to California.	Look for answers that show: by sea, by wagon train, by horseback.
What were these people seeking?	Answers that range from gold to a better way of life.
Draw a picture showing some important ideas about early California history.	Check to see whether the pictures represent the time period and idea (e.g., Gold Rush, San Francisco fire, and so on).

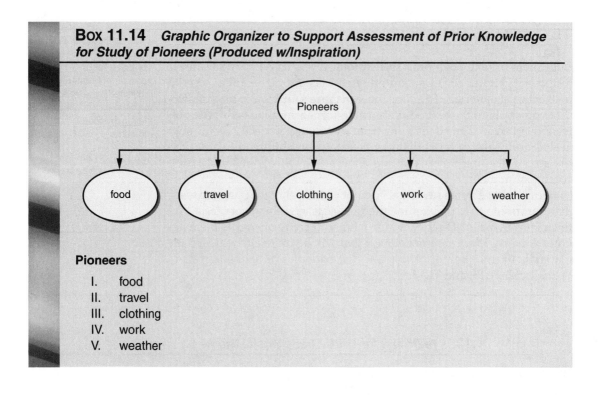

Box 11.14 *Graphic Organizer to Support Assessment of Prior Knowledge for Study of Pioneers (Produced w/Inspiration)*

Pioneers

I.   food
II. travel
III. clothing
IV. work
V.   weather

INDIVIDUALIZED ACADEMIC TESTS

Sometimes it may be convenient to use an individualized academic test for determining reading or math instructional level. These instruments may be particularly helpful when children move to the classroom without records or when you are puzzled about how a child is learning. **Individualized academic tests** are formal interviews of children on a topic such as reading or mathematics. Through the standardized interview process, the teacher not only learns firsthand what the second or third grader knows, but also how he or she approached the task. For example, if assessing knowledge of double-digit addition, watch Marcey at work. Give her some double-digit addition problems. You can readily assess Marcey's ability with this problem, 22 + 49 = 611, which shows she does not understand place value.

Such information can be gathered through informal means if that is the only question. But if more information is needed about math facts, math concepts, or math vocabulary, spend 30 minutes in a structured interview with an individualized math test and Marcey to gather this information—it may take several days of observation. Used selectively, tests can be helpful efficiency tools.

individualized academic tests formal interviews of children on specific topics.

348

TEST PREP

As the stakes for achievement testing increase, school districts and teachers have increased their use of test prep materials. Thus, the issue of teaching to the test emerges. If teaching to the test means aligning the curriculum and assessment procedures, this practice assures stakeholders—parents and the public—that students learn what they need to know; teachers, students, and administrators are accountable. If teaching to the test means *item-teaching*, teachers organize their instruction around the actual items found either on a test or around a set of look-alike items. For instance: "Gloria has 14 pears but ate 3." The test-taker must choose from four choices the number of pears that Gloria has now. Suppose the teacher revised this item slightly: "Joe has 14 bananas but ate 3." The test-taker chooses from the same four answers, ordered slightly differently (Popham, 2001).

Such practice blows the predictive validity of test scores and in the end cheats students. As you cope with the high-stakes demands of your curriculum, you will want to avoid the use of such materials and concentrate on matching your teaching to the concepts in the best interests of your students. You will use the results of your classroom-based authentic assessments and occasional paper-and-pencil tests to assess the effectiveness of your program so that your students will be successful on the standardized achievement tests aligned with the outcome expectations of your state.

In addition to school test-prep programs, many books are available for parents to use to assess their children against state standards. Some parents enroll their children in test-prep classes, as well. As an early childhood teacher, you will reassure parents that the best preparation for success is the holistic, outcome-based program that you create with rich opportunities for children to investigate projects, obtain skills as part of this work, and sustain learning curiosity that will last a lifetime.

SUMMARY

At the primary level, tests and testing become a formal part of student life. Though best early childhood practice eschews the use of tests for the most part, assessment in the service of instruction is required. Sometimes tests are the most efficient way to gather information quickly. Sometimes tests are required as part of the accountability mechanism, particularly in third grade. Teachers must pick the procedure to match the philosophy of their school's program and be prepared to answer responsibly when asked to describe child progress.

FIELD ACTIVITIES

1. With a small group of children, try one or more of the informal assessment measures described. Report the results—respecting confidentiality—to your class.

2. For your state, find out about the required learning goals or learning outcomes. Make a plan for assessing children for the acquisition of these for a grade level of your choice.

3. Examine portfolios in a local school. Discuss with your classmates the similarities or differences across grades and schools.

4. Look at textbook tests and compare them to the curricular goals for a theme of your choice. How would these measures assist your efforts in assessment? What limitations did you find?

5. Review an individualized academic test. Try administering part or all of it to a volunteer child. How will you use these measures in your program of the future?

IN-CLASS ACTIVITIES

1. Review the test manual for a standardized achievement test. Try giving the test to a classmate. Analyze your efforts. Discuss ways to improve performance on subsequent administrations.

2. Bring to class a state report card for your state, or another. Review the assessment results reported statewide and one urban, one rural, and one suburban district. For each of the districts, identify curricular modifications that may be appropriate for enhanced student achievement.

3. In a small group, plan a presentation to a group of parents about portfolios. Describe how you will involve children in their own assessment and why you will do so. In addition, identify ways that parents will be involved in the process.

STUDY QUESTIONS

1. Define learner outcomes. Who establishes these and what is the early childhood teacher's role in the assessment of learner outcomes? What influence should learner outcomes have on curriculum or program goals? What responsibility do teachers have in accountability within their program goals?

2. How does informal assessment fit into a typical school day?

3. How do you integrate content as seen in the examples of classroom activities? How do you likewise integrate assessment?

4. Why is it important for assessments to remain dynamic and inclusive? How do portfolios accomplish this?

5. How are achievement tests often misused in schools? How can parents be encouraged to advocate for their children in schools where readiness tests form the basis for placement?

6. What are some steps teachers can take to ensure their students are treated fairly and appropriately throughout the testing

process? What should teachers keep in mind while using readiness tests?

7. In which classroom situations will textbook tests be used? How can teachers ensure each child is appropriately assessed by textbook tests?

REFLECT AND RE-READ

- I understand achievement tests and their role in primary education.
- I can develop a reasonable approach toward portfolios and know the limitations of these documentation procedures.
- I can link standards to planning and assessment.

CASE VIGNETTE

Sabah, the oldest son of recent immigrant parents, is 7 years old. The native language is spoken at home; Sabah seems to experience some difficulty in understanding English conversation with the observer, herself fluent in the child's language. Mrs. Shakil, his mother, reports that Sabah's grades in school since kindergarten have been C's and D's; she expects him to do well in school and sits him down after school to do homework. This process takes forever, more than an hour, and is accomplished with much yelling and cajoling. Often, Sabah doesn't complete homework, begging to go play; Mrs. Shakil finally relents.

What should the second-grade teacher do to assist Sabah and his family? What assessments should be planned?

Source: From S. Umar, 2004, submitted in partial fulfillment of ECE 375 Early Childhood Assessment: DePaul University. Used by permission.

TECHNOLOGY LINKS

http://www.ncrel.org

North Central Regional Educational Laboratory. Publishes links to curricular and assessment materials for use in the primary years.

http://www.nctm.org

National Council of Teachers of Mathematics. Practical examples for implementation of standards in the classroom.

http://www.reading.org

International Reading Association. Position papers and publications on teaching reading.

http://www.nsta.org

National Science Teachers Association. Standards, position papers, and examples for teaching.

http://www.socialstudies.org

National Council for Social Studies. Standards, position papers, and publications on teaching the social studies.

http://intranet.cps.k12.il.us/Assessments

Chicago Systemic Initiative. Lesson plans, test prep suggestions, K–2 Handbook, and much more.

http://www.makingstandardswork.com

Center for Performance Assessment. On this site, there are examples of teaching plans and position papers.

http://www.whatworks.ed.gov/

What Works Clearinghouse. This website presents classroom practice that shows promise for success.

SUGGESTED FURTHER READINGS

Barrentine, S. J., & Stokes, S. M. (2005). *Reading assessment: Principles and practices for elementary teachers* (2nd ed.). Newark, DE: International Reading Association.

Bickart, T. S., Dodge, D. T., & Jablon, J. R. (2004). *What every parent needs to know about 1st, 2nd & 3rd graders: An essential guide to your child's education.* Washington, DC: Teaching Strategies.

Bickart, T. S., Jablon, J. R., & Dodge, D. T. (2001). *Building the primary classroom: A complete guide to teaching and learning.* Washington, DC: Teaching Strategies.

Harp, B. (2000). *The handbook of literacy assessment and evaluation* (2nd ed.). Norwood, MA: Christopher-Gordon.

Kauffman, J. M., & Hallahan, D. P. (2005). *Special education: What it is and why we need it.* Boston: Allyn & Bacon.

Popham, W. J. (2005). *Classroom assessment: What teachers need to know* (4th ed.). Boston: Allyn & Bacon.

Strickland, K. (2005). *What's after assessment? Follow-up instruction for phonics, fluency, and comprehension.* Portsmouth, NH: Heinemann.

Appendices

Appendix A

Self-Assessment Pretest Associated with Terms to Know

Early Childhood Preassessment Inventory	
I am familiar with methods of observation and recording of children's behavior for purposes of assessing goals, providing for individual needs, and appropriately teaching young children. I am familiar with terms such as • observations • observation records • anecdotal notes • running records • class journals • checklists • frequency records • event sampling • time sampling • rating scales • portfolios • documentation panel • formative evaluation • summative evaluation	I need to know more about _____.
I can create assessment plans for learning environments that address the needs of young children from culturally diverse backgrounds and including both typical and atypical children. I am knowledgeable about the related terms, such as • intrinsically motivating • ecological assessment • resiliency • authentic assessment • task analysis • presentation mode • response mode • dynamic assessment • mediated learning experience (MLE) • functional assessment	I need to know more about _____.

• strength-based assessment • multiple intelligences theory • prereferral screening • diagnostic tests • curriculum-based measures • criterion-referenced measures • performance assessment • portfolios • Child Find team • diagnostic evaluation • referral question • psychoeducational evaluation • Individualized Family Service Plans (IFSP) • multidisciplinary staffing • play-based assessment	
I am aware of value issues regarding assessment best practice and the existence of codes of ethics in professional life. I am knowledgeable of the related terms, such as • stakeholders • accountability • high-stakes measure • confidentiality • child study	I need to know more about _____.
I am familiar with ways to gather information through the use of library resources, the Internet, professional and organizational resources, and community resources. I know what role the following play in assessment: • NAEYC, CEC, AERA, Buros Institute, Chicago Public Schools, ISBE	I need to know more about _____.
I am acquainted with the physical, cognitive, emotional, social, and spiritual developmental milestones of young children. I know about typical and atypical development. I am familiar with the following related terms: • case finding • screening • diagnosis • Apgar Rating Scale • prenatal testing • amniocentesis • ultrasound • chorionic villus biopsy (CVS) • gestational age • established risk • biological risk • environmental risk • drug-exposed babies • fetal alcohol syndrome (FAS)	I need to know more about _____.

(continued)

I can choose, administer, and interpret correctly various assessment techniques appropriate for the early childhood age span. I am familiar with the statistics of testing and terms such as:	I need to know more about _____.
<ul><li>mean</li><li>raw score</li><li>range</li><li>standard deviation</li><li>normal curve</li><li>standardized test</li><li>norm-referenced test</li><li>population</li><li>normative sample</li><li>norms</li><li>criterion-referenced test</li><li>derived scores</li><li>age-equivalent scores</li><li>grade-equivalent scores</li><li>interpolated score</li><li>extrapolated score</li><li>percentile ranks</li><li>deviation quotients</li><li>normal-curve equivalents</li><li>stanines</li><li>reliability</li><li>test-retest reliability</li><li>interscorer reliability</li><li>correlation coefficient</li><li>correlation coefficient</li><li>standard error of measurement (SEM)</li><li>validity</li><li>face validity</li><li>content validity</li><li>criterion-related validity</li><li>concurrent validity</li><li>predictive validity</li><li>sensitivity</li><li>specificity</li><li>construct validity</li><li>objectivity</li><li>scale scores</li></ul>	
I am aware of the complex social and cultural context in which child-care and educational settings are embedded. I know how these issues apply to assessment of young children: <ul><li>developmentally appropriate practice</li><li>portfolios</li><li>accountability</li><li>learner outcomes</li><li>informal evaluation</li><li>portfolios</li><li>individualized academic tests</li></ul>	I need to know more about _____.

<ul><li>textbook tests</li><li>standards-based teaching</li><li>achievement testing</li><li>test prep</li></ul>	
I appreciate the family role in the assessment process. I know the differences and the roles for stakeholders on the <ul><li>multidisciplinary team</li><li>interdisciplinary team</li></ul>	I need to know more about _____.
I know that I must commit to an assessment system that is comprehensive, multidimensional, and holistic for the diverse population of young learners and their families. I am familiar with the following terms and practices: <ul><li>tests</li><li>norm-based instruments</li><li>screening tests</li><li>inventory</li><li>rubric</li><li>interrater reliability</li><li>accountability</li><li>report card</li><li>grades</li><li>student-led conferences</li><li>stakeholders</li><li>accountability</li></ul>	I need to know more about _____.
I appreciate the role of assessment processes and results in IEP and IFSP development. I know about the role that the following play in the process: <ul><li>parent perspective</li><li>developmental questionnaires</li><li>parental reports</li><li>behavioral questionnaires</li><li>parental questionnaires</li><li>parent interview</li></ul>	I need to know more about _____.
I am aware of legislation and public policy as it affects children, families, and programs for young children, particularly the issues of high-stakes testing. For example: IDEA No Child Left Behind Act Head Start Performance Standards	I need to know more about _____.

(continued)

If asked, I would define *assessment* as

My most recent positive experience with *assessment* is

The worst experience of my life with *assessment* is

Appendix B

Child Development Chart for Typical Development

Sources: Adapted from the following: *The Carolina Curriculum for Handicapped Infants and Infants at Risk*, by N. Johnson-Martin, K. G. Jens, and S. M. Attermeier, 1986, Baltimore: Brookes; *The Carolina Curriculum for Preschoolers with Special Needs*, by N. Johnson-Martin, S. M. Attermeier, and B. Hacker. 1990, Baltimore: Brookes; *Help for Special Preschoolers Assessment Checklist*. 1987. Palo Alto. CA: VORT Corporation; *HELP Hauraii Early Learning Profile Activity Guide*, by S. Furuno. K. A. O'Reiley, C. M. Hosaka, T. T. Inatsoka, T. L. Allman, and B. Zeisloft, 1985, Palo Alto, CA: VORT Corporation; *Mainstreaming Preschoolers*, by CRC Education and Human Development, Inc. for the Administration for Children, Youth and Families, 1978. Washington, DC: U.S. Government Printing Office (1979620-182/5708); *Transdisciplinary Play-Based Assessment: A Functional Approach to Working with Young Children*, by T. W. Linder, 1990 Baltimore: Brookes.

Child Development Chart for Typical Development

	Gross-Motor Skills	Fine-Motor Skills	Language Comprehension	Expressive Communication	Cognitive Skills	Self-Help Skills	Social Skills
0–3 Months	Holds head up in prone position. Lifts head when held at shoulder. Kicks reciprocally. Rolls from side to supine position.	Moves arms symmetrically. Follows with eyes to midline. Brings hands to midline in supine position. Activates arms on sight of toy.	Responds to voice. Watches speaker's eyes and mouth. Searches with eyes for sound.	Cries when hungry or uncomfortable. Makes comfort sounds.	Inspects surroundings. Shows anticipation. Inspects own hands.	Opens mouth in response to food stimulus. Coordinates sucking, swallowing, and breathing.	Regards face. Enjoys physical contact: molds, relaxes body when held. Makes eye contact. Expresses distress.
3–6 Months	Holds head in line with body when pulled to sitting. Bears weight on hands in prone position. Sits with light support. Holds head steady in supported sitting position. Rolls from supine position to side.	Follows with eyes without moving head. Keeps hands open most of time. Uses palmar grasp. Reaches and grasps objects.	Quiets to mother's voice. Distinguishes between friendly and angry voices. Responds to own name.	Coos variety of vowel sounds. Laughs. Takes turns. Responds to speech by vocalizing. Expresses displeasure and excitement.	Begins rattle play. Repeats/continues familiar activity. Uses hands and mouth for sensory exploration of objects. Plays with own hands, fingers, toes.	Brings hand to mouth holding toy or object. Swallows strained or pureed foods. Inhibits rooting reflex.	Smiles socially. Discriminates strangers. Demands attention. Vocalizes pleasure or displeasure. Enjoys social play, e.g., "This Little Piggy." Lifts arms to mother.
6–9 Months	Exhibits body-righting reaction. Extends arms protectively. Sits independently, but may use hands. Stands holding on. Pulls to stand. Crawls backward. Gets into sitting position without assistance.	Transfers object. Manipulates toy actively with wrist movement. Reaches and grasps with extended elbow.	Looks at pictures briefly. Looks for family members or pets when named. Responds to simple requests with gesture.	Babbles to people. Produces variety of consonants in babbling. Babbles with adult inflection. Babbles reduplicated syllables. "mama." "baba." etc. Vocalizes loudly to get \vattention.	Works to obtain desired out-of-reach object. Finds object observed being hidden. Touches adult's hand or toy to restart an activity. Plays 2 to 3 minutes with single toy. Follows trajectory of fast-moving object. Shows interest in sounds of object.	Uses tongue to move food in mouth (4–8 months). Holds own bottle. Mouths and gums solid foods. Bites voluntarily: inhibits bite reflex. Feeds self a cracker.	Recognizes mother (4–8 months). Displays stranger anxiety. Smiles at mirror image. Shows anxiety to separation from mother.

Age	Gross Motor	Fine Motor	Language (Receptive)	Language (Expressive)	Cognitive	Self-Help	Social/Emotional
9–12 Months	Creeps on hands and knees. Moves from sitting to prone position. Stands momentarily. Walks holding on to furniture (cruises).	Takes objects out of container. Uses both hands freely. Tries to imitate scribble. Puts object into container. Releases object voluntarily. Pokes with index finger. Uses neat pincer grasp.	Understands "no no." Listens selectively to familiar words. Enjoys looking at books.	Babbles single consonant-vowel syllables, e.g., "ba." Responds to certain words (e.g., "wave bye bye") with appropriate gesture. Uses behaviors and vocalization to express needs.	Overcomes obstacle to obtain object. Retrieves object using other material. Imitates gestures. Unwraps a toy. Enjoys looking at books.	Finger feeds variety of foods. Holds spoon. Cooperates with dressing by extending arm or leg. Chews by munching.	Enjoys turn-taking game. Resists supine position. Shows like and dislike for certain people, objects, or situations. Shows toys to others; does not release. Tests parents' reactions at feeding and bedtime by new and mischievous behavior.
12–18 Months	Stands from supine position. Walks without support. Throws ball. Creeps up stairs. Pulls toy while walking. Carries large toy while walking. Moves to music.	Uses two hands in midline, one holding, one manipulating. Scribbles spontaneously. Place pegs in pegboard. Builds two- to three-cube tower.	Responds to simple verbal requests; identifies one body part. Understand many nouns. Brings objects from another room on request.	Combines gestures and vocalizations to express a variety of communicative functions. Says "Dada" or "Mama" purposefully. Uses single words. Uses exclamations, e.g., "Oh, oh!" Says "no" meaningfully. Uses 10–15 words (by 18 months).	Understands adult's pointing. Hands toy back to adult. Matches objects. Places round and square pieces in form board. Nests two or three cans. Identifies self in mirror.	May refuse food; appetite decreases. Brings spoon to mouth. Drinks from cup with some spilling. Indicates discomfort over soiled pants. Removes socks.	Displays independent behavior; may be difficult to discipline. May display tantrum behavior. Demonstrates sense of humor. Is easily distractible; has difficulty sitting still.
18–24 Months	Moves on "ride-on" toys without pedals. Walks upstairs holding railing, both feet on step. Picks up toy from floor without falling. Runs.	Imitates circular scribble. Imitates horizontal stroke. Holds crayon with fist.	Identifies three to six body parts. Matches sounds to animals. Understands personal pronouns, some action verbs, and some adjectives. Enjoys nursery rhymes.	Uses intelligible words about 65% of the time. May use jargon (syllable strings that sound like speech). Tells experience using jargon and words. Uses two-word sentences. Names two or three pictures. Attempts to sing songs with words. Imitates three- to four-word phrase.	Finds object not observed being hidden. Activates mechanical toy. Matches objects to pictures. Sorts objects. Explores cabinets and drawers. Remembers where objects belong. Recognizes self in photo.	Scoops food, feeds self with spoon. Chews with rotary jaw movements. Plays with food. Removes shoe when laces undone. Zips/unzips large zipper. Shows awareness of need to eliminate.	Expresses affection. Expresses wide range of emotions including jealousy, fear, anger, sympathy, embarrassment, anxiety, and joy. Attempts to control others; resists control: somewhat Aggressive. Engages in parallel play. Enjoys solitary play occasionally.

(continued)

	Gross-Motor Skills	Fine-Motor Skills	Language Comprehension	Expressive Communication	Cognitive Skills	Self-Help Skills	Social Skills
24–36 Months	Runs forward well. Jumps in place, two feet together. Stands on one foot, with aid. Walks on tiptoe. Kicks ball forward.	Strings four large beads. Turns pages singly. Snips with scissors. Holds crayon with thumb and fingers, not fist. Uses one hand consistently in most activities. Paints with some wrist action; makes dots, lines, circular strokes. Rolls, pounds, squeezes, and pulls clay.	Points to pictures of common objects when they are named. Can identify objects when told their use. Understands question forms what and where. Understands negative no, not, can't, and don't. Enjoys listening to simple storybooks and requests them again.	Joins vocabulary words together in two-word phrases. Gives first and last name. Asks what and where questions. Makes negative statements (e.g., "Can't open it"). Shows frustration at not being understood. Sustains conversation for two or three turns.	Selects and looks at picture books, names pictured objects, and identifies several objects within one picture. Matches and uses associated objects meaningfully (e.g., given cup, saucer, and head, puts cup and saucer together). Stacks rings on peg in order of size. Uses self and objects in pretend play. Can talk briefly about what he or she is doing. Imitates adult actions (e.g., housekeeping play). Has limited attention span; learning is through exploration and adult direction (as in reading of picture stories). Is beginning to understand functional concepts of familiar objects (e.g., that a spoon is used for eating) and part/whole concepts (e.g., parts of the body).	Gets drink from fountain or faucet unassisted. Open door by turning handle. Takes off coat. Puts on coat with assistance. Washes and dries hands with assistance.	Watches other children; joins briefly in their play. Defends own possessions. Begins to play house. Participates in simple group activity (e.g., sings, claps, dances). Knows gender identity.
36–48 Months	Runs around obstacles. Walks on a line. Balances on one foot for 5 to 10 seconds. Hops on one foot. Pushes, pulls, steers wheeled toys. Rides (i.e., steers and pedals) tricycle. Uses slide without assistance. Jumps over 15 cm (6 in.) high object, landing on both feet together. Throws ball over head. Catches ball bounced to him or her.	Builds tower of nine small blocks. Drives nails and pegs. Copies circle. Imitates cross. Manipulates clay materials (e.g., rolls balls, snakes, cookies).	Begins to understand sentences involving time concepts (e.g., "We are going to the zoo tomorrow"). Understands size comparatives such as big and bigger. Understands relationships expressed by if . . . then or because sentences. Carries out a series of two to four related directions. Understands when told, "Let's pretend."	Talks in sentences of three or more words, which take the form agent-action-object ("I see the ball") or agent-action-location ("Daddy sit on chair"). Tells about past experiences. Uses -s on nouns to indicate plurals. Uses -ed on verbs to include past tense. Refers to self using pronouns I or me. Repeats at least one nursery rhyme and can sing a song. Speech is understandable to strangers, but there are still some sound errors.	Recognizes and matches six colors. Intentionally stacks blocks or rings in order of size. Draws somewhat recognizable picture that is meaningful to child, if not to adult; names and briefly explains picture. Asks questions for information: why and how questions requiring simple answers. Knows own age. Knows own last name. Has short attention span; learns through observing and imitating adults, and by adult instruction and explanation; is easily distracted. Has increased understanding of concepts of the functions and grouping of objects (e.g., can put doll house furniture in correct rooms); part/whole (e.g.,) can identify pictures of hand and foot as parts of body. Begins to be aware of past and present (e.g., "Yesterday we went to the park. today we go to the library.").	Pours well from small pitcher. Spreads soft butter with knife. Buttons and unbuttons large buttons. Washes hands unassisted. Blows nose when reminded. Uses toilet independently.	Joins in play with other children; begins to interact. Shares toys; takes turns with assistance. Begins dramatic play, acting out whole scenes (for example, traveling, playing house, pretending to be animals). Comforts peers in distress.

Age								
48–60 Months	Walks backward toe-heel. Jumps forward 10 times without falling. Walks up and down stairs alone, alternating feet. Turns somersault.	Cuts on line continuously. Copies cross. Copies square. Prints a few capital letters.	Follows three unrelated commands in proper order. Understands comparatives such as *pretty*, *prettier*, and *prettiest*. Listens to long stories, but often misinterprets the facts. Incorporates verbal directions into play activities. Understands sequencing of events when told them (e.g., "First we have to go to the store, then we can make the cake, and tomorrow we will eat it").	Asks *when, how,* and *why* questions. Uses modals such as *can, will, shall, should,* and *might.* Joins sentences together (e.g., "I went to the store and I bought some ice cream"). Talks about causality by using *because* and *so.* Tells the content of a story but may confuse facts.	Points to and names four to six colors. Matches pictures of familiar objects (e.g., show, sock, foot, apple, orange, banana). Draws a person with two to six recognizable parts, such as head, arms, legs; can name or match drawn parts to own body. Draws, names, and describes recognizable picture. Rote counts to 5, imitating adults. Describes what will happen next. Dramatic play is closer to reality; with attention paid to detail, time, and space.	Knows own street and town. Has more extended attention span; learns through observing and listening to adults as well as through exploration; is easily distracted. Has increased understanding of concepts of function, time, part/whole relationships. Function or use of objects may be stated in addition to names of objects. Time concepts are expanding. The child can talk about yesterday or last week (a long time ago), about today, and about what will happen tomorrow.	Cuts easy foods with a knife (e.g., hamburger patty, tomato slice). Laces shoes.	Plays and interacts with other children. Plays dress-up. Shows interest in exploring gender differences.
60–72 Months	Runs lightly on toes. Walks on balance beam. Can cover 2 meters (6½ feet) hopping. Skips on alternate feet. Jumps rope. Skates.	Cuts out simple shapes. Copies triangle. Traces diamond. Copies first name. Prints numerals 1 to 5. Colors within lines. Has adult grasp of pencil. Has handedness well established (i.e., child is left- or right-handed). Pastes and glues appropriately. Uses classroom tools appropriately.	Demonstrates preacademic skills.	There are few obvious differences between child's grammar and adult's grammar. Still needs to learn such things as subject-verb agreement and some irregular past-tense verbs. Can take appropriate turns in a conversation. Gives and receives information. Communicates well with family, friends or strangers. Retells story from picture book with accuracy.	Names some letters and numerals. Rote counts to 10. Sorts objects by single character-istics (e.g., by color, shape, or size—if the difference is obvious). Is beginning to use accurately time concepts of *tomorrow* and *yesterday.*	Begins to relate check time to daily schedule. Attention span increases noticeably; learns through adult instruction; when interested, can ignore distractions. Concepts of function increase as well as understanding of why things happen; time concepts are expanding into an understanding of the future in terms of major events (e.g., "Christmas will come after two weekends").	Dresses self completely. Ties shoes. Brushes teeth unassisted. Crosses street safely.	Chooses own friend(s). Plays simple table games. Plays competitive games. Engages in cooperative play with other children involving group decisions, role assignments, fair play.

Appendix C

Selected Early Childhood Tests to Consider for Use in Educational and Child-Care Settings

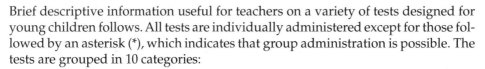

Brief descriptive information useful for teachers on a variety of tests designed for young children follows. All tests are individually administered except for those followed by an asterisk (*), which indicates that group administration is possible. The tests are grouped in 10 categories:

1. School Readiness and Screening Tests
2. Diagnostic Tests of Development, Ability, and Aptitude
3. Tests of Academic Achievement
4. Tests of Achievement in Language
5. Tests of Achievement in Reading
6. Tests of Achievement in Spelling
7. Tests of Achievement in Mathematics
8. Tests to Identify Giftedness
9. Tests of Perceptual and/or Motor Skills
10. Tests of Behavior and Conduct

Source: The material in this appendix was compiled originally by Lynn Van Stee, Loyola University of Chicago; updated and enlarged for the 2nd edition by Meredith Dodd, DePaul University School of Education graduate student; updated for the 3rd edition by Joshua Sheppard, DePaul University School of Education graduate student.

1. School Readiness and Screening Tests

Name	Author	Publisher	Copyright Date	Age Range	Purpose	Approximate Testing Time	Types of Response
Ages and Stages Questionnaires (ASQ)	Bricker, D., et al.	Paul H. Brookes	1998	4 months to 4 years	A parent-completed questionnaire used to identify children at risk for developmental delays and to monitor the child's progress at 4- to 6-month intervals. Records child's abilities in five areas: gross motor, fine motor, communication, personal-social, and problem solving. Also available in Spanish.	10 minutes	Rater
Boehm Test of Basic Concepts–Revised (BTBC–3)*	Boehm, A.	Psychological Corporation	2000	3 to 5 and kindergarten to second grade	Measures children's mastery of the concepts considered necessary for achievement in the first years of school. Concepts tested include those of space (location, direction, orientation, and dimension), time, and quantity (number).	15–30 minutes	Nonverbal (pencil and booklet)
Bracken School Readiness Assessment: BSRA	Bracken, B. A.	PsychCorp	2002	2 to 7 years	To help determine if a child may have an underlying language disorder that requires further evaluation.	10 to 15 minutes	Verbal
Brigance Infant and Toddler Screens	Brigance, A. H., & Glascoe, F. P.	Curriculum Associates	2002	birth–21 months	Assesses infant and toddler developmental skills and observes caregivers' involvement and interactions.	10–12 minutes	Verbal and nonverbal
Brigance Early Preschool Screen II	Brigance, A. H.	Curriculum Associates	2005	2–5 years and 11 months	Assesses children's skills in developmental areas.	10–15 minutes	Verbal and nonverbal
Brigance K and 1 Screen II	Brigance, A. H.	Curriculum Associates	2005	2–5 years and 11 months	Indicates developmental problems—language, learning, or cognitive delays. Identifies children who are talented or gifted. Also assists teachers with program planning.	10–15 minutes	Verbal and nonverbal

(continued)

Name	Author	Publisher	Copyright Date	Age Range	Purpose	Approximate Testing Time	Types of Response
Children-At-Risk Screener: Kindergarten & Preschool (CARS)	Aaronson, M., & Aaronson, D.	CTB/McGraw-Hill	1991	2 to 6	Designed to identify children at risk for educational failure and in need of more in-depth assessment. CARS tests a variety of skills including following directions, abstract reasoning, spatial relationships, receptive language, and cognitive concepts. Includes a magnetic board and figures as testing tools.	8–15 minutes	Expressive language not necessary.
Child Development Inventory (CDI)	Ireton, H.	American Guidance Service	2004	15 months to 6 years	Measures a young child's present development according to the parent's report. Includes eight scales: Social Development, Self Help, Gross Motor, Fine Motor, Expressive Language, Language Comprehension, Letters, and Numbers. Also a 30-item problems checklist. Profiles child's development, strengths, and problems.	45 minutes	Verbal, nonverbal, rater
Comprehensive Identification Process (CIP)	Zehrbach, R.	Scholastic Testing Service	1997	2-5 to 5-5	Identifies children who may need special medical, psychological, or educational assistance before they enter school. Assesses various areas of development: fine motor, gross motor, cognitive-verbal, speech-expressive, language, hearing, vision, social-affective, and medical.	30 minutes	Verbal and nonverbal
Developmental Indicators for the Assessment of Learning–Revised (DIAL–3)	Mardell-Czudnowski, C., & Goldenberg, D.	American Guidance Service	1998	2-0 to 5-11	Designed to identify children with potential learning problems or potential giftedness. Areas measured include motor, concepts, self-help, social development, and language. Although this test is administered individually, it is designed to handle screening of large numbers of children with different examiners administering each of the three areas.	20–30 minutes	Verbal, nonverbal

Early Screening Inventory–Revised (ESI–R)	Meisels, S., & Wiske, M.	Pearson Early Learning	1997		Identifies children who are at-risk in the areas defined by IDEA (Individuals with Disabilities Education Act). Domains include cognition, communication, and motor. An optional social-emotional scale and adaptive behavior checklist are also available.	15 minutes	Verbal, nonverbal, rater
AGS Early Screening Profiles: ESP	Harrison, P., Kaufman, A., Kaufman, N., Bruininks, R., Rynders., Ilmer,	S., Sparrow, S., & Cicchetti, D. AGS Publishing	1990	2 to 6 years	Screens cognitive, language, motor, self-help, and social performances in the major developmental areas.	15–40 minutes	Verbal and written
FirstSTEp: Screening Test for Evaluating Preschoolers	Miller, L. J.	PsychCorp	1993	3 to 6 years	To identify preschoolers who are at risk for developmental delays.	15 minutes	Verbal
Kent Inventory of Developmental Skills (KIDS)	Reuter, J., Katoff L., & Gruber, C.	Western Psychological	2004	birth–6 years	Used to asses the developmental status infants and children with severe developmental disabilities.	45 minutes	Nonverbal
LAP Kindergarten Screen	Chapel Hill Training Outreach Project	Kaplan School Supply	1997	5	Provides a measure of skills in the areas of fine-motor writing and manipulation, language comprehension and naming, gross motor, and cognitive.	15 minutes	Verbal and nonverbal
Minneapolis Preschool Screening Instrument Revised (MPSI)	Lichtenstein, R.	Minneapolis Public Schools	1991	3-7 to 5-4	Measures skills in various areas that are combined into a single score to determine referrals for further assessment. Domains include building, copying shapes, information, matching, sentence completion, hopping and balancing, naming colors, prepositions, identifying body parts, and repeating sentences.	12–15 minutes	Verbal, nonverbal, rater

(continued)

Name	Author	Publisher	Copyright Date	Age Range	Purpose	Approximate Testing Time	Types of Response
Miller Assessment for Preschoolers (MAP)	Miller, L. J.	Western Psychological	2002	2.9–5.8	Evaluates young children for mild to moderate developmental delays.	30–40 minutes	Verbal and nonverbal
Pervasive Developmental Disorders Screening Test-II: PDDST-II	Siegel, B.	PsychCorp	2004	18 months and up	Designed to detect autism at an early age.	10 to 20 minutes	Verbal
School Readiness Test Revised (SRT)*	Anderhalter, O., & Perney, J.	Scholastic Testing Service	1992	End of kindergarten to first 3 weeks of first grade	A tool for evaluating a child's readiness for first grade. The eight subtests are administered over several sessions and include vocabulary, identifying letters, visual discrimination, auditory discrimination, comprehension and interpretation, number knowledge, handwriting ability, and developmental spelling ability.	90 minutes	Nonverbal (pencil and booklet)
Wide Range Achievement Test–Expanded Edition	Robertson, G. J.	PsychCorp	2001	5 years and up	Designed to comprehensively assess reading comprehension, mathematics, and nonverbal reasoning.	2001	Written

2. Diagnostic Tests of Development, Ability, and Aptitude

Name	Author	Publisher	Copyright Date	Age Range	Purpose	Approximate Testing Time	Types of Response
Batelle Developmental Inventory–2nd ed. (BDI)	Jean Newborg & Batelle Memorial Institute	Thomson Nelson	2004	Birth to 0-8	A measure of basic developmental skills in five domains: personal-social, adaptive, motor, communication, and cognitive. Information is gained by means of observations of the child in a natural setting, parent interview, and a structured test format. Developed for planning and designing educational programs and for program evaluation. A 10–30 minute screening component is also available.	Varies	Verbal, nonverbal, rater
Bracken Basic Concept Scale–Revised (BBCS)	Bracken, B.	Psychological Corporation	1998	2-6 to 8-0	Measures knowledge of general concepts usually acquired during preschool and early school years. Subtests include colors, letter identification, numbers and counting, comparisons, shapes, direction/position, social/emotional, size, texture/material, quantity, and time/sequence.	20–30 minutes	Nonverbal
Brigance Inventory of Early Development II	Brigance, A.	Curriculum Associates	2004	Early development, birth to 7; Basic Skills, kindergarten to sixth grade	This easel format, criterion-referenced inventory is part of a three-part series that provides information on mastered and unmastered skills, concepts, and behavior. This information can be used to determine strengths and weaknesses and to plan instruction.	Not reported (test is untimed)	Verbal and nonverbal

(continued)

Name	Author	Publisher	Copyright Date	Age Range	Purpose	Approximate Testing Time	Types of Response
Brigance Inventory of Basic Skills–Revised	Brigance, A. H.	Curriculum Associates	1999	PK–9	Identify performance levels, set instructional goals, report progress on basic skills. Norm options. Available in Spanish.	Varies by age and items presented	Written and verbal
Carolina Developmental Profile–2nd ed. (CDP)	Harbin, G., & Lillie, D.	Kaplan School Supply	1990	2 to 5	An observation tool for monitoring progress of individual students so that goals and instruction can be personalized for each child. The skills are divided into major developmental categories: gross motor, fine motor, reasoning, receptive and expressive language, and social-emotional. A Spanish edition is available.	Varies	Verbal and nonverbal
Child Observation Record Revised (COR)	Publisher	High/Scope Educational Research Foundation	2003	21/2 to 6	Measures a young child's developmental status using teacher observations throughout the year. The teacher makes note of child behavior in six domains: initiative, social relations, creative representation, music and movement, language and literacy, and logic and mathematics. The information gained from ongoing administration of the COR is useful for evaluating programs, monitoring progress, and planning developmentally appropriate experiences for each child. Initial training is recommended.	Varies (ongoing process)	Rater
Children's Category Test: CCT	Boll, T.	PsychCorp	1993	5 to 16 years	To measure complex intellectual functioning of higher-order cognitive abilities.	15–20 minutes	Written

Comprehensive Scale of Student Abilities (CSSA)	Hammill, D., & Hresko, W.	Pro-Ed	1994	6 to 16	A rating scale to quantify students' school-related developmental abilities. For use in referral for special education services.	Varies	Rater
Developmental Assessment of Young Children (DAYC)	Voress, J. K., & Maddox, T.	Pro-Ed	1998	5–11	Identifies possible delays within cognition, communication, social-emotional development, physical development, and adaptive behavior.	10–20 minutes	Verbal and nonverbal
Developing Skills Checklist (DSC)	Publisher	CTB/McGraw-Hill	1990	4 to 6-2	A comprehensive assessment package that measures a full range of skills and behavior that children typically develop between pre-kindergarten and the end of kindergarten. Test domains include mathematical concepts and operations, language, memory, visual, auditory, print concepts, writing and drawing concepts, plus a social-emotional observational record. A Spanish edition is available.	30–45 minutes total administered over three sessions	Verbal, nonverbal, rater
Developmental Observation Checklist System (DOCS)	Hresko, W., et al.	Pro-Ed	1994	Birth to 6	A checklist completed by parents or caregivers. DOCS uses a systems approach, assessing three areas: general development, adjustment behavior, and parent stress and support.	Varies	Rater
Draw-A-Person Intellectual Ability Test for Children, Adolescents, and Adults (DAP:IQ)	Reynolds, C. R., & Hickman, J. A.	Pro-Ed	2004	4-0 through 89-11	Measures cognitive ability by scoring elements representative of universal features of the human figure.	10–12 minutes	Nonverbal (drawing)
Early Learning Accomplishment Profile–Revised (E-LAP)	Glover, M., et al.	Kaplan School Supply	1995	Birth to 36 months	A criterion-referenced measure of gross- and fine-motor, cognitive, language, self-help, and social/emotional development.	Varies	Verbal, nonverbal, rater

(continued)

Name	Author	Publisher	Copyright Date	Age Range	Purpose	Approximate Testing Time	Types of Response
Early School Assessment (ESA)*	Publisher	CTB/McGraw-Hill	1990	Pre-kindergarten to beginning first grade	Assesses pre-math and pre-reading skills to guide the teacher in developing appropriate instruction and identifying children who qualify for Chapter 1 programs. The ESA probes language, visual, auditory, number concepts, logical operations, and memory.	15–30 minutes for each of six sessions	Nonverbal (pencil and booklet)
Gesell Developmental Schedules–Revised	Knobloch, H., et al.	Gesell Institute	1987	4 weeks to 36 months	Designed to assist in the early identification of developmental problems in infants and young children. The schedules sample a variety of behaviors: adaptive, gross motor, fine motor, language, and personal-social. Test data is gathered through both observation and direct testing. A parent questionnaire can also be administered.	45 minutes	Verbal, nonverbal, rater
Hiskey-Nebraska Test of Learning Aptitude (NTLA)	Hiskey, M.	Author	1966	3 to 16	An assessment of learning aptitude for deaf and hearing children with separate norms for each. Instructions for the deaf are pantomimed.	50 minutes	Nonverbal
Inventory of Early Development–Revised (IED)	Brigance, A.	Curriculum Associates	1991	Birth to 7	In addition to helping identify at-risk infants and preschoolers, the IED tracks development, assists with instructional planning, and assists in communicating with parents. It includes 11 major skill areas: pre-ambulatory motor, gross motor, fine motor, self-help, speech and language, general knowledge and comprehension, social and emotional development, readiness, basic reading, manuscript writing, and basic math.	Varies	Verbal, nonverbal, and rater

Test	Author	Publisher	Year	Age Range	Description	Time	Format
Learning Accomplishment Profile Diagnostic Assessment Kit (LAP–D Screens)*	Sanford, A., et al.	Kaplan School Supply	2003	2-6 to 6-0	Originally a criterion-referenced test, the LAP–D is now norm-referenced. It provides assessment in five areas of development: motor, social, self-help, language, and cognition.	45 minutes	Verbal, nonverbal, and rater (parent)
Metropolitan Readiness Tests–6th Edition (MRT)*	Nurss, J., & McGauvran, M.	Psychological Corporation	1995	Preschool to fall of first grade	The MRT consists of two levels. Level 1, for preschool through fall of kindergarten, measures a wide range of prereading skills. Level 2, for spring of kindergarten through fall of first grade, measures more advanced beginning reading and math skills. The 6th edition, a component of a new program called M-KIDS, is designed for optional one-on-one administration in order to aid teachers in assessing emergent literacy strategies and processes in their students.	80–100 minutes total administered over five to seven sittings	Nonverbal (booklet and pencil)
Mullen Scales of Early Learning AGS EDITION	Mullen, E.	American Guidance Service	1995	Birth to 36 months and 36 to 69 months	These scales provide an assessment of the child's learning style, strengths, and needs, focusing on five areas: visual receptive organization, visual expressive organization, language receptive organization, language expressive organization, and gross-motor base. These scales are available in two levels: infant and preschool. Administration of this test requires training in clinical infant assessment.	10–45 minutes	Verbal and nonverbal
Process Assessment of the Learner: PAL	Berninger, W. W.	PsychCorp	2001	4 to 11 years	Provides an individual assessment of the reading and writing skills of students from kindergarten through grade 6.	30–60 minutes	Writing

(continued)

373

Name	Author	Publisher	Copyright Date	Age Range	Purpose	Approximate Testing Time	Types of Response
The Rivermead Behavioral Memory Test for Children: RBMT-C	Wilson, B. A., Ivani-Chalian, R., & Aldrich, F.	PsychCorp	1991	5 to 11 years	To study a number of attributes through subjects in order to provide an objective measure of a range of everyday memory problems reported and observed in children.	25 to 30 minutes	Verbal
System to Plan Early Childhood Services (SPECS)	Bagnato, S., et al.	American Guidance Service	1990	2 to 6	SPECS is a three-part system: first, "Developmental Specs" is a rating scale for the child's developmental and behavioral status and is to be completed by all members of the child's team; next, "Team Specs" provides a summary of the individual ratings of the team members; and finally, "Program Specs" helps the team design an individualized plan and evaluate progress.	Not reported	Rater

3. Tests of Academic Achievement

Name	Author	Publisher	Copyright Date	Age Range	Purpose	Approximate Testing Time	Types of Response
Aprenda: La prueba de logros en espanol–2nd ed.*	Publisher	Psychological Corporation	1997	Kindergarten to eighth grade	A norm-referenced test of achievement for Spanish-speaking students. This is not a translation of an English language test, rather, it was specifically developed for the Spanish-speaking population. Subtests include sounds and letters, word reading, sentence reading, listening to words and stories, and mathematics.	2 hours 25 minutes for kindergarten, ranging to 4 hours 45 minutes at higher levels	Nonverbal (pencil and booklet)

	Publisher/Author	Publisher	Year	Age/Grade	Description	Time	Format
Basic Achievement Skills Individual Screener (BASIS)	Sonnenschein, J.	Psychological Corporation	1983	1st to 12th grade	A norm- and criterion-referenced test to assess the basic skill areas of reading, mathematics, spelling, and writing.	Less than 1 hour	Verbal and nonverbal
California Achievement Tests–6th ed. (CAT–6)*	Publisher	CTB/McGraw-Hill	2002	Kindergarten to 12th grade	A set of norm-referenced tests that assess mastery of instructional objectives. Content areas include reading, spelling, language, mathematics, study skills, science, and social studies. Braille and large-print editions are available.	1 hour 30 minutes for kindergarten, ranging to 5 hours 30 minutes at higher levels	Nonverbal (pencil and booklet)
Child Observation Record, 2nd ed.	High Scope	High Scope		2 1/2 years to 6	Measures child progress on 32 dimensions of learn in six broad categories: Initiative, Social Relations, Creative Representation, Movement and Music, Language and Literacy, Mathematics, and Science.	Record child progress throughout the year	Checklist for teacher completion. Electronic versions available.
Child Observation Record for Infants and Toddlers	High Scope	High Scope	2003	6 weeks to 3 years	Assesses broad areas of child development.	Checklist for teacher completion	Electronic versions available.
Comprehensive Tests of Basic Skills–5th ed. (CTBS/5)*	Publisher	CTB/McGraw-Hill	1992	Kindergarten to 12th grade	Used to assess academic achievement progress in basic skills areas: reading, language, spelling, mathematics, study skills, science, and social studies. Braille and large-print editions are available.	1 hour 30 minutes for kindergarten, ranging to 5 hours 15 minutes at higher levels	Nonverbal (pencil and booklet)
Diagnostic Achievement Battery–3rd ed. (DAB–3)*	Newcomer, P.	Pro-Ed	Copyright Date: 2001	6 to 14	Assesses performance in listening, speaking, reading, writing, and mathematics.	40–50 minutes	Verbal and nonverbal

(continued)

Name	Author	Publisher	Copyright Date	Age Range	Purpose	Approximate Testing Time	Types of Response
Diagnostic Screening Test: Achievement–Revised (DSTA)*	Gnagey, T., & Gnagey, P.	Slosson Educational Publications	2002	Kindergarten to 12th grade	Provides a measure of achievement in science, social studies, literature, and the arts, plus a total achievement score and an estimated mental age.	5–10 minutes	Nonverbal (pencil and booklet)
GOALS: A Performance-Based Measure of Achievement*	Publisher	Psychological Corporation	1994	1st to 12th grade	An assessment of academic achievement that uses open-ended questions and requires students to use reasoning skills while writing, drawing diagrams, completing charts and pictures, and editing. The test items are designed to resemble classroom activities. Can be used alone or in combination with more traditional achievement tests.	One class period	Nonverbal (pencil and booklet)
Hammill Multiability Achievement Test (HMAT)	Hammill, D., Hresko, W., Ammer, J., Cronin, M., & Quinby S.	Pro-Ed	1998	7–0	A quick assessment of student ability that reflects the content of today's school curriculum.	30–60 minutes	Nonverbal
Iowa Tests of Basic Skills (ITBS)*	Hieronymus, A., et al.	Riverside	2001	Kindergarten to 9th grade	A criterion- and norm-referenced set of tests that measure overall functioning rather than specific content. The tests can provide a continuous measure of the development of fundamental skills necessary for school and life success.	125–150 minutes	Nonverbal (pencil and booklet)
Kaufman Test of Educational Achievement–2nd ed. (KTEA)	Kaufman, A., & Kaufman, N.	American Guidance Service	2003	1st to 12th grade	A norm-referenced, easel-format test of multiple skills. The KTEA contains both a Brief and Comprehensive Form. Either can be used for program planning and placement decisions. Additionally, the Brief Form is useful for screening, and the Comprehensive Form for identifying strengths and weaknesses.	Brief Form, 10–35 minutes; Comprehensive, 20–75 minutes	Verbal and nonverbal

		Publisher					
Metropolitan Achievement Tests–7th ed. (MAT–7)*	Prescott, G., et al.	Psychological Corporation	1993	Kindergarten to grade 12-9	The MAT-7 provides a global assessment of the student's skill development in reading, mathematics, language, social studies, and science. The battery is useful for screening, monitoring group performance, and evaluating programs. A short form is also available.	1 hour 35 minutes for kindergarten, ranging to 4 hours 10 minutes at higher levels	Nonverbal (pencil and booklet)
Monitoring Basic Skills Progress–2nd ed. (MBSP)	Fuchs, L., et al.	Pro-Ed	1997	First to Sixth grade	A computer-assisted measurement program that both tests and monitors progress in reading, math, and spelling. Students are tested at the computer, each time with a different test form. Results are computer-plotted graphically over time so that teachers can easily monitor progress. The program also reports a performance analysis and remedial program recommendations.	Varies	Nonverbal (keyboard)
The Ounce Scale	Meisels, S. J., Marsden, D. B., Dombro, A. L., Weston, D. R., & Jewkes, A. M.	Pearson Early Learning Group	2004	birth to $3\frac{1}{2}$	Provides information about infants' and young children's development.	Varies	Visual
Peabody Individual Achievement Test–Revised	Markwardt, F.	American Guidance Service	1998	Kindergarten to 12th grade	Provides a wide-range screening of basic curriculum areas: mathematics, reading recognition, reading comprehension, spelling, general information, and written expression. This test is useful for individual evaluation, guidance and counseling, admissions and transfers, grouping students, and progress evaluation.	30–40 minutes	Verbal and nonverbal
Riverside Performance Assessment Series (R–PAS)*	Riverside		1993	1st to 12th grade	A set of free-response assessments for reading, mathematics, and writing. For each activity, students are presented with a scenario in which they must take an active part, using strategic thinking and problem-solving skills while writing and completing charts and diagrams. A Spanish edition is available.	Varies	Nonverbal

(continued)

377

Name	Author	Publisher	Copyright Date	Age Range	Purpose	Approximate Testing Time	Types of Response
SRA Achievement Series*	Naslund, R., et al.	Science Research Associates	1978	Kindergarten to 12th grade	A norm- and criterion-referenced test battery that assesses skill development in reading, mathematics, language arts, social studies, sciences, and use of reference materials.	2 hours to 2 hours 47 minutes for grades K–3	Nonverbal (pencil and booklet)
The Stanford Early School Achievement Test–4th ed. (SESAT)*	**Madden, R.,** et al.	Psychological Corporation	1996	Kindergarten to first grade	The first of a series of three tests (SESAT, SAT, TASK) that provide comprehensive, continuous assessment of skill development in key content areas: sounds and letters, word reading, sentence reading, mathematics, environment, and listening to words and stories.	Level 1 (K-0 to K-5), 3 hours 10 minuts; Level 2 (K-5 to 1-5), 3 hours 45 minutes	Nonverbal (pencil and booklet)
Test of Memory and Learning: TOMAL	Reynolds, C. R., & Bigler, E. D.	AGS Publishing	2004	5 to 19 years	Allows the assessment of strengths and weakness in a child's memory as well as potentially pathologic indicators of memory disturbances.	45 minutes	Verbal
Wechsler Individual Achievement Test–2nd ed. (WIAT)	Publisher	Psychological Corporation	2001	5 to 19	A comprehensive battery for measuring academic difficulties. Measures eight areas: basic reading, mathematics reasoning, spelling, reading comprehension, numerical operations, listening comprehension, oral expression, and written expression. A shorter screening battery can also be given.	Comprehensive Battery, 30–50 minutes for young children; Screener, 10–18 minutes	Verbal and nonverbal
Wide Range Achievement Test–3 (WRAT–3)* **(Group administration for spelling and arithmetic sections only)**	Wilkinson, G.	Jastak Associates	1993	5 to 75	Measures achievement with a focus on the coding skills of reading, spelling, and arithmetic.	15–30 minutes	Verbal and nonverbal

Woodcock-Johnson Psycho-Educational Battery–Revised (WJ–R): Tests of Achievement	Woodcock, R., & Johnson, M.	1990	2 to 90	An easel-format set of tests for assessing achievement level in reading, mathematics, written language, and knowledge. The standard battery yields five cluster scores and includes nine tests. A supplemental battery of five additional tests can also be administered if additional diagnostic information is needed. Computer scoring and books on test interpretation are available.	(Information not found)	Verbal and nonverbal
Work Sampling for Head Start	L., Dorfman, A. B., & Jablon, J. R., Pearson Early Learning Group	2005	P3–P4	Assessment that tracks progress and improves learning.	Varies	Visual
Work Sampling System	Meisels, Jablon, et al.	1995	Preschool through grade 5	An ongoing evaluation process designed as an alternative to standardized achievement tests. The system is composed of three elements: developmental checklists, portfolios, and summary reports, which are all intended to be classroom-focused and relevant to instruction.	Varies (ongoing process)	Verbal, nonverbal, rater
Young Children's Achievement Test (YCAT)	Hresko, W., Peak, P., Herron, S., & Bridges, D.	2000	4-0 through 7-11	Identifies children at risk for school failure at a young age.	25–45 minutes	Verbal and nonverbal

(continued)

4. Tests of Achievement in Language

Name	Author	Publisher	Copyright Date	Age Range	Purpose	Approximate Testing Time	Types of Response
Bankson Language Test–2nd ed. (BLT–2)	Bankson, N.	Pro-Ed	1990	3-0 to 6-11	Useful for establishing the presence of a language disorder or need for further testing. The BLT–2 provides a measure of a child's linguistic skills in terms of semantic knowledge, morphological/ syntactical rules, and pragmatics. A short form is also available for screening purposes.	30 minutes	Verbal and nonverbal
Clinical Evaluation of Language Fundamentals, Fourth Edition: CELF-4	Semel, E., Wiig, E. H., & Secord, W. A.	PsychCorp	2003	5 to 21 years	Provides the bridge that helps you understand a child's need for classroom language adaptations, enhancements, or curriculum accommodations.	30–60 minutes	Verbal
Clinical Evaluation of Language Fundamentals– Preschool-2 (CELF–Preschool)	Wiig, E., et al.	Psychological Corporation	2005	3 to 6	Assesses a wide range of expressive and receptive language skills: basic concepts, sentence structure, word structure, formulating labels, recalling sentences in context, and linguistic concepts.	30–45 minutes	Verbal and nonverbal
Comprehensive Assessment of Spoken Language: CASL	Carrow-Woolfolk, E.	AGS Publishing	1999	3 years and up	CASL is comprised of 15 tests that measure language processing skills, comprehension, expression, retrieval, etc., in four language structure categories: lexical, syntactic, supralinguistic, and pragmatic.	30 to 45 minutes	Verbal
Comprehensive Receptive and Expressive Vocabulary Test–2nd ed. (CREVT)	Wallace, G., & Hammill, D.	Pro-Ed	2002	4 to 17	Used to identify students with difficulties, define strengths and weaknesses, and measure progress. The CREVT measures two skills: receptive language, for which the student points to the correct picture for the word spoken by the examiner, and expressive language, for which the student defines the word spoken.	20–30 minutes	Verbal and nonverbal

380

DELV–Norm Referenced	Seymour, H. N., Roeper, T. W., & de Villiers, J.	PsychCorp	2005	4 to 12 years	Used to accurately diagnose child's speech and language disorder.	45 to 50 minutes	Written, verbal
Expressive One-Word Picture Vocabulary Test–Revised (EOWPVT–R)	Gardner, M.	Academic Therapy Publications	1990	2-0 to 11-11	Provides a measure of a child's expressive vocabulary through the presentation of picture cards. The test can be used to appraise definitional and interpretational skills, estimate fluency in English, and indicate possible speech or language difficulties.	5–10 minutes	Verbal
Expressive Vocabulary Test: EVT	Williams, K. T.	AGS Publishing	1997	2 to 6 years	EVT is an individually administered, norm-referenced test of expressive vocabulary and word retrieval.	15 minutes	Visual and verbal
EOWPVT (Expressive One-Word Picture Vocabulary Test)	Brownell, R.	Harcourt	2000	2–18 years	Assesses how a person processes language and other elements of verbal expression.	10–15 minutes	Verbal
Goldman-Fristoe-Woodcock Test of Auditory Discrimination 2 (G-F-WTAD)	Goldman, R., Fristoe, M., & Woodcock, R.	American Guidance Service	2000	3-8 to adult	Evaluates an individual's ability to discriminate among speech sounds in both quiet and noisy backgrounds. Words are presented on cassette.	15 minutes	Nonverbal
Illinois Test of Psycholinguistic Abilities–3rd ed. (ITPA–3)	Hammill, D. Mather, N., & Roberts, R.	Pro-Ed	2001	2-4 to 10-3	Assesses both verbal and nonverbal psycholinguistic ability. The "representation level" tests skills with language symbols, and the "automatic level" assesses skills in retention and retrieval of language.	1 hour	Verbal and nonverbal
Kaufman Survey of Early Academic and Language Skills (K-SEALS)	Kaufman, A., & Kaufman, N.	American Guidance Service	1993	3 to 6	A norm-reference measure of children's language (expressive and receptive), articulation, and preacademic skills with numbers, letters, and words.	15–25 minutes	Verbal and nonverbal

(continued)

Name	Author	Publisher	Copyright Date	Age Range	Purpose	Approximate Testing Time	Types of Response
Kindergarten Language Screening Test (KLST)	Gauthier, S., & Madison, C.	Pro-Ed	1998	Kindergarten	A screener to identify children with language problems either in reception or expression.	Less than 5 minutes	Verbal and nonverbal
Language Arts Assessment Portfolio (LAAP)	Karlsen, B.	American Guidance Service	1992	First to Sixth grade	A classroom assessment system of student progress in four areas of language arts: reading, writing, listening, and speaking. It provides a means for individualizing both assessment and instruction, using teacher evaluation and a portfolio of student work documenting student growth.	Varies (ongoing process)	Verbal, nonverbal, rater
Oral and Written Language Scales (OWLS)	Carrow-Woolfolk, E.	American Guidance Service	1995	3 to 21	OWLS samples a wide range of language tasks: listening comprehension, oral expression, and written expression. The scales assess semantic, syntactic, pragmatic, and supralinguistic (higher-order thinking) aspects of language.	Listening Comprehension, 5–15 minutes; Oral Expression, 10–25 minutes. (Written Expression time not reported.)	Verbal and nonverbal
Peabody Picture Vocabulary Test–Revised, 3rd ed. (PPVT–III)	Dunn, L., & Dunn, L.	American Guidance Service	1997	2-6 to 40	An easel-format, receptive vocabulary test intended to measure verbal ability and scholastic aptitude. A suitable test for students with reading or writing difficulties or those who are severely physically impaired because any method of indicating "yes" or "no" is an acceptable response.	10–15 minutes	Verbal and nonverbal
Pre-LAS (Language Assessment Scales)	Duncan, S., & DeAvila, F.	CTB/McGraw-Hill	2000	Preschool to First grade	Assesses the oral language proficiency of children in three areas: morphology, syntax, and semantics. There are two separate tests, English and Spanish. Useful for identifying limited or non-English speaking students.	10 minutes	Verbal and nonverbal

Test	Author	Publisher	Year	Age	Description	Time	Type
Preschool Language Scale–4 (PLS-4)	Zimmerman, I., et al.	Psychological Corporation	2002	Birth to 6	A norm-referenced test of prelanguage skills (attention, vocal development, social communication), and receptive and expressive skills (semantics, structure, and integrative thinking skills). Uses playlike test activities. Spanish edition available.	20–30 minutes	Verbal and nonverbal
Prueba del Desarrollo Inicial del Lenguaje	Hresko, W., et al.	Pro-Ed	1982	3 to 7	A measure of both receptive and expressive spoken Spanish.	15 minutes	Verbal and nonverbal
Receptive-Expressive Emergent Language Test–3rd ed. (REEL–3)	Bzoch, K., & League, R.	Pro-Ed	2003	Birth to 3	Measures children's language development in the first 3 years of life. The test covers areas of receptive, expressive, and inner language through an interview with a parent or other caregiver. The REEL–2 is useful for developing interventions for at-risk infants and toddlers.	30–40 minutes	Rater
Receptive One-Word Picture Vocabulary Test, 2000 Edition (ROWPVT)	Brownel, R.	Academic Therapy Publications	2000	2-0 to 11-11	Designed as a companion test to the EOWPVT, this test assesses receptive language skills and is especially useful for bilingual, speech-impaired, immature and withdrawn, and emotionally or physically impaired children.	20 minutes	Nonverbal
Test of Articulation in Context (TAC)	Lanphere, T.	Pro-Ed	1998	3–12	Assesses articulation and phonological skills by using familiar context and spontaneous reaction.	15 to 20 minutes	Verbal
Test of Early Language Development–3rd ed. (TELD-3)	Hresko, W., et al.	Pro-Ed	1999	2-0 to 7-11	Provides an overall score of language proficiency as well as a diagnostic profile of a child's language skills in both reception and expression.	20 minutes	Verbal and nonverbal

(continued)

Name	Author	Publisher	Copyright Date	Age Range	Purpose	Approximate Testing Time	Types of Response
Reynell Developmental Language Scales	Reynell, J. K., & Gruber, C.	Western Psychological	1990	1–6	Measures language skills in developmentally delayed children.	30 minutes	Verbal and nonverbal
Test of Pragmatic Language (TOPL)	Phelps-Terasaki D., & Phelps-Gun, T.	Western Psychological	1992	5–adult	Assesses the effectiveness and appropriateness of a student's pragmatic language skills.	30–45 minutes.	Verbal and nonverbal
Test of Early Written Language–2nd ed. (TEWL–2)	Hresko, W., Herron, S., & Peak, P.	Pro-Ed	1996	3 to 7	An assessment of emergent written language skills. Useful for measuring progress and evaluating programs and appropriate for identifying mildly handicapped students.	10–30 minutes	Verbal and nonverbal
Test of Language Development–Primary, 3rd ed. (TOLD–P3)	Newcomer, P., & Hammill, D.	Pro-Ed	1997	4-0 to 8-11	Designed to identify and isolate disorders through testing the basic linguistic skills of listening, speaking, semantics, syntax, and phonology.	30–60 minutes	Verbal and nonverbal
Test of Narrative Language (TNL)	Gillam, R. B., & Pearson, N. A.	Pro-Ed	2004	5-0 through 11-11	Assesses how well children use their knowledge of the components of language while they engage in functional discourse.	15–20 minutes	Verbal
Test of Phonological Awareness (TOPA)*	Torgesen, J., & Bryant, B.	Pro-Ed	1994	Kindergarten to second grade	Provides a measure of a child's ability to hear individual sounds in words. Because this ability is related to ease in learning to read, this test can be used to identify children in kindergarten who may benefit from specialized instruction to prepare them for reading. One test is available for kindergarten and another for first and second grade.	20 minutes	Nonverbal

Name	Author	Publisher	Copyright Date	Age Range	Purpose	Approximate Testing Time	Types of Response
Test of Pragmatic Language (TOPL)	Phelps-Terasaki, D., & Phelps-Gunn, T.	Pro-Ed	1992	5-0 to 13-11	A comprehensive test of the student's pragmatic language, meaning language used socially and for a purpose. It is a measure of not just what is said, but why.	45 minutes	Verbal
Test of Written Language–3rd ed. (TOWL–3)	Hammill, D. D., Larsen, S. C.	AGS Publishing	1996	7 to 17 years	Contains both essay analysis and traditional test formats to assess important aspects of written language.	90 minutes	Written

5. Tests of Achievement in Reading

Name	Author	Publisher	Copyright Date	Age Range	Purpose	Approximate Testing Time	Types of Response
The Classroom Reading Inventory–10th ed.	Silvaroli, N., & Wheelock, W.	McGraw-Hill	2004	5-0 to 24-11	An informal reading inventory test to help identify students' reading problems.	Varies	Oral
Comprehensive Test of Phonological Processing (CTOPP)	Wagner, R., Torgesen, J., & Rashotte, C.,	Pro-Ed	1999	5-0 to 24-11	Assesses phonological awareness, phonological memory, and rapid naming.	30 minutes	Nonverbal
Comprehensive Assessment of Reading Strategies (CARS Series)	Adcock, D.	Curriculum Associates	2005	Grades 1–8	Diagnoses students' strength and weaknesses. Builds and reinforces reading skills.	Varies	Nonverbal
Dynamic Indicators of Basic Early Literacy Skills (DIBELS)	Good, R., & Kaminski, R.	University of Oregon	2005	4 to 11 years	DIBELS is designed to use short (1 minute) fluency measures—sound, letter naming, phoneme segmentation, nonsense word, oral reading fluency, word use—to regularly monitor the development of prereading and early reading skills.	5–10 minutes	Written or verbal
Early Reading Diagnostic Assessment–2nd ed. (ERDA–2)	PsychCorp	PsychCorp	2003	4 to 8 years	Administered to identify young children at risk for reading difficulty or failure.	45–60 minutes	Visual, verbal

(continued)

385

Name	Author	Publisher	Copyright Date	Age Range	Purpose	Approximate Testing Time	Types of Response
Early Reading Success Indicator: ERSI	PsychCorp	PsychCorp	2004	5 to 10 years	Helps to prevent reading failure and enriches the WISC–IV tests.	20–25 minutes	Verbal, reading
Gray Oral Reading Test–4th ed	Wiederholt, L., & Bryant, B.	Harcourt	2001	6.0 through 18.0	This test requires students to read passages aloud and answer literal, inferential, critical, and affective comprehension questions. The GORT–R identifies students who may benefit from additional help, indicates strengths and weaknesses, and monitors progress.	15–30 minutes	Verbal
Gray Silent Reading Tests (GSRT)	Wiederholt, J. L., & Blalock, G.	Pro-Ed	2000	7–25	Measures a person's silent reading comprehension ability.	20 minutes	Written
Group Reading Assessment and Diagnostic Evaluation: GRADE	Williams, K. T.	AGS Publishing	2001	3 years and up	To deliver reliable reading diagnostics for individual students, including intervention suggestions that profile both individual and classroom strengths and weaknesses.	45–90 minutes	Written
Khan-Lewis Phonological Analysis–2nd ed. (KLPA–2)	Khan, L., & Lewis, N.	AGS Publishing	2002	2 years and up	Provides a comprehensive diagnosis of both articulation and use of the phonological process.	10–30 minutes	Verbal
Reading Fluency Indicator: RFI	Williams, K. T.	AGS Publishing	2004	5 to 18 years	Provides information about a student's ability both to read independently and participate in classroom activities that require reading.	5–10 minutes	Written
Slosson Oral Reading Test–Revised (SORT–R)	Slosson, R.	Slosson Educational Publications	1994	Preschool to adult	A quick estimate of target-word recognition useful for identifying individuals with reading difficulties.	3–5 minutes	Verbal

Sounds and Symbols Early Reading Program	Goldman, R., & Lynch, M.	AGS Publishing	2005	3 to 8 years	Addresses the five building blocks of early reading development outlined in the No Child Left Behind Act.	Varies	Verbal
Stanford Diagnostic Reading Test–4th ed. (SDRT)*	Karlsen, B., & Gardner, E.	Psychological Corporation	1995	Late first grade to post-high school	A norm- and criterion-referenced test designed to indicate areas of strength and weakness in reading decoding, vocabulary, comprehension, and rate of reading. The SDRT is primarily for use with low achievers and thus contains a greater number of easy items than some other achievement tests.	105 minutes for grades K–3	Nonverbal (pencil and booklet)
Test of Early Reading Ability–3rd ed. (TERA–3)	Reid, D. K., Hresko, W. P., & Hammill, D. D.	AGS Publishing	2005	3 to 6 years	Screens children's early reading abilities through the measurement of knowledge of contextual meaning, the alphabet, and conventions such as reading from left to right.	30 minutes	Visual and verbal
Test of Early Reading Ability–Deaf or Hard of Hearing (TERA–D)	Reid, D., et al.	Pro-Ed	1991	3-0 to 13-11	An adaptation of the TERA–2 designed for simultaneous communication or American Sign Language.	20–30 minutes	Verbal or sign language
Test of Phonological Awareness in Spanish (TPAS)	Riccio, A. C., Imhoff, B., Hasbrouck, J. E., & Davis, G. N.	Pro-Ed	2004	4-0 through 10-11	Measures phonological awareness ability in Spanish-speaking children.	15–30 minutes	Verbal
Test of Phonological Awareness Skills (TOPAS)	Newcomer, P., & Barenbaum, E.	Pro-Ed	2004	5–10	Helps identify children who have problems in phonological awareness.	15–30 minutes	Verbal
Test of Reading Comprehension–3rd ed. (TORC–3)	Brown, V., Hammill, D. D., & Wiederholt, J. L.	AGS Publishing	1995	7 to 17 years	To strengthen reading comprehension in general vocabulary, syntactic similarities, paragraph reading, and sentence sequencing.	30 minutes for each subtest	Written

(continued)

Name	Author	Publisher	Copyright Date	Age Range	Purpose	Approximate Testing Time	Types of Response
Test of Word Reading Efficiency (TOWRE)	Torgesen, J., Wagner, R., & Rashotte, C.	Pro-Ed	1999	6-0 through 24-11	Measures word reading accuracy and fluency.	5–10 minutes	Verbal
Woodcock Reading Mastery Tests–Revised (WRMT–R/NU)	Woodcock, R.	American Guidance Service	1998	5 to 751	Provides an assessment of reading skills in six areas: visual-auditory learning, letter identification, word identification, word attack, word comprehension, and passage comprehension. Computer scoring is available.	10–30 minutes	Verbal

6. Tests of Achievement in Spelling

Name	Author	Publisher	Copyright Date	Age Range	Purpose	Approximate Testing Time	Types of Response
Test of Written Spelling–4th ed. (TWS–4)*	Larsen, S., & Hammill, D.	Pro-Ed	1999	1st to 12th grade	An assessment of spelling ability that includes a comparison between ability with predictable sound-letter patterns and with less predictable patterns.	20 minutes	Nonverbal

7. Tests of Achievement in Mathematics

Name	Author	Publisher	Copyright Date	Age Range	Purpose	Approximate Testing Time	Types of Response
Group Mathematics Assessment and Diagnostic Evaluation (G.MADE)	Williams, K. T.	AGS Publishing	2004	5 years and up	Provides a clear, accurate account of a student's mathematics skills and a direct link to effective intervention if necessary.	50–90 minutes	Written

Name	Author	Publisher	Copyright Date	Age Range	Purpose	Approximate Testing Time	Types of Response
Keymath–Revised/NU Norms Update	Connolly, A.	American Guidance Service	1998	Kindergarten to ninth grade	A norm- and criterion-referenced, easel-format test of math skills in three areas: basic concepts, operations, and applications. Two forms and computer scoring are available.	35–50 minutes	Verbal and nonverbal
Test of Early Mathematics Ability–3rd ed. (TEMA–3)	Ginsburg, H., & Baroody, A.	Pro-Ed	2003	3-0 to 8-11	Measures both formal and informal math skills and identifies specific strengths and weaknesses. Useful for assessing specific difficulties, measuring progress, designing instruction and remediation, and identifying gifted students. A book of remedial techniques and instructional activities for each area tested is also available.	20–30 minutes	Verbal and nonverbal
Test of Mathematical Abilities for Gifted Students (TOMAGS)	Ryser, G. R., & Johnsen, S. K.	Pro-Ed	1998	Grades K–3 and 4–6	Identifies children gifted in mathematics through use of mathematical reasoning and mathematical problem solving.	20–30 minutes	Nonverbal (written)

8. **Tests to Identify Giftedness**

Name	Author	Publisher	Copyright Date	Age Range	Purpose	Approximate Testing Time	Types of Response
Creativity Assessment Packet (CAP)*	Williams, F.	Pro-Ed	1980	6 to 18	The CAP is a set of three instruments for identifying creativity. Two are completed by the student: the Test of Divergent Thinking and the Test of Divergent Feeling. The third instrument, the Williams Scale, is a rating scale completed by teachers or parents. Factors measured include fluency, flexibility, elaboration, originality, vocabulary, and comprehension.	Divergent thinking, 25 minutes for younger students; Divergent Feeling, 20–30 minutes; Williams Scale, 30 minutes	Nonverbal (pencil and booklet), rater

(continued)

389

Name	Author	Publisher	Copyright Date	Age Range	Purpose	Approximate Testing Time	Types of Response
Gifted Rating Scales	Pfeiffer, S., & Jarosewich, T.	PsychCorp	2003	4 to 6 years	Norm referencing rating scales based on current theories of giftedness and federal and state guidelines regarding the definition of gifted and talented students.	5–10 minutes	Written
Screening Assessment for Gifted Elementary Students–Primary (SAGES–P)*	Johnson, S., & Corn, A.	Prufrock	1992	5-0 to 8-11	Useful for helping to identify gifted children in grades K to 3. SAGES–P contains two sections: a reasoning subtest that serves as a measure of aptitude, and a general information subset that serves as a measure of achievement.	30 minutes	Nonverbal (pencil and booklet)
Torrance Tests of Creative Thinking: Figural (TTCT:F)*	Torrance, E.	Scholastic Testing Service	1998	Kindergarten to adult	Evaluates creative potential in a wide variety of areas. The test has two sections: Figural (involves thinking creatively with pictures) and Verbal (involves thinking creatively with words). Tests of thinking creatively with actions and movement are also available for ages 3 to kindergarten.	Figural, 30 minutes; Verbal, 45 minutes	Nonverbal

9. Tests of Perceptual and/or Motor Skills

Name	Author	Publisher	Copyright Date	Age Range	Purpose	Approximate Testing Time	Types of Response
Bruininks-Oseretsky Test of Motor Proficiency	Buininks, R.	American Guidance Service	1999	4 1/2 to 14 1/2	A measure of both gross- and fine-motor functioning. Skills sampled include running, speed and agility, balance, bilateral coordination, strength, upper limb coordination, response speed, visual-motor control, and upper limb speed and dexterity.	45–60 minutes	Nonverbal

Test	Author	Publisher	Year	Age	Description	Time	Verbal/Nonverbal
Developmental Test of Visual Perception–2nd ed. (DTVP–2)	Hammill, D., et al.	Pro-Ed	1993	4 to 10	An eight-subtest measure of visual-perception and visual-motor integration skills. Useful for identifying children with difficulties in these areas, determining eligibility for special programs, and monitoring intervention progress.	35 minutes	Nonverbal
Developmental Test of Visual-Motor Integration: 5th ed. (VMI)*	Beery, K., Beery, N., & Buktenica, N.	Modern Curriculum Press	2004	2 to 15	Designed to determine the level at which visual-motor perception and motor performance are integrated. The VMI consists of geometric figures that are copied by the student as accurately as possible.	15–20 minutes	Nonverbal
Motor-Free Visual Perception Test–3 (MVPT–3)	Colarusso, R., & Hammill, D.	Academic Therapy Publications	2002	4-0 to 8-0	Useful for screening or diagnosis with learning disabled, mentally challenged, or physically challenged children. The MVPT measures visual perception by presenting a student with a line drawing that he or she must match with an identical drawing presented in a multiple-choice format.	10 minutes	Nonverbal
Peabody Developmental Motor Scales–2 (PDMS–2)	Folio, M., & Fewell, R.	Western Psychological Services	2000	Birth to 83 months	Assesses both gross- and fine-motor skills in children. The PDMS was developed to meet the programming needs of handicapped children in physical education. Gross-motor items are classified into five skill categories: reflexes, balance, non-locomotor, locomotor, and receipt and propulsion of objects. Fine-motor items are classified into four skill categories: grasping, hand use, eye-hand coordination, and manual dexterity.	45–60 minutes	Nonverbal
Test of Auditory-Perceptual Skills–Revised (TAPS–R)	Gardner, M.	Pro-Ed	1997	4 to 12	Useful for identifying auditory-perceptual difficulties, imperceptions of auditory modality, and language and learning problems.	10–15 minutes	Verbal

(continued)

Name	Author	Publisher	Copyright Date	Age Range	Purpose	Approximate Testing Time	Types of Response
Test of Gross Motor Development–2 (TGMD–2)	Ulrich, D.	Pro-Ed	2000	3 to 10	Assesses appropriate motor skills in the areas of locomotion and object control. The TGMD is useful for identifying children who are significantly behind their peers and may be eligible for special physical education services.	15 minutes	Nonverbal

10. Tests of Behavior and Conduct

Name	Author	Publisher	Copyright Date	Age Range	Purpose	Approximate Testing Time	Types of Response
Adaptive Behavior Assessment System–2nd ed. (ABAS–II)	Harrison, P., & Oakland, T.	PsychCorp	2003	3 years and up	Measures eligibility under IDEA.	15–20 minutes	Verbal and written
Academic Competence Evaluation Scales: ACES	DiPerna, J. C., & Elliott, S. N.	PsychCorp	2000	4 years and up	A standardized instrument to screen students who have difficulty learning, determine how the student functions in the classroom, and prioritize skills that may need intervention.	10 to 15 minutes	Written
AAMR Adaptive Behavior Scale–School Edition (ABS–S:2)	Nihira, K., & Lambert, N.	American Association on Mental Retardation	1993	3 to 16	A 16-domain measure of social competence and independence for use with mentally retarded, emotionally maladjusted, and developmentally disabled individuals.	60–90 minutes	Rater (teacher or other school personnel)
Anxiety Scales for Children and Adults (ASCA)*	Battle, J.	Pro-Ed	1993	School-age to adult	A series of self-report scales to identify individuals experiencing intense anxiety.	15 minutes	Nonverbal (pencil and booklet)

Asperger Syndrome Diagnostic Scale: ASDS	Myles, B., Bock, S., & Simpson, R.	Western Psychological Services	2001	ASDS helps to quickly rule out other possible diagnoses and determine the likelihood that a child or adolescent has Asperger syndrome.	5 minutes	Parent or therapist questionnaire
Autism Diagnostic Interview–Revised (ADI–R)	Rutter, M., LeCouteur, A., & Lord, C.	Western Psychological Services	2003	ADI–R attempts to assess individuals suspected of having autism or other autism spectrum disorders. Useful for formal diagnosis as well as treatment and educational planning.	1.5–2.5 hours	Verbal
Behavior Assessment System for Children–2 (BASC–2)	Reynolds, C., & Kamphaus, R.	American Guidance Service	2004	A set of rating scales for describing an individual's behavior and emotions. Contains teacher, parent, and self-reports plus directly observed classroom behavior and a structured developmental history. Computer scoring is available.	Varies	Nonverbal (pencil and booklet), rater
Comprehensive Test of Adaptive Behavior–Revised (CTAB–R)	Adams, G.	Psychological Corporation	2000	Assesses level of independent behavior in individuals with mental and/or physical disabilities. Includes both a student test and a parent/guardian survey.	Varies	Rater
Connors' Rating Scales–Revised	Conners, C.	Multi-Health Systems	1997	A standard scale for identifying attention deficit disorder and other problem behaviors. The test can also be used for charting progress and evaluating intervention programs. A "Hyperactivity Index" is included or can be administered separately as "Connors' Abbreviated Symptom Questionnaire" (CASQ). Long and short forms of the CRS are available for both teachers and parents.	Varies	Rater

(continued)

Name	Author	Publisher	Copyright Date	Age Range	Purpose	Approximate Testing Time	Types of Response
Culture-Free Self-Esteem Inventories–3rd ed. (CFSEI-3)	Battle, J.	Pro-Ed	2004	5-0 to adult	A series of self-report scales that measure an individual's self-esteem in a variety of contexts: general, peers, school, and parents. A "lie" (defensiveness) scale is also included.	15–20 minutes	Verbal and nonverbal
Depression and Anxiety in Youth Scale (DAYS)	Newcomer, P., et al.	Pro-Ed	1994	6-0 to 19-0	Used to identify major depressive disorder and overanxious disorders in children. The teacher and parent scales have a true/false format regarding the presence or absence of a symptom. Students also report the degree to which they experience certain feelings.	Student scale, 15–20 minutes for readers and 30 minutes when items must be read to the student; teacher and parent scales, 5–10 minutes	Nonverbal or verbal, rater
Krug Aspergers Disorder Index (KADI)	Krug, D., & Arick, J.	Western Psychological Services	2003	6 to 22 years	Helps clinicians distinguish individuals with Asperger's disorder from those who have other forms of high-functioning autism.	15–20 minutes	Parent or therapist questionnaire
Outcomes PME: Planning, Monitoring, Evaluating	Stoiber, K. C., & Kratochwill, T. R.	PsychCorp	2001	5 years and up	To evaluate a student's progress toward identified behavior improvement goals.	Varies	Written and verbal
Scales of Independent Behavior–Revised (SIB–R)	Bruininks, R., et al.	DLM Teaching Resources	1996	Infant to adult	Assesses functional independence and adaptive behavior in motor, social, and communication, and personal-living and community-living skills. A Spanish edition is available.	45–50 minutes	Rater
Autism Diagnostic Observation Schedule (ADOS)	Lord, C., Rutter, M., DiLavore, P. C., & Risi, S.	Western Psychological Services	2001	2 years or older	ADOS is used to evaluate almost anyone suspected of having autism, from toddlers to adults, and children with no speech to adults who are fluent.	160 minutes	Verbal

Name	Authors	Publisher	Year	Age	Description	Time	Format
Beck Youth Inventories of Emotional & Social Impairment	Beck, J. S., Beck, A. T., & Jolly, J.	PsychCorp	2001	7 to 14 years	Assesses symptoms of depression, anxiety, anger, disruptive beavior, and self-concept in children and adolescents.	5–10 minutes	Written
Behavior Assessment System for Children–2nd ed. (BASC-2)	Reynolds, C. R., & Kamphaus, R. W.	AGS Publishing	2004	2 to 21 years	Examines adaptive and maladaptive behavior in reference to IDEA.	10 to 30 minutes	Written
Behavior Rating Inventory of Executive Function (BRIEF)	Gioia, G. A., Espy, K. A., & Isquith, P. K.	PsychCorp	2002	2 to 5 years	To assess impairment of executive function in children and young people from preschool age through adolescents.	10–15 minutes	Verbal
Brown Attention-Deficit Disorder Scales	Brown, T. E.	PsychCorp	2001	3 to 7 years	Identifies ADHD in primary-grade students.	10 to 20 minutes	Verbal
Caregiver-Teacher's Report Form	Achenbach, T., & Edelbrock, C.	Author	2000	6 to 11 and 12 to 16	Provides a profile of problem-behavior syndromes, adaptive behavior, and school performance. Eight scales are included: anxious, social withdrawal, unpopular, self-destructive, obsessive-compulsive, inattentive, nervous-overactive, and aggressive.	Varies	Rater
Carey Temperament Scales (CTS)	Carey, W. B., & McDevitt, S. C.	PsychCorp	1995	1 month to 12 years	To quickly and accurately gain a deeper understanding of a children's temperament or behavioral style.	20 minutes	Written
Piers-Harris Children's Self-Concept Scale, 2nd ed. (Piers-Harris 2)	Piers, E., Harris, D., & Herzberg, D.	Western Psychological Services	2002	7–18	To quickly identify youngsters who need further testing or treatment, based on self-concept in ages 7–18.	10–15 minutes	Written
Social-Emotional Dimension Scale–2 (SEDS–2)	Hudson, J., & Roberts, T.	Pro-Ed	2004	5 1/2 to 18 1/2	A rating scale to screen for students at risk for conduct disorders, behavior problems, or emotional disturbance.	Not reported	Rater

(continued)

Name	Author	Publisher	Copyright Date	Age Range	Purpose	Approximazte Testing Time	Types of Response
Social Communication Questionnaire (SCQ)	Rutter, M., Bailey, A., & Lord, C.	Western Psychological Services	2003	4 years and older	This instrument helps evaluate communication skills and social functioning in children who may have autism or autism spectrum disorders.	10 minutes	Written, by parent.
Social Skills Rating System (SSRS)	Gresham, F. M., & Elliott, S. N.	AGS Publishing	1990	3 to 18 years	To obtain a complete picture of social behaviors from teachers, parents, and even from students themselves that affect teacher-student relationships, peer acceptance, academic performance, etc.	10–25 minutes	Verbal and written
Vineland Social-Emotional Early Childhood Scales (Vineland SEEC)	Sparrow, S. S., Balla, D. A., & Cicchetti, D. V.	AGS Publishing	1998	Birth through 6 years	Measures early childhood social-emotional development, including interpersonal relationships, play and leisure time, and coping skills.	15–25 minutes	Verbal

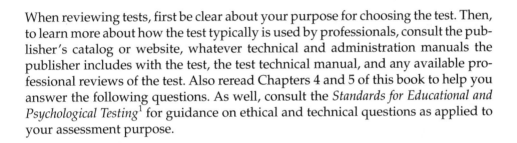

Appendix D

*Test Evaluation Guidelines**

When reviewing tests, first be clear about your purpose for choosing the test. Then, to learn more about how the test typically is used by professionals, consult the publisher's catalog or website, whatever technical and administration manuals the publisher includes with the test, the test technical manual, and any available professional reviews of the test. Also reread Chapters 4 and 5 of this book to help you answer the following questions. As well, consult the *Standards for Educational and Psychological Testing*[1] for guidance on ethical and technical questions as applied to your assessment purpose.

[1]AERA, APA, & NCME. (1999). *Standards for educational and psychological testing*. Washington, DC: American Educational Research Association.

DESCRIPTIVE INFORMATION

Title	
Author	
Copyright date/edition	
Publisher	
Stated purpose of test	

Are there subtests?	Separate scores for these?

Standardized	Criterion referenced
	Portfolio

Multipurpose (screening, monitoring, etc.)

Appropriate number of items for age range?

Qualifications for administrator:

Components in the kit (manual, equipment):

Individual	Group

Total time required to administer

Age range	Available in other languages?

Cost

What behavior or knowledge is sampled in the test?

Whom is the test designed to assess?

If there are subtests, how do these relate to each other?

How clear are the directions?

Is extra equipment required?

How easy is it to administer?

What kinds of space and room conditions are necessary in order to administer the test?

What special training is needed to administer?

Can it be administered by paraprofessionals?

What kinds of scores does the test yield?

Does it have suggestions for communicating results to parents?

Do the projected results contribute to parents' understanding of their child as a learner?

Does the information obtained yield useful information for planning intervention or instruction?

What information is given about the technical qualities?

- norms (Do these match the population you are teaching?)
- reliability
- validity

If this is a high-stakes test, are the technical qualities appropriate for this use? (The available technical information convinces you research is solid and in keeping with the *Standards for Educational and Psychological Testing.*)

Summary of strengths
- technical adequacy
- efficiency
- matches purpose planned

ANALYSIS AND CONCLUSION

Do the claims or interpretations made about the child's performance match the evidence you have available?

Is the evidence clear, credible, easily located, and easily understood?

Does the test have suggestions for collection, use, and interpretation of appropriate collateral information?

Does this measure provide the most efficient manner for gathering the needed information?

Do the gathered data facilitate or enhance your work with the child?

Does it match your purpose?

Appendix E

*Choosing Technology and Software to Support Assessment**

When you choose software to support your assessment program, you will find a wide variety of available programs. Choices include the following:

- Links to state and national association goals, Head Start Outcomes, NCLB
- Record-keeping capacity
- Lesson plan suggestions
- Specially formulated "tests" for students
- Report-generation capacity
- Web-based format with access by multiple stakeholders

The programs are available on CD-ROM and on the Internet, specially formulated for your program, and are released commercially every day. So, you will need to keep in mind several principles when evaluating programs that might meet your needs. The evaluation process will call upon your knowledge of child development, instructional methodology, and assessment. You are in effect choosing an electronic tool to facilitate your work with young children. Some of the relevant issues and questions to think about follow.

The first step in the process of decision-making is the *evaluation of your hardware.* Most sophisticated assessment systems utilizing CD-ROM technology will require not only storage for the electronic files but also a good amount of memory for on-screen viewing and processing of your data collection. The electronic files may be stored on CD-ROMs, on a school network server, or on your hard drive. If you use external storage of student records, lesson plans, or whatever, you will want to have enough storage on your hard drive so that you can effectively sort data and use it in planning for your students. If stored elsewhere, you will want to know about the developer's reputation for security of data, including backup systems.

More and more, assessment systems utilize the World Wide Web. For these programs you will want to have high-speed cable or DSL access to the Internet for ease of use. Once you have evaluated your hardware, you will want to think about the content of the *software programs* themselves. You will need to think about the program from the perspective of each of the stakeholders in the system: child, family, administrator, community, and of course, you—the teacher. These perspectives overlap, but the primary interests of the various stakeholders follow.

Child and family perspective

- Does the program provide appropriate safeguards for confidentiality?
- Is the material free from obvious cultural bias?
- Can the materials be used in multiple languages?
- Are there options for children and family members with disabilities?
- Who has access to stored data on individual children?
- Where are the data stored?
- What is the deletion policy for stored data, both formative and summative?
- Can the family access the stored information? Under what conditions?

Child perspective

- If children will be using the program to assess themselves, is it simple enough for them to use independently?
- Does the program provide options for cooperative use, if this is part of your assessment program?
- Is the program design intuitive? Familiar?
- Does the program provide sufficient branching to assess in-depth?
- Is the program enticing for children? Similar to classroom curriculum?
- Can a child review answers or process? Change answers if necessary?
- Does the material provide a challenge?
- Are the items in keeping with best developmentally appropriate practice?
- Are there links to support additional learning or assessment opportunities?
- Does the program support diverse levels of computer literacy for the spectrum of learners?
- How much adult help is required? Initially? Ongoing?

Administrator perspective

- Does the technology match program goals?
- Does the program add efficiency?
- Does the program provide maintenance support and regular updates? Is the fee for this service reasonable?
- Does the program combine many instructional and assessment decisions in a useable format with appropriate confidentiality safeguards?
- Does the program support all the accountability demands? Link appropriately to existing databases?

Community

- Do the reports support accountability goals?
- Are the prepared reports nontechnical, jargon-free, and easily understood?
- Do the reports model best practice in accountability reporting?
- Does the program answer the questions of Head Start and NCLB?

Teacher

- Does the program provide appropriate, but not cumbersome, password protection to guard the privacy of individual children?
- Is the scope and sequence of the program appropriate for the children you are teaching?
- Does the program help individualize instruction?
- Does the program provide easy ways to navigate through it—table of contents, easy access to help?
- Does the program include the capacity to sort the standards and goals that you must achieve with your students?
- Is the technology user-friendly? Can you point-and-click your way through the program? Is it intuitive? Does it contain effective and efficient search capacities?
- Does the program accomplish what you want it to do?
  - Provide class summaries?
  - Link to standards?
  - Link to lesson planning?
  - Provide suggestions for curriculum integration?
  - Generate accountability reports?
  - Generate parent reports?

- Are the technical manuals or online support well organized and clearly written in teacher-friendly language?
- Does the promotional material show examples that are compatible to your classroom situation? Are they believable?

Note: Technology resource to consult: International Society for Technology in Education at http://www.iste.org. See also ISTE. (2000). *National Educational Technology Standards for Students Connecting Curriculum and Technology.* Eugene, OR: ISTE.

Appendix F

*Portfolio Template**

Name	**School**

Teacher's name _____   Grade _____

A picture of me in school.

Table of Contents

Date Added	Portfolio Artifact[1]	How I feel about my work
	Reading/Writing Artifacts	☺ ☺ ☹
	Math/Science Artifacts	☺ ☺ ☹
	Social Studies Artifacts	☺ ☺ ☹
	Cooperative Project Artifacts	☺ ☺ ☹
	Art/Music/Drama Artifacts	☺ ☺ ☹
	School Social Skills	☺ ☺ ☹
	Self-efficacy Development	☺ ☺ ☹
	Other	☺ ☺ ☹

[1]Insert spaces as needed for the year.

Note: Artifacts may be drawings, writings, interviews, graphic organizers, peer evaluations, self-assessments—narrative or in response to rubric or checklist, teacher-completed checklists, log or journal, record of performance recorded by rubric, photos, video, graphic organizer, or any other demonstration/documentation of academic progress.

Did you think about the following artifacts . . .? (Teacher: Select those appropriate for age/grade and ask child to reflect upon choices).

1. poems written
2. songs composed
3. handwriting samples
4. stories written or narrated
5. math problems solved
6. PowerPoint presentations created
7. audiotapes or videos made
8. photos of projects
9. dioramas
10. science lab notes

Selection process includes:

1. all subject areas or learning domains
2. reference to all required standards or outcomes
3. student reflection
4. teacher guidance in selection
5. parent review

Artifacts included for the fall quarter:

Drawings that show [in this space each child can show reflections about work completed or can dictate to the teacher the reasons why the material is in the portfolio] _____

_____

_____

_____

_____

Samples of work showing that I can solve problems [again include the reflections about why each is included] _____

_____

_____

_____

_____

My strengths as a learner include

1. _____

2. _____

3. _____

I am working on

_____

_____

_____

_____

My learning challenges are

_____

_____

_____

_____

Standards for my grade (you will need the teacher's assistance with the next section)

In this space list all that you will evaluate for the quarter in each subject area.

Standard1:[2] Students will use mathematical analysis, scientific inquiry [etc.] as appropriate, to pose questions, seek answers, and develop solutions.

Evidence for progress toward this standard

1. _____
2. _____
3. _____
4. _____
5. _____

[continue with all required standards]

Bull's eye![3] I hit the target on this standard!

Standard: [insert learning standard here]

Achieving this standard was

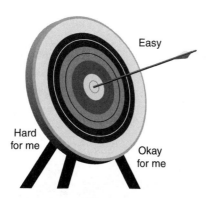

To achieve this standard, I include the following artifacts

_____
_____
_____

[2]New York State Mathematics and Science Partnership Program.
[3]Developed by Bridget Amory, Assistant Principal, Morris Early Childhood Center, Milford School District, Delaware.

Parent Review

1. I appreciated seeing

    _____
    _____
    _____
    _____
    _____
    _____

2. How this compares to what I see at home

    _____
    _____
    _____
    _____
    _____
    _____

3. Next quarter I hope to see

    _____
    _____
    _____
    _____
    _____
    _____

Appendix G

*Child Interview Protocols**

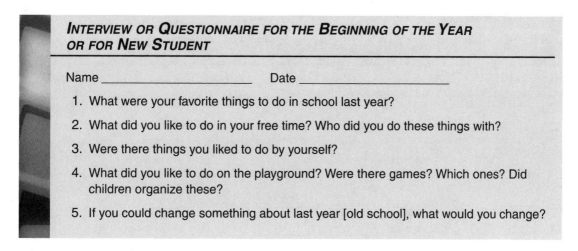

INTERVIEW OR QUESTIONNAIRE FOR THE BEGINNING OF THE YEAR OR FOR NEW STUDENT

Name _____ Date _____

1. What were your favorite things to do in school last year?

2. What did you like to do in your free time? Who did you do these things with?

3. Were there things you liked to do by yourself?

4. What did you like to do on the playground? Were there games? Which ones? Did children organize these?

5. If you could change something about last year [old school], what would you change?

INTERVIEW OF CHILD TO DETERMINE ACADEMIC INTERESTS

Name _____ Date _____

1. I have time to play before school and like to . . .

2. After school, I go to . . . We usually . . . [have a snack—your favorite?], then . . .

3. I do my homework . . . [e.g., right after school, after dinner, right before bed]

4. On weekends, I like to . . .

5. My favorite books that my mom/dad/babysitter read to me are . . .

6. My favorite game is . . .

7. I like to learn . . .

8. My favorite field trip of all time was . . .

READING QUESTIONS

Name _____   Date _____

1. Do you like to read? Why? Why not?

2. Do you like to have others read to you?

3. What do you look at when someone reads to you?

4. Does everyone read to you in English?

5. What are your favorite things to read?

6. If we added books to our library, what should we get?

7. When you get a book that is too hard to read, what do you do?

Appendix H

*Example Forms for Collecting Assessment Information**

Name _____ Date _____

Motor Skills for 5/6-Year-Old

Skill	Evident	Emerging
Zips		
Buttons		
Ties shoes		
Strings beads		
Uses scissors with accuracy		
Controls writing tools		
Throws large ball		
Catches large ball		

Event Checklist for Whole Class

Color Concepts[1]

Names of Children in the Class	Matches Basic Colors	Points to When Named	Names Basic Colors	Names Many Other Colors
1.				
2.				
3.				
4.				
[...]				
17.				
18.				
19.				
20.				

Checklists

Name _____   Date _____

Skill of Interest (e.g., Using Ruler Can Measure to the Nearest Inch)	Child's Name (for Ease, Preprint all the Children's Names in a Group or in Your Class)	Yes	No
	1.		
	2.		
	3.		
	4.		
	5.		
	[...]		
	25.		
	26.		
	27		

---

[1]Insert date of observation or of assessment conducted. For example, 3/15/07 8/8 colors or 3/15/07 attempted, emerging, not observed/completed.

Event to Record, (e.g., Gets folder out promptly; puts books away quietly)

Name	Mon	Tues	Wed	Thur	Fri	Mon	Tues	Wed

Rating Scales[2]

Skill	Child's Name	All of the time	Some of the time	None of the time
Uses a variety of reading strategies				
Shows oral reading fluency				
Reads fiction and nonfiction				
Interprets pictures				
Interprets charts and graphs				
Responds orally to reading				
Responds in writing to reading				

[2] Make these charts for each member of your class. Choose skills to rate that are of interest for report cards or other data collection demands.

End-of-Day Summative and Formative Evaluation   Date _____

As you think about the day, what worked well?

_____

_____

_____

_____

_____

_____

_____

_____

_____

_____

List three or four main ideas that you will ponder during the week.

_____

_____

_____

_____

_____

_____

_____

_____

_____

_____

What additional information do you need from the instructor that will clarify the experience of today?

_____

_____

_____

_____

_____

_____

_____

_____

_____

_____

Teacher's Name: _____

Appendix I

CHICAGO EARLY DEVELOPMENT SCREENING INVENTORY FOR TEACHERS II

By: Evelyn Baumann, Jack Kavanagh, and Gayle Mindes

CEDSIT II: Version of Screening Inventory for Teachers of 4 and 5 Year Olds

IDENTIFYING INFORMATION

Date: _____

Child's Name:_____ Sex: _____
              first   middle   last

Parent or Guardian: _____

Date of Birth:_____ Age: _____
            year   month   day

Preschool Center:_____ Teacher:_____

BACKGROUND INFORMATION

- This checklist has been designed as a screening instrument to identify those children who are "at high risk". It is developed to quickly find those children who may require referral and special services. It has been standardized on Head Start children and is designed to reflect each child's strengths and special needs.

- For greater accuracy in using this checklist, it is recommended that it be completed after the child has been in the program for a period of four weeks. Also, it is recommended that teachers or other program staff complete a parent interview, as the child enters the program. The **CEDSI II,** the parent interview instrument has been specifically designed for this purpose and has been standardized on Head Start children.

- Following the scoring of the **CEDSIT II**, if the child is found to be at risk for special needs, an appropriate referral for professional diagnosis should be made. The **CEDSI II** Interview Form and the **CEDSIT II** Form can be of help to the diagnostians and should be utilized for periodic review.

DIRECTIONS

- Please read over the entire checklist before planning to complete the **CEDSIT II**. You will then be familiar with the kinds of skills that you must plan to observe.

- Plan to complete the **CEDSIT II** on individual children when you can observe the child. Answer each item carefully with a firm decision that the child does or does not possess the particular skill on the checklist.

- It will ordinarily take 30 to 40 minutes to complete this observation on each child.

KBM DEVELOPMENTAL ASSESSMENT, INC. • 507 N. Elmhurst Road • Prospect Heights, Illinois 60070

CHICAGO EARLY DEVELOPMENT SCREENING INVENTORY FOR TEACHERS II
(CEDSIT II)

Motor / Communication / Cognitive Skills

This child: YES   NO

1. Often bumps into things
2. Seems unusually clumsy
3. Has trouble using buttons
4. Has trouble using zippers
5. Has trouble putting on coat
6. Has trouble tying shoes
7. Has trouble washing self when told to do so
8. Has trouble hopping on one foot
9. Has trouble catching a ball
10. Has trouble copying a square
11. Has trouble copying a circle
12. Tends to scribble rather than draw shapes or pictures of things
13. Has trouble using scissors
14. Has trouble assembling puzzles
15. Has trouble naming the primary colors (red, blue, yellow)
16. Has trouble counting beyond three
17. Has trouble naming the letters of the alphabet
18. Has trouble telling how old he/she is (or showing the correct number of fingers)
19. Has trouble stating correctly whether he/she is a boy or girl
20. Has trouble naming more than one or two body parts of his/her body
21. Has trouble stating his/her full name

Social / Emotional Skills

This child: YES   NO

1. Has difficulty sitting still seems to be in continual motion
2. Frequently has temper tantrums
3. Often provokes other children (starts fights, hits, and throws things)
4. Has trouble accepting limits
5. Shows considerable frustration when his/her activities are interferred with
6. Is excessively demanding of the teacher
7. Very seldom shares with others
8. Seems more restless and fidgety than other children
9. Is easily distracted from his activities
10. Often asks for food other than at snack or mealtimes
11. Tends to cry easily or frequently
12. Mostly whines and complains when asked to do or get something
13. Often pouts and is sullen when he/she doesn't get what he/she wants
14. Tends to react to strange adults by clinging to that person
15. Tends to react to strange adults by showing fear and withdrawal
16. Tends to give up easily when things are not going his/her way
17. Seems mostly shy and withdrawn
18. Tends to interact more with adults than with other children
19. Seems to prefer toys or activities more appropriate for younger children (pull toys, stack blocks or rings)

22. Has trouble describing items in a picture ____ ____
23. Has trouble repeating a sentence spoken to him/her ____ ____
24. Has trouble singing songs or nursery rhymes ____ ____
25. Has trouble telling a story about a picture shown to him/her ____ ____
26. Has trouble repeating (in his/her own words) a simple story ____ ____
27. Has trouble when required to do two things, one right after the other ("Put the book on the table and close the door.") ____ ____
28. Has trouble following directions ____ ____
29. Does not seem to like to look at books ____ ____
30. Often says "huh?" or "what?" or asks for repetition of what is said ____ ____
31. Very seldom copies actions he/she has seen others perform ____ ____
32. Very seldom uses two or more sentences to tell me something ____ ____
33. Very seldom asks questions ____ ____
34. Very seldom asks questions about how things work ____ ____
35. Very seldom asks questions about why ____ ____
36. Has trouble understanding and responding when I talk to him/her ____ ____
37. Seems to have trouble hearing from across the room ____ ____
38. Seems to have trouble hearing when spoken to in a whisper ____ ____
39. May have a speech problem ____ ____
40. Tends to stutter ____ ____
41. Speech seems unclear and hard to understand ____ ____
42. Seems afraid to talk ____ ____
43. Tends to use "me" rather than "I" when speaking ____ ____

20. Seems to prefer repetitious involvement with records, puzzles or other toys ____ ____
21. In general does not seem to be liked by other children ____ ____
22. In general does not find eating pleasurable ____ ____
23. Tends to wet his/her pants more than other children ____ ____
24. Seems to often indulge in body-play (rocking, finger-twiddling, or masturbation) ____ ____

Teacher notes: _____
_____
_____
_____
_____
_____
_____
_____
_____
_____
_____
_____
_____
_____
_____
_____
_____
_____
_____
_____
_____
_____
_____
_____
_____
_____
_____

CEDSIT II SCORING

DIRECTIONS

1. Give one point for each **YES** answer on the **Motor** / **Communication** / **Cognitive Skills Scale**. Add the points together to make a total.

2. Give one point for each **YES** answer on the **Social** / **Emotional Skills Scale**. Add the points together to make a total.

3. Record the scores in the space provided below and interpret the scales according to the directions.

INTERPRETATION

TOTALS: _____ Motor / Communication / Cognitive

_____ Social / Emotional

Refer for evaluation:

12 – 20*on Motor / Communication / Cognitive Scale

7 – 11*on Social / Emotional Scale

Observe further:

4 – 11 on Motor / Communication / Cognitive Scale

2 – 6 on Social / Emotional Scale

Not likely to require referral:

0 – 3 on Motor / Comminication / Cognitive Scale

0 – 1 on Social / Emotional Scale

*or scores above

PLEASE NOTE A high score on either scale indicates a need to refer the child for an in-depth diagnostic assessment.

Teacher's Comments _____

_____

_____

_____

_____Teacher's Signature

Glossary

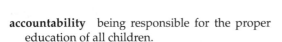

accountability being responsible for the proper education of all children.

age-equivalent score derived score giving a child's performance as that which is normal for a certain age.

amniocentesis a prenatal test in which amniotic fluid is withdrawn from the embryonic sac of a fetus.

anecdotal notes brief notes of significant events or critical incidents in a particular child's day.

Apgar Rating Scale screening test given to newborn infants 1 minute and 5 minutes after birth.

artifacts the materials that children produce to demonstrate knowledge, skills, or dispositions.

assessment process for gathering information to make decisions.

atypical development unusual developmental pattern of children.

authentic assessment *see* performance assessment.

behavioral intervention plans plans made based on assessment of young children who present troubling behavior. Modifications to the regular program are made and monitored.

behavior questionnaires questionnaires designed to give parents an opportunity to report any behavior problems of their children.

biological risk risk to infant because of prenatal, perinatal, or neonatal difficulty.

checklists forms for recording the skills or attributes of the children in a class.

Child Find federal requirement for teachers (and others working with young children) to identify young children with disabilities so they may receive appropriate services and interventions to ameliorate such disabilities.

Child Find team group of professionals whose responsibility it is to determine children with special needs.

child study in-depth look at a particular child at a specific point in time.

chorionic villus biopsy a prenatal test in which chorionic tissue is removed from the developing placenta.

class journals diaries that teachers keep about a group's progress toward meeting educational goals.

concurrent validity relationship between a test and another criterion when both are obtained at about the same time.

confidentiality allowing a child's assessment and other records to be available only to school personnel, agency officials, and parents.

content validity extent of how well a test tests the subject matter it is supposed to test.

construct validity the extent to which a test measures a theoretical characteristic or trait.

constructivist perspective views teaching and learning as a process of discovery for the learner, based on the learner's prior knowledge. Teacher facilitates knowledge, skills, and attitude learning to support individual development.

convergent validity is demonstrated when similar instruments measuring similar constructs yield comparable results.

correlation coefficient degree of relationship between two variables.

criterion-based instruments are those based on a learning goal or standard. Finite steps in the learning of particular concepts are measured.

criterion-referenced measures tests that compare performance in certain skills to accepted levels.

criterion-referenced test a standardized test that compares a child's performance to his or her own progress in a certain skill or behavior.

criterion-related validity relationship between the scores on a test and another criterion.

curriculum-based language assessment a process for determining a child's functional language skills and vocabulary related to the subject matter being studied.

curriculum-based measures diagnostic tests for specific subjects.

derived score score obtained by comparing the raw score with the performance of children of known characteristics on a standardized test.

developmentally appropriate practice planning instruction for preschool children around topics rooted in the children's social world.

deviation quotients standard scores with a mean of 100 and a standard deviation of usually 15.

diagnostic evaluation *see* diagnostic tests.

diagnostic measures are those used by psychologists and others who receive special training, and often certification for using these specialized instruments, that become a key determinant to entitle young children for special educational intervention and service.

diagnostic tests tests used to identify a child's specific areas of strength and weakness, determine the nature of the problems, and suggest the cause of the problems and possible remediation strategies.

documentation collection of artifacts to support record keeping of child's progress in learning.

documentation panel is the part of the Reggia Emilio process that shows, publicly, the learning accomplishments of young children.

dynamic assessment one-to-one interview approach between teacher and student using available assessment information for teaching a specific skill.

ecological assessment an approach that includes the classroom environment, personal interactions, and the learning tasks as variables in the collection of evidence for the measure of learning for individuals.

event sampling record of skills or behaviors a teacher wants the children to know or to do.

extrapolated score derived score estimated from norm scores because the raw score is either less than or greater than anyone in the normative sample.

face validity whether a test looks as if it is testing what it is supposed to be testing.

family involvement including the parents in all phases of the assessment of a child with a developmental problem.

formative evaluation (assessment) an approach to examining young children that holds assessment is an ongoing process. It is similar to the scientific approach where a query is generated, validated or not, and then another query is formed.

frequency records checklists for recording the presence or absence of, frequency of, or quality of selected behaviors.

functional assessment focused observational method that links individual assessment to curricular intervention for one student.

grade-equivalent score derived score giving a child's performance as that which is normal for a certain grade.

grades letters or numbers ascribed to child-performance, based on a summative judgment by the teacher regarding child accomplishment of a task, a course, or a marking period—quarter, semester, year.

high-stakes decision is any test applied to make life-affecting decisions for the educational futures of young children.

IDEA federal law that governs the practices for delivery of educational services to all children with disabilities.

IEP goals the specified learning goals for children with disabilities. These are established by a multidisciplinary team that includes the child's parents.

individualized academic tests formal interviews of children on specific topics.

Individualized Educational Plan (IEP) the formal document that governs the contract for educational intervention for a young child with disabilities.

Individualized Educational Plan conference (IEP conference) the multidisciplinary meeting where parents and those involved in intervention with a young child with disabilities meet to assess progress, or review initial assessment results, and plan educational interventions to support the child's learning.

Individualized Family Service Plan (IFSP) specific plan for the assessing of needs and for the services needed for a child with a developmental problem.

informal evaluation task activities used to assess the instructional needs and levels of children.

initial referral conference the meeting where teachers and parents meet to share concerns about a child's progress in the learning situation.

interpolated score derived score estimated from norm scores because no one with that particular score was actually part of the normative sample.

interrater reliability *see* interscorer reliability.

interscorer reliability ability of a test to produce the same results regardless of who administers it.

intrinsically motivating causing a child to do something or continue doing something because of the nature of the thing or activity itself.

inventory test to assess overall ability in a given area.

learner outcomes expectations for children's performances.

mastery learning the philosophy that promotes the idea that everyone should learn particular concepts or skills and that teachers are responsible for teaching toward this level of accomplishment for all children.

mean the arithmetic average of a group of scores.

mediated learning experience (MLE) teaching approach in which the teacher uses questions, suggestions, and cues to prompt the child to think more consciously about the task and to expand learner expertise.

multidisciplinary staffing group of professionals involved in the assessment of children with special needs, the teaching of these children, and the evaluation of their progress.

multiple intelligence theory theory that children have seven areas of intellectual competence that are relatively independent of each other.

normal curve bell-shaped curve representing the usual distribution of human attributes.

normal-curve equivalents standard scores for group tests; scale has 100 equal parts, mean is usually 50, and standard deviation is usually 21.06.

normative sample subset of a population that is tested for a standardized test.

norm-based instruments tests that compare children to others of similar age, grade level, or other important characteristics.

norm-referenced test *see* standardized test.

norms scores obtained from the testing of a normative sample for a standardized test.

objectivity implies that a scoring scheme is sufficiently clear and discrete so that all those applying the criteria will obtain similar scores.

observation records written records of the observations of a child including anecdotes, daily logs, and in-depth running records.

observations systematic means of gathering information about children by watching them.

outcomes are the specifications used by school districts, states, and professional associations to describe measurable educational goals.

parent interview an interview of a child-care professional with a parent for determining how well a child is doing.

parent perspective a parent's perception of a child's development, learning, and education.

parent questionnaires questionnaires given by child-care professionals to parents for obtaining information about a child.

parental reports information from a parent concerning a child.

parents' rights as specified in state and federal law, parents are assured that schools and agencies will fully involve and inform parents in the care and education of their children.

percentile ranks derived scores indicating the percentage of individuals in the normative group whose test scores fall at or below a given raw score.

performance refers to actions on the part of learners that can be assessed through observation, review of child-produced documents, or other learning products.

performance assessment determining developmental progress of children through a variety of means, including observations and special problems or situations.

performance-based assessment is based on child-action related to an educational activity. That is, the child does the task and the teacher watches and scores the results.

P.L. 99–457 Education of the Handicapped Act Amendments, 1986.

play-based assessment relies on the teacher's knowledge of child's play to judge the social/emotional, language, cognitive, and physical development of a young child. This can be conducted in a natural situation or by interview.

population group of individuals on which a standardized test is normed.

portfolios places, such as folders, boxes, or baskets, for keeping all the information known about the children in a class.

predictive validity how accurately a test score can be used to estimate performance on some variable or criterion in the future.

prenatal testing testing done prior to the birth of a baby.

prereferral screening refers to the evidence that you gather to substantiate a developmental concern regarding child progress.

presentation mode way a task or learning situation is presented to a child as part of instruction.

primary responsibility the person expected to perform a certain task.

project-based learning curricula organized on the basis of child-generated curiosities.

psychological evaluation assessment that incorporates developmental psychological and educational tasks.

range the spread of the scores or the difference between the top score and the bottom score on a test.

rating scales methods of recording whether or not children possess certain skills or attributes and to what extent.

raw score the number of items that a child answered correctly on a test.

referral questions questions posed in a child study to aid in the determination of the specific problems and needs of a child and the assessing of the developmental progress of the child.

Reggio Emilia approach holistic community way to develop early childhood programs that includes all stakeholders—child, parents, teachers, school leaders, and the community at-large.

reliability consistency, dependability, or stability of test results.

report card formal, written documents that form a legal academic history for a child.

reporting ways that teachers generate their knowledge about children's accomplishments.

resiliency ability to cope in a challenging environment.

response mode how a child responds to a direction or instruction.

rubrics scoring criteria for performance tasks.

running records notes made of routine functioning of an individual child or a small group of children.

scaled score statistically determined scores that are used to derive total scores or that refer to results on subtests of an instrument.

screening results documentation of broad-based, quick overview of child's developmental or educational progress on a set of objectives/milestones.

screening test test used to identify children who may be in need of special services, as a first step in identifying children in need of further diagnosis; focuses on the child's ability to acquire skills.

social validity describes the usefulness of assessment information for the teacher in the educational setting.

specificity percentage of children without developmental problems who are correctly identified by a developmental screening test.

stakeholders people important in the lives of children, especially regarding the assessment of children.

standard deviation the distance scores depart from the mean.

standard error of measurement (SEM) estimate of the amount of variation that can be expected in test scores as a result of reliability correlations.

standard score is created statistically. This process converts raw scores to numbers that can be used to compare child progress on a particular dimension.

standardized test test that interprets a child's performance in comparison to the performance of other children with similar characteristics.

standards-based teaching an approach to teaching that requires teachers to coordinate instruction to specified standards or goals.

stanines standard scores with nine unequal bands; bands four, five, and six represent average performance.

strength-based assessment requires the assessor to focus on a child's capacities to plan intervention.

student-led conferences are those meetings between teacher and child where the learner holds the responsibility for reviewing and judging self-progress in relationship to class standards and teacher judgment. May include parents.

summative evaluation reports the final results of a given assessment. For teachers, this often means the end-of-the-year-summary of child progress.

task analysis process in which large goals are broken down into smaller objectives or parts and sequenced for instruction.

technical issues variables of task, learner, and context that can cause problems with performance assessment.

techniques methods, whether formal or informal, for gathering assessment information.

test instrument for measuring skills, knowledge, development, aptitudes, and so on.

test-retest reliability ability to get the same results from a test taken twice within two weeks.

textbook tests assessment materials published by textbook publishers to accompany their instructional materials.

time sampling checklist for determining what is happening at a particular time with one or more children.

treatment validity the usefulness of test results for planning intervention.

typical development the usual or expected developmental pattern of children.

ultrasound a prenatal test in which sound waves are used to determine a fetus's development.

validity the extent to which a test measures what it is supposed to measure.

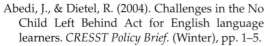

References

Abedi, J., & Dietel, R. (2004). Challenges in the No Child Left Behind Act for English language learners. *CRESST Policy Brief.* (Winter), pp. 1–5.

Abel, E. L. (1998). *Fetal alcohol abuse syndrome.* New York: Plenum.

Airasian, P. W. (2005). *Classroom assessment: Concepts and applications* (5th ed.). New York: McGraw-Hill.

Almy, M., & Genishi, C. (1979). *Ways of studying children* (rev. ed.). New York: Teachers College Press.

American Academy of Pediatrics Committee on Children with Disabilities. (2001). Developmental surveillance and screening of infants and young children. *Pediatrics, 108*(1), 192–196.

American Cancer Society. (2005). Women and smoking: An epidemic. Available online at http://amc.org.

American College of Obstetricians and Gynecologists. (2005). *Screening tests for birth defects.* Washington, DC: Author.

American Educational Research Association, American Psychological Association, & the National Council on Measurement in Education. (1999). *Standards for educational and psychological testing.* Washington, DC: American Psychological Association.

American Educational Research Association. (2000). *AERA position statement concerning high-stakes testing in Pre-K–12 education.* Washington, DC: Author.

American Speech and Hearing Association. (2005). Cultural differences in communication and learning styles. Available online at http://asha.org.

Apfel, N. H. (2001). The birth of a new instrument: The Infant-Toddler and Family Instrument (ITFI). *Zero to Three, 21*(4), 29–35.

Apgar, V. (1953). Proposal for a new method of evaluating the newborn infant. *Anesthesia and Analgesia, 32,* 260–267.

Armour-Thomas, E. (2004). What is the nature of evaluation and assessment in an urban context? In S. R. Steinberg, & J. L. Kincheloe (Eds.), *19 Urban questions: Teaching in the city.* New York: Peter Lang.

ASCD. (2005). NCLB update: Measuring student learning. *EdPolicy Update, 4*(6), 1. Available online at http://www.ascd.org.

Aschbacher, P. R. (2000). Developing indicators of classroom practice to monitor and support school reform. *The CRESST Line,* Winter 2000, pp. 6–8.

Atkins, A. (1990). Do kindergarten tests fail our kids? Don't let a misused test direct your child to the wrong classroom. *Better Homes and Gardens, 68,* 22–24.

Austin, T. (1994). *Changing the view: Student-led parent conferences.* Portsmouth, NH: Heinemann.

Baca, L. M., & Cervantes, H. T. (2004). *The bilingual special education interface* (4th ed.). Upper Saddle River, NJ: Merrill/Prentice Hall.

Bagnato, S. J., Neisworth, J. T., & Munson, S. M. (1997). *Linking assessment and early intervention: An authentic curriculum-based approach.* Baltimore: P. H. Brookes Pub.

Bailey, J. M., & Guskey, T. R. (2001). *Implementing student-led conferences.* Thousand Oaks, CA: Corwin.

Bailey, J. M., & Guskey, T. R. (2001). *Implementing student-led conferences.* Thousand Oaks, CA: Corwin.

Barnett, D., Macmann, G., & Carey, K. (1992). Early intervention and the assessment of developmental skills: Challenges and directions. *Topics in Early Childhood Special Education, 12*(1), 21–43.

Baum, S., Viens, J., & Slatin, B. (2005). *Multiple intelligences in the elementary classroom: A teacher's toolkit.* New York: Teachers College.

Baumann, E., McDonough, S., & Mindes, G. (1974). *Classroom observation guide for Head Start teachers.* Chicago: City of Chicago, Department of Human Services.

Beaty, J. J. (2006). *Observing the development of the young child* (6th ed.). Upper Saddle River, NJ: Merrill/Prentice Hall.

Bell, G. E. (1989). Making the most of parent–teacher conferences: Tips for teachers. *Focus on Early Childhood, 2,* 2.

Benson, B. (2003). *How to meet standards, motivate students, and still enjoy teaching.* Thousand Oaks, CA: Corwin.

Berger, E. H. (2004). *Parents as partners in education: The school and home working together* (6th ed.). Upper Saddle River, NJ: Merrill/Prentice Hall.

Berk, L. E. (2005). *Infants, children and adolescents* (5th ed.). Boston: Allyn & Bacon.

Berlin, L. J., Brooks-Gunn, J., McCarton, C., & McCormick, M. C. (2004). The effectiveness of early intervention: Examining risk factors and pathways to enhanced development. In M. Batshaw, (Ed.), *Children with disabilities.* (5th ed.). Baltimore: Paul H. Brookes.

Berns, R. A. (2004). *Child, family, community: Socialization and support* (6th ed.). Belmont, CA: Wadsworth.

Berry, C. F., & Mindes, G. (1993). *Planning a theme-based curriculum: Goals, themes, and planning guides for 4s and 5s.* Glenview, IL: Good Year Books.

Bielenberg, B., & Fillmore, L. W. (2005). The English they need for the test. *Educational Leadership, 62*(4), 45–49.

Bigge, J., & Stump, C. (1999). *Curriculum, assessment, and instruction for students with disabilities.* Belmont, CA: Wadsworth.

Bodrova, E., & Leong, D. J. (1996). *Tools of the mind: The Vygotskian approach to early childhood education.* Upper Saddle River, NJ: Merrill/Prentice Hall.

Borich, G. D., & Tombari, M. L. (2004). *Educational assessment for the elementary and middle school classroom* (2nd ed.). Upper Saddle River, NJ: Merrill/Prentice Hall.

Bracey, G. W. (2004). *Setting the record straight: Responses to misconceptions about public education in the US* (2nd ed.). Portsmouth, NH: Heinemann.

Bracken, B. (1987a). Limitations of preschool instruments and standards for minimal levels of technical adequacy. *Journal of Psychoeducational Assessment, 4,* 313–326.

Bracken, B. (1987b). The technical side of preschool assessment: A primer of critical issues. *Preschool Interests, 2,* 6–9.

Braun, H. I., & Mislevy, R. (2005). Intuitive test theory. *Phi Delta Kappan, 86*(7), 489–497.

Brazelton, T. B., & Nugent, J. K. (1995). *Brazelton Neonatal Assessment Scale* (3rd ed.). London: McKeith Press.

Bredekamp, S., & Copple, C. (Eds.). (1997). *Developmentally appropriate practice in early childhood programs serving children from birth through age 8* (Rev. ed.). Washington, DC: National Association for the Education of Young Children.

Bredekamp, S., & Rosegrant, T. (1992). *Reaching potentials: Appropriate curriculum and assessment for young children* (Vol. 1). Washington, DC: National Association for the Education of Young Children.

Bricker, D. (1989). *Early intervention for at-risk and handicapped infants, toddlers and children* (2nd ed.). Baltimore: Paul H. Brookes.

Bricker, D. (2002). *Assessment, Evaluation, and Programming System (AEPS®) for Infants and Children, Second Edition.* Baltimore: Paul H. Brookes.

Bricker, D., & Squires, J. (1999). *Ages and stages questionnaires: A parent-completed child monitoring system* (2nd ed.). Baltimore: Paul H. Brookes.

Bricker, D., Pretti-Frontczak, K., & McComas, N. (1998). *An activity-based approach to early intervention* (2nd ed.). Baltimore: Paul H. Brookes.

Brigance, A. (2004). *BRIGANCE® Inventory of Early Development–II (IED–II).* North Billerica, MA: Curriculum Associates.

Brofenbrenner, U. (1979). *The ecology of human development.* Cambridge, MA: Harvard.

Brookhart, S. (2004). *Grading.* Upper Saddle River, NJ: Merrill/Prentice Hall.

Brown-Chidsey, R. (Ed.). (2005). *Assessment for intervention.* Baltimore: Guilford.

Bruner, C. Goldberg, J. & Kot U (1999). *The abc's of early childhood: Trends, information, and evidence for use in developing on early childhood system of case and education.* Child and Family Policy Center Website: www.cfpcinwa.org

Busse, R. T. (2005). Rating scale applications within the problem-solving model. In R. Brown-Chidney (Ed.), *Assessment for intervention.* New York: Guilford.

Carr, J. F., & Harris, D. E. (2001). *Succeeding with standards: Linking curriculum, assessment and action planning.* Alexandria, VA: Association for Supervision and Curriculum Development.

Cegelka, P. T., & Berdine, W. H. (1995). *Effective instruction for students with learning problems.* Boston: Allyn & Bacon.

Chalufour, I., & Worth, K. (2004). *Building structures with young children.* St. Paul, MN: Redleaf Press.

Chandler, L. K., & Dahlquist, C. M. (2006). *Functional assessment: Strategies to prevent and remediate challenging behavior in school settings* (2nd ed.). Upper Saddle River, NJ: Merrill/ Prentice Hall.

Charlesworth, R. (2005). *Experiences in math for young children* (5th ed.). Clifton Park, NY: Delmar/Thomson.

Children's Defense Fund Mission Statement and Leave No Child Behind® movement. Available online at http://www.childrensdefensefund.org.

Children's Defense Fund. (2004). *The state of America's children.* Washington, DC: Author.

Clay, M. (1993). *An observational survey of early literacy achievement.* Portsmouth, NH: Heinemann.

Cochran-Smith, M. (2005). No Child Left Behind: Three years and counting. *Journal of Teacher Education, 56*(2), 99–103.

Cohen, R., Stern, V., & Balaban, N. (1997). *Observing and recording the behavior of young children* (4th ed.). New York: Teachers College Press.

Committee on Economic Development. (2002). *Preschool for all: Investing in a productive and just society.* Washington, DC: CED. http:// www.ced.org/.

Connolly, A.J. (1998). *Key Math Revised: A diagnostic inventory of essential mathematics.* Circle Pines, MN: American Guidance.

Cook, R. E., Klein, M. D., & Tessier, A. (2004). *Adapting early childhood curricula for children in inclusive settings* (6th ed.). Upper Saddle River, NJ: Merrill/Prentice Hall.

Cook, R. E., Tessier, A., & Klein, M. D. (2004). *Adapting early childhood curriculum for children with special needs* (6th ed.). Upper Saddle River, NJ: Merrill/Prentice Hall.

Costa, A. L., & Kallick, B. (2003). *Assessment strategies for self-directed learning.* Thousand Oaks, CA: Corwin.

Council of Chief State School Officers (2003). *State content standards: A 50 state resource.* Washington, DC: Author. http://www.ccsso.org.

Cromwell, E. S. (2000). *Early childhood education: A whole curriculum for ages 2–5* (2nd ed.). Needham Heights,: M.A. Allyn & Bacon.

DAP in 2005 Thematic Issue. (2005). *Young Children, 60*(4).

de Bettencourt, L. U. (1987). How to develop parent partnerships. *Teaching Exceptional Children, 19,* 26–27.

Deno, S. (1985). Curriculum-based measurement: The emerging alternative. *Exceptional Children, 52,* 219–232.

Deno, S. (1990). Individual differences and individual difference: The essential difference in special education. *Journal of Special Education, 24,* 160–173.

Dewey, D., Crawford, S. G., & Kaplan, B. J. (2003). Clinical importance of parent ratings of everyday cognitive abilities in children with learning and attention problems. *Journal of Learning Disabilities, 36*(1), 87–95.

Dewey, D., Crawford, S. G., Creighton, D. E., & Sauve, R. S. (2000). Parents' ratings of everyday cognitive abilities in very low birth weight children. *Journal of Developmental and Behavioural Pediatrics, 21,* 37–43.

Dietel, R. (2001). How is my child doing in school? Ten research-based ways to find out. *National PTA: Our Children.* Available online at *http://www.pta.org*

Diffily, D., & Sassman, C. (2002). *Project-based learning with young children.* Portsmouth, NH: Heinemann.

Division for Early Childhood, Council for Exceptional Children. (1998). *Position statement on services for children birth to age eight with special needs.* Denver: Author.

Doctoroff, G., & Arnold, D. H. (2004). Parent-rated externalizing behavior in preschoolers: The predictive utility of structured interviews, teacher reports, and classroom observations. *Journal of Clinical Child & Adolescent Psychology, 33*(4), 813–818.

Dodge, D. T., & Colker, L. J. (2002). *The creative curriculum for early childhood* (4th ed.). Washington, DC: Teaching Strategies.

Dombro, A.L., Colker, L.J., Dodge, D.T. (1999). *The Creative curriculum for infants & toddlers* (Rev. ed.). Washington, DC: Teaching Strategies.

Donovan, M. (1995). *Parent response form for Chicago Public Schools Project.* Chicago: Erikson Institute on Early Education.

Duckworth, E. (1987). *The having of wonderful ideas and other essays on teaching and learning.* New York: Teachers College Press.

Eckert, T. L., & Arbolino, L. A. (2005). The role of teacher perspectives in diagnostic and program evaluation decision making. In R. Brown-Chidsey (Ed.), *Assessment for intervention: A problem-solving approach.* New York: Guilford.

Educational Testing Service. (1990). Testing in the schools. *ETS Policy Notes, 2*(3).

Educational Testing Service. (1993). Learning by doing: A manual for teaching and assessing higher-order thinking in science and mathematics. In *Performance assessment sampler: A workbook.* Princeton: Author.

Eggers-Pierola, C. (2005). *Connections and commitments: Reflecting Latino values in early childhood programs.* Portsmouth, NH: Heinemann.

Eisner, E. (2002). *The educational imagination: On the design and evaluation of educational programs* (3rd ed.). New York: Macmillan.

Elliott, J. L., & Thurlow, M. L. (2005). *Improving test performance of students with disabilities . . . on district and state assessments* (2nd ed.). Thousand Oaks, CA: Corwin.

Elliott, S. N. (1993). *Creating meaningful performance assessments: Fundamental concepts.* Reston, VA: Council for Exceptional Children.

Elliott, S., & Braden, J. (2000). *Educational assessment and accountability for all students: Facilitating the meaningful participation of students with disabilities in district and statewide assessment programs.* Madison: Wisconsin Department of Public Instruction.

Epps, S., & Jackson, B. J. (2000). *Empowered families, successful children: Early intervention programs that work.* Washington, DC: American Psychological Association.

Epstein, M. H. (1998). Using strength-based assessment in programs for children with emotional and behavioral disorders. *Beyond Behavior, 9*(2), 25–27.

Escamilla, K., Chavez, L., & Vigil, P. (2005). Rethinking the gap: High stakes testing and Spanish-speaking students in Colorado. *Journal of Teacher Education, 56*(2), 132–144.

Eyer, D. W., & Gonzalez-Mena, J. (2004). *Infants, toddlers, and caregivers* (6th ed.). New York: McGraw-Hill.

Family Educational Rights and Privacy Act (FERPA) of 1974. 20 U.S.C.A. Section 123g, with accompanying regulations set forth in 45 C.F.R. part 99.

Farr, R., & Tone, B. (1998). *Portfolio and performance assessment: Helping students evaluate their progress as readers and writers* (2nd ed.). Fort Worth: Harcourt.

Feeney, S., & Kipnis, K. (1989). The National Association for the Education of Young Children code of ethical conduct and statement of commitment. *Young Children, 45,* 24–29.

Feeney, S., Christensen, D., & Moravcik, E. (2006). *Who am I in the lives of children?* (7th ed.). Upper Saddle River, NJ: Merrill/Prentice Hall.

Feldman, M. A. (Ed.). (2004). *Early intervention: The essential readings.* Malden, MA: Blackwell.

Feuer, M. J., & Fulton, K. (1993). The many faces of performance assessment. *Phi Delta Kappan, 74,* 478.

Feuerstein, R. (1979). *The dynamic assessment of retarded performers: The learning potential assessment device, theory, instruments, and techniques.* Baltimore: University Park Press.

Fewell, R., & Glick, M. (1998). The role of play in assessment. In D. P. Fromberg & D. Bergen (Eds.), *Play from birth to twelve and beyond: Contexts, perspectives, and meanings.* New York: Garland.

Flesch, R. (1955). *Why Johnny can't read.* New York: Harper.

Fredericks, A. D., & Rasinski, T. V. (1990). Involving parents in the assessment process. *The Reading Teacher, 44,* 346–349.

Fromberg, D. P. (2002). *Play and meaning in early childhood education.* Boston: Allyn & Bacon.

Fuchs, L. S. (1993). *Connecting performance assessment to instruction.* Reston, VA: Council for Exceptional Children.

Gardner, H. (1999). *The disciplined mind: What all students should understand.* New York: Simon & Schuster.

Gardner, H. (2004). *Frames of mind: The theory of multiple intelligences.* New York: Basic Books.

Garfinkle, A. N. (2004). *Assessing play skills.* In M. McLean, M. Worley, & D. B. Bailey (Eds.), *Assessing infants and preschoolers with special needs* (3rd ed.). Upper Saddle River, NJ: Merrill/Prentice Hall.

Gargiulo, R. M., & Kilgo, J. L. (2005). *Young children with special needs* (2nd ed.). Clifton Park, NY: Thomson/Delmar.

Garvey, C. (1993). Special topic: New directions in studying pretend play. *Human Development, 35*(4), 235–240.

Gelfer, J. I., & Perkins, P. G. (1992). Constructing student portfolios: A process and product that fosters communication with families. *Day Care and Early Education, 20,* 9–13.

Genishi, C. (Ed.). (1992). *Ways of assessing children and curriculum: Stories of early childhood practice.* New York: Teachers College Press.

Gesell, A. L., & Amatruda, C. S. (1954). *Developmental diagnosis* (3rd ed.). New York: Hoeber.

Gestwicki, C. (2004). *Home, school and community relations* (4th ed.). Albany, NY: Delmar.

Gil, E., & Drewes, J. C. (Eds.) (2005). *Cultural issues in play therapy.* New York: Guilford.

Glascoe, F. P. (1998). *Collaborating with parents: Using parents' evaluation of developmental status to detect and address developmental and behavioral problems.* Nashville, TN: Ellsworth & Vanderneer Press.

Glascoe, F. P. (1999). Communicating with parents. *Young Exceptional Children, 2*(4), 17–25.

Glascoe, F. P., MacLean, W. E., & Stone, W. L. (1991). The importance of parents' concerns about their child's behavior. *Clinical Pediatrics, 30,* 8–11.

Goffin, S. G., & Wilson, C. (2001). *Curriculum models and early childhood education: Appraising the relationship* (2nd ed.). Upper Saddle River NJ: Merrill/Prentice Hall.

Gonzalez-Mena, J. (2006). *The child in the family and the community* (4th ed.). Upper Saddle River, NJ: Merrill/Prentice Hall.

Goodenough, F. L. (1949). *Mental testing: Its history, principles, and applications.* New York: Rinehart.

Goodwin, W. L., & Goodwin, L. D. (1997). Using standardized measures for evaluating young children's learning. In B. Spodek & O. N. Saracho (Eds.), *Issues in early childhood education assessment and evaluation.* New York: Teachers College Press.

Gould, P. & Sullivan, J. (2005). *The inclusive early childhood classroom: Easy ways to adapt learning centers for all children.* Upper Saddle River, NJ: Merrill/Prentice Hall.

Gredler, G. R. (1992). *School readiness: Assessment and educational issues.* Brandon, VT: Clinical Psychology Publishing.

Green, B. F., Jr. (1981). A primer of testing. *American Psychologist, 36,* 1001–1011.

Greenfield, P. M., & Cocking, P. R. (2003). *Cross-cultural roots of minority child development.* Hillsdale, NJ: Laurence Erlbaum Associates.

Greenspan, S. I. (2003). *The clinical interview of the child* (3rd ed.). Washington, DC: American Psychiatric Association.

Greenspan, S. I., & Wieder, S. (1997). An integrated developmental approach to interventions for young children with severe difficulties in relating and communicating. In S. I. Greenspan, B. Kalmanson, R. Shahmoon-Shanok, S. Wieder, G. G. Williamson, & M. Anzalone (Eds.), *Assessing and treating infants and young children with severe difficulties in relating and communicating.* Washington, DC: National Center for Infants, Toddlers, and Families.

Greenspan, S. I., & Wieder, S. (1998). *The child with special needs: Encouraging intellectual and emotional growth.* Reading, MA: Perseus.

Gronlund, G., & Engel, B. (2001). *Focused portfolios™: A comprehensive assessment for the young child.* St. Paul, MN: Redleaf Press.

Guerin, G. R., & Maier, A. S. (1983). *Informal assessment in education.* Palo Alto: Mayfield.

Guidry, J., van den Pol, R., Keely, E., & Neilson, S. (1996). Augumenting traditional assessment and information: The videoshare model. *Topics in Early Childhood Special Education, 16*(1), 51–65.

Gullo, D. F. (2005). *Understanding assessment and evaluation in early childhood education* (2nd ed.). New York: Teachers College.

Gunning, T. J. (2005). *Creating literacy instruction for all children* (5th ed.). Needham Heights, MA: Allyn & Bacon.

Guralnick, M. J. (Ed.). (2000). *Interdisciplinary clinical assessment of young children with developmental disabilities.* Baltimore: Paul H. Brookes.

Guskey, T. R. (2001). *Implementing mastery learning* (2nd ed.). Belmont, CA: Wadsworth.

Guskey, T. R. (Ed.). (1994). *High-stakes performance assessment: Perspectives on Kentucky's educational reform.* Thousand Oaks, CA: Corwin.

Guskey, T. R., & Bailey, J. M. (2001). *Developing grading and reporting systems for student learning.* Thousand Oaks, CA: Corwin.

Hannon, J.H. (2000). Learning to like Matthew. *Young Children, 55,* 24–28.

Hanson, M. J. (2004). Ethnic, cultural, and language diversity in intervention settings. In E. W. Lynch, & M. J. Hanson (Eds.), *Developing cross-cultural competence: A guide for working with children and their families* (3rd ed.). Baltimore: Paul H. Brookes.

Harp, B., & Brewer, J. (2000). Assessing reading and writing in the early years. In D. S. Stickland & L. M. Morrow (Eds.), *Beginning reading and writing* (Chap. 13). New York: Teachers College Press.

Hauser-Cram, P., & Shonkoff, J. (1988). Rethinking the assessment of child-focused outcomes. In

H. Weiss & F. Jacobs (Eds.), *Evaluating family programs* (pp. 73–94). Hawthorne, NY: Aldine.

Head Start. (2002). Technical Assistance Paper No. 4. Developmental Screening, Assessment, and Evaluation: Key Elements for Individualizing Curricula in Early Head Start Programs. Washington, DC: Author. Available online at http://www.headstartinfo.org/.

Head Start. (2003 July). Head Start Child Outcomes—Setting the Context for the National Reporting System. *Head Start Bulletin No. 76.*

Hebert, E. A. (2001). *The power of portfolios: What children can teach us about learning and assessment.* San Francisco: Jossey Bass.

Helm J. H., & Beneke, S. (Eds.). (2003). *The power of projects: Meeting contemporary challenges in early childhood classrooms—strategies & solutions.* New York: Teachers College.

Helm, J. H., Beneke, S., & Steinheimer, K. (1997). *Windows on learning: Documenting young children's work.* New York: Teachers College Press.

Henning-Stout, M. (1994). *Responsive assessment: A new way of thinking about learning.* San Francisco: Jossey-Bass.

Herman, J., Aschbacher, P., & Winters, L. (1992). *A practical guide to alternative assessment.* Alexandria, VA: Association for the Supervision of Curriculum Development.

Heward, W. L. (2006). *Exceptional children: An introduction to special education* (8th ed.). Upper Saddle River, NJ: Merrill/Prentice Hall.

Higginbotham, M. L. O., & Pretzello, L. (n.d.). *Observation: Implications for appropriate early childhood assessment.* Unpublished manuscript. Louisiana State University Medical Center, New Orleans.

Hill, B. C., Kamber, P., & Norwick, L. (1994). Six ways to make student portfolios more meaningful and manageable: Involving students, peers, and parents in portfolio assessment. *Instructor, 104,* 118–120.

Hilliard, A. G. (2000). Excellence in education versus high-stakes standardized testing. *Journal of Teacher Education, 51*(4), 293–304.

Hills, T. W. (1987). *Screening for school entry, ERIC Digest.* Champaign, IL: ERIC Clearinghouse on Elementary and Early Childhood Education.

Hills, T. W. (1992). Reaching potentials through appropriate assessment. In S. Bredekamp & T. Rosegrant (Eds.), *Reaching potentials: Appropriate curriculum and assessment for young children* (Vol. 1). Washington, DC: National Association for the Education of Young Children.

Hirsch, E. S. (Ed.). (1984). *The block book* (Rev. ed.). Washington, DC: National Association for the Education of Young Children.

Hirshberg, L. (1996). History-making, not history-taking: Clinical interviews with infants and their families. In S. J. Meisels & E. Genichel (Eds.), *New visions for the developmental assessment of infants and young children.* Washington, DC: Zero to Three: National Center for Infants, Toddlers, and Families.

Hohmann, M., & Weikart, D. P. (2002). *Educating young children: Active learning practices for preschool and child care programs* (2nd ed.). Ypsilanti, MI: High Scope.

Hooper, S. R., & Umansky, W. (2004). *Young children with special needs* (4th ed.). Upper Saddle River, NJ: Merrill/Prentice Hall.

Hoover, H. D. et al. (2001). *Message to parents: Iowa Test of Basic Skills.* Itasca, IL: Riverside Publishing.

Hoover, H. D., Hieronymous, A. N., Frisbie, D. A., & Dunbar, S. B. (1996). *Iowa Tests of Basic Skills.* Chicago: Riverside Publishing Company.

Howard, V. F., Williams, B. F., & Lepper, C. (2005). *Very young children with special needs: A formative approach for today's children* (3rd ed.). Upper Saddle River, NJ: Merrill/Prentice Hall.

Hoy, C., & Gregg, N. (1994). *Assessment: The special educator's role.* Pacific Grove, CA: Brooks/Cole.

Illinois State Board of Education. (2001). Illinois learning standards. Available online at http://www.isbe.net/ils/standards.html.

Illinois State Board of Education. (2005). English language learning proficiency standards. Available online at http://www.isbe.net/bilingual/htmls/elp_standards.htm..

Inger, M. (1993). Authentic assessment in secondary education. *Institute on Education and the Economy Brief, 6,* 4.

Innovative Education. (2005). http://www.innovativeeducation.com.

Interdisciplinary Council on Developmental and Learning Disorders (ICDL). (2000). *ICDL clinical practice guidelines.* Bethesda, MD: Author.

Interdisciplinary Council on Developmental and Learning Disorders. (2000). *ICDL clinical practice guidelines for infants, children, and families with special needs.* Bethesda, MD: Author.

International Reading Association Board of Directors. (1980, June). Board action. *Reading Today,* p. 1.

Ireton, H. R. (1994). *The child development review manual.* Minneapolis: Behavior Science Systems.

Ireton, H. R. (1997). *Child development inventories in education and health care.* Minneapolis: Behavior Science Systems.

Jablon, J. R., Dombro, A. L., & Dichtelmiller, M. L. (1999). *The power of observation.* Washington, DC: Teaching Strategies.

Jacobson, J., & Raymer, A. (1999). *The big book of reproducible graphic organizers: 50 great templates to help kids get more out of reading, writing, social studies & more.* New York: Scholastic.

Johnson, J. E., Christie, J. F., & Wardle, F. (2005). *Play, development and early education.* Needham Heights, MA: Allyn & Bacon.

Jones, E., & Reynolds, G. (1992). *The play's the thing: Teachers' roles in children's play.* New York: Teachers College Press.

Jordan, L., Reyes-Blanes, M. E., Peel, B. B., Peel, H. A., & Lane, H. B. (1998). Developing teacher–parent partnerships across cultures: Effective parent conferences. *Intervention in School and Clinic, 33*(3), 141–147.

Kamii, C. (1990). *Achievement testing in the early grades: The games grown-ups play.* Washington, DC: National Association for the Education of Young Children.

Kamii, C. (with Joseph, L.). (2000). *Young children reinvent arithmetic: Implications of Piaget's theory.* 2nd ed. New York: Teachers College.

Kamii, C., & Rosenblum, V. (1990). An approach to assessment in mathematics. In C. Kamii (Ed.), *Achievement testing in the early grades: The games grown-ups play.* Washington, DC: National Association for the Education of Young Children.

Katz, L., & Chard, S. (2000). *Engaging children's minds: The project approach.* Norwood, NJ: Ablex.

Kentucky State Department of Education. (2005) What's new. Available online at http://www.education.ky.gov.

Kerr, M. M., & Nelson, C. M. (2006). *Strategies for addressing behavior problems in the classroom.* (5th ed.). Upper Saddle River, NJ: Merrill/Prentice Hall.

Knobloch, H., Steven, F., Malone, A., Ellison, P., & Risemberg, H. (1979). The validity of parental reporting of infant development. *Pediatrics, 63,* 873–878.

Kohn, A. (2004). *What does it mean to be well educated? And more essays on standards, grading, and other follies.* Boston: Beacon.

Kostelnik, M. J., Stein, L. C., Whiren, A. P., Soderman, A. K., & Gregory, K. (2006). *Guiding children's social development* (5th ed.) Clifton Park, NY: Delmar.

Kostelnik, M. J., Whiren, A. P., & Soderman, A. K. (2004). *Developmentally appropriate curriculum: Best practices in early childhood education* (3rd ed.). Upper Saddle River, NJ: Merrill/Prentice Hall.

Kovas, M. A. (1993). Making your grading motivating: Keys to performance-based evaluation. *Quill and Scroll, 68,* 10–11.

Krechevsky, M. et al. (2003). *Making teaching visible: Documenting individual and group learning as professional development.* Cambridge, MA: Harvard Project Zero.

Kroth, R. L., & Edge, D. (1997). *Strategies for communicating with parents and families of exceptional children.* Denver: Love.

Kubiszyn, T., & Borich, G. (2003). *Educational testing and measurement: Classroom application and practice* (7th ed.). New York: Wiley.

Kuhs, T. M., Johnson, R. L., Agruso, S. A., & Monrad, D. M. (2001). *Put to the test: Tools and techniques for classroom assessment.* Portsmouth, NH: Heinemann.

Lantz, H. B. (2004). *Rubrics for assessing student achievement in science, grades K–12.* Thousand Oaks, CA: Corwin.

Lee-Katz, L., Ellis, M., & Jewett, J. (1993). *There's math in deviled eggs: Strategies for teaching young children.* Bloomington, IN: Agency for Instructional Technology.

Lee, J. M., & McDougal, O. (2000). Guidelines for writing notes to families of young children. *Focus on Pre-K and K, 13*(2), 4–6.

Lerner, J., Lowenthal, B., & Egan, R. (1998). *Preschoolers with special needs: Children-at-risk or who have disabilities.* Needham Heights, MA: Allyn & Bacon.

Lewis, R. B., & Doorlag, D. H. (2006). *Teaching special students in general education classrooms* (7th ed.). Upper Saddle River, NJ: Merrill/Prentice Hall.

Lichtenstein, R., & Ireton, H. R. (1984). *Preschool screening: Early identification of school problems.* New York: Grune & Stratton.

Lidz, C. (2003). *Early childhood assessment.* New York: Wiley.

Lieber, J., Schwartz, I., Sandall, S., Horn, E., & Wolery, R. A. (1999). Curricular considerations for young children in inclusive settings. In C. Seefeldt (Ed.), *The early childhood curriculum: Current findings in theory and practice* (3rd ed.). New York: Teachers College Press.

Linder, T. (1993). *Transdisciplinary play-based assessment: A functional approach to working with young children* (Rev. ed.). Baltimore: Paul H. Brookes.

Linn, R. (2003), Accountability, responsibility and reasonable expectations. *Educational Researcher, 32*(7), 3–13.

Linn, R. L., & Miller, D. M. (2005). *Measurement and assessment in teaching* (9th ed.). Upper Saddle River, NJ: Merrill/Prentice Hall.

Losardo, A., & Notari-Syverson, A. (2001). *Alternative approaches to assessing young children*. Baltimore: Paul H. Brookes.

Lynch, E. W., & Hanson, M. J. (2004). *Developing cross-cultural competence: A guide for working with children and their families* (3rd ed.). Baltimore: Paul H. Brookes.

MacDonald, S. (2001). *Block play: The complete guide to learning and playing with blocks*. Beltsville, MD: Gryphon House.

Maldonado-Duran, J. M. (Ed.). (2002). *Infant and toddler mental health: Models of clinical intervention with infants and their families*. Washington, DC: American Psychiatric Association.

Mapp, K., & Henderson, A. (2005). *A new wave of evidence: The impact of school, family, and community connections on student achievement*. Reported in *Education Update*, March 2005. Alexandria, VA: Association for Supervision and Curriculum Development.

Martin-Kniep, G. O. (1998). *Why am I doing this? Purposeful teaching through portfolio assessment*. Portsmouth, NH: Heinemann.

Martin-Kniep, G. O. (2000). *Becoming a better teacher: Eight innovations that work*. Alexandria, VA: Association for Supervision and Curriculum Development.

Marzano, R. J., Pickering, D., & McTighe, J. (1993). *Assessing student outcomes: Performance assessment using the dimensions of learning model*. Alexandria, VA: Association for the Supervision of Curriculum Development.

Maxwell, K. L., & Clifford, R. M. (2004). School readiness assessment. *Beyond the Journal, Young Children on the Web*. Available online at http://www.naeyc.org.

Maxwell, K. L., & Clifford, R. M. (2004). School readiness assessment. *Young Children, 59*(1) 42–49.

McCollum, J., Azar-Mathis, R., Henderson, K., & Kusmierek, A. (1989). Assessment of infants and toddlers: Supporting developmentally and ecologically relevant intervention. *Illinois technical assistance project*. Springfield, IL: Illinois State Board of Education.

McGee, L. M., & Morrow, L. M. (2005). *Teaching literacy in kindergarten*. Baltimore: Paul H. Brookes.

McGonigel, M. J., Woodruff, G., & Roszmann-Millican, M. (1994). Parents in the infant-toddler assessment process. *Zero to Three, 14*, 59–65.

McLaughlin, M. J., & Warren, S. H. (1994). *Performance assessment and students with disabilities: Usage in outcomes-based accountability systems*. Reston, VA: Council for Exceptional Children.

McLean, M., Wolery, M., & Bailey, D. B. (2004). *Assessing infants and preschoolers with special needs* (3rd ed.). Upper Saddle River, NJ: Merrill/Prentice Hall.

McLoughlin, J. A., & Lewis, R. B. (2005). *Assessing special students* (6th ed.). Upper Saddle River, NJ: Merrill/Prentice Hall.

McTighe, J., & Wiggins, G. (2005). *The understanding by design handbook* (2nd ed.). Alexandria, VA: Association for the Supervision of Curriculum Development.

McWilliam, R. A., Wolery, M., & Odom, S. L. (2001). Instructional perspectives in inclusive preschool classrooms. In M. J. Guralnick (Ed.), *Early childhood inclusion: Focus on change*. Baltimore: Paul H. Brookes.

Meisels, S. (2000). On the side of the child: Personal reflections on testing, teaching, and early childhood education. *Young Children, 55*(6), 16–19.

Meisels, S. J. (2001). Fusing assessment and intervention: Changing parents' and providers' views of young children. *Zero to Three, 21*(4), 4–10.

Meisels, S. J., & Provence, S. (1989). *Screening and assessment: Guidelines for identifying young disabled and developmentally vulnerable children and their families*. Washington, DC: National Center for Clinical Infant Programs.

Meisels, S. J., & Steele, D. M. (1991). *The early childhood portfolio collection process*. Ann Arbor: Center for Human Growth and Development, The University of Michigan.

Meisels, S. J., Dombro A.L., Marsden, D.B., Western, D.R., Jewkes, A.M. 2003. *Ounce Scale™*. Rebus Inc., a Pearson Education Inc., Company.

Meisels, S. J., Jablon, J. R., Dichtelmiller, M. L., Dorfman, A. B., & Marsden, D. B. (2001). *The Work Sampling System™* (4th ed.). Rebus, Inc., a Pearson Education Inc., Company. http://www.pearsonearlylearning.com.

Mercer, C. D., & Mercer, A. R. (2005). *Teaching students with learning problems* (7th ed) Upper Saddle River, NJ: Merrill/Prentice Hall.

Million, J. (2005). Getting teachers set for parent conferences. *Communicator, 28* (February), 5–6.

Mindes, G. (1982). Social and cognitive aspects of play in young handicapped children. *Topics of Early Childhood Special Education, 2,* 14.

Mindes, G. (1990). Kindergarten in our nation. In C. Seefeldt (Ed.), *Continuing issues in early childhood education.* Upper Saddle River, NJ: Merrill/Prentice Hall.

Mindes, G., & Donovan, M. A. (2001). *Building character: Five enduring themes for a stronger early childhood curriculum.* Boston: Allyn & Bacon.

Morris, D., & Perney, J. (1984). Developmental spelling as a predictor of first grade reading achievement. *Elementary School Journal, 84,* 441–457.

Morrow, L. M. (2005). *Literacy development in the early years: Helping children read and write* (5th ed.). Boston: Allyn & Bacon.

Morse, B. A., & Weiner, L. (2005). Fetal alcohol syndrome. In S. Parker B. Zuckerman & M. Augustyn (Eds.). *Developmental and behavioral pediatrics: A handbook for primary care* (2nd ed.). Philadelphia: Lippincott Williams & Wilkins.

National Association for Education of Young Children (NAEYC) (1996). NAEYC position statement: Responding to linguistic and cultural diversity—recommendations for effective early childhood education. *Young Children, 51*(2), 4–12+.

National Association for Elementary School Principals (2006). *Leading early childhood communities: What principals should know & be able to do.* Alexandria, VA: Author.

National Association for the Education of Young Children (NAEYC) & National Association of Early Childhood Specialists in State Departments of Education (NAECS/SDE). (2003). *Position statement on early childhood curriculum, assessment, and program evaluation.* Washington, DC: Author. Available online at http://www.naeyc.org.

National Association for the Education of Young Children and National Association of Early Childhood Specialists in State Departments of Education. (2003). *Early childhood curriculum, assessment, and program evaluation: Building an effective, accountable system in programs for children birth through age 8.* Washington, DC: Author. Available online at http://www.naeyc.org and http://naecs.crc.uiuc.edu/.

National Association for the Education of Young Children. (1995). Position statement on school readiness. *Young Children, 46,* 21–23.

National Association for the Education of Young Children. (2005). *NAEYC code of ethical conduct and statement of commitment.* Washington, DC: author. Available online at http://www.naeyc.org.

National Association of Early Childhood Specialists in State Departments of Education & National Association for the Education of Young Children. (2001). Still unacceptable trends in kindergarten entry and placement. *Young Children, 56*(5), 59–62.

National Association of Elementary School Principals (NAESP). (2005). *Leading early childhood learning communities: What principals should know and be able to do.* Washington, DC: Author.

National Commission on Excellence in Education. (1983). *A nation at risk: The imperative for school reform.* Washington, DC: U.S. Government Printing Office.

National Council for Teachers of Mathematics. (2005). *Illuminations.* Available online at http://illuminations.nctm.org/.

National Council of Teachers of Mathematics. (2000). *Principles and standards for school mathematics.* Reston, VA: National Council for Teachers of Mathematics.

National Council of Teachers of Mathematics. (2000). *Principles and standards: Setting higher standards for our students, higher standards for ourselves.* Washington, DC: Author.

National Education Goals Panel. (1997). *Getting a good start in school.* Washington, DC: US Government Printing Office.

Neisworth, J. T., & Bagnato, S. J. (2000). Recommended practices in assessment. In S. Sandall, M. E. McLean, & B. J. Smith (Eds.), *DEC recommend practices in early intervention/early childhood special education.* Denver: Division for Early Childhood.

Neuman, S. B., Copple, C., & Bredekamp, S. (2000). *Learning to read and write: Developmentally appropriate practices for children.* Washington, DC: National Association for the Education of Young Children.

No Child Left Behind Act of 2001. U.S. Public Law 107–110. 107th Congress, 8 January 2002.

Noonan, M. J., & McCormick, L. (1993). *Early intervention in natural environments.* Pacific Grove, CA: Brooks/Cole.

Ohio Department of Education. (1990a). *Study skills begin at home: Book 1: Preschool.* Columbus, OH.

Ohio Department of Education. (1990b). *Study skills begin at home: Book 2: Kindergarten–Grade 3.* Columbus, OH: Ohio Department of Education.

Otto, B. (2006). *Language development in early childhood* (2nd ed.). Upper Saddle River, NJ: Merrill/Prentice Hall.

Paley, V. G. (2004). *A child's work: The importance of fantasy play.* Chicago: University of Chicago.

Papalia, D. E., Olds, S. W., & Feldman, R. D. (2006). *A child's world: Infancy through adolescence* (10th ed.). New York: McGraw-Hill.

Pavri, S. (2001). Developmental delay or cultural difference? *Young Exceptional Children, 4*(4), 2–9.

Pearson Early Learning (2005). *The work sampling system*™. http://www.pearsonearlylearning.com/.

Pellegrini, A. D. (2004). *Observing children in their natural worlds: A methodological primer* (2nd ed.). Mahwah, NJ: Lawrence Erlbaum.

Perrin, E. C. (1995). Behavioral screening. In S. Parker & B. Zukerman (Eds.), *Behavioral and developmental pediatrics: A handbook for primary care* (pp. 22–23). Boston: Little, Brown & Company.

Pianta, R. C., & Kraft-Sayre, M. (2003). *Successful kindergarten transition: Your guide to connecting children, families & schools.* Baltimore: Paul H. Brookes.

Pierangelo, R. & Giuliani, G.A. (2006) *Assessment in special education: A practical approach.* (2nd ed.). Boston: Allyn & Bacon.

Plake, B. S., & Impara, J. C. (Eds.). (2003). *The fifteenth mental measurements yearbook.* Lincoln: Buros Institute.

Popham, W. J. (2000). *Testing! Testing! What every parent should know about school tests.* Boston: Allyn & Bacon.

Popham, W. J. (2001). *The truth about testing: An educator's call to action.* Alexandria, VA: Association for Supervision and Curriculum Development.

Popham, W. J. (2001). Teaching to the test? *Educational Leadership, 58*(6), 16–21.

Popham, W. J. (2003). *Test better, teach better: The instructional role of assessment.* Alexandria, VA: Association for Supervision and Curriculum Development.

Popham, W. J. (2004). *America's "failing" schools.* New York: Routledge/Falmer.

Popham, W. J. (2005). *Classroom assessment: What teachers need to know* (4th ed.). Boston: Allyn & Bacon.

Popham, W.J. (1997). Consequential validity: Fight concern, wrong concept. *Education Measurement: Issues and Practices, 16*(2), 9–13.

Popp, R. J. (1992). *Family portfolios: Documenting change in parent–child relationships.* Louisville, KY: National Center for Family Literacy, occasional paper.

Potter, L., & Bulach, C. (2001). Do's and don'ts of parent–teacher conferences. *Here's How, 19* (Spring), 1–4.

Pretti-Frontczak, K., & Bricker, D. (2004). *An activity-based approach to early intervention* (3rd ed.). Baltimore: Paul H. Brookes.

Project Zero. (2005). Project Zero at the Harvard Graduate School of Education. Available online at *http://www.pz.harvard.edu/index.htm.*

Provence, S., & Apfel, N. H. (2001). *Infant-Toddler and Family Instrument (ITFI).* Baltimore: Paul H. Brookes.

Pugach, M. C., & Warger, C. L. (Eds.). (1996). Challenges for the special education-curriculum reform partnership. *In curriculum trends, special education and reform: Refocusing the conversation.* New York: Teachers College Press.

Quinn, K. (2005). *Ivy chronicles.* New York: Penguin.

Raab, M. M., Whaley, K. T., & Cisar, C. L. (1993). Looking beyond instructional interactions: An ecological perspective of classroom programming. Presentation made at the 20th International Early Childhood Conference on Children with Special Needs, San Diego, CA, December.

Ramey, C. T., & Ramey, S. L. (2000). Early intervention and early experience. In P. K. Smith & A. D. Pellegrini (Eds.), *Psychology of education: Major themes (Vol. 2).* London: Routledge.

Ramsey, P. G. (2004). *Teaching and learning in a diverse world: Multicultural education for young children* (3rd ed.). New York: Teachers College.

Reed, V. A. (2005). *Introduction to children with language disorders* (3rd ed.). Needham Heights, MA: Allyn & Bacon.

Reeves, D. B. (2000). *Accountability in action: A blueprint for learning organizations.* Denver: Center for Performance Assessment.

Renzulli, P. (2005). Philadelphia Public Schools Online Report Cards (http://www.phila.k12.pa.us.)

Rhodes, R. L., Ochoa, S. H., & Ortiz, S. O. (2005). *Assessing culturally and linguistically diverse students: A practical guide.* New York: Guilford.

Robinson, J. (1988). *The baby boards: A parents' guide to preschool & primary school entrance tests.* New York: Arco.

Romero, I. (1999). Individual assessment procedures with preschool children. In E. V. Nuttall,

434

I. Romero, & J. Kalesnik (Eds.), *Assessing and screening preschoolers: Psychological and education dimensions* (2nd ed.). Needham Heights, MA: Allyn & Bacon.

Rosenkoetter, S. E., & Squires, S. (2000). Writing outcomes that make a difference for children and families. *Young Exceptional Children, 4*(1), 2–8.

Rothstein, R. (2000). Toward a composite index of school performance. *The Elementary School Journal, 100*(5), 409–442.

Sacks, P. (1999). *Standardized minds: The high price of America's testing culture and what we can do to change it.* Cambridge, MA: Perseus Books.

Sadowski, M. (Ed.). (2004). Teaching the new generation of US students. *Teaching immigrant and second-language students: Strategies for success.* Cambridge, MA: Harvard.

Salvia, J., & Ysseldyke, J. (2004). *Assessment* (9th ed.). Boston: Houghton Mifflin.

Sandall, S. R., & Schwartz, I. S. (2002). *Building blocks for teaching preschoolers with special needs.* Baltimore, MD: Paul H. Brookes.

Sandall, S., McLean, M. E., & Smith, B. J. (2000). *DEC recommended practices in early intervention/ early childhood special education.* Longmont, CO: Sopris West.

Sanford, A. R., & Zelman, J. G. (1981). *Learning Accomplishment Profile–Revised.* Winston-Salem, NC: Kaplan School Supply.

Santos, R. M., & Ostrosky, M. M. (2005). Understanding the impact of language difference on classroom behavior. *What works briefs.* Champaign, IL: Center on the Social and Emotional Foundations for Early Education. Available online at *http:// csefel.uiuc.edu.*

Schmid, R. E. (1999). An elementary school application of pre-referral assessment and intervention. *Diagnostique, 25*(1), 59–70.

Schonberg, R. L., & Tifft, C. J. (2002). Birth defects, prenatal diagnosis, and fetal therapy. In M. Batshaw (Ed.), *Children with disabilities* (5th ed.) Baltimore: Paul H. Brookes.

Schroeder, F. C., & Pryor, S. (2001). Multiple measures: Beginning with ends. *The School Administrator, 58*(11), 22–25.

Schultz, K.A., Colarusso, R.P., & Strawderman, V.W. (1989). *Mathematics for every young child.* Columbus, OH: Merrill/Prentice Hall.

Seefeldt, C. & Barbour, N. (1998). *Early Childhood education: An introduction* (4th ed.). Columbus, OH: Merrill/Prentice Hall.

Seligman, M. (2000). *Conducting effective conferences with parents of children with disabilities: A guide for teachers.* New York: Guilford.

Seplocha, H. (2004). Partnerships for learning: Conferencing with families. *Beyond the Journal, Young Children on the Web,* September. Available online at http://naeyc.org.

Serafini, F. (2001). Three paradigms of assessment: Measurement, procedure, and inquiry. *Reading Teacher 54*(4), 384–393.

Serna, L. A., Nielsen, E. Mattern, N., & Forness, S. (2003). Primary prevention in mental health for Head Start classrooms: Partial replication with teachers as interveners. *Behavioral Disorders, 28*(2), 124–129.

Shackelford, J. (2000). State and jurisdictional eligibility definitions for infants and toddlers with disabilities under IDEA. *NECTAS notes.* Issue No: 5, revised. Available online at http:// www.nectas.unc.edu.

Shepard, L. A. (2000). The role of assessment in a learning culture. *Educational Researcher, 29*(7), 4–14.

Shepard, L. A., Hammerness, K., Darling-Hammond, L., & Rust, F. (2005). Assessment. In L. Darling-Hammond & J. Bransford (Eds.), *Preparing teachers for a changing world: What teachers should learn and be able to do.* San Francisco: Jossey-Bass.

Sheridan, S. M., & McCurdy, M. (2005). Ecological variables in school-based assessment and intervention planning. In R. Brown-Chidsey (Ed.), (pp. 43–64). *Assessment for intervention: A problem-solving approach.* New York: Guilford.

Shonkoff, J. P. (2004). *Science, policy and the young developing child: Closing the gap between what we know and what we do.* Chicago: Ounce of Prevention.

Shonkoff, J. P., & Meisels, S. J. (Eds.). (2000). *Handbook of early intervention* (2nd ed.). New York: Cambridge.

Shores, E. F., & Grace, C. (2005). *The portfolio book: A step-by-step guide for teachers.* Upper Saddle River, NJ: Merrill/Prentice Hall.

Smith, A. F. (2000). Reflective portfolios: Preschool possibilities. *Childhood Education, 76*(4), 204–208.

Smith, D., & Goldhaber, J. (2004). *Poking, pinching & pretending: Documenting toddlers' explorations with clay.* St Paul: Redleaf Press.

Smith, T., Pretzel, R., & Landry, K. (2001). Infant assessment. In R. J. Simeonsson & S. Rosenthal (Eds.), *Psychological and developmental assessment:*

Children with disabilities and chronic conditions. New York: Guilford.

Spieker, S. J., Solchany, J., McKenna, M., DeKlyen, M., & Barnard, K. E. (2000). The story of mothers who are difficult to engage in prevention programs. In J. D. Osofsky & H. E. Fitzgerald (Eds.), *WAIMH handbook of infant mental health. Vol. 3: Parenting and child care.* New York: John Wiley.

Spodek, B., & Saracho, O. N. (Eds.). (2005). *Handbook of research on the education of young children.* Hillsdale, NJ: Lawrence Erlbaum.

Stefanakis, E. H. (1998). *Whose judgment counts? Assessing bilingual children, K–3.* Portsmouth, NH: Heinemann.

Stenmark, J. K. (1991). Math portfolios: A new form of assessment. *Teaching K–8, 21,* 62–68.

Stenmark, J. K. (Ed.). (1991). *Mathematics assessment: Myths, models, good questions, and practical suggestions.* Reston, VA: National Council of Teachers of Mathematics.

Sternberg, R. J., & Grigorenko, E. L. (2002). *Dynamic testing: The nature and measurement of learning potential.* New York: Cambridge.

Stiggins, R. J. (2005). *Student-involved assessment for learning* (4th ed.). Upper Saddle River, NJ: Merrill/Prentice Hall.

Strickland, K. (2005). *What's after assessment? Follow-up instruction for phonics, fluency, and comprehension.* Portsmouth, NH: Heinemann.

Strickland, K., & Strickland, J. (2000). *Making assessment elementary.* Portsmouth, NH: Heinemann.

Sulzby, E. (1985). Children's emergent reading of favorite storybooks. *Reading Research Quarterly, 20,* 458–481.

Sulzby, E. (1989). Assessment of writing and children's language while writing. In L. M. Morrow & J. K. Smith (Eds.), *Assessment of instruction in early literacy.* Upper Saddle River, NJ: Prentice Hall.

T.H.E. Journal. (2005). http://www.edtechinfocenter.com.

Takushi, R., & Uomoto, J. M. (2001). The clinical interview from a multicultural perspective. In L. A. Suzuki, J. G. Ponterotto, & P. J. Meller (Eds.), *Handbook of multicultural assessment* (2nd ed.). San Francisco: Jossey-Bass.

Taylor, C. S., & Nolen, S. B. (2005). *Classroom assessment: Supporting teaching and learning in real classrooms.* Upper Saddle River, NJ: Merrill/Prentice Hall.

Taylor, R. (1998). Check your cultural competence. *Nursing Management, 29*(8), 30–32.

Teale, W. H. (1990). The promise and challenge of informal assessment in early literacy. In L. M. Morrow & J. K. Smith (Eds.), *Assessment for instruction in early literacy.* Upper Saddle River, NJ: Prentice Hall.

Teale, W. H., & Sulzby, E. (Eds.). (1986). *Emergent literacy: Writing and reading.* Norwood Park, NJ: Ablex.

Thomas, R. M. (2005). *High stakes testing: Coping with collateral damage.* Mahwah, NJ: Lawrence Erlbaum.

Thompson, S. J., & Quenemoen, R. F. (2001). Eight steps to effective implementation of alternate assessments. *Assessment for Effective Intervention, 26*(2), 67–74.

Thurlow, M. L. (2001). Special issue: Students with disabilities and high stakes testing. *Assessment for Effective Intervention, 26*(2).

Thurlow, M. L., Elliott, J. L., & Ysseldyke, J. E. (2003). *Testing students with disabilities: Practical strategies for complying with district and state requirements* (2nd ed.). Thousand Oaks, CA: Corwin.

Tompkins, G. E. (2006). *Literacy for the 21st century: A balanced approach* (4th ed.). Upper Saddle River, NJ: Merrill/Prentice Hall.

Turnbull, A. Turnbull, R. Erwin, E & Soodak, L. (2006). *Families, professionals & exceptionality: positive outcomes through partnership and trust* (5th ed.). Upper Saddle River, NJ: Merrill/Perntice Hall.

Turnbull, A.P. Turnbull, R., Shank, M. & Smith, S.S. (2007). *Exceptional lives: Special education in today's schools* (5th ed.). Upper Saddle River, NJ: Merrill/Prentice Hall.

Turnbull, R., Huerta, N., & Stowe, M. (2006). *The Individuals with Disabilities Act as amended in 2004.* Upper Saddle River, NJ: Merrill/Prentice Hall.

Twombly, E., & Fink, G. (2004). *Ages & stages learning activities.* Baltimore: Paul H. Brookes.

U. S. Department of Education. (2005a). CFDA Number: 84.357 Reading First. http://ed.gov.

U. S. Department of Education. (2005b). CFDA Number: 84.359 Early Reading First. http://ed.gov.

U.S. Department of Education. (1991). *America 2000: An educational strategy sourcebook.* Washington, DC: Author.

U.S. Department of Education. (1991). *Individuals with Disabilities Education Act.* Washington, DC: Author.

U.S. Department of Education. (1997). *Individuals with Disabilities Education Act (IDEA).* Washington, DC: Author.

U.S. Department of Education. (2004). *Individuals with Disabilities Education Act (IDEA)*. Washington, DC: Author.

Urbina, S. (2004). *Essentials of psychological testing*. New York: Wiley.

Valencia, R. R., & Suzuki, L. A. (2001). *Intelligence testing and minority students: Foundations, performance factors, and assessment issues*. Thousand Oaks, CA: Sage.

Van Hoorn, J., Nourot, P., Scales, B., & Alward, K. (2003). *Play at the center of the curriculum* (3rd ed.). Upper Saddle River, NJ: Merrill/Prentice Hall.

Vermont Department of Education. (2005). Programs and services: Assessment. Available online at http://www.state.vt.us/educ/new/html/pgm_assessment.html.

Vygotsky, L. (1978). Mind in society: The development of higher psychological processes (M. Cole, V. John Steiner, S.Scribner, & E. Souberman, Eds.). Cambridge, MA: Harvard University Press.

Vygotsky, L. (1986). *Thought and language* (A. Kozulin, Trans.). Cambridge, MA: MIT Press.

Walker, D. K., & Wiske, M. S. (1981). *A guide to developmental assessments for young children* (2nd ed., p. 32). Boston: Massachusetts Department of Education, Early Childhood Project.

Weber, C., Behl, D., & Summers, M. (1994). Watch them play; watch them learn. *Teaching Exceptional Children*, (Fall), 30–35.

Weinstein, R. S. (2004). *Reaching higher: The power of expectations in schooling*. Cambridge, MA: Harvard. *Young Children*. (2005). Special issue: DAP in 2005, *60*(4).

West, J., Denton, K., & Germino-Hausken, E. (2000). *America's kindergarteners: Findings from the Early Childhood Longitudinal Study, Kindergarten Class of 1998–99, Fall 1998*. Washington, DC: U.S. Department of Education, National Center for Educational Statistics.

Widerstrom, A. H. (2005). *Achieving learning goals through play: Teaching young children with special needs* (2nd ed.). Baltimore, MD: Paul H. Brookes.

Wieder, S., & Greenspan, S. (2001). The DIR (developmental, individual-difference, relationship-based) approach to assessment and intervention planning. *Zero to Three, 21*(4), 11–19.

Wiggins, G. (1994). Toward better report cards. *Educational Leadership, 52*, 28–37.

Williams, D. (2003). The complexities of learning in a small group. In R. Kantor & D. Fernie (Eds.), *Early childhood classroom processes*. Cresskill, NJ: Hampton Press.

Winsch, M. J., Conlon, C. J., & Scheidt, P. C. (2002). Substance abuse: A preventable threat to development. In M. Batshaw (Ed.), *Children with disabilities* (5th ed.). Baltimore: Paul H. Brookes.

Wood, J. W. (2006). Teaching students in inclusive settings: Adopting and accommodating instruction. (5th ed.). Upper Saddle River, NJ: Merrill/Prentice Hall.

Wortham, S. C. (2006). *Early childhood curriculum: Developmental bases for learning and teaching* (4th ed.). Upper Saddle River, NJ: Merrill/Prentice Hall.

Wurm, J. P. (2005). *Working in the Reggio way: A beginner's guide for American teachers*. St. Paul, MN: Redleaf Press.

Yelland, N. J. (Ed.). (2000). *Promoting meaningful learning: Innovations in educating early childhood professionals*. Washington DC: National Association for the Education of Young Children.

Zero to Three Work Group. (1994). Toward a new vision for the developmental assessment of infants and young children. *Zero to Three, 14*, 1–8.

Zero to Three. (1995). *Diagnostic classification: 0–3*. Arlington, VA: National Center for Clinical Infant Programs.

Zero to Three. (2003). Infant and early childhood mental health: Promoting healthy social and emotional development. Washington, DC: Author. Available online at http://www.zerotothree.org.

Zero to Three. (2005). Laying the foundation for successful prekindergarteners by building bridges to infants and toddlers. Washington, DC: Author. Available online at http://www.zerotothree.org.

Zvetina, D., & Guiter'ez, J. (1994). *Social emotional observation criteria*. Chicago: Erikson Institute.

Name Index

Subject Index